Five Restoration Adaptations of Shakespeare

# FIVE RESTORATION
ADAPTATIONS OF
SHAKESPEARE
EDITED WITH AN INTRODUCTION BY
CHRISTOPHER SPENCER

UNIVERSITY OF ILLINOIS PRESS · URBANA, 1965

A grant from the Ford Foundation has helped to defray the cost of publishing this work.

© 1965 by the Board of Trustees of the University of Illinois. Manufactured in the United States of America. Library of Congress Catalog Card No. 65-10401.

PREFACE

The present volume contains the texts of the three most popular Restoration adaptations of Shakespeare — the operatic *Tempest,* Tate's *King Lear,* and Cibber's *Richard III.* A fourth play, Davenant's *Macbeth,* is one of the earliest and best-known of the adaptations. The fifth, Granville's *Jew of Venice,* adds variety in that it is a revision of an early Shakespeare comedy; and, moreover, it is of special interest since it contains the turn-of-the-century metamorphosis of one of Shakespeare's best-known and most controversial characters. Dryden's *All for Love* has been omitted because it is very easily available elsewhere and because it is so far removed from Shakespeare's *Antony and Cleopatra* as not to belong in a collection of this kind. Of these five adaptations only *Macbeth* has been edited recently. Except for some passages in the Furness *Variorum* edition of *The Merchant of Venice,* Granville's *Jew* has not been reprinted since the early eighteenth century. Editions of the other adaptations from the late eighteenth and early nineteenth centuries offer the plays as they were done in the theater of their day, but often not as they were done in the period of adaptation; and the editions in the adapters' collected works are not always reliable. In fact, very little is known about the early texts. In her *Stage History of Shakespeare's King Richard the Third* (1909), Alice I. P. Wood did not consult the earliest text of Cibber's adaptation and, consequently, did not know that the adapter had written a scene in which the young princes are murdered on the stage. The scene was discovered by Hazelton Spencer and was published in

Modern Language Notes in 1927 by A. C. Sprague, but it is available only there and in the original quarto. Individual acts or scenes from the adaptations have sometimes been reprinted, but it is ironic to read and judge by snippets the work of an age that was especially conscious of unity. It seems, therefore, that complete texts should be made available, together with some assembly of what is known about the plays from the widely scattered sources in which this information is now located and with discussion of the early editions.

It is time, too, that we reviewed our opinion of the adaptations. Our attitude toward them has remained largely unchanged since the appearance of Hazelton Spencer's *Shakespeare Improved* in 1927; he concluded (pp. 373-374) that "concerning [the adapters'] efforts as a whole I am not aware that anything good can be said, though, as we have seen, there is occasional merit in detail" (these details were rare). During the past third of a century our knowledge of Restoration and eighteenth-century drama has increased, and our understanding of the Augustan point of view has broadened and deepened. Some of this knowledge and understanding has been applied to a group of plays by George C. Branam in his *Eighteenth-Century Adaptations of Shakespearean Tragedy* (1956), but we still have no convincing answer to the question why some of the adaptations were so immensely popular for so long on the stage and, publishers evidently thought, in the study as well. I think that some of the adaptations are good drama if they are read not as (inevitably) bad Shakespeare but as new plays. In the Introduction I develop this thesis and attempt to suggest briefly how the five plays in this volume might be regarded.

I am grateful to Charles T. Prouty for encouraging me to study the adaptations of Shakespeare and to Maynard Mack for introducing me to the "Augustan Age." More recently, I am indebted to G. Blakemore Evans and Richard E. Allen for their criticisms and suggestions, and to James G. McManaway for his answers to my queries. I also wish to thank the librarians and libraries that have been generous with their collections and have supplied me with microfilm and Xerox prints: Miss Isabelle F. Grant and the University of Illinois Library, the Folger Shakespeare Library, the William A. Clark Library, the Henry E. Huntington Library, and the libraries of the University of Chicago, Harvard University, the University of Michigan, the University of Texas, and Yale University. Materials from the Yale Manuscript of *Macbeth* are reproduced with the permission of the Yale University

Library and the Yale University Press; and the Prologue and Epilogue to *The Tempest* from Egerton MS 2623 are published with the permission of The Trustees of the British Museum. My thanks are also due the Council on Research Grants of Illinois State University for financial assistance, and Karen Little Satterlee and Carmelita Edgerton for typing the manuscript. Finally, I must thank my family for their forbearance while this book was being written.

Normal, Illinois
April, 1964

Abbreviations

Dates are given New Style: thus, January, 1663/64 is listed as January, 1664. In addition to conventional abbreviations of titles of periodicals, the following shortened references are used for the most frequently cited works:

B. M. Catalogue	The British Museum Catalogue of Printed Books, 58 vols., 10 supplements, Ann Arbor, 1946. Also, General Catalogue of Printed Books, London, 1931— (in progress; through Vol. CCXXX [1964]).
Branam	George C. Branam, Eighteenth-Century Adaptations of Shakespearean Tragedy, Berkeley, 1956.
CBEL	Cambridge Bibliography of English Literature, ed. F. W. Bateson, 4 vols., New York, 1941. Also Supplement, ed. George Watson, Cambridge, England, 1957.
Cibber, Apology	An Apology for the Life of Mr. Colley Cibber, ed. Robert W. Lowe, 2 vols., London, 1889.
Downes	John Downes, Roscius Anglicanus, ed. Montague Summers, London, n.d.
First Folio (F1)	Mr. William Shakespeares Comedies, Histories, & Tragedies, facsimile ed. Helge Kökeritz and C. T. Prouty, New Haven, 1954.
Ford	H[erbert] L. Ford, Shakespeare 1700-1740, Oxford, 1935.
Handasyde	Elizabeth Handasyde, Granville the Polite, London, 1933.
Hogan, I, II	Charles Beecher Hogan, Shakespeare in the Theatre 1701-1800, 2 vols., Oxford, 1952-57.
Jaggard	William Jaggard, Shakespeare Bibliography, New York, 1959. First published in 1911.
Lawrence	W. J. Lawrence, The Elizabethan Playhouse and Other Studies [First Series], New York, 1963. First published in 1913.
London Stage	The London Stage 1660-1800, Part II, ed. E. L. Avery, 2 vols., Carbondale, Ill., 1960; Part III, ed. A. H. Scouten, 2 vols., 1961; Part IV, ed. G. W. Stone, Jr., 3 vols., 1962.
Macdonald	Hugh Macdonald, John Dryden: A Bibliography, Oxford, 1939.

Nicoll, *History,* I, II, III	Allardyce Nicoll, *A History of English Drama, 1660-1900,* rev. ed., Vols. I-III, Cambridge, England, 1952.
Odell, I, II	G. C. D. Odell, *Shakespeare from Betterton to Irving,* 2 vols., New York, 1920.
C. Spencer, *Macbeth*	Christopher Spencer, *Davenant's* Macbeth *from the Yale Manuscript:* An Edition, with a Discussion of the Relationship of Davenant's Text to Shakespeare's, New Haven, 1961.
H. Spencer	Hazelton Spencer, *Shakespeare Improved,* Cambridge, Mass., 1927.
Summers, *Adaptations*	Montague Summers, ed., *Shakespeare Adaptations,* Boston, 1922.
The Term Catalogues	*The Term Catalogues, 1668-1709 A. D.,* ed. Edward Arber, 3 vols., London, 1903-06.
Wood	Alice I. P. Wood, *The Stage History of Shakespeare's King Richard the Third,* New York, 1909.
Woodward and McManaway	G. L. Woodward and J. G. McManaway, *A Check List of English Plays 1641-1700,* Chicago, 1945.

CONTENTS

INTRODUCTION

The idea of substantially altering Shakespeare's plays seems to have come primarily from the ingenious, experimental mind of Sir William Davenant, who, at the Restoration, was anxious to show the new court and a younger generation that his taste was up to date and that Shakespeare, whom he admired greatly, could be made attractive to the new patrons of the theater. Upon Charles's return Davenant petitioned for the right of "reformeinge" and "makeinge . . . fitt" earlier plays; and in a warrant dated December 12, 1660, his actors were given exclusive rights to eleven plays, including *The Tempest, King Lear, Macbeth,* and six others of Shakespeare's works. Almost eight years later the Duke's Company was granted rights to five more Shakespearean dramas, and shortly thereafter a long list of plays was alloted to the rival King's Company, including *The Merchant of Venice, Richard III,* and nineteen others by Shakespeare.[1] Although the King's Men received three-fifths of the thirty-five Shakespearean plays that were assigned, most of the adapting during the early years was done for the Duke's Company: previous to December, 1680, when Tate's *Richard II* was given, only Lacy's *Sauny the Scot* in the 1660's and Dryden's *All for Love* and Ravenscroft's *Titus Andronicus* in the 1670's were performed by the King's Company.

Three clusters of adaptations appeared between 1660 and 1710.[2]

---

[1] The warrants are printed in Nicoll, *History,* I, 352-354.
[2] The following survey of adaptations is indebted to the list of 123 adaptations of 35 Shakespearean plays made between 1660 and 1820 in Branam,

Davenant himself combined *Much Ado about Nothing* and *Measure for Measure* to make *The Law Against Lovers,* as well as adapting *Macbeth* and (probably) *Hamlet* and (possibly) *Julius Caesar.*[3] He also altered *The Two Noble Kinsmen* to form *The Rivals,* and he collaborated with Dryden in *The Tempest;* it was his company that performed the nonextant tragicomedy which was made from *Romeo and Juliet* by James Howard and which, according to Downes, was played alternately with the tragedy.[4] The second cluster includes eleven adaptations which appeared between 1677 and 1683, when the uniting of the companies had ended competition and had given the actors a plentiful stock of plays. Several of this group were frankly political, including Crowne's *Misery of Civil War* (from *II* and *III Henry VI*) and *Henry the Sixth, the First Part* (from the first three acts of *II Henry VI*); the former was directed particularly against the Whigs and the latter against Popery. Tate's *Richard II* was forbidden after two performances, but his *Ingratitude of a Commonwealth* was allowed. Apparently, officialdom did not see any objectionable political reference — even in 1681 — in the story of a king who arranges the succession stupidly, and *King Lear* was undisturbed. Dryden's *All for Love* and *Troilus and Cressida* also appeared with this group.

The third cluster, made up of comedies and histories, appeared in 1700 and 1701. Granville's *Jew of Venice* was accompanied by Gildon's *Measure for Measure,* Dennis' *Comical Gallant,* and Burnaby's *Love Betrayed* (from *Twelfth Night*); all but Dennis' included masques. The histories were Betterton's cut version of *Henry IV* and Cibber's *Richard III.* The Master of the Revels insisted that Cibber omit the first act of his adaptation on the ground that Henry VI would remind people of James II, but luckily the official did not further conclude that Henry's nemesis, Richard, would remind people of James's

---

pp. 179-192. The total is really larger than 123: Hogan lists several adaptations not in Branam, and Herschel Baker, *John Philip Kemble* (Cambridge, Mass., 1942), pp. 328-329, lists five adaptations by Kemble that are not included in Branam. Perhaps seventeenth-century prompt books, principally those of the Smock Alley Theatre in Dublin from the 1670's and early 1680's, should also be added; on these see R. C. Bald, "Shakespeare on the Stage in Restoration Dublin," *PMLA,* LVI (1941), 369-378; and G. Blakemore Evans, ed., *Shakespearean Prompt-Books of the Seventeenth Century,* Vol. I, Part I (Charlottesville, Va., 1960). My survey is also indebted to Odell and H. Spencer.

[3] Nicoll, *History,* I, 401-402.

[4] Downes, p. 22.

nemesis, King William. Although Cibber was surely innocent of intentional political reference, the disgruntled Jacobite statesman, Granville, just as surely did mean to refer to King William's countrymen through Portia's new and most unpleasant suitor, Myn Heer Van Gutts.

The age of Cibber (1711-43) produced eighteen versions: a cluster of comedies around 1716; a group of histories and Roman plays around 1719, all of which, as Branam points out, moralized about the dangers of civil war and referred more or less obliquely to the uprising of 1715;[5] and another group of comedies in 1735-39. Cibber himself made a second adaptation of Shakespeare, *Papal Tyranny in the Reign of King John,* which, however, was not successfully performed until 1745.[6]

Throughout the ages of Betterton and Cibber, Shakespeare's plays (original and adapted) were performed frequently. Between one-eighth and one-ninth of the dramatic performances Pepys attended were of Shakespeare's plays; he saw twelve different Shakespearean dramas on forty-one occasions between 1660 and 1669 — *Macbeth* nine times and *The Tempest* eight, both in adapted form on most if not all occasions.[7] However, G. E. Bentley, relying primarily on allusions of various types, concludes that the last two decades of the seventeenth century "seem to mark the beginning of the flood tide of Shakespeare's reputation, especially as seen in quotations from his works and references to his characters."[8] A. H. Scouten states that about 11 per cent of performances in the London theaters between 1703 and 1710 were of Shakespeare (original and adapted); about 14 per cent between 1710 and 1717; about 17 per cent in 1717-23; a dip to about 12 per cent in 1723-34; and then a rise to about 25 per cent in 1740-41, shortly before the arrival of Garrick.[9] Undoubtedly the encouragement of the Shakespeare Ladies Club in 1736-38 and the restricting

---

[5] Branam, pp. 61-63.

[6] E. L. Avery, "Cibber, *King John,* and the Students of the Law," *MLN,* LIII (1938), 272-275, quotes a letter published by Cibber in the *Daily Advertiser* for Feb. 4, 1737: "I had finish'd the Revisal of [*King John*] Ten Years since." John J. McAleer, "Colley Cibber — Shakespeare Adapter," *Shakespeare Newsletter,* XI (Dec., 1961), 42, states that Cibber's *King John* was given once in 1703 and was rehearsed both in 1723 and in 1736.

[7] Odell, I, 22.

[8] *Shakespeare & Jonson: Their Reputations in the Seventeenth Century Compared* (Chicago, 1945), I, 64.

[9] "The Shakespearean Revival" in *London Stage,* Part III, Vol. I, pp. cxlix-clii.

effect on new plays of the Licensing Act of 1737, as well as the extraordinary success of Macklin's performance of Shylock, contributed to this increase.[10] During the age of Garrick, as is shown in the recently published statistical study by G. W. Stone, Jr., of performances from 1747 to 1776, Shakespeare contributed almost 20 per cent of Drury Lane and about 16 per cent of Covent Garden performances.[11]

Stone's lists and the statistics provided by Hogan also reveal much about the popularity of individual plays during the eighteenth century, relative both to other Shakespearean dramas (original and adapted) and to non-Shakespearean plays. Thus, Stone lists as the five most frequently performed tragedies at Drury Lane from 1747 to 1776 *Romeo and Juliet, Hamlet, King Lear, The Mourning Bride,* and *Macbeth* (if *Richard III* had been counted a tragedy, it would have ranked third, ahead of *King Lear*); and at Covent Garden *Romeo and Juliet* had more than twice as many performances as runner-up *Jane Shore* (here *Richard III* would have rated second), followed by *Hamlet, Alexander the Great, Othello,* and *Macbeth.* In comedy *Much Ado about Nothing* was second at Drury Lane; *Cymbeline* was fifth; and *The Tempest* was ninth. *The Merry Wives of Windsor* was fourth at Covent Garden and *The Merchant of Venice* tenth. In tragedy 29 per cent of performances at the two theaters were of Shakespeare's plays (985 of 3,412), and in comedy 14 per cent (737 of 5,179) were Shakespearean. According to Hogan's count, *Hamlet* was first in total recorded performances of Shakespeare's plays during the eighteenth century with 601 performances; *Macbeth* (45 per cent Davenant's adaptation) was second; *Richard III* (Cibber's version) was third; *Romeo and Juliet* (largely Garrick's version) fourth; *Othello* (comparatively unadapted)[12] fifth; *King Lear* (in Tate's, Garrick's, and Coleman's adaptations) sixth; *I Henry IV* seventh; *The Taming of the Shrew* (in various adaptations) eighth; *The Merchant of Venice* (Granville's *Jew* in the first half of the century, the original in the sec-

---

[10] See E. L. Avery, "The Shakespeare Ladies' Club," *SQ,* VII (1956), 153-158. Frederick T. Wood, *"The Merchant of Venice* in the Eighteenth Century," *English Studies,* XV (1933), 212-214, quotes conveniently Genest's, Kirkman's, and Cooke's accounts of Macklin's dramatic first night as Shylock (Feb. 14, 1741); see also Chapter III, "Shylock," in William W. Appleton, *Charles Macklin: An Actor's Life* (Cambridge, Mass., 1960), pp. 43-55.

[11] *London Stage,* Part IV, Vol. I, pp. clxiv, clxvi.

[12] Marvin Rosenberg, "The 'Refinement' of *Othello* in the Eighteenth Century British Theatre," *SP,* LI (1954), 75-94, emphasizes the very substantial cutting, which included the omission of IV.i and the role of Bianca.

ond half) ninth; and *The Tempest* (the Davenant-Dryden-Shadwell version until 1750, and other versions from 1750 to 1800) tenth.[13] Even if Garrick's *Romeo and Juliet* is counted as the Shakespearean original rather than as an altered version, more than 40 per cent of the performances of these ten plays were of adaptations (1,853 of 4,424). Furthermore, the many editions of some of the altered versions suggest that their popularity was not limited to the stage: there seem to be at least fifteen editions of Cibber's *Richard III* between 1700 and Cibber's death in 1757, plus that in the adapter's *Plays.* Shakespeare contributed a very substantial part of eighteenth-century theater fare, and a considerable portion of the contribution was in adapted form.

However, by the second half of the eighteenth century the attitude toward Shakespeare was changing:[14] the romantic comedies were becoming more popular; critics began to mention reading the plays in their discussions of theater performances;[15] respect paid to rules and decorum was declining as interest in psychological realism was increasing; and attacks on adapting Shakespeare began to appear. There was more interest in antiquarian matters, of which evidence appeared in Farmer's *Essay on the Learning of Shakespeare* (1767) and in the historical accuracy of costumes, as in the performance of *Richard III* at Drury Lane in 1764 billed as "in the habits of the Times," and Macklin's appearance as Macbeth at Covent Garden in 1773 in "ancient dresses."[16] Also, new understanding of the text of Shakespeare's plays was being contributed in the later part of the century by Capell, Dr. Johnson, Steevens, and Malone.

With the changing attitude toward Shakespeare, many of the adaptations in the ages of Garrick and Kemble were milder in their alterations and often restored some of Shakespeare's lines: G. W. Stone, Jr.,

---

[13] Hogan, I, 460-461; II, 716-719.

[14] On the restoration of Shakespeare see R. W. Babcock, *The Genesis of Shakespeare Idolatry* (Chapel Hill, 1931).

[15] James J. Lynch, *Box, Pit, and Gallery* (Berkeley, 1953), p. 91. Lynch devotes two chapters, pp. 57-115, to Shakespeare before and during "Johnson's London."

[16] M. St. Clare Byrne, "The Stage Costuming of *Macbeth* in the Eighteenth Century," *Studies in English Theatre History in Memory of Gabrielle Enthoven* (London, 1952), pp. 52-64. See also Nicoll, *History*, III, 36-38, and Lily B. Campbell, "A History of Costuming on the English Stage Between 1660 and 1823," *University of Wisconsin Studies in Language and Literature*, No. 2 (1918), 187-223. Denis Donoghue, "Macklin's Shylock and Macbeth," *Studies: An Irish Quarterly Review*, XLIII (1954), 421-430, emphasizes Macklin's importance in restoring the "Shakespearean texts" to the stage.

has shown how Garrick consulted expert opinion in his redaction of *Macbeth*, which brings back much of Shakespeare, though it also expands the dying speech of the protagonist. Stone further suggests that Garrick's realistic style of acting (he did eighteen Shakespearean roles) helped increase interest in the characters.[17] Garrick's and Coleman's versions of *King Lear*, too, included some restoration of Shakespeare; but Tate's redaction continued and outlived its later competitors. J. P. Kemble, although he adapted twenty-two of Shakespeare's plays and frequently used material from earlier adaptations, made only negligible additions from his own pen.[18]

Garrick's and Kemble's reworkings of earlier adaptations raise the question of definition: what constitutes an adaptation? In compiling his list of 123 items, Branam omitted "plays that differ from the original only in being cut or in having the order of scenes altered" and "plays that, though treating similar material, are not based on Shakespeare and do not use any of his scenes or lines in recognizable form."[19] Branam's net is wide; and although such inclusiveness is desirable in a bibliography, we need at least rough distinctions for purposes of dis-

---

[17] "Garrick's Handling of *Macbeth*," *SP*, XXXVIII (1941), 609-628, and "David Garrick's Significance in the History of Shakespearean Criticism," *PMLA*, LXV (1950), 183-197, esp. p. 187. A. H. Scouten disagrees with Stone's estimate of Garrick's importance in the Shakespeare revival in "Shakespeare's Plays in the Theatrical Repertory When Garrick Came to London," *Studies in English, Department of English, University of Texas* (Austin, 1945), pp. 257-268, and in "The Increase in Popularity of Shakespeare's Plays in the Eighteenth Century," *SQ*, VII (1956), 188-202. Other articles on Garrick's adaptations by Stone include "Garrick's Long Lost Alteration of *Hamlet*," *PMLA*, XLIX (1934), 890-921; "*A Midsummer Night's Dream* in the Hands of Garrick and Colman," *PMLA*, LIV (1939), 467-482; "Garrick's Production of *King Lear*," *SP*, XLV (1948), 89-103; "The God of His Idolatry," *Joseph Quincy Adams Memorial Studies* (Washington, D. C., 1948), pp. 115-128; and "Shakespeare's *Tempest* at Drury Lane During Garrick's Management," *SQ*, VII (1956), 1-7. Several Shakespearean performances of Garrick are discussed in detail by Kalman A. Burnim, *David Garrick, Director* (Pittsburgh, 1961).

[18] In addition to Baker's biography (note 2 above), see Harold Child, *The Shakespearean Productions of John Philip Kemble* (London, 1935), and James Boaden, *Memoirs of the Life of John Philip Kemble Esq.* (London, 1825). According to Boaden (II, 2) Kemble would "consider [the play] attentively in the author's genuine book: then . . . examine what corrections could be properly admitted into his text; and, finally, what could be cut out in the representation, not as disputing the judgment of the author, but as suiting the time of the representation to the habits of his audience, or a little favouring the powers of his actors, in order that the performance might be as uniformly good as it was practicable to make it."

[19] Branam, p. 179.

cussion. The typical adaptation includes substantial cuts of scenes, speeches, and speech assignments; much alteration of language; and at least one and usually several important (or scene-length) additions. Accompanying these measurable changes are alterations or at least new emphases in tone, in character, and in theme. About one-third of Branam's 123 adaptations are of this type, as are the five in this volume. To one side of this main group stand those redactions (about one-fifth of the total) in which the text is cut, speech assignments are shifted, and the language is somewhat altered, but in which there are no major additions. The *Hamlet* attributed to Davenant, the Bettertonian *Henry IV,* and a number of redactions by Kemble belong here. To the other side of the main group are plays which are almost entirely rewritten, either retaining the basic Shakespearean structure or providing a new one, as in Dryden's *All for Love.* There remain a number of partial restorations of the original play — such as Garrick's or Kemble's versions of *King Lear* — and also adaptations of parts of plays — such as Lampe's and Leveridge's one-act presentations of *Pyramus and Thisbe* and Bullock's and Johnson's reworkings of the Induction to *The Taming of the Shrew.* The following remarks apply principally to the kind of adaptation I have described as typical.

Since the end of the eighteenth century two approaches have dominated criticism of the Augustan versions of Shakespeare. On the one hand the adaptations have been studied clinically as products of the rules and Restoration and eighteenth-century stage conditions and conventions, often with a classification of changes by type. Branam's *Eighteenth-Century Adaptations of Shakespearean Tragedy* approaches its subject in this way. On the other hand the adaptations are compared critically with the Shakespearean originals as a part of the history of attitudes toward Shakespeare; the critic expresses himself in tones of horror, dismay, disgust, or amusement, with very rare touches of grudging praise. The usual criticism is that the adaptations are made superficial in language, in character, in subject, and in overexplicit statement of theme, or "preaching." Moreover, the indictment continues, the alterations go much further than necessary: *The Tempest* could have been adapted to the Restoration theater without adding sisters for Miranda and Caliban, a female companion for Ariel, and a man who has never seen a woman. Furthermore, critics object, the additions are often incongruous with what remains of the original: by changing too little or too much, the adapters created their own indecorum, in which their additions seem superficial and thin beside the Shakespearean material. Finally, it appalls modern critics that these versions should have been considered "improved" Shakespeare in an age that prided itself on its taste; and therefore the adapters and their works are felt to deserve the most unmerciful treatment.[20]

The first kind of approach, that concerned with conditions and types of changes, is a useful preliminary to understanding the adaptations; but the common critical judgment of the second approach I believe to be pointless. At one time the harsh judgment was worth making. When Tate's *King Lear* had only recently been displaced, H. N. Hudson coined the word "Tatification" and referred to the Restoration *King Lear* as "this shameless, this execrable piece of dementation. Tate improve Lear? Set a tailor at work, rather, to improve Niagara! Withered be the hand, palzied be the arm, that ever dares to touch one of Shakespeare's plays."[21] As a larger and larger portion of the public had adopted this point of view, more and more of Shakespeare had been restored. However, with the possible exception of Cibber's *Richard III*, the adaptations are now dead *as Shakespeare* and are most unlikely ever again to replace their betters. Although as cadavers they may serve for dissection by graduate students, to belabor them as bad Shakespeare is like kicking a carcass. Nevertheless, the adaptations were popular on the Restoration and eighteenth-century stage, and to ignore them is to overlook a substantial part of the drama that the Augustan audience saw and read. It is not, then, worth our while to berate the adapters or their versions of the plays, but it is worth an effort to try to understand them.

We can best understand the adaptations if we regard them as new plays. We recognize that *All for Love* is thin when placed beside *Antony and Cleopatra,* but that it is a very good play when placed beside the tragedies of its own age. Similarly, although an adaptation of Shakespeare's *King Lear* should not refocus the play on a love story, we do not object per se to dramas that focus on young lovers whose

---

[20] The word "improved" is an unfortunate choice. One may "improve" something — an old house, for example — without necessarily having either a low opinion of the original maker or a higher opinion of oneself. The Augustans were full of praise of Shakespeare and were often modest about their own contributions. The arrogance implied by "Shakespeare improved" is frequently overestimated.

[21] *Lectures on Shakespeare,* II (New York, 1848), 277-278.

parents behave so blindly that they cause extremely serious trouble for themselves and others. Viewed as an adaptation, *The Tempest* is cheapened by the addition of Dorinda, Hippolito, Sycorax, and Milcha; but, if we are in the proper mood, we can enjoy a play containing two women who have never seen a man, a man who has never seen a woman, brother and sister monsters, and male and female spirits. Employing this approach, we should consider the Shakespearean original as the source, which the Augustan dramatist followed closely at times, but in which he made changes that are keys to *his* vision of the potentialities of story, character, and theme.

It might be objected that these Restoration plays were written and performed as if they were Shakespeare "altered" or "adapted," and that therefore the approach I suggest is not natural. However, part of our inability to see much worthy of praise in the adaptations comes from the false expectations established by the words "alteration" and "adaptation." They seem to suggest that an original is being adjusted only as much as necessary to meet new conditions; and the adapters themselves have contributed to this misunderstanding at times by saying that they are merely polishing Shakespeare's gems that he was too ignorant (or that he lived in an age too ignorant) to polish himself. Nevertheless, it is certainly true that they often did more than "alter" or "adapt" or "polish gems" in the sense those words usually have for us; and we can more reasonably judge in terms of what they did than of what they often said they did. In discussing translation Dryden distinguished among metaphrase, paraphrase, and "imitation," the last being "where the translater (if now he has not lost that name) assumes the liberty, not only to vary from the words and sense, but to forsake them both as he sees occasion; and taking only some general hints from the original, to run division on the groundwork, as he pleases." Later in the same essay Dryden elaborated on the term: "I take imitation of an author . . . to be an endeavour of a later poet to write like one who has written before him, on the same subject; that is, not to translate his words, or to be confined to his sense, but only to set him as a pattern, and to write, as he supposes that author would have done, had he lived in our age, and in our country."[22] It is hard to believe that a Shakespeare living in the Restoration would have written some of the lines the adapters wrote; but, responsive as he was to the interests of his

---

[22] "Preface to the Translation of Ovid's Epistles" (1680), in W. P. Ker, ed., *Essays of John Dryden* (Oxford, 1926), I, 237, 239.

time, he might have included a love story in *King Lear*. The term "imitation" as Dryden glosses it here seems closer to what the adapters did than are the terms "adaptation" or "alteration."

Yet to think of these reworkings of Shakespeare's plays as "imitations" is not really to recommend them to modern sensibilities. Behind this kind of imitation were so many assumptions foreign to our attitude toward literature that they block our understanding. Consider, for example, Dryden's position in his "Grounds of Criticism in Tragedy" (1679) as he discussed his adaptation of *Troilus and Cressida*. He began by comparing his revision of Shakespeare's plays to the treatment given Aeschylus' dramas in making them suitable for later generations of Athenians. Like Aeschylus, Dryden said, Shakespeare is an extraordinary genius; but his greatness lies buried under the unrefined language of his day, a plot that needs remodeling, an incoherent succession of scenes, and unnecessary and incompletely developed characters. Among the implications of Dryden's attitude seem to be these: first, that a lesser man could — indeed, Dryden implies, should — tamper with what seems to him the disorder of a greater man; second, that the work is not primarily the expression of an individual consciousness and is therefore subject to tampering without destroying the fragile vision of an individual mind; third, that the work is mechanical rather than organic and is therefore subject to disassembly, repair, substitution for worn or inferior parts, and reassembly — not worse, of course, but better than before; fourth, that the quality of such parts as language has improved greatly since the Elizabethan age; and fifth, that the mechanic's knowledge of how to put all kinds of parts together has also improved. These are common assumptions before the Romantic period, but modern readers are unlikely to sympathize with them. Thus, the conventional terminology, supported by the adapters' statements, establishes unsuitable expectations; and the adapters' own premises hinder our understanding of their performance. Rather than untying the Gordian knot of no longer acceptable assumptions, we can try to cut through it by attempting to regard the adaptations as new plays. Furthermore, such an approach today can bring us closer to the Augustan attitude toward the altered plays, for, in spite of the efforts of some adapters to distinguish carefully between their work and Shakespeare's, neither they nor their audience were primarily interested in comparing the rewritten versions with the originals.

In presenting the variety of life itself, Shakespeare gave more than the Restoration and eighteenth-century adapters wanted: they were interested in the sense of harmony and pattern and consistency and order that they felt art should offer. By its nature a play should be a useful and harmonious part of the great pattern of Nature, reflecting order in itself even as it revealed and "taught" the order that exists in Nature: Nature is "At once the source and end and test of Art." Since poetic justice reveals what is felt to be a natural pattern of things rather than accidental exceptions, guilty characters are regularly punished; and those who are more sinned against than sinning, including Lear, Cordelia, and Gloucester, are usually permitted to live. Further, the explicitly stated moral pulls the parts of the play together at the same time that it fits the play into its niche in the order of Nature. For example, Macbeth's "Farewell vain World, and what's most vain in it, Ambition" not only says something about Nature in terms of human existence, but it also incorporates the moralizing of Lady Macduff, the comparisons and contrasts that have been developed between the Macbeths and the Macduffs in the adaptation, and the argument between Macbeth and his wife over responsibility for their behavior (IV.iv), as well as several other passages in the play.

Moral, then, is closely related to structure, which is a part both of making apparent the order in Nature that art is supposed to show and of conveying the sense of a finished product. Hazelton Spencer complains that "Structure is . . . an accidental matter, dependent on stage and age and climate and a local technique. What avails it that the adapter has tinkered up a bit of plotting more neatly for a special stage, if he has obscured a great character or spoiled a great phrase?"[23] But this view does not recognize that structure is a part of an attitude toward life. Furthermore, one's reaction depends on what he is looking for: one does not expect a tight structure in Shakespeare, and he should not demand profound characterization or a richly imaginative style in the adaptations. Cibber omits quantities of unnecessary material in *Richard III* and adds an explanatory first act and a scene between Richard and Anne that rounds out the latter's story. Granville prunes much of the expansive material, including the Gobbos, from *The Merchant of Venice* and concentrates on friendship and love and music — with a pinch of smut. Davenant and Dryden extend the comparisons and contrasts of Shakespeare's *Tempest* with additions and

---

[23] H. Spencer, p. 374.

new characters. The resulting plays are more tightly coherent and are primarily *social:* they emphasize permanent patterns of human relationships with less attention to the depths of individual experience.

The characters, then, tend to become generalized as the adapter fits them into his mould, where they serve the stronger interests of moral clarity, of easily understandable motivation, of sharpened comparison and contrast, or simply of balance and unity. Edgar becomes a heroic lover and thereby helps to unite the Gloucester and Lear stories; to motivate himself and Cordelia; to set off the lust of Edmund, Goneril, and Regan; and to give a firm, happy ending to the play. After Act I Cordelia is the typically dutiful and "virtuous" daughter of Lear, the typically obstructive father. Prospero, on the other hand, is the oppressively careful father, at times reminiscent of Polonius. Ferdinand and Hippolito are sparks — one wise and one foolish, as if fresh from the country. Perhaps the most extraordinary metamorphosis is the Macbeth who must choose between Love and Ambition in IV.iv. This generalizing, conventionalizing tendency also helps to make the character more crude: in the plays of the adapters the evil of Richard III, Goneril, Regan, Edmund, and Shylock is laid out before us more directly.[24] Characters who repent are explicit about their reformation (Alonzo and Antonio in *The Tempest,* for example).

Three points should be emphasized about the style of the adaptations: first, that in part the adapters did not *understand* the aims of Shakespeare's style; second, that they did not *like* certain aspects of his style; and third, that they nevertheless made some effort to imitate his manner of writing, though dislike and lack of understanding (as well as sheer lack of ability) hindered their efforts. Granville assured his readers that "all imaginable Care has been taken to imitate the same fashion of Period, and turn of Stile and Thought with the Original," and Cibber did his "best to imitate [Shakespeare's] Style, and manner of thinking"; but the most revealing statement is Tate's: *"I have us'd less Quaintness of Expression even in the newest Parts of this Play. I confess 'twas Design in me, partly to comply with my Author's Style to make the Scenes of a Piece, and partly to give it some Resemblance of the Time and Persons here Represented."* "Quaintness" is

---

[24] This generalizing of character is, of course, a part of the eighteenth century's tendency to move toward the abstract, a matter that is discussed with much clarity and insight by B. H. Bronson, "Personification Reconsidered," *ELH,* XIV (1947), 163-177.

best understood here not as "old-fashioned prettiness," but rather as what in this context is almost its contrary, "highly elegant or refined" speech (*OED*, s.v. "Quaint," adj., 6). It looks as if some of Tate's bad lines were deliberately not polished for the double reason that if they had been refined, they would not have resembled Shakespeare's, and that primitive people (Lear and his contemporaries) talked clumsily. In other words, Tate had difficulty distinguishing between inelegant poetry and bad poetry in the style of an age other than his own, and he allowed this insensitivity to corrupt his own style: perhaps Cordelia's sudden collapse into very prosaic verse at I.i.213 should be attributed to Tate's efforts to avoid "Quaintness" in the language of primitive lovers in an old-fashioned play.

And yet we still wonder why the Augustans could not see the difference between a partly polished Restoration or eighteenth-century style and Shakespeare's. One reason is that they were blocked from seeing the indecorum by their assumption that Elizabethan English was inferior. We recognize two styles, the Shakespearean and the Augustan, each legitimate in itself — but we find a mixture unpleasant. The Augustans, however, tended to feel that there was only one standard of excellence and that therefore no really uncrossable chasm existed between styles: other manners of writing were merely imperfect efforts to reach an ideal to which the age of the adapters was closer.[25] On the one hand, then, they imitated Shakespeare's style, mixing their intentional crudeness with what they considered his ignorance or lack of technical proficiency. And on the other hand, they deliberately rewrote some of his lines to make them measure up to theirs in polish.

Much of the beauty and variety — the richness — of Shakespeare's language is in its ability to suggest. The Augustans, however, wanted the plays to be explicit. Just as characters were conventionalized and generalized, the language was often modified so that it would be more direct. For example, Davenant's Macbeth soliloquizes

> If it were well when done; then it were well
> It were done quickly; if his Death might be
> Without the Death of nature in my self,
> And killing my own rest; it wou'd suffice;

The soliloquy is cut from twenty-eight lines to sixteen. Davenant tells us what his hero thought without the deep insight into Macbeth's state

---

[25] Earl R. Wasserman, *Elizabethan Poetry in the Eighteenth Century* (Urbana, 1947), pp. 14-20, discusses the early Augustan attitude toward the Elizabethan style.

of mind that Shakespeare provided; a minimum of emotion accompanies the thought. This tendency to discuss moves easily into sententiousness, and all five adaptations contain considerable moralizing. However, what happens to the language is appropriate to the revised plays' emphasis on a clear structure which defines both characters' relationships to each other and the audience's attitude toward them, to simplifying and standardizing the characters themselves, to concentrating on a moral, and to exploiting theatrical situations. As much as possible is made direct, explicit, clear, and on the surface.

As successful acting vehicles in their own day the adaptations are not difficult to defend. They worked in the Augustan theater when the original plays either would not have succeeded at all or would not have done as well. At a time when Shakespeare's reputation was not yet established, the adapters fitted the plays to the public taste and to the new theater and acting companies: women's parts, for example, were expanded in *Macbeth, The Tempest,* and *King Lear.*[26] However, I have suggested that the Augustan plays have value in the study also, a value much less than that of Shakespeare's dramas, but nonetheless sufficient to put them among the better plays of their own age. That value will appear only when the adaptations are viewed not as glasses that distort the rays that shine through them from Shakespeare, but as opaque objects to be studied for their own less brilliant light.[27]

Although the Restoration adaptation of *Macbeth* was not published until six years after Davenant's death in 1668, it is universally attributed to the manager of the Duke's Company on the basis of John Downes's statement that it was his, the resemblance of the structural alterations to those Davenant suggested for *The Tempest,* and the absence of any other probable contender.[28] The adapted version was probably made in 1663-64, for echoes and imitations of *Macbeth* — some of them of the Restoration adaptation — appear in the first act of Davenant's *Rivals,* which Pepys saw on September 10, 1664. Pepys saw *Macbeth* first on November 5, 1664, and frequently thereafter; and Henry Her-

---

[26] On the influence of actresses on the adaptations, see Lucyle Hook, "Shakespeare Improv'd, or A Case for the Affirmative," *SQ,* IV (1953), 289-299.

[27] Ruth Wallerstein, "Dryden and the Analysis of Shakespeare's Technique," *RES,* XIX (1943), 165-185, approaches her subject in a similar manner. C. Spencer, "A Word for Tate's *King Lear,*" *SEL,* III (1963), 241-251, attempts an analysis of this type.

[28] The problems of date and authorship are discussed in C. Spencer, *Macbeth,* pp. 1-16.

bert had listed it as a "Revived play" a year earlier.[29] Betterton played Macbeth until 1710, when the part was taken by Mills at Drury Lane, and, after 1718, by Quin at Lincoln's Inn Fields and later at Covent Garden and Drury Lane. Garrick performed the title role in his adaptation on January 7, 1744, although Davenant's version continued to be acted at theaters other than Drury Lane through 1746 and was acted again in 1749-51. When it was announced that Garrick would restore much of Shakespeare in his version, Quin is reported to have asked, "What does he mean? Don't I play *Macbeth* as written by Shakespeare?" Garrick omitted both Lady Macduff scenes added by Davenant in Act III, the Shakespearean Porter's speech, and the scene involving young Macduff. He kept the witch material, of course, and added the following death speech, reminiscent of Marlowe's *Dr. Faustus*, for the protagonist:

> 'Tis done! the scene of life will quickly close.
> Ambition's vain, delusive dreams are fled,
> And now I wake to darkness, guilt and horror.
> I cannot bear it! let me shake it off —
> 'Two' not be; my soul is clogg'd with blood —
> I cannot rise! I dare not ask for mercy —
> It is too late, hell drags me down. I sink,
> I sink — Oh! — my soul is lost forever!
>
> > [Dies.[30]

Phelps removed the witch material and restored young Macduff and the custom of bringing Macbeth's head onstage in 1847.[31]

In addition to revising the language thoroughly, dropping the Porter's speech, reducing the cast (the "bleeding Sergeant," Ross, Angus, Menteth, Cathnes, Seyward's Son, Macduff's Son, the Scottish and English Doctors, the Old Man, and "another Lord" are missing), and reassigning speeches as an inevitable product of omitting characters, Davenant added five major passages: three new scenes of dialogue between the Macduffs, one of which involves the witches as well; a new scene between the Macbeths; and a passage between Lady Macduff and Lady Macbeth just before the latter opens the letter from her husband (I.v). Many factors influenced these additions, but whatever else they do, they also fit the moral which is the

---

[29] Joseph Q. Adams, *The Dramatic Records of Sir Henry Herbert* (New Haven, 1917), p. 138.

[30] Quoted by Stone, *SP*, XXXVIII (1941), 620. Quin's remark is quoted by Stone, p. 610, from Murphy's *Life of Garrick*, I, 71.

[31] Odell, II, 274.

organizing principle behind the adaptation Davenant produced. Shakespeare's play was a study in evil, its growth and effects on Lady Macbeth and Macbeth, particularly the latter. Altering the focus from evil to the less profound subject of ambition, the adapter is more interested in discussing his subject and in showing its effect on characters' actions than in revealing the state of a character's outlook as it becomes increasingly diseased.

In the new scene in Act IV, after contrasting the pulls of Love and Ambition, Macbeth decides that the latter is more important. Soon a distracted Lady Macbeth enters and asserts, "I stand so high that I am giddy grown," to which her husband replies that she blew his "Ambition up into a Flame," and they argue about degrees of responsibility. Earlier (I.v) Lady Macduff has assured Lady Macbeth that "the glories gain'd in war" are worthless, and has distrusted her husband's desire to oppose Macbeth; they argue the nature of Ambition in III.ii. 38-58 and its relation to public responsibility. In a passage added to V.ii in the Yale MS (but not in the printed versions of the play), Lenox remarks to Malcolm and his army,

> Ambition is a tree whose Roots are small,
> Whose growth is high: whose shadow ever is
> The blackness of the deed attending it,
> Under which nothing prospers. All the fruit
> It beares are doubts and troubles, with whose crowne
> The over burdend tree at last falls downe.

This would serve as well as Macbeth's dying line for the motto of Davenant's play. The theme of the evils of ambition, with a young king returning amid a chorus of praise to ascend his murdered father's throne, was no doubt complimentary to Charles II in the early 1660's; one notes that Davenant has Charles's ancestor Fleance return from France for the victory. In addition to stressing the theme of ambition, these added scenes develop the Macduffs as foils to the Macbeths, give more opportunity to the actresses, allow the witches additional scope for display, and fill out a short play with more action. Although Davenant removed *Macbeth* to the comparatively superficial level on which Restoration tragedy customarily operates and although the poetry of his lines is not distinguished, his version of the play is a coherent and forceful presentation of his chosen theme.

The most harshly criticized of the adapted versions is *The Tempest*: Furness reprinted the operatic version in the *Variorum* as an "object-

lesson of prime importance . . . to be fully hated it must be fully seen";
Lounsbury remarked of the Miranda-Dorinda conversation that "however true to the life then lived, it was certainly not true to any life
worth living"; Odell called the play "the worst perversion of Shakespeare in the two-century history of such atrocities. . . . I doubt if
sillier stuff was ever written by two poets, laureate or other"; and
Hazelton Spencer observed, "One aim and one alone animated its
authors: to pander."[32] A reason for this reaction is, I suspect, that
the Davenant-Dryden version in the context of Shakespeare's play
seems irreverent: Shakespeare's noble, mature, philosophical play contrasts sharply with the adolescent humor of the *double-entendres* and
the added buffoonery in the subplot. Yet Mrs. Inchbald is probably
correct in saying that *The Tempest* "would never have become a
favourite on the stage without the aid of Dryden's alteration. The
human beings in the original drama had not business enough on the
scene to make human beings anxious about them; and the preternatural
characters were more wonderful than pleasing."[33] Moreover, the
production of the operatic *Tempest* at the Old Vic in June, 1959, on
the tercentenary of Henry Purcell's birth, did not offend the sensibilities of many who wrote about it: M. St. Clare Byrne, for example,
found it "a spirited and pleasing entertainment of more than merely
antiquarian interest."[34]

The original adaptation of *The Tempest* — the one Pepys saw eight
times between November 7, 1667, and 1669 — was apparently made at
Davenant's suggestion: according to Dryden, the older man invented
Hippolito and *"the Comical parts of the Saylers"* (which were *"for
the most part his writing"*), and corrected Dryden's contributions.
Dryden himself, then, wrote the new scenes involving Hippolito, Ferdinand, Dorinda, and Miranda; made other but comparatively lesser
additions; and revised Shakespeare's lines. This adaptation was published in 1670 and again in Dryden's *Works* in 1701; but the interven-
ing editions as well as modern editions before 1922 that presented

---

[32] H. H. Furness, *A New Variorum*, IX, *The Tempest* (Philadelphia, 1897),
p. viii; T. R. Lounsbury, *Shakespeare as a Dramatic Artist* (New York, 1901),
p. 306; Odell, I, 31; H. Spencer, p. 201.

[33] Quoted by John R. Brown, "Three Adaptations," *Shakespeare Survey*, XIII
(1960), 139.

[34] "The Shakespeare Season at The Old Vic, 1958-59 . . . ," *SQ*, X (1959),
550. See also J. R. Brown (note 33 above). The operatic *Tempest* had last
been performed by the Old Vic in 1844.

themselves as Dryden's (including those of Scott-Saintsbury and Furness) were actually the operatic version of the play made, probably, in 1673 and first published in 1674.[35] In comparison with the 1670 text there are transpositions (Act II begins with the low comedy instead of the nobles, who appear later; and the Ferdinand-Ariel scene is removed from II to the beginning of III); additions (principally, a passage in I.ii introducing Milcha there instead of at the end of the play, and a masque at the end); comparatively minor alterations and omissions; and, most important to contemporary theatergoers, new and elaborate staging. The confusion of these versions was encouraged by Herringman's printing Dryden's original Preface, Prologue, and Epilogue with the 1674 version, although Dryden was writing for the rival theater. The opera continued on the stage until 1750 (Hogan lists six performances of "the original" in 1746);[36] thereafter the original play or Garrick's or Sheridan's version was usually performed. Hippolito and Dorinda were not banished permanently until 1838.[37]

The play has been the subject of much controversy concerning the linked problems of authorship, date, and versions.[38] In an article entitled "Did Thomas Shadwell Write an Opera on 'The Tempest'?" W. J. Lawrence argued that Shadwell was responsible for the operatic revision of the Davenant-Dryden adaptation;[39] his evidence was that Downes named Shadwell as the reviser, that Pietro Reggio attributed the song "Arise, arise" to Shadwell, and (on the basis of style) that the Prologue and Epilogue to *The Tempest* in Egerton MS 2623 were Shadwell's. In 1925 Thorn-Drury pointed out the weakness of Lawrence's evidence and argued that Dryden was responsible for the operatic additions. The following year Walmsley disagreed with Thorn-Drury and urged the claims of Shadwell. Thorn-Drury replied, asking whether anyone can make an opera out of what is already operatic; he apparently felt that the play was revised from time to time rather than all at once and that at least most of the work was presumably

---

[35] The discovery was made independently by W. J. Lawrence and by Sir Ernest Clarke (*The Athenaeum*, Aug. 25, 1906). See also Summers, *Adaptations*, pp. xi-xii, xli ff.

[36] Hogan, I, 434.

[37] Odell, II, 201.

[38] Nicoll, *History*, I, 430, considers that "there has been more controversy over this than over any other Restoration play."

[39] *Anglia*, XXVII (1904), 205-217, revised and reprinted in Lawrence, pp. 193-206.

done by Dryden. Walmsley's rejoinder added little to the discussion.[40]
The matter was taken up again twenty years later by Charles E. Ward,
who argued that Betterton was responsible for the operatic version:
Ward emphasized that Shadwell was busy with *Psyche* in the autumn
of 1673 when *The Tempest* was being prepared for the elaborate Dorset
Garden production. Betterton was "the most likely person to have had
the legal right to Davenant's *Tempest*, the interest, the knowledge, and
the skill to make it an opera."[41] The following year W. M. Milton
summarized the arguments and suggested that the opera was probably
a cooperative venture, perhaps a "filler" used while the more elaborate
Psyche was being prepared. In any case, Betterton would have had
much to do with it, but "Lawrence's conclusion, that Shadwell was
responsible for the revisions in this version, appears to be, on the whole,
still sound."[42] This seems a sensible view of the matter, except that
there is no internal evidence of haste, and the history of the play
("probably the most popular play of the Restoration period")[43] does
not confirm the suggestion that it was a "filler." The matter of dating
has also been discussed. Downes gave 1673, but Lawrence favored
about April 30, 1674. (However, if Downes was thinking by the Old
Style calendar, with the year ending on March 25, the two dates are
not as far apart as they might at first appear to be.) Nicoll states that
the opera "was in preparation by Aug. 22, 1673";[44] and Dryden's
"Prologue Spoken at the Opening of the New House, March 26, 1674,"
refers to "Machines and Tempests."[45] In his discussion of the Folger
Shakespeare Library's librettos "Songs and Masques in *The Tempest*,"

---

[40] G. Thorn-Drury, "Some Notes on Dryden," *RES*, I (1925), 327-330, and
"Shadwell and the Operatic *Tempest*," *RES*, III (1927), 204-208. D. M.
Walmsley, "Shadwell and the Operatic *Tempest*," *RES*, II (1926), 463-466,
and a note by the same title in *RES*, III (1927), 451-453.

[41] Charles E. Ward, "*The Tempest*: A Restoration Opera Problem," *ELH*,
XIII (1946), 119-130, p. 128.

[42] W. M. Milton, "'*Tempest*' in a Teapot," *ELH*, XIV (1947), 207-218, p.
218.

[43] George R. Noyes, ed., *The Poetical Works of Dryden* (Cambridge, Mass.,
1950), p. 1052.

[44] Downes, p. 34; Lawrence, p. 203; Nicoll, *History*, I, 430. H. Spencer, pp.
94, 109, accepts Lawrence's dating; Nicoll, citing H. Spencer, agrees.

[45] H. M. Hooker, "Dryden's and Shadwell's *Tempest*," *HLQ*, VI (1943),
224-228, cites a manuscript of this Prologue at the Huntington Library, in
which the variant "Tempests and Operas" appears. She suggests that whereas
"Machines and Tempests" might conceivably be taken to refer only to *Macbeth*,
"Tempests and Operas" clearly refers to *The Tempest* as well. However,
Macbeth was considered an opera — by Downes, for example (p. 33).

which were apparently distributed at the theater for the audience's use, McManaway supports Downes's dating.[46] On the music, which has also received much attention, see the note to I.i of *The Tempest* below.

Davenant's *Macbeth* had been largely concerned with Ambition, but both Love and Ambition are important in *The Tempest*. In Shakespeare's play the lines are distributed about as follows: 256 for the lovers, 428 for the low comedy characters, 436 for the nobles, and 925 not exclusively attached to any one group. The corresponding figures for the operatic version are 1,227 for the lovers, 444 for the low comedy, 188 for the nobles, and 849 for more than one group. These figures support Norman Holland's emphasis on the lovers in his interpretation of the play: "What Davenant saw [in *The Tempest*] was a study of the 'natural man.' For the Restoration writer, serious or comic, sex provided a lowest common denominator for all mankind — the animal level of man. Davenant's *The Tempest* uses the natural man's intuitive sexuality to generate an action of rivalry, to say, much in the manner of Locke and Hobbes: 'Because men are naturally this way, struggles and rivalries arise and government is needed.' "[47] What Holland says is true, but it does not include an important part of the play — the punishment and repentance of the nobles. Even though there are fewer lines devoted to them in the Restoration version of the play, the focus on their Ambition is much greater (omission of the Francisco-Adrian-Gonzalo witbout and the plot against Alonzo cut 327 lines from Shakespeare's play).

An insight into this aspect of the adapted *Tempest* is provided by Davenant's remarks in his *Preface to Gondibert* (1650) concerning his

---

[46] J. G. McManaway, "Songs and Masques in *The Tempest*," *Theatre Miscellany, Luttrell Society Reprints*, No. 14 (1953), 71-96, p. 83. On this libretto see also the note to III.v.23 of *The Tempest* below. Charles Haywood, "*The Songs and Masque in the New Tempest*: An Incident in the Battle of the Two Theaters, 1674," *HLQ*, XIX (1955), 39-56, discusses and reprints a libretto for Duffett's "Mock-Tempest," which was being played at Drury Lane during the winter of 1674-75. Carroll Camden, "*Songs and Chorusses in The Tempest*," *Studies in English Drama Presented to Baldwin Maxwell, PQ*, XLI (1962), No. 1, pp. 114-122, discusses an apparently unique copy at Rice University of the booklet whose title is the title of his article. This booklet contains eleven songs, two of which are not known to have been published elsewhere until Kemble's edition of 1789. Camden suggests that these are the songs of Sheridan's version (which was not published), first performed in January of 1777.

[47] *The First Modern Comedies* (Cambridge, Mass., 1959), p. 221. Frank H. Moore, *The Nobler Pleasure: Dryden's Comedy in Theory and Practice* (Chapel Hill, 1963), pp. 68-75, defends the lovers' behavior as "natural."

choice of persons for his epic.[48] Characters whose example should be
avoided are "deriv'd from the distempers of Love or Ambition, for
Love and Ambition are too often the raging Feavers of great minds."
Although Ambition is "necessary for every vertuous breast," "the world
is onely ill govern'd because the wicked take more paines to get authority then the vertuous, for the vertuous are often preach'd into
retirement" or into "Lasynesse." His "considered definition" of Love
is "that indefinite Love is Lust, and Lust when it is determin'd to one
is Love"; moreover, "Love is the most acceptable imposition of Nature,
the cause and preservation of Life, and the very healthfulnesse of the
mind as well as of the Body, but Lust, our raging Feaver, is more
dangerous in Cities then the Calenture in Ships." Hippolito suffers
from Lust according to Davenant's definition, and, until he learns
better, he causes the trouble his originator predicts. Ferdinand, the
romantic hero who has something of the fantastic sense of honor of
the heroic lover (e.g., IV.iii.138-140), is never attracted to anyone but
Miranda, although, being wise, he is ready to mistrust even the one he
loves. Prospero paid so little attention to Ambition (unlike Macbeth,
who paid too much) that he lost his kingdom and almost his life;
having recognized his fault he returns to his responsibilities. By contrast, Antonio and Alonzo are guilty of the excess of Ambition; they
are among those who are allowed to govern ill by default in others,
such as Prospero, who would govern well. Their penance (destroying
the Moors and suffering on the island), their penitence (e.g., II.iv.
14-34), and their retirement from politics are sufficient to entitle them
to Prospero's forgiveness. Ferdinand is quick to think of himself as
"Savoy" when he sees a young lady (III.vi.28), but he is not over-
ambitious, as he insists a few lines later. In the main plot, then, the
nobles and Prospero are presented in terms of Ambition; the young
people are presented largely in terms of Love. Both are combined and
parodied in Davenant's subplot. When Sycorax tells Trincalo, "I'll be
kind to all of 'em, just as I am to thee" (IV.ii.9-10), she reflects Hip-

---

[48] Shakespeare's *Tempest* was probably in Davenant's mind as he wrote
Gondibert. Sir A. W. Ward, *A History of English Dramatic Literature* (London, 1899), II, 200, exaggerates when he asserts that Davenant "plagiarised
characters and situations from *The Tempest*" for *Gondibert.* More carefully in
III, 169n, Ward says that the Astragon-Birtha section "in its earliest passages at
all events [is] obviously modelled on the scenes between Prospero, Miranda, and
Ferdinand." Quotations from Davenant's *Preface* are from Joel E. Spingarn,
ed., *Critical Essays of the Seventeenth Century* (Bloomington, Ind., 1957), II,
14-16.

polito's point of view (but without his hope for salvation); and the sailors' struggle for power is a parody both of excessive and deficient Ambition — as Prospero observes, "And now their Wine is gone, they will not quarrel" (V.ii.212).

Shakespeare wrote of the uncivilized world of nature and the civilized world of man and saw good and evil in each. Davenant and Dryden, writing in a more cynical and "civilized" age, had a more limited admiration for the uncivilized world: Hippolito's lack of knowledge leads to lust and almost to death. Prospero is punished by being banished from Milan, and he can think of little but returning to his rightful authority. Civilization, on the other hand, is to be desired, although its representatives in the play are not all desirable — one, Ferdinand, is to be imitated, while the others show passions that are to be avoided.

Downes says that *King Lear* was performed "exactly as *Mr. Shakespear* Wrote it" between the Restoration and the appearance of Tate's version; but we know little more about the play during the 1660's and 1670's.[49] Much later, there were continual assaults upon Tate's text: playbills of 1743 advertise performances "With Restorations from Shakespeare";[50] Garrick, whose greatest role seems to have been Lear,[51] adapted the play in 1756, restoring some of Shakespeare but keeping the love story and Tate's ending, and not bringing back the Fool; Colman in his adaptation, which was performed at Covent Garden from 1768-73 as Garrick's was being played at Drury Lane and (in 1770) Tate's was used at the Haymarket,[52] omitted the Fool and the love story as well, though he kept the happy ending; J. P. Kemble made three versions of the play.[53] But Tate's *Lear* survived all of these; and it was not until 1823 that Kean restored the tragic ending (though he kept the love story) and 1838 that Macready hesitantly restored the Fool, played by Phyllis Horton.[54] It was 157 years since

---

[49] Downes, p. 33. H. Spencer, p. 75, lists a performance in June, 1675. Leland E. Derrick, "The Stage History of *King Lear*," unpub. dissertation (Texas, 1940), quotes much contemporary criticism and commentary in the 150 pages he devotes to the fortunes of the play from the Restoration through Macready's era.

[50] Hogan, I, 263.

[51] G. W. Stone, Jr., *SP*, XLV (1948), 101; Burnim, *David Garrick, Director*, p. 141.

[52] Hogan, II, 345-350.

[53] H. Baker, *John Philip Kemble*, pp. 328-329.

[54] Odell, II, 154, 194-195.

Tate's adaptation had first appeared; evidently, the Romantic critics never saw Shakespeare's play performed.[55] Moreover, there were purchasers and, presumably, readers for the more than twenty editions that had appeared even by the time Garrick revised the play.

Robert Ornstein has observed that "though good usually triumphs and evil is destroyed at the close of Jacobean tragedy, we are made to feel how vulnerable are the walls — the political, religious, legal, and familial institutions — which seek to check or contain the uncivilized fury of civilized man."[56] Of no play would this observation be more true than of Shakespeare's *King Lear*. The destruction of evil involves the destruction of such an extraordinary amount of good that many critics, including Dr. Johnson and A. C. Bradley, have been unhappy with the ending.[57] The Augustan Age, especially, was more interested in thickening the walls than in being shown the nearness of chaos, and Tate's revision pulls the play down within the literary expectations of his audience.[58] Cordelia's lying (in Tate's version) to her father for the calculated purpose of preventing her marriage to the hated Burgundy supplies her with the conventional motivation of a stage heroine; her father's angry reaction — disinheritance — is equally to be expected. Edgar's laying his heart before Cordelia; her pretending indifference to "prove" him; his staying in disguise to protect her; his rescuing her from ruffians sent by the lustful villain; his appearing from a victory over the villain and at the last moment to rescue the heroine and her father from death — all these are in the conventional pattern of romantic story and drama. Lear himself is an angry and confused parent who, maltreated by ungrateful daughters, goes mad upon the heath. The Fool is quite properly omitted; he would have no function in Tate's version, and he occupies time needed for the love story. The action leads up to the moral that "Truth and Vertue shall at last succeed" in spite of "Storms of Fortune," a statement that applies to the Lovers, but that has little to do with Lear.

Thus, the complex and uncertain problem of Lear and Gloucester is removed to the background in Tate's adaptation, and the black-and-

---

[55] D. Nichol Smith, *Shakespeare in the Eighteenth Century* (Oxford, 1928), p. 25.

[56] *The Moral Vision of Jacobean Tragedy* (Madison, 1960), p. 44.

[57] Johnson's opinion was expressed in the notes to his edition of 1765; A. C. Bradley, *Shakespearean Tragedy* (New York, 1904), pp. 251-252.

[58] The point of view outlined in this paragraph is expressed more fully in C. Spencer, *SEL*, III (1963), 241-251.

white conflict is brought to the fore. The Villains are more obviously evil: Edmund plots to rape Cordelia; Regan commits adultery with Edmund; and it is Goneril who orders the execution of her father and sister. The first two of these additions provide sensational new scenes to add to (and in III.ii to blend with) the new passages written for the lovers. We see the lustful sisters who have poisoned each other quarreling at length over the dying Edmund; and, of course, we are shown the exciting last-minute rescue of Lear and Cordelia. This desire to exploit the theatrical possibilities of the story appears also in the characters' tendency to soliloquize, to make explicit their states of mind at points of emotional crisis: soliloquies not in Shakespeare are given by Edmund at III.ii.1-26 and 112-125 (also a long aside at 52-59), by Gloster at V.iii.6-23, and by Cordelia over the sleeping Lear at V.vi.1-12. Critics who have complained about what Tate added and what he omitted have usually failed to see that the alterations made in the play are related to each other. Tate gives us a coherent combination of theatrical scenes moving along a story line that is complex but yet clear and unified; he deserves A. W. Ward's accolade, "a painstaking and talented writer who, with enduring success, adapted *King Lear*."[59]

We know little about *Richard III* during the Restoration. John Caryll's *English Princess; or, The Death of Richard the III* was performed at Lincoln's Inn Fields in 1667 with "Applause from the Town, as well as profit to the whole Company," and was published in 1667 and again in 1673 and 1674.[60] However, Caryll's play is not an adaptation; it presents in rhymed couplets the courtship of Elizabeth by Richard, Richmond, and Stanley, and borrows little more from Shakespeare's *Richard III* than the idea of Richard's being visited by ghosts (see my note to *The Tempest*, Epilogue, l. 9, below). Nevertheless, there are several unconnected pieces of evidence that *Richard III* was performed in the original or in adapted form before Cibber's version appeared. First in importance is a copy of the 1634 quarto of Shakespeare's play with a Restoration cast in a contemporary hand: the actors include Betterton as Edward IV, Kynaston as Clarence, Sandford as Richard, [Joseph] Williams as Buckingham, Mountfort as

---

[59] In *The Cambridge History of English Literature* (Cambridge, England, 1934), VIII, 41.
[60] The quotation is from Downes, p. 27; the dates are from Nicoll, *History*, I, 395.

Richmond, Hodgson as Rivers, and Michael Lee as Vaughan.[61] Although Summers preferred a date of 1689-90 for the cast, Van Lennep's revised dating of between 1690 (when Lee seems to have joined the company) and July, 1692, seems preferable (in August, Joseph Williams left the company and did not return until after Mountfort's death in December). Cibber's parenthesis "had he ever acted it" in his discussion of Sandford as Richard (see the note to the Persons in *Richard III* below) is not conclusive evidence against Sandford's having played the role, since it is possible that Cibber was ignorant of a performance that took place or that, in context, Cibber is referring to acting in Shakespeare's day. Second is a "Prologue to Richard the third" by A. B., printed in *Covent Garden Drollery* (London, 1672). Third are two allusions which are discussed by Summers: a reference to "visions bloodier than King *Dicks*" with a note referring to *Richard III* in Henry Higden's *A Modern Essay on the Thirteenth Satyr of Juvenal* (1686), and also "A Horse; a Horse; my Kingdom for a Horse" in D'Urfey's *A Fool's Preferment* (1688).[62]

Published early in 1700, Cibber's *Richard III* was presumably first performed near the beginning of that year or at the end of 1699. Perhaps because of the censorship to which it was subjected (see Cibber's Preface and my note to it below), and perhaps because of poor acting (see the note to V.viii.14 below), it was not successful: Cibber says in his "To the Reader" in *Ximena* (1719) that *Richard III* "did not raise me £5 on the third day," and it was apparently not tried again until 1704, nor, as far as we know definitely, republished before the revised version of 1718. The play's popularity increased slowly, and it was not performed frequently until Garrick made his famous first appearance on the London stage in the title role on October 19, 1741. J. P. Kemble played Richard from 1783 to 1802 at Drury Lane, Richmond until 1810 at Covent Garden (George Frederick Cooke playing

---

[61] The cast is printed and discussed by Montague Summers, *Playhouse of Pepys* (New York, 1935), pp. 101, 224-225, and by J. G. McManaway in a letter published in *TLS*, June 27, 1935, p. 416. Summers and William Van Lennep discuss the cast further in *TLS*, July 4, 1935, and April 30, May 7, and June 18, 1938.

[62] The Prologue is readily available in John Munro *et al.*, eds., *The Shakspere Allusion-Book* (London, 1932), II, 103. Summers, who discusses the allusions in his *Playhouse of Pepys*, pp. 223-225, thinks the Prologue "affords proof of a revival at some time before (and probably near to)" 1672. However, *The Shakspere Allusion-Book* suggests that 1661 is the date and (p. 104) that Alexander Brome may be the author.

Richard), and then Richard again from 1810 to 1817.[63] His version of *Richard III,* published in 1810, omits 126½ lines of Cibber's play, restores 4½ from Shakespeare, and adds 1½ by Kemble.[64] Lamb and Hazlitt attacked Cibber's version,[65] and at Covent Garden in 1821 the attempt was made, unsuccessfully, to restore much of Shakespeare, including Queen Margaret and Clarence; Phelps, too, tried to make restorations in 1845.[66] Irving was more successful in 1877, but Wood commented in 1909 that "Cibber's form, while nominally despised by first-class actors and the critical public, is still holding the stage and is still preferred by a large part of the community whose opinions cannot be ignored."[67] A. C. Sprague tells of going to see *Richard III* in Boston

---

[63] Wood, p. 110.

[64] This count is given by Wood, p. 113, who, however, goes on to say (p. 114) that there is "little variation" from this in Inchbald's *British Theatre* (1806-09), XVII, and Oxberry's *New English Drama*, III (1818). I have compared the latter with Cibber's version, and the number of omitted lines seems to be about eighty. See also Alan S. Downer's facsimile of and Introduction to his *Oxberry's 1822 Edition of King Richard III with the Descriptive Notes Recording Edmund Kean's Performance Made by James H. Hackett* (London, 1959).

[65] Lamb's comment is in his "On the Tragedies of Shakespeare, Considered with Reference to Their Fitness for Stage Representation," originally published in 1811: "I am almost disposed to deny to Garrick the merit of being an admirer of Shakspeare. . . . I believe it impossible that he could have had a proper reverence for Shakspeare, and have condescended to go through that interpolated scene in Richard the Third, in which Richard tries to break his wife's heart by telling her he loves another woman, and says, 'if she survives this she is immortal.' Yet I doubt not he delivered this vulgar stuff with as much anxiety of emphasis as any of the genuine parts; and for acting, it is as well calculated as any." T. Hutchinson, ed., *Works of Charles Lamb* (London, 1924), I, 134. Hazlitt's remarks are in his *Characters of Shakespear's Plays* and include: "Some of the most important and striking passages in the principal character have been omitted, to make room for idle and misplaced extracts from other plays; the only intention of which seems to have been to make the character of Richard as odious and disgusting as possible. It is apparently for no other purpose than to make Gloucester stab King Henry on the stage, that the fine abrupt introduction of the character in the opening of the play is lost in the tedious whining morality of the uxorious king (taken from another play); — we say *tedious,* because it interrupts the business of the scene, and loses its beauty and effect by having no intelligible connection with the previous character of the mild, well-meaning monarch. The passages which the unfortunate Henry has to recite are beautiful and pathetic in themselves, but they have nothing to do with the world that Richard has to 'bustle in.' In the same spirit of vulgar caricature is the scene between Richard and Lady Anne (when his wife) interpolated without any authority, merely to gratify his favourite propensity to disgust and loathing." P. P. Howe, ed., *Complete Works of William Hazlitt* (London, 1930), IV, 300-301.

[66] Odell, II, 153, 268-271.

[67] Wood, p. 133.

in 1930 and being treated to "the Cibber text practically in its entirety. Leiber even included the appalling scene in which Richard visits Lady Anne, now Queen, and tries to induce her to take her own life, and played it so well that not a soul laughed." "Cibber, by the way, was nowhere mentioned in the programme."[68]

The unusual endurance of Cibber's *Richard III* doubtless resulted largely from the two main changes in the adaptation. The first is the more compact structure and sharper focus that Cibber provides in his version. Queen Margaret, Edward IV, and Clarence are omitted, and with them go many scenes: Act I is reduced from four scenes to three; Act II from four to two; Act III from seven to two; Act IV from five to four; and Act V loses the scene of Buckingham's execution, although Cibber's method of staging results in nine scenes instead of Shakespeare's five. The historical background of the play is less complex; and the new first act, as well as the choral comments of Stanley, the Lieutenant, and Tressel, provide additional clarity. Further, the adaptation contains about 2,150 lines, instead of 3,619.[69] The focus is even more exclusively on Richard: Cibber's protagonist speaks 39.9 per cent of the lines in the play, whereas Shakespeare's spoke 31.2 per cent; Cibber's Richard appears in fifteen of twenty scenes, whereas Shakespeare's appeared in fifteen of twenty-five; and Cibber provides seven new soliloquies for his central character.[70] This opportunity for a great actor such as Garrick undoubtedly contributed to the adaptation's enduring success.

These soliloquies are part of the second main change in the play, the less obvious but extremely significant alteration in Richard's character. As Eugene M. Waith has pointed out, the increasing moral tone at the end of the seventeenth century accompanied the decline of the "Herculean Hero";[71] in such a climate the intellectually malignant but fascinating hero of Shakespeare was no longer appropriate. As a substitute Cibber attempted to provide a new basis for Richard's character in a series of soliloquies which is designed less to reveal the man or his motives than to relate him to familiar character types and to conven-

---

[68] *Shakespearian Players and Performances* (Cambridge, Mass., 1953), pp. 151, 212.

[69] 3,619 is the number given by E. K. Chambers, *William Shakespeare: A Study of Facts and Problems* (Oxford, 1930), II, 398.

[70] I count as new soliloquies II.i.54-66, II.ii.128-140, III.i.154-178, III.ii.24-33 (technically an aside), III.ii.270-282, IV.iii.19-38 (not in the 1700 version), and the new lines in V.v.

[71] *The Herculean Hero* (New York, 1962), pp. 200-201.

tional morality. For example, he is an Ambitious Lover who actually suffers from pangs of love in II.i.31-34 and III.ii.24-33. Particularly significant is the soliloquy of the Villain at the end of III.i, in which Richard argues against Conscience with two extended similes, one of five lines in which Conscience is compared to a scarecrow and one of nine lines in which it is compared to money ("we live by parting with it"). The speech is less what a man of Richard's actions would think than what, according to conventional morality, he ought to think; that is, he should recognize the pull of Conscience (as he also does while the Princes are being murdered — IV.iii.19-38 — and in V.v), but he resists it. A further consequence is that rather than making Richard an individual, the soliloquy has the opposite effect of making him like all other Villains.

Richard is also the Heroic Warrior. Like the Dauphin of *Henry V*, he suggests clothing and feeding his enemies before he fights with them. Moreover, he is concerned about his Fame (III.i.175-176, III.ii.278-280, and IV.iii.26-36) and thereby shows again the conventional attitude and reveals his awareness of another relationship with society. The Heroic Warrior and Villain meet (not very smoothly) in Richard's death speech, where first, Hotspur-like, Richard laments the Fame that Richmond has gained from him, and then, with words borrowed from Northumberland in *II Henry IV*, calls down destruction upon the world. These last lines seem more appropriate to the death of a real arch-villain than to the Villain who talks about Conscience and Fame. Richard forgets Love at the end of the play, but Richmond is not allowed to ignore it: on being informed that Princess Elizabeth is approaching, he observes, "Ay, there indeed my toil's rewarded."

Shakespeare wrote for an audience that responded to the Machiavellian with mingled fascination and horror, and a modern audience responds to Richard the colorful politician, brilliantly articulate and clever. Cibber, however, chose another way in which to relate his protagonist to the audience: instead of dazzling or horrifying them, his hero is designed to shock and to irritate them — apparently Cibber the actor played the role that way. The audience is pleased to see the source of irritation destroyed, and one wonders whether some of the sneers at Cibber the actor as Richard do not result in some measure at least from a confusion of the irritating stage character with the irritating man.[72]

---

[72] Steele suggested as much in *The Theatre*, No. 7, Jan. 23, 1720: John Loftis,

The Jew of Venice, adapted by George Granville, later Lord Lans-
downe, was evidently first performed before the middle of 1701.[73]
Hogan records a total of thirty-six performances through 1748;[74] and,
in addition, it was a birthday play for Queen Anne: on September 8,
1711, it was advertised "As it was perform'd before her Majesty on her
Birth day [Feb. 6] at St. James's."[75] However, *The Jew*'s success was
really ended in 1741, when Macklin played "the Jew that Shakespeare
drew":[76] from his first performance to the end of the century 316
performances of the original are recorded, twenty-six in 1741 alone.[77]
Granville's Shylock, originated by Thomas Doggett (c. 1670-1721),
was also played by Griffin, Boheme, Ogden, Aston, and Arthur.

Critics' views of Granville's Shylock are almost as varied as their
views of Shakespeare's. Hazelton Spencer felt that Granville "has not
altered Shylock's character" and that Doggett "may have played Shylock as a comic spectacle — I hope he did. But there is no evidence
that he caricatured him." For Lounsbury Granville's Jew "is not indeed a comic character, as has been so persistently asserted; but he is
essentially a vulgar one." Handasyde, who considered "obviously un-
true" the notion that Shylock was "broadly comic," observed that
"Shylock's passionate lust for revenge is transformed into a cold and

---

ed., *Richard Steele's* The Theatre *1720* (Oxford, 1962), p. 29. Loftis, p. 128,
points out that Steele had made the point earlier in *Town-Talk*, No. 2, Dec.
23, 1715.

[73] There has been confusion about the date of publication (and, based on it,
of probable first performance). Alfred Jackson, "Play Notices from the Burney
Newspapers, 1700-1703," *PMLA*, XLVIII (1933), 823, cites an announce-
ment of the publication of *The Jew* in *The London Gazette* for Jan. 19-23,
1701, dates given also by Avery, *London Stage*, Part II, Vol. I, p. 7. Nicoll,
History, II, 333, gives the date of publication as Jan. 17 and cites *The London
Gazette* and *Post-Man*. The Prologue and Epilogue of *The Jew* refer to *All
for Love* and *Timon of Athens*, both of which were performed in January, 1701.
However, Hogan, I, 2, 309, gives the date of publication as June 17, 1701,
and the date of first performance as "probably May"; June 17 is also the date
in the 1929 edition of Nicoll, *History*, II. I have not seen the *Post-Man*, but
the correct date in *The London Gazette* is June 19-23, 1701.

[74] Hogan, I, 461. "An excellent Droll, called, *The Distressed Merchant*; or
The Jew of Venice" was performed six times at Phillip's Booth, Bowling Green,
Southwark, in 1754 (Hogan, II, 415). *The Jew* was performed later in the
provinces: Sybil Rosenfeld, *Strolling Players & Drama in the Provinces 1660-
1765* (Cambridge, England, 1939), lists performances at York in 1755-56 and
on the Kentish circuit in 1752-53 and 1764.

[75] *London Stage*, Part II, Vol. I, p. 255.

[76] On Macklin's performance see notes 10 and 16 above.

[77] Hogan, I, 313, 461; II, 717.

motiveless cruelty."[78] However, Granville's Jew was surely comic:
Thomas Doggett was a comedian; and it is presumably to his performance that Rowe referred in 1709 when he complained that "tho' we
have seen [The Merchant of Venice] receiv'd and acted as a Comedy,
and the part of the Jew perform'd by an excellent Comedian, yet I
cannot but think it was design'd tragically by the Author."[79] Moreover,
Downes described Doggett as "the only Comick Original now Extant:
Witness . . . The Jew of Venice."[80] J. H. Wilson, after summarizing the
various points of view and examining the evidence, has come to the
conclusion that Granville's Shylock was "intended to evoke laughter,"
that he "is a petty villain of an exaggeratedly melodramatic type, a
most unconvincing rascal exposed to ridicule. He is a stock-jobbing
[cheating] Jew who has overreached himself and is properly punished."[81] Wilson is probably correct in describing the class to which
Shylock belongs, but in Granville's play the Jew overreaches himself
not as a stock-jobber but as a hater. By omitting most of Shakespeare's
III.i, Granville shows us much less of Shylock's suffering, and, as a
result, Shylock's part in the action is more obviously that of the Villain,
the impediment to happiness of the friends and even of the lovers:
Shylock remarks that neither friend will be willing long to survive the
other, and it seems as if Bassanio may lose his life in a hopeless attempt
to save Antonio. He is fitted into his part in the eternal stage struggle
between Villain and Hero; and individual character is subordinated to
conventional conflict.

Granville cut the number of scenes and the cast by half: he omitted
II.i-iv, II.vii-ix, III.i, and III.iv-v, and, with them, Morocco, Arra-
gon, Salanio, Salarino, Tubal, Launcelot, and Old Gobbo. The material Granville added develops the theme of the adaptation — the
support of love and friendship for each other: Antonio the friend
helps Bassanio the lover win his lady, and the lovers then save the
friend. Although the theme is in Shakespeare's play, it is stressed
heavily in Granville's additions, the most substantial of which deal with
Love (III.i.20-60 and 177-183, and V.i.159-212) or with Friendship

---

[78] H. Spencer, p. 343; T. R. Lounsbury, Shakespeare as a Dramatic Artist,
p. 338; Handasyde, pp. 58, 61.
[79] Nicholas Rowe, "Some Account of the Life &c. of Mr. William Shakespear," in D. Nichol Smith, ed., Eighteenth Century Essays on Shakespeare
(New York, 1962), p. 12.
[80] Downes, p. 52.
[81] J. H. Wilson, "Granville's 'Stock-Jobbing Jew,'" PQ, XIII (1934), 1-15,
p. 12.

(I.i.63-73 and IV.i.179-218) or with Love and Friendship (III.i.188-221 and 284-297, and V.i.230-261). The new scene (II.ii) is built around Antonio's toast to Friendship, Bassanio's toast to Love, and Shylock's unacceptable toast to Money. Then (in the earlier version) the "Masque of Peleus and Thetis" emphasizes the power of Love and Friendship; the Lovers are saved from Jupiter's wrath by means of the prophecy given by Peleus' friend Prometheus, who is then freed himself. In the play proper Friendship stands for Honor, as Portia points out in the last lines of Act III. An extravagant display of this Honor follows in the exciting climax of IV, when Bassanio draws his sword and places himself between Shylock, who is ready to begin cutting his pound of flesh, and Antonio, who has given his "death" speech. Before Portia can act, the Duke orders Bassanio's arrest. It takes not only Portia's ingenuity but also the Duke's recognition of noble motives ("Virtue") to save the characters. Later, Granville suggests the potential conflict between Love and Honor (Friendship) as Bassanio momentarily turns on Antonio, who shames him (V.i.183-185). However, all is resolved happily, and Bassanio has learned that enduring love is based on "Gratitude" — presumably, both to Portia and to Antonio.

This sententiousness is omnipresent in *The Jew*, and most of the characters participate in the moralizing. Four of the acts end with sententious couplets: Antonio on the joys of giving in I; Bassanio on the difficulties "Lovers and Friends" experience in parting in II; Nerissa on the ability of women to deceive men in IV; and Bassanio on gratitude at the end. The main characters tend to do their moralizing about such grand subjects as Friendship, Love, Fame, and Chance. The secondary figures, however, are allowed more cynical observations, such as Nerissa's couplet at the end of IV and Gratiano's repeated equation of "Matters of State" and "A Rape and a Robbery" at the end of II.i, followed immediately by his observation that Jew, Turk, and Christian "all jog on — unerring, to the Devil." Decorum of character seems to operate here: since Gratiano is not heroic (he would not choose the lead casket), he is allowed the kind of reflection that the nobler lovers would not use. Bassanio emerges as a more important character in Granville than in Shakespeare; he has more than his share of sententious lines to speak, and he acts heroically in the trial scene. He also gains, of course, from the omission of the other suitors and from the lesser interest in Shylock's character. In addition, he is presented in a more realistic manner, for Granville's Portia and Bassanio are more the familiar young lady and gentleman than the fairy tale princess and the exotic young aristocrat.

Love supported by Friendship is the theme of the masque as of the play, and, of course, the masque itself adds to the interest in music expressed in the play. Granville probably included it originally as a concession to the current enthusiasm for "operatic" entertainments; but he seems to have been proud of it, for he included it in his *Poems upon Several Occasions* (1712, 1716, 1721, 1726, 1732).[82] Although he removed the masque from the final version of *The Jew of Venice* in the second volume of the *Genuine Works* (1732), he included it in Vol. I. Others, though not Dr. Johnson, who commented unfavorably on the masque in his *Life* of Granville, seem to have shared the author's opinion, for the masque was performed and separately reprinted later in the century.[83]

I have urged that the adaptations should be read as if they were new plays. Such a reading will be worthwhile in three ways. First, the best of the adaptations are enjoyable in themselves if they are read for themselves, some of the enjoyment coming originally from Shakespeare and some from the adapter. Second, the adaptations read as new plays will add to our understanding of the age that produced them. And third, we may broaden and deepen our understanding of Shakespeare — not by praising him at the adapters' expense, but by comprehending *their* vision of the Shakespearean material with which they were working. We might compare what is to be gained here with the value of an interpretation of a Shakespearean play from a particular point of view or in terms of a particular theme: we may not wish to adopt the interpreter's understanding to the exclusion of other insights — indeed, we may on the whole dislike it — but his view may still add significantly to a comprehensive reading of the play. Every age tends to admire what interests it in Shakespeare and to ignore or lament the rest; and the more evidence we obtain of this fact, the more we should exert ourselves to profit from the insight of our predecessors.

---

[82] Handasyde, pp. 125, 273-274.

[83] Nicoll, *History*, II, 333, lists a performance of the masque at the Swan Tavern on April 28, 1747. The *B. M. Catalogue*, Vol. XC, col. 659, lists texts of [1740?] and 1781, the latter on a single leaf included in a volume of that date. At the University of Illinois Library there is an undated copy (catalogued as 178-) of the masque printed on a single leaf.

MACBETH,

A

TRAGÆDY.

With all the

ALTERATIONS,
AMENDMENTS,
ADDITIONS,

AND

NEW SONGS.

As it's now Acted at the Dukes Theatre.

By Sr Wm Davenant

LONDON,

Printed for *P. Chetwin,* and are to be Sold
by most Booksellers, 1674.

THE ARGUMENT.

Duncan, *King of the* Scots, *had two Principal Men, whom he Im-*
ployed in all Matters of Importance, Macbeth *and* Banquo, *These*
two Traveling together through a Forrest, were met by three Fairie
Witches (Weirds the Scots *call them) whereof the first making*
Obeysance unto Macbeth, *saluted him,* Thane (*a Title unto which*
that of Earl *afterwards succeeded) of* Glammis, *the second* Thane
of Cowder, *and the third King of* Scotland: *This is unequal deal-*
ing, saith Banquo, *to give my Friend all the Honours, and none*
unto me: To which one of the Weirds made Answer, That he
indeed should not be a King, but out of his Loyns should come a   10
Race of Kings; that should for ever Rule the Scots. *And having*
thus said, they all suddenly Vanished, Upon their Arrival to the
Court, Macbeth *was immediately Created* Thane *of* Glammis; *and*
not long after some new Service of his, requiring new Recompence,
he was Honoured with Title of Thane *of* Cowder. *Seeing then*
how happily the Prediction of the three Weirds fell out in the
former, he Resolved not to be wanting to himself in fulfilling the
third; and therefore first he Killed the King, and after by reason
of his Command among the Souldiers and Common People, he
Succeeded in his Throne. Being scarce warm in his Seat, he called   20
to mind the Prediction given to his Companion Banquo: *Whom*
hereupon suspected as his Supplanter, he caused to be Killed, to-
gether with his Posterity: Flean *one of his Sons, Escaped only,*
with no small difficulty into Wales, *Freed as he thought from all*
fear of Banquo *and his Issue; he Built* Dunsinan *Castle, and made*
it his Ordinary Seat: And afterwards on some new Fears, Con-
sulted with certain of his Wizards about his future Estate: Was
told by one of them, that he should never be Overcome, till Birnam *Wood (being some Miles distant) came to* Dunsinan *Castle;*
and by another, that he should never be Slain by any Man which   30
was Born of a Woman. Secure then as he thought, from all future
Dangers; he omitted no kind of Libidinous Cruelty for the space
of 18 Years; for so long he Tyrannized over Scotland. *But having*

then made up the Measure of his Iniquities, Macduff *the Governor of* Fife, *associating to himself some few Patriots (and being assisted with Ten Thousand* English) *equally hated by the Tyrant, and abhorring the Tyranny, met in* Birnam *Wood, & taking every one of them a Bough in his hand (the better to keep them from discovery) Marching early in the Morning towards* Dunsinan *Castle, which they took by* Scalado. Macbeth *escaping, was pursued by* 40 Macduff, *who having overtaken him, urged him to the Combat; to whom the Tyrant, half in scorn, returned this Answer: That he did in Vain attempt to Kill him, it being his Destiny never to be Slain by any that was Born of Woman. Now then said* Macduff, *is thy fatal end drawing fast upon thee, for I was never Born of Woman, but violently Cut out of my Mothers Belly: Which words so daunted the cruel Tyrant, though otherways a Valiant man and of great Performances, that he was very easily slain; and* Malcolm Conmer, *the true Heir, Seated in his Throne.*

THE PERSONS NAMES.

King of *Scotland,*	Mr. *Lee.*
Malcolm his Son, Prince of *Cumberland,*	Mr. *Norris.*
Donalbain,	Mr. *Cademan.*
Lenox,	Mr. *Medbourn.*
Macbeth,	Mr. *Batterton.*
Banquo,	Mr. *Smith.*
Macduff,	Mr. *Harris.*
Seymour,	
Seyton,	
Fleance, Boy to *Banquo,*	
2 Murderers,	
Macbeth's Wife,	Mrs. *Batterton.*
Macduff's Wife,	Mrs. *Long.*
[Maid,]	
Waiting Gentlewoman,	
Ghost of *Banquo,*	
Heccate,	Mr. *Sanford.*
Witches,	
Servants, [Soldiers, Messengers,] and Attendants.	

37

ACT I, SCENE I

Thunder and Lightening.

Enter three Witches.

1. *Witch.* When shall we three meet again,
In Thunder, Lightning, and in Rain?
  2. When the Hurly-burly's done,
When the Battle's lost and won.
  3. And that will be e're set of Sun.
  1. Where's the place?
  2.   Upon the Heath.
  3. There we resolve to meet *Macbeth.* . . . .   [*A shriek like an Owl.*
  1. I come Gray *Malkin.*
  All.   *Paddock* calls!
To us fair weather's foul, and foul is fair!
Come hover through the foggy, filthy Air. . . . .   [*Exeunt flying.*

[ACT I, SCENE II]

Enter King, Malcolm, Donalbain *and* Lenox, *with Attendants
meeting* Seyton *wounded.*

  King. What aged man is that? if we may guess
His message by his looks, He can relate
The Issue of the Battle!
  Mal. This is the valiant *Seyton,*
Who like a good and hardy Souldier fought

38

To save my liberty. Hail, Worthy Friend,
Inform the King in what condition you
Did leave the Battle?
    Seyt.   It was doubtful;
As two spent swimmers, who together cling
And choak their Art: the merciless *Mackdonald*   10
(Worthy to be a Rebel, to which end
The multiplying Villanies of Nature
Swarm'd thick upon him) from the western Isles
With Kernes and Gallow-glasses was supply'd.
Whom Fortune with her smiles oblig'd a-while;
But brave *Macbeth* (who well deserves that name)
Did with his frowns put all her smiles to flight:
And Cut his passage to the Rebels person:
Then having Conquer'd him with single force,
He fixt his Head upon our Battlements.   20
    King. O valiant Cousin! Worthy Gentleman!
    Seyt. But then this Day-break of our Victory
Serv'd but to light us into other Dangers
That spring from whence our hope did seem to rise,
Produc'd our hazard: for no sooner had
The justice of our Cause, Sir, (arm'd with valour,)
Compell'd these nimble Kernes to trust their Heels,
But the *Norweyan* Lord, (having expected
This opportunity) with new supplies
Began a fresh assault.
    King.   Dismaid not this   30
Our Generals, *Macbeth* and *Banquo?*
    Seyt. Yes, as sparrows Eagles, or as hares do Lions;
As flames are heighten'd by access of fuel,
So did their valours gather strength, by having
Fresh Foes on whom to exercise their Swords:
Whose thunder still did drown the dying groans
Of those they slew, which else had been so great,
Th'had frighted all the rest into Retreat.
My spirits faint: I would relate the wounds
Which their Swords made; but my own silence me.   40
    King. So well thy wounds become thee as thy words:
Th'are full of Honour both: Go get him Surgeons ——
                [*Exeunt* Seyton *and Attendants.*

Enter Macduff.

But, who comes there?
 Mal.   Noble *Macduff!*
 Len. What haste looks through his eyes!
 Don. So should he look who comes to things strange.
 Macd. Long live the King!
 King.   Whence com'st thou, worthy *Thane?*
 Macd. From *Fife,* Great King; where the *Norweyan* Banners
Darkned the Air; and fann'd our people cold:
Norwey himself, with infinite supplies,
(Assisted by that most disloyal *Thane*   50
Of *Cawdor*) long maintain'd a dismal Conflict,
Till brave *Macbeth* oppos'd his bloody rage,
And check'd his haughty spirits, after which
His Army fled: Thus shallow streams may flow
Forward with violence a-while; but when
They are oppos'd, as fast run back agen.
In brief, the Victory was ours.
 King.   Great Happiness!
 Mal. And now the *Norwey* King craves Composition.
We would not grant the burial of his men,
Until at *Colems-Inch* he had disburs'd   60
Great heaps of Treasure to our Generals use.
 King. No more that *Thane* of *Cawdor* shall deceive
Our confidence: pronounce his present Death;
And with his former Title greet *Macbeth.*
He has deserv'd it.
 Macd.   Sir! I'll see it done.
 King. What he has lost, Noble *Macbeth* has won. . . . . [*Exeunt.*

[ACT I, SCENE III]

Thunder and Lightening.
Enter three Witches flying.

1. *Witch.* Where hast thou been, Sister?
2. Killing Swine!
3. Sister; where thou?
1. A Sailor's wife had Chestnuts in her lap,
And mounch'd, and mounch'd, and mounch'd; give me quoth I;
Anoint thee, Witch, the rump-fed Ronyon cry'd,
Her Husband's to the *Baltick* gone, Master o'th'*Tyger.*
But in a sieve I'll thither sail,
And like a Rat without a tail
I'll do, I'll do, and I will do.   10
2. I'll give thee a wind.
1. Thou art kind.
3. And I another.
1. I my self have all the other.
And then from every Port they blow;
From all the points that Sea-men know.
I will drain him dry as hay;
Sleep shall neither night nor day
Hang upon his pent-house lid;
My charms shall his repose forbid,   20
Weary sen-nights nine times nine,
Shall he dwindle, waste, and pine.
Though his Bark cannot be lost,
Yet it shall be Tempest-tost.
Look what I have.
2. Shew me, shew me, ——
1. Here I have a Pilot's thumb
Wrack'd, as homeward he did come!   [*A Drum within.*
3. A Drum, a Drum:
Macbeth does come.   30
1. The weyward Sisters hand in hand,
Posters of the Sea and Land
Thus do go about, about,
Thrice to thine.
2. And thrice to mine.
3. And thrice agen to make up nine.
2. Peace, the Charms wound up.
        Enter Macbeth *and* Banquo *with Attendants.*
Macb. Command they make a halt upon the Heath. ——

So fair, and foul a day I have not seen!
    Banq. How far is't now to *Forres?* what are these   40
So wither'd, and so wild in their attire?
That look not like the Earths Inhabitants,
And yet are on't? Live you? or are you things
Crept hither from the lower World to fright
Th'Inhabitants of this? You seem to know me
By laying all at once your choppy fingers
Upon your skinny-lips; you shou'd be women,
And yet your looks forbid me to interpret
So well of you. ——
    Macb. Speak, if you can, what are you?   50
    1. *Witch.* All hail, *Macbeth,* Hail to thee *Thane of Glamis.*
    2. All hail, *Macbeth,* Hail to thee *Thane of Cawdor.*
    3. All hail, *Macbeth,* who shall be King hereafter.
    Banq. Good Sir, what makes you start? and seem to dread
Events which sound so fair? I'th'name of Truth
Are you fantastical? or that indeed
Which outwardly you shew? my noble Partner,
You greet with present Grace, and strange prediction
Of noble Fortune, and of Royal hope;
With which he seems surpriz'd: To me you speak not.   60
If you can look into the seeds of Time,
And tell which grain will grow, and which will not,
Speak then to me; who neither beg your favours,
Nor fear your hate. ——
    1. *Witch.*   Hail!
    2.   Hail!
    3.   Hail!
    1. Lesser than *Macbeth,* and greater.
    2. Not so happy, yet much happier.
    3. Thou shalt get Kings, thou shalt ne'r be one.
So all Hail *Macbeth* and *Banquo.* ——
    1. *Banquo* and *Macbeth,* all Hail . . . .   [*Going.*
    Macb. Stay! you imperfect Speakers! tell me more;   70
By *Sinel's* death I know I am *Thane* of *Glamis;*
But how of *Cawdor,* whilst that *Thane* yet lives?
And, for your promise, that I shall be King,
'Tis not within the prospect of belief,

No more than to be *Cawdor:* say from whence
You have this strange Intelligence: or why
Upon this blasted Heath you stop our way
With such prophetick greeting? Speak, I charge you. [*Witches vanish.*
Ha! gone! . . . .
   Banq.   The earth has Bubbles like the water:
And these are some of them: how soon they are vanish'd!   80
   Macb. . . . Th' are turn'd to Air; what seem'd Corporeal
Is melted into nothing; would they had staid.
   Banq. . . . Were such things here as we discours'd of now?
Or have we tasted some infectious Herb
That captivates our Reason?
   Macb. Your Children shall be Kings.
   Banq.   You shall be King.
   Macb. And *Thane* of *Cawdor* too, went it not so?
   Banq. Just to that very tune! who's here?

Enter Macduff.

   Macd. Macbeth the King has happily receiv'd
The news of your success: And when he reads   90
Your pers'nal venture in the Rebels fight,
His wonder and his praises then contend
Which shall exceed: when he reviews your worth,
He finds you in the stout *Norweyan*-ranks;
Not starting at the Images of Death
Made by your self: each Messenger which came
Being loaden with the praises of your Valour;
Seem'd proud to speak your Glories to the King;
Who, for an earnest of a greater Honour
Bad me, from him, to call you *Thane* of *Cawdor:*   100
In which Addition, Hail, most Noble *Thane!*
   Banq. What, can the Devil speak true?
   Macb. The *Thane* of *Cawdor* lives!
Why do you dress me in his borrow'd Robes?
   Macd. 'Tis true, Sir; He, that was the *Thane,* yet lives;
But under heavy judgment bears that life
Which he in justice is condemn'd to lose.
Whether he was combin'd with those of *Norway,*
Or did assist the Rebel privately;

Or whether he concurr'd with both, to cause   110
His Country's danger, Sir, I cannot tell:
But, Treasons Capital, confess'd, and prov'd,
Have over-thrown him.
    Macb.   *Glamis* and *Thane* of *Cawdor!*
The greatest is behind; my noble Partner!
Do you not hope your Children shall be Kings?
When those who gave to me the *Thane* of *Cawdor*
Promis'd no less to them.
    Banq.   If all be true,
You have a Title to a Crown, as well
As to the *Thane* of *Cawdor.* It seems strange;
But many times to win us to our harm,   120
The Instruments of darkness tell us truths,
And tempt us with low trifles, that they may
Betray us in the things of high concern.
    Macb. Th'have told me truth as to the name of *Cawdor,*   [*Aside.*
That may be prologue to the name of King.
Less Titles shou'd the greater still fore-run,
The morning Star doth usher in the Sun.
This strange prediction in as strange a manner
Deliver'd, neither can be good nor ill:
If ill; 'twou'd give no earnest of success,   130
Beginning in a truth: I'm *Thane* of *Cawdor;*
If good? why am I then preplext with doubt?
My future bliss causes my present fears,
Fortune, methinks, which rains down Honour on me,
Seems to rain bloud too: *Duncan* does appear
Clowded by my increasing Glories: but
These are but dreams.
    Banq.   Look how my Partner's rap'd!
    Macb. If Chance will have me King; Chance may bestow
A Crown without my stir.
    Banq. His Honours are surprizes, and resemble   140
New Garments, which but seldom fit men well,
Unless by help of use.
    Macb.   Come, what come may;
Patience and time run through the roughest day.
    Banq. Worthy *Macbeth!* we wait upon your leisure.

Macb. I was reflecting upon late transactions;
Worthy *Macduff;* your pains are registred
Where every day I turn the leaf to read them.
Let's hasten to the King: we'll think upon
These accidents at more convenient time.
When w'have maturely weigh'd them, we'll impart   150
Our mutual judgments to each others breasts.
   Banq. Let it be so.
   Macb.   Till then, enough. Come Friends . . . .   [*Exeunt.*

[ACT I, SCENE IV]

    Enter King, Lenox, Malcolm, Donalbain, *Attendants.*
   King. Is execution done on *Cawdor* yet?
Or are not they return'd, who were imploy'd
In doing it?
   Mal.   They are not yet come back;
But I have spoke with one who saw him die,
And did report that very frankly, he
Confess'd his Treasons; and implor'd your pardon,
With signs of a sincere and deep repentance.
He told me, nothing in his life became him
So well, as did his leaving it. He dy'd
As one who had been study'd in his Death,   10
Quitting the dearest thing he ever had,
As 'twere a worthless trifle.
   King.   There's no Art
To find the minds construction in the face:
He was a Gentleman on whom I built
An absolute trust.

        Enter Macbeth, Banquo, *and* Macduff.
        O worthy'st Cozen!
The sin of my Ingratitude even now

Seem'd heavy on me. Thou art so far before,
That all the wings of recompence are slow
To overtake thee: would thou hadst less deserv'd,
That the proportion both of thanks and payment   20
Might have been mine: I've only left to say,
That thou deserv'st more than I have to pay.
   Macb. The service and the loyalty I owe you,
Is a sufficient payment for it self:
Your Royal part is to receive our Duties;
Which Duties are, Sir, to your Throne and State,
Children and Servants; and when we expose
Our dearest lives to save your Interest,
We do but what we ought.
   King.   Y'are welcome hither;
I have begun to plant thee, and will labour   30
Still to advance thy growth: And noble *Banquo,*
(Who ha'st no less deserv'd; nor must partake
Less of our favour,) let me here enfold thee,
And hold thee to my heart.
   Banq.   There if I grow,
The harvest is your own.
   King.   My joys are now
Wanton in fulness; and wou'd hide themselves
In drops of sorrow. Kinsmen, Sons, and *Thanes;*
And you, whose places are the nearest, know
We will establish our estate upon
Our Eldest, *Malcolm,* whom we name hereafter   40
The Prince of *Cumberland:* nor must he wear
His Honours unaccompany'd by others,
But marks of nobleness, like Stars shall shine
On all deservers. Now we'll hasten hence
To *Enverness:* we'll be your guest, *Macbeth,*
And there contract a greater debt than that
Which I already owe you.
   Macb.   That Honour, Sir,
Out-speaks the best expression of my thanks:
I'll be my self the Harbinger, and bless
My wife with the glad news of your approach.   50
I humbly take my leave.   [Macbeth *going out, stops, and speaks*
                 whilst the King talks with Banq. *&c.*

King. My worthy *Cawdor!* . .
Macb. Prince of *Cumberland!* that is a step
On which I must fall down, or else o're-leap;
For in my way it lies. Stars! hide your fires,
Let no light see my black and deep desires.
The strange Idea of a bloudy act
Does into doubt all my resolves distract.
My eye shall at my hand connive, the Sun
Himself should wink when such a deed is done . . . .   [*Exit.*
    King. True, Noble *Banquo,* he is full of worth;   60
And with his Commendations I am fed;
It is a Feast to me. Let's after him,
Whose care is gone before to bid us welcome:
He is a matchless Kinsman . . . .   [*Exeunt.*

[ACT I, SCENE V]

Enter Lady Macbeth, *and Lady* Macduff. *Lady* Macbeth
having a Letter in her hand.

    La. Macb. Madam, I have observ'd since you came hither,
You have been still disconsolate. Pray tell me,
Are you in perfect health?
    La. Macd. Alas! how can I?
My Lord, when Honour call'd him to the War,
Took with him half of my divided soul,
Which lodging in his bosom, lik'd so well
The place, that 'tis not yet return'd.
    La. Macb. Methinks
That should not disorder you: for, no doubt
The brave *Macduff* left half his soul behind him,
To make up the defect of yours.
    La. Macd. Alas!   10
The part transplanted from his breast to mine,
(As 'twere by sympathy) still bore a share

In all the hazards which the other half
Incurr'd, and fill'd my bosom up with fears.

    La. Macb. Those fears, methinks, should cease now he is safe.

    La. Macd. Ah, Madam, dangers which have long prevail'd
Upon the fancy; even when they are dead
Live in the memory a-while.

    La. Macb. Although his safety has not power enough to put
Your doubts to flight, yet the bright glories which   20
He gain'd in Battel might dispel those Clowds.

    La. Macd. The world mistakes the glories gain'd in war,
Thinking their Lustre true: alas, they are
But Comets, Vapours! by some men exhal'd
From others bloud, and kindl'd in the Region
Of popular applause, in which they live
A-while; then vanish: and the very breath ——
Which first inflam'd them, blows them out agen.

    La. Macb. I willingly would read this Letter; but
Her presence hinders me; I must divert her.   30
If you are ill, repose may do you good;
Y'had best retire; and try if you can sleep.

    La. Macd. My doubtful thoughts too long have kept me waking,
Madam! I'll take your Counsel. . . . .   [*Exit Lady* Macduff.

    La. Macb. Now I have leisure, peruse this Letter.
His last brought some imperfect news of things
Which in the shape of women greeted him
In a strange manner. This perhaps may give
More full intelligence.   [*She reads.*

They met me in the day of success; and I have been told they have 40
more in them than mortal Knowledg. When I desir'd to question
them further; they made themselves air. Whilst I entertain'd my
self with the wonder of it, came Missives from the King, who call'd
me Thane *of* Cawdor: *by which Title, these weyward Sisters had*
saluted me before, and referr'd me to the coming on of time; with,
Hail King that shall be. This have I imparted to thee, (my dearest
partner of Greatness) that thou might'st not lose thy rights of
rejoycing, by being ignorant of what is promis'd. Lay it to thy
heart, and farewel.

Glamis thou art, and *Cawdor,* and shalt be   50
What thou art promis'd: yet I fear thy Nature

Has too much of the milk of humane kindness
To take the nearest way: thou would'st be great:
Thou do'st not want ambition: but the ill
Which should attend it: what thou highly covet'st
Thou covet'st holily! alas, thou art
Loth to play false; and yet would'st wrongly win!
Oh how irregular are thy desires?
Thou willingly, Great *Glamis,* would'st enjoy
The end without the means! Oh haste thee hither,   60
That I may pour my spirits in thy ear:
And chastise with the valour of my tongue
Thy too effeminate desires of that
Which supernatural assistance seems
To Crown thee with.

Enter Servant.

　　　　　　　What may be your news?
　　Serv. The King comes hither to night.
　　La. Macb.　　　　　　　　　　Th'art mad to say it:
Is not thy Master with him? were this true,
He would give notice for the preparation.
　　Serv. So please you, it is true: our *Thane* is coming;
One of my fellows had the speed of him;   70
Who, almost dead for breath, had scarcely more
Than would make up his Message.
　　La. Macb. See him well look'd too: he brings welcome news.

　　　　　　　　　　　　　　　　[Exit Servant.]

There wou'd be musick in a Raven's voice,
Which should but croke the Entrance of the King
Under my Battlements. Come all you spirits
That wait on mortal thoughts: unsex me here:
Empty my Nature of humanity,
And fill it up with cruelty: make thick
My bloud, and stop all passage to remorse;   80
That no relapses into mercy may
Shake my design, nor make it fall before
'Tis ripen'd to effect: you murthering spirits,
(Where ere in sightless substances you wait
On Natures mischief) come, and fill my breasts
With gall instead of milk: make haste dark night,

And hide me in a smoak as black as hell;
That my keen steel see not the wound it makes:
Nor Heav'n peep through the Curtains of the dark,
To cry, hold! hold!

Enter Macbeth.

Great *Glamis*! worthy *Cawdor*!   90
Greater than both, by the all-Hail hereafter;
Thy Letters have transported me beyond
My present posture; I already feel
The future in the instant.
   Macb.   Dearest Love,
Duncan comes here to night.
   La. Macb.   When goes he hence?
   Macb. To morrow, as he purposes.
   La. Macb.   O never!
Never may any Sun that morrow see.
Your face, my *Thane,* is as a book where men
May read strange matters to beguile the time.
Be chearful, Sir; bear welcome in your eye,   100
Your hand, your tongue: Look like the innocent flower,
But be the serpent under't: He that's coming
Must be provided for: And you shall put
This nights great bus'ness into my dispatch;
Which shall to all our future nights and daies
Give soveraign Command: we will with-draw,
And talk on't further: Let your looks be clear,
Your change of Count'nance does betoken fear.   [*Exeunt.*

[ACT I, SCENE VI]

Enter King, Malcolm, Donalbain, Banquo, Lenox,
Macduff, *Attendants.*

King. This Castle has a very pleasant seat;

The air does sweetly recommend it self
To our delighted senses.
   Banq.   The Guest of Summer,
The Temple-haunting *Martin* by his choice
Of this place for his Mansion, seems to tell us,
That here Heavens breath smells pleasantly. No window,
Buttrice, nor place of vantage; but this Bird
Has made his pendant bed and cradle where
He breeds and haunts. I have observ'd the Air,
'Tis delicate.
                  Enter Lady Macbeth.

   King.   See, see our honoured Hostess,   10
By loving us, some persons cause our trouble;
Which still we thank as love: herein I teach you
How you should bid us welcome for your pains,
And thank you for your trouble.
   La. Macb.   All our services
In every point twice done, would prove but poor
And single gratitude, if weigh'd with these
Obliging honours which your Majesty
Confers upon our house; for dignities
Of old and later date (being too poor
To pay) we must be still your humble debtors.   20
   Macd. Madam, we are all joyntly, to night, your trouble;
But I am your trespasser upon another score.
My wife, I understand, has in my absence
Retir'd to you.
   La. Macb. I must thank her: for whilst she came to me
Seeking a Cure for her own solitude,
She brought a remedy to mine: her fears
For you, have somewhat indispos'd her, Sir,
She's now with-drawn, to try if she can sleep:
When she shall wake, I doubt not but your presence   30
Will perfectly restore her health.
   King. Where's the *Thane* of *Cawdor*?
We cours'd him at the heels, and had a purpose
To be his purveyor: but he rides well,
And his great love (sharp as his spur) has brought him
Hither before us. Fair and Noble Lady,

We are your Guests to night.
   La. Macb.   Your servants
Should make their Audit at your Pleasure, Sir,
And still return it as their debt.
   King. Give me your hand.   40
Conduct me to *Macbeth:* we love him highly,
And shall continue our affections to him.   *[Exeunt.*

[ACT I, SCENE VII]

Enter Macbeth.

   Macb. If it were well when done; then it were well
It were done quickly; if his Death might be
Without the Death of nature in my self,
And killing my own rest; it wou'd suffice;
But deeds of this complexion still return
To plague the doer, and destroy his peace:
Yet let me think; he's here in double trust.
First, as I am his Kinsman, and his Subject,
Strong both against the Deed: then as his Host,
Who should against his murderer shut the door,   10
Not bear the sword myself. Besides, this *Duncan*
Has born his faculties so meek, and been
So clear in his great Office; that his Vertues,
Like Angels, plead against so black a deed;
Vaulting Ambition! thou o're-leap'st thy self
To fall upon another:
                    Enter Lady Macbeth.
           Now, what news?
   La. Macb. H'has almost supp'd: why have you left the
    chamber?
   Macb. Has he enquir'd for me?
   La. Macb.   You know he has!

Macb. We will proceed no further in this business:
H'has honour'd me of late; and I have bought   20
Golden opinions from all sorts of people,
Which should be worn now in their newest gloss,
Not cast aside so soon.
    La. Macb.   Was the hope drunk
Wherein you dress'd your self? has it slept since?
And wakes it now to look so pale and fearful
At what it wish'd so freely? Can you fear
To be the same in your own act and valour,
As in desire you are? would you enjoy
What you repute the Ornament of Life,
And live a Coward in your own esteem?   30
You dare not venture on the thing you wish:
But still wou'd be in tame expectance of it.
    Macb. I prithee peace: I dare do all that may
Become a man; he who dares more, is none.
    La. Macb. What Beast then made you break this Enterprize
To me? when you did that, you were a man:
Nay, to be more than what you were, you would
Be so much more the man. Nor time nor place
Did then adhere; and yet you wish'd for both;
And now th'have made themselves; how you betray   40
Your Cowardize? I've given suck, and know
How tender 'tis to love the Babe that milks me:
I would, whilst it was smiling in my face,
Have pluck'd my Nipple from his boneless gums,
And dash'd the brains out, had I so resolv'd,
As you have done for this.
    Macb. If we should fail: ——
    La. Macb.   How, fail! ——
Bring but your Courage to the fatal place,
And we'll not fail; when *Duncan* is a-sleep,
(To which, the pains of this daies journey will   50
Soundly invite him) his two Chamberlains
I will with wine and wassel so convince
That memory (the centry of the brain)
Shall be a fume; and the receipt of reason,
A limbeck only: when, in swinish sleep,

Their natures shall lie drench'd, as in their Death,
What cannot you and I perform upon
His spungy Officers? we'll make them bear
The guilt of our black Deed.

    Macb. Bring forth men-children only;   60
For thy undaunted temper should produce
Nothing but males: but yet when we have mark'd
Those of his Chamber (whilst they are a-sleep)
With *Duncan's* bloud, and us'd their very daggers;
I fear it will not be, with ease, believ'd
That they have don't.

    La. Macb.   Who dares believe it otherwise,
As we shall make our griefs and clamours loud
After his death?

    Macb.   I am setl'd, and will stretch up
Each fainting sinew to this bloudy act.
Come, let's delude the time with fairest show,   70
Fain'd looks must hide what the false heart does know.   *[Exeunt.]*

ACT II, SCENE I

Enter Banquo *and* Fleance.

    Banq. How goes the night, Boy?
    Flea. I have not heard the Clock,
But the Moon is down.
    Banq. And she goes down at twelve.
    Flea.   I take't 'tis late, Sir.
                         [Exit Fleance.

    Banq. An heavy summons lies like lead upon me;
Nature wou'd have me sleep, and yet I fain
Wou'd wake: Merciful powers restrain me in
These cursed thoughts that thus disturb my rest.

        Enter Macbeth and *Servant.*

Who's there?

   Macb.   A friend.

   Banq. What, Sir, not yet at rest? the King's a-bed;   10
He has been to night in an unusual pleasure:
He to your servants has been bountiful,
And with this Diamond he greets your wife
By the obliging name of most kind Hostess.

   Macb. The King taking us unprepar'd, restrain'd our power
Of serving him; which else should have wrought more free.

   Banq. All's well.
I dream'd last night of the three weyward Sisters;
To you they have shewn some truth.

   Macb.   I think not of them;
Yet, when we can intreat an hour or two,   20
We'll spend it in some words upon that business.

   Banq. At your kindest leisure.

   Macb. If when the Prophesie begins to look
Like truth you will adhere to me, it shall
Make honour for you.

   Banq.   So I lose none in seeking
To augment it, but still keeping my bosom free,
And my Allegiances dear, I shall be counsell'd.

   Macb. Good repose the while.

   Banq.   The like to you, Sir.   [*Exit* Banquo.

   Macb. Go bid your Mistress, when she is undrest,
To strike the Closet-bell, and I'll go to bed.   [*Exit Servant.*]
Is this a dagger which I see before me?   31
The hilt draws towards my hand; come, let me grasp thee:
I have thee not, and yet I see thee still;
Art thou not, fatal Vision, sensible
To feeling as to sight? or, art thou but
A dagger of the mind, a false creation
Proceeding from the brain, opprest with heat.
My eyes are made the fools of th'other senses;
Or else worth all the rest: I see thee still,
And on thy blade are stains of reeking bloud.   40
It is the bloudy business that thus
Informs my eye-sight; now, to half the world
Nature seems dead, and wicked dreams infect

The health of sleep; now witchcraft celebrates
Pale *Heccate's* Offerings; now murder is
Alarm'd by his nights Centinel: the wolf,
Whose howling seems the watch-word to the dead:
But whilst I talk, he lives: hark, I am summon'd;
O *Duncan,* hear it not, for 'tis a bell
That rings my Coronation, and thy Knell.   [*Exit.*

[ACT II, SCENE II]

Enter Lady Macbeth.

La. Macb. That which made them drunk, has made me bold;
What has quenched them, hath given new fire to me.
Heark; oh, it was the Owl that shriek'd;
The fatal Bell-man that oft bids good night
To dying men, he is about it; the doors
Are open, and whilst the surfeited Grooms neglect
Their charges for sleep, Nature and death are now
Contending in them.

Enter Macbeth.

Macb. Who's there?

La. Macb. Alas, I am afraid they are awak'd,   10
And 'tis not done; the attempt without the deed
Would ruine us. I laid the daggers ready,
He could not miss them; and had he not resembl'd
My Father, as he slept, I would have don't.
My Husband.

Macb. I have done the deed, didst thou not hear a noise?

La. Macb. I heard the Owl scream, and the Crickets cry,
Did not you speak?

Macb.   When?

La. Macb.   Now.

Macb. Who lies i'th' Anti-chamber?

La. Macb.   *Donalbain.*

Macb. This is a dismal sight.   20

La. Macb. A foolish thought to say a dismal sight.

Macb. There is one did laugh as he securely slept,
And one cry'd Murder, that they wak'd each other.
I stood and heard them; but they said their Prayers,
And then addrest themselves to sleep again.

La. Macb. There are two lodg'd together.

Macb. One cry'd, Heaven bless us, the other said, *Amen:*
As they had seen me with these Hang-mans hands,
Silenc'd with fear, I cou'd not say *Amen*
When they did say, Heaven bless us.   30

La. Macb. Consider it not so deeply.

Macb. But, wherefore could not I pronounce, *Amen?*
I had most need of blessing, and *Amen*
Stuck in my throat.

La. Macb. These deeds shou'd be forgot as soon as done,
Lest they distract the doer.

Macb. Methoughts I heard a noise cry, sleep no more:
Macbeth has murder'd sleep, the innocent sleep;
Sleep, that locks up the senses from their care;
The death of each daies life; tir'd labours bath;   40
Balm of hurt minds; great natures second course;
Chief nourisher in life's feast.

La. Macb. What do you mean?

Macb. Still it cry'd, sleep no more, to all the house.
Glamis hath murder'd sleep, and therefore *Cawdor*
Shall sleep no more; *Macbeth* shall sleep no more.

La. Macb. Why do you dream thus? go, get some water,
And cleanse this filthy witness from your hands.
Why did you bring the daggers from the place?
They must be there, go carry them, and stain   50
The sleepy Grooms with bloud.

Macb.   I'll go no more;
I am afraid to think what I have done.
What then, with looking on it, shall I do?

La. Macb. Give me the daggers, the sleeping and the dead
Are but as pictures; 'tis the eye of childhood
That fears a painted Devil: with his bloud

I'll stain the faces of the Grooms; by that
It will appear their guilt.   [*Exit Lady* Macbeth.
                                                          [*Knock within.*

    Macb.   What knocking's that?
How is't with me, when every noise affrights me?
What hands are here! can the Sea afford   60
Water enough to wash away the stains?
No, they would sooner add a tincture to
The Sea, and turn the green into a red.

              Enter Lady Macbeth.

    La. Macb. My hands are of your colour; but I scorn
To wear an heart so white. Heark,   [*Knock.*
I hear a knocking at the Gate: to your Chamber;
A little water clears us of this deed.
Your fear has left you unman'd; heark, more knocking.
Get on your Gown, lest occasions call us,
And shews us to be watchers; be not lost   70
So poorly in your thoughts.   [*Exit.*
    Macb. Disguis'd in blood, I scarce can find my way.
Wake *Duncan* with this knocking, wou'd thou could'st.   [*Exit.*

[ACT II, SCENE III]

          Enter Lenox *and* Macbeth's *Servant.*

    Len. You sleep soundly, that so much knocking
Could not wake you.
    Serv. Labour by day causes rest by night.
              Enter Macduff.
    Len. See the Noble *Macduff.*
Good morrow, my Lord, have you observ'd
How great a mist does now possess the air;
It makes me doubt whether't be day or night.
    Macd. Rising this morning early, I went to look out of my
Window, and I cou'd scarce see farther than my breath:

The darkness of the night brought but few objects   10
To our eyes, but too many to our ears.
Strange claps and creekings of the doors were heard;
The *Screech-Owl* with his screams, seem'd to foretell
Some deed more black than night.

Enter Macbeth.

Is the King stirring?
    Macb.   Not yet.
    Macd. He did command me to attend him early;
I have almost slip'd the hour.
    Macb. I'll bring you to him.
    Macd. I know this is a joyful trouble to you.
    Macb. The labour we delight in, gives Ease to it self.   20
That door will bring you to him.
    Macd. I'll make bold to call; for 'tis my limited service.

[*Exit* Macduff.

    Len. Goes the King hence to day?
    Macb.   So he designs.
    Len. The night has been unruly:
Where we lay, our chimneys were blown down;
And, as they say, terrible groanings were heard i'th'air:
Strange screams of death, which seem'd to prophesie
More strange events, fill'd divers Ears:
Some say the Earth shook.
    Macb.   'Twas a rough night.
    Len. My young remembrance cannot recollect its fellow.   30

Enter Macduff

    Macd. Oh horror! horror! horror!
Which no heart can conceive, nor tongue can utter.
    Macb. ⎫
    Len. ⎬ What's the matter?
          ⎭
    Macd.   Horror has done its worst:
Most sacrilegious murder has broke open
The Lord's anointed Temple, and stole thence
The life o'th'building.
    Macb.   What is't you say; the life?
    Len. Meaning his Majesty.
    Macd. Approach the Chamber, and behold a sight
Enough to turn spectators into stone.

59

I cannot speak, see, and then speak your selves: 40
Ring the Alarum-bell. Awake, awake,   [*Exeunt* Macbeth *and* Lenox.
Murther, Treason; *Banquo, Malcolm,* and *Donalbain,*
Shake off your downy sleep, Death's counterfeit;
And look on Death it self; up, up, and see,
As from your Graves, rise up, and walk like spirits
To countenance this horror: ring the bell.   [*Bell rings.*

Enter Lady Macbeth.

   La. Macb. What's the business, that at this dead of night
You alar'm us from our rest?
   Macd.   O, Madam!
'Tis not for you to hear what I can speak:
The repetition in a womans ear   50
Would do another murther.

Enter Banquo.

Oh *Banquo, Banquo,* our Royal Master's murther'd!
   La. Macb. Ah me! in our house?
   Banq. The deed's too cruel any where. *Macduff,*
Oh, that you could but contradict your self,
And say it is not true.

Enter Macbeth *and* Lenox.

   Macb. Had I but dy'd an hour before this chance,
I had liv'd a blessed time; for, from this instant,
There's nothing in it worth a good mans care;
All is but toyes, Renown and Grace are dead.   60

Enter Malcolm *and* Donalbain.

   Donal. What is amiss?
   Macb.   You are, and do not know't:
The spring, the head, the fountain of your bloud
Is stop'd; the very source of it is stop'd.
   Macd. Your Royal Father's murther'd.
   Mal.   Murther'd! by whom?
   Len. Those of his Chamber, as it seem'd, had don't;
Their hands and faces were all stain'd with bloud:
So were their Daggers, which we found unwip'd,
Upon their pillows. Why was the life of one,
So much above the best of men, entrusted
To the hands of two, so much below   70
The worst of beasts.

Macb. Then I repent me I so rashly kill'd e'm.
Macd. Why did you so?
Macb. Who can be prudent and amaz'd together;
Loyal and neutral in a moment? no man.
Th' expedition of my violent love
Out-ran my pausing reason: I saw *Duncan,*
Whose gaping wounds look'd like a breach in nature,
Where ruine enter'd. There I saw the murtherers
Steep'd in the colour of their trade; their Daggers   80
Being yet unwip'd, seem'd to own the deed,
And call for vengeance; who could then refrain,
That had an heart to love; and in that heart
Courage to manifest his affection.
   La. Macb. Oh, oh, oh.   [*Faints.*
   Macd.   Look to the Lady.
   Mal. Why are we silent now, that have so large
An argument for sorrow?
   Donal. What should be spoken here, where our fate may rush
Suddenly upon us, and as if it lay
Hid in some corner, make our death succeed   90
The ruine of our Father e're we are aware.
   Macd. I find this place too publick for true sorrow:
Let us retire, and mourn: but first,
Guarded by Vertue, I'm resolv'd to find
The utmost of this business.
   Banq.   And I.
   Macb.   And all.
Let all of us take manly resolution;
And two hours hence meet together in the Hall
To question this most bloudy fact.
   Banq. We shall be ready, Sir.
                  [*Exeunt all but* Malcolm *and* Donalbain.
   Mal. What will you do?   100
Let's not consort with them:
To shew an unfelt-sorrow, is an office
Which false men do with ease.
I'll to *England.*
   Donal. To *Ireland* I'm resolv'd to steer my course;
Our separated fortune may protect our persons.
Where we are, Daggers lie hid under mens smiles,

And the nearer some men are allied to our bloud,
The more, I fear, they seek to shed it.
   Mal. This murtherous shaft that's shot,   110
Hath not yet lighted; and our safest way
Is, to avoid the aim: then let's to horse,
And use no ceremony in taking leave of any.   *[Exeunt.*

ACT II, SCENE IV

Enter Lenox *and* Seyton.

   Seyt. [Three score and one] I can remember well,
Within the compass of which time I've seen
Hours dreadful, and things strange; but this one night
Has made that knowledge void.
   Len. Thou seest the Heavens, as troubled with mans act,
Threaten'd this bloudy day: by th'hour 'tis day,
And yet dark night does cover all the skie,
As if it had quite blotted out the Sun.
Is't nights predominance, or the daies shame
Makes darkness thus usurp the place of light.   10
   Seyt. 'Tis strange and unnatural,
Even like the deed that's done; on Tuesday last,
A *Faulcon* towring in her height of pride,
Was by a mousing *Owl* hawk'd at, and kill'd.
   Len. And *Duncan's* Horses, which before were tame,
Did on a sudden change their gentle natures,
And became wild; they broke out of their Stables,
As if they would make war with mankind.
   Seyt. 'Tis said they eat each other.
   Len.   They did so,
To th'amazement of those eyes that saw it.   20
                Enter Macduff.
Here comes the good *Macduff:*
How goes the world, Sir, now?

Is't known who did this more than bloudy deed?
   Macd. Those that *Macbeth* hath slain, are most suspected.
   Len. Alas, what good could they pretend?
   Macd. It is suppos'd they were suborn'd.
Malcolm and *Donalbain,* the Kings two Sons,
Are [secretly] stoln away from Court,
Which puts upon them suspition of the deed.
   Len. Unnatural still.   30
Could their ambition prompt them to destroy
The means of their own life?
   Macd. You are free to judge
Of their deportment as you please; but most
Men think e'm guilty.
   Len. Then 'tis most like the Soveraignty will fall
Upon *Macbeth.*
   Macd. He is already nam'd, and gone to *Scone*
To be invested.
   Len.   Where's *Duncan's* body?
   Macd. Carried to *Colmehill,*   40
The sacred Store-house of his Predecessors.
   Len. Will you to *Scone?*
   Macd.   No, Cousin, I'll to *Fyfe:*
My wife and children frighted at the Alar'm
Of this sad news, have thither led the way,
And I'll follow them: may the King you go
To see invested, prove as great and good
As *Duncan* was; but I'm in doubt of it.
New Robes ne're as the old so easie sit.   *[Exeunt.*

[ACT II, SCENE V]

Scene An Heath.
Enter Lady Macduff, *Maid, and Servant.*
La. Macd. Art sure this is the place my Lord appointed

Us to meet him?

Serv. This is the entrance o'th' Heath; and here
He order'd me to attend him with the Chariot.

La. Macd. How fondly did my Lord conceive that we
Should shun the place of danger by our flight
From *Everness?* The darkness of the day
Makes the Heath seem the gloomy walks of death.
We are in danger still: they who dare here
Trust Providence, may trust it any where.   10

Maid. But this place, Madam, is more free from terror:
Last night methoughts I heard a dismal noise
Of shrieks and groanings in the air.

La. Macd. 'Tis true, this is a place of greater silence;
Not so much troubled with the groans of those
That die; nor with the out-cries of the living.

Maid. Yes, I have heard stories, how some men
Have in such lonely places been affrighted
With dreadful shapes and noises.   [Macduff *hollows.*

La. Macd. But heark, my Lord sure hollows;   20
'Tis he; answer him quickly.

Serv. Illo, ho, ho, ho.

Enter Macduff.

La. Macd. Now I begin to see him: are you on foot,
My Lord?

Macd. Knowing the way to be both short and easie,
And that the Chariot did attend me here,
I have adventur'd. Where are our children?

La. Macd. They are securely sleeping in the Chariot.

First Song by Witches.

1. *Witch.* Speak, Sister, speak; is the deed done?

2. Long ago, long ago: 30
Above twelve glasses since have run.

3. Ill deeds are seldom slow nor single:
Following crimes on former wait.
The worst of creatures fastest propagate.
Many more murders must this one ensue,
As if in death were propagation too.

2. He will.

1.   He shall.

3.   He must spill much more bloud;
And become worse, to make his Title good.
  1. Now let's dance.
  2.   Agreed.
  3.   Agreed.
  4.   Agreed.
  Chorus. We shou'd rejoyce when good Kings bleed.   40
When cattel die, about we go,
What then, when Monarchs perish, should we do?
  Macd. What can this be?
  La. Macd. This is most strange: but why seem you affraid?
Can you be capable of fears, who have
So often caus'd it in your enemies?
  Macd. It was a hellish Song: I cannot dread
Ought that is mortal; but this is something more.

                     Second Song.

    Let's have a dance upon the Heath;
    We gain more life by *Duncan's* death.   50
    Sometimes like brinded Cats we shew,
    Having no musick but our mew.
    Sometimes we dance in some old mill,
    Upon the hopper, stones, and wheel,
    To some old saw, or Bardish Rhime,
    Where still the Mill-clack does keep time.

    Sometimes about a hollow tree,
    A round, a round, a round dance we.
    Thither the chirping Cricket comes,
    And Beetle, singing drowsie hums.   60
    Sometimes we dance o're Fens and Furs,
    To howls of wolves, and barks of curs.
    And when with none of those we meet,
    We dance to th'ecchoes of our feet.

    At the night-Raven's dismal voice,
    Whilst others tremble, we rejoyce;
    And nimbly, nimbly dance we still
    To th'ecchoes from a hollow Hill.
  Macd. I am glad you are not affraid.

65

La. Macd. I would not willingly to fear submit: 70
None can fear ill, but those that merit it.

    Macd. Am I made bold by her? how strong a guard
Is innocence? if any one would be
Reputed valiant, let him learn of you;
Vertue both courage is, and safety too.

                Enter Witches.   [*A dance of witches.*

    Macd. These seem foul spirits; I'll speak to e'm.
If you can any thing by more than nature know;
You may in those prodigious times fore-tell
Some ill we may avoid.

    1. *Witch.* Saving thy bloud will cause it to be shed. 80

    2. He'll bleed by thee, by whom thou first hast bled.

    3. Thy wife shall shunning danger, dangers find,
And fatal be, to whom she most is kind.   [*Exeunt witches.*

    La. Macd. Why are you alter'd, Sir? be not so thoughtful:
The Messengers of Darkness never spake
To men, but to deceive them.

    Macd. Their words seem to fore-tell some dire predictions.

    La. Macd. He that believes ill news from such as these,
Deserves to find it true. Their words are like
Their shape; nothing but fiction. 90
Let's hasten to our journey.

    Macd. I'll take your counsel; for to permit
Such thoughts upon our memories to dwell,
Will make our minds the Registers of Hell.   [*Exeunt omnes.*

ACT III, SCENE I

Enter Banquo.

    Banq. Thou hast it now, King, *Cawdor, Glamis,* all,
As the three Sisters promis'd; but I fear
Thou plaid'st most foully for't: yet it was said

It should not stand in thy Posterity:
But that my self should be the Root and Father
Of many Kings; they told thee truth.
Why, since their promise was made good to thee,
May they not be my Oracles as well.

Enter Macbeth, Lenox, *and Attendants.*

Macb. Here's our chief Guest, if he had been forgotten,
It had been want of musick to our Feast.   10
To night we hold a solemn supper, Sir;
And all request your presence.
Banq. Your Majesty layes your commands on me,
To which my duty is to obey.
Macb. Ride you this afternoon?
Banq.   Yes, Royal Sir.
Macb. We should have else desir'd your good advice,
(Which still hath been both grave and prosperous)
In this daies Counsel; but we'll take to morrow.
Is't far you ride?
Banq. As far, Great Sir, as will take up the time   20
Twixt this and Supper; and go not my Horse the better,
I must become a borrower of the night,
For a dark hour or two.
Macb.   Fail not our Feast.
Banq. My Lord, I shall not.
Macb. We hear our bloudy Cousins are bestow'd
In *England,* and in *Ireland;* not confessing
Their cruel Parricide; filling their hearers
With strange invention. But, of that to morrow.
Goes your Son with you?
Banq. He does; and our time now calls upon us.   30
Macb. I wish your Horses swift, and sure of foot.
Farewel.   [*Exit* Banquo.
Let every man be master of his time
Till seven at night, to make society
The more welcome; we will our selves withdraw,
And be alone till supper.   [*Exeunt Lords.*
Macduff departed [privately], perhaps
He is grown jealous [. I have sent for him
To come to supper]; he and *Banquo* must

[Meet] the same fate.   40
Do those men attend our pleasure?
  Serv. They do; and wait without.
  Macb.   Bring them before us.
                                                     [Exit Servant.

I am no King till I am safely so.
My fears stick deep in *Banquo's* successors;
And in his Royalty of Nature reigns that
Which wou'd be fear'd. He dares do much;
And to that dauntless temper of his mind,
He hath a wisdom that doth guide his valour
To act in safety. Under him
My genius is rebuk'd: he chid the Sisters   50
When first they put the name of King upon me,
And bade them speak to him. Then, Prophet like,
They hail'd him Father to a line of Kings.
Upon my head they plac'd a fruitless Crown,
And put a barren Scepter in my hand:
Thence to be wrested by anothers race;
No son of mine succeeding: if't be so;
For *Banquo's* Issue, I have stain'd my soul,
For them the gracious *Duncan* I have murder'd:
Rather than so, I will attempt yet further,   60
And blot out, by their bloud, what e're
Is written of them in the book of Fate.

          Enter Servant, and two Murtherers.

Wait you without, and stay there till we call.   *[Exit Servant.*
Was it not yesterday we spoke together?
  1. *Mur.* It was; so please your Highness.
  Macb. And have you since consider'd what I told you?
How it was *Banquo,* who in former times
Held you so much in slavery;
Whilst you were guided to suspect my innocence.
This I made good to you in our last conference;   70
How you were born in hand; how crost:
The Instruments, who wrought with them.
  2. *Mur.* You made it known to us.
  Macb. I did so; and now let me reason with you:
Do you find your patience so predominant

In your nature,
As tamely to remit those injuries?
Are you so Gospell'd to pray for this good man,
And for his Issue; whose heavy hand
Hath bow'd you to the Grave, and begger'd yours for ever?   80
   1. *Mur.* We are men, my Liege.
   Macb. Ay, in the catalogue you go for men;
As hounds, and grey-hounds, mungrels, spaniels, curs,
Shoughs, water-rugs, and demi-wolves, are all
Call'd by the name of dogs: the list of which
Distinguishes the swift, the slow, the subtil,
The house-keeper, the hunter, every one
According to the gift which bounteous Nature
Hath bestow'd on him; and so of men.
Now, if you have a station in the list,   90
Nor i'th' worst rank of manhood; say't,
And I will put that business in your bosoms,
Which, if perform'd, will rid you of your enemy,
And will endear you to the love of us.
   2. *Mur.* I am one, my Liege,
Whom the vile blows, and malice of the Age
Hath so incens'd, that I care not what I do
To spight the World.
   1. *Mur.*   And I another,
So weary with disasters, and so inflicted by fortune,
That I would set my life on any chance,   100
To mend it, or to lose it.
   Macb. Both of you know *Banquo* was your enemy.
   2. *Mur.* True, my Lord.
   Macb. So is he mine; and though I could
With open power take him from my sight,
And bid my will avouch it: yet I must not;
For certain friends that are both his and mine;
Whose loves I may not hazard; would ill
Resent a publick process: and thence it is
That I do your assistance crave, to mask   110
The business from the common eye.
   2. *Mur.* We shall, my Lord, perform what you command us.
   1. *Mur.* Though our lives ——

Macb.   Your spirits shine through you.
Within this hour, at most,
I will advise you where to plant your selves;
For it must be done to night:
And something from the Palace; alwaies remember'd,
That you keep secrecy with the prescribed Father.
Flean, his Son too, keeps him company;
Whose absence is no less material to me   120
Than that of *Banquo's:* he too must embrace the fate
Of that dark hour. Resolve your selves apart.
    Both Mur. We are resolv'd, my Liege.
    Macb. I'll call upon you streight.   [*Exeunt Murtherers.*
Now, *Banquo,* if thy soul can in her flight
Find Heaven, thy happiness begins to night.   [*Exit.*

[ACT III, SCENE II]

Enter Macduff *and Lady* Macduff.

    Macd. It must be so. Great *Duncan's* bloudy death
Can have no other Author but *Macbeth.*
His Dagger now is to a Scepter grown;
From *Duncan's* Grave he has deriv'd his Throne.
    La. Macd. Ambition urg'd him to that bloudy deed:
May you be never by Ambition led:
Forbid it Heav'n, that in revenge you shou'd
Follow a Copy that is writ in bloud.
    Macd. From *Duncan's* Grave, methinks, I hear a groan
That call's a loud for justice.
    La. Macd.   If the Throne   10
Was by *Macbeth* ill gain'd, Heavens Justice may,
Without your Sword, sufficient vengeance pay.
Usurpers lives have but a short extent,
Nothing lives long in a strange Element.

Macd. My Countreys dangers call for my defence
Against the bloudy Tyrants violence.
    La. Macd. I am affraid you have some other end,
Than meerly *Scotland's* freedom to defend.
You'd raise your self, whilst you wou'd him dethrone;
And shake his Greatness, to confirm your own.   20
That purpose will appear, when rightly scan'd,
But usurpation at the second hand.
Good Sir, recall your thoughts.
    Macd.   What if I shou'd
Assume the Scepter for my Countrey's good?
Is that an usurpation? can it be
Ambition to procure the liberty
Of this sad Realm; which does by Treason bleed?
That which provokes, will justifie the deed.
    La. Macd. If the Design should prosper, the Event
May make us safe, but not you Innocent: 30
For whilst to set your fellow Subjects free
From present Death, or future Slavery,
You wear a Crown, not by your Title due,
Defence of them, is an Offence in you;
That Deed's unlawful though it cost no Blood,
In which you'l be at best unjustly Good.
You, by your Pitty which for us you plead,
Weave but Ambition of a finer thread.
    Macd. Ambition do's the height of power affect,
My aim is not to Govern, but Protect: 40
And he is not ambitious that declares,
He nothing seeks of Scepters but their cares.
    La. Macd. Can you so patiently your self molest,
And lose your own, to give your Countrey rest!
In *Plagues* what sound Physician wou'd endure
To be infected for another's Cure.
    Macd. If by my troubles I cou'd yours release,
My Love wou'd turn those torments to my ease:
I shou'd at once be sick and healthy too,
Though Sickly in my self, yet Well in you.   50
    La. Macd. But then reflect upon the Danger, Sir,
Which you by your aspiring wou'd incur.

From Fortunes Pinacle, you will too late
Look down, when you are giddy with your height:
Whilst you with *Fortune* play to win a Crown,
The Peoples Stakes are greater than your own.
   Macd. In hopes to have the common Ills redrest,
Who wou'd not venture single interest.

Enter Servant.

   Serv. My Lord, a Gentleman, just now arriv'd
From Court, has brought a Message from the King.   60
   Macd. One sent from him, can no good Tidings bring?
   La. Macd. What wou'd the Tyrant have?
   Macd.   Go, I will hear
The News, though it a dismal Accent bear;
Those who expect and do not fear their Doom,
May hear a Message though from Hell it come.   *[Exeunt.*

[ACT III, SCENE III]

Enter Macbeth's *Lady and Servant.*

   La. Macb. Is *Banquo* gone from Court?
   Serv. Yes Madam, but returns again to night.
   La. Macb. Say to the King, I wou'd attend his leisure
For a few words.   *[Exit Servant.*
Where our desire is got without content,
Alass, it is not Gain, but punishment!
Tis safer to be that which we destroy,
Then by Destruction live in doubtful joy.

Enter Macbeth.

How now my Lord, why do you keep alone?
Making the worst of Fancy your Companions,   10
Conversing with those thoughts which shou'd ha' dy'd
With those they think on: things without redress

Shou'd be without regard: what's done, is done.
    Macb. Alas, we have but scorch'd the Snake, not kill'd it,
She'l close and be her self, whilst our poor malice
Remains in danger of her former Sting.
But let the frame of all things be disjoynt
E're we will eat our bread in fear; and sleep
In the affliction of those horrid Dreams
That shake us nightly! Better be with him   20
Whom we to gain the Crown, have sent to peace;
Then on the torture of the Mind to lye
In restless Agony. *Duncan* is dead;
He, after life's short feavor, now sleeps Well:
Treason has done it's worst; nor Steel, nor Poyson,
No Ferreign force, nor yet Domestick Malice
Can touch him further.
    La. Macb. Come on, smooth your rough brow:
Be free and merry with your guests to night.
    Macb. I shall, and so I pray be you but still,   30
Remember to apply your self to *Banquo:*
Present him kindness with your Eye and Tongue.
In how unsafe a posture are our honors
That we must have recourse to flattery,
And make our Faces Vizors to our hearts.
    La. Macb. You must leave this.
    Macb. How full of Scorpions is my mind, Dear Wife!
Thou know'st that *Banquo* and his *Flean* lives.
    La. Macb. But they are not Immortal, there's comfort yet in
      that.
    Macb. Be merry then, for e're the *Bat* has flown   40
His Cloyster'd flight; e're to black *Heccate's* Summons,
The sharp brow'd Beetle with his drowsie hums,
Has rung night's second Peal:
There shall bee done a deed of dreadful Note.
    La. Macb. What is't?
    Macb. Be innocent of knowing it, my Dear,
Till thou applaud the deed. Come dismal Night,
Close up the Eye of the quick sighted Day
With thy invisible and bloody hand.

The Crow makes wing to the thick shady Grove,   50
Good things of day grow dark and overcast,
Whilst Night's black Agent's to their Preys make hast,
Thou wonder'st at my Language, wonder still,
Things ill begun, strengthen themselves by ill.   *[Exeunt.*

[ACT III, SCENE IV]

Enter three Murtherers.

1. *Mur.* The time is almost come,
The *West* yet glimmers with some streaks of day,
Now the benighted Traveller spurs on,
To gain the timely Inn.
  2. *Mur.* Hark, I hear Horses, and saw some body alight
At the Park gate.
  3. *Mur.*   Then tis he; the rest
That are expected are i'th'court already.
  1. *Mur.* His Horses go about almost a Mile,
And men from hence to th' *Pallace* make it their usual walk. *[Exeunt.*

Enter Banquo *and* Fleance.

Banq. It will be Rain to night.
Flea.   We must make hast.   10
Banq. Our hast concerns us more then being wet.
The King expects me at his feast to night,
To which he did invite me with a kindness,
Greater then he was wont to express.   *[Exeunt.*

Re-enter Murtherers with drawn Swords.

  1. *Mur. Banquo,* thou little think'st what bloody feast
Is now preparing for thee.
  2. *Mur.* Nor to what shades the darkness of this night,
Shall lead thy wandring spirit.   *[Exeunt after* Banquo.
      [Clashing of Swords is heard from within.

74

Re-enter Fleance *pursu'd by one of the Murtherers.*

Flea. Murther, help, help, my Father's kill'd.　　　[*Exeunt running.*

[ACT III, SCENE V]

Scene opens, a Banquet prepar'd.

Enter Macbeth, *Lady* Macbeth, Seyton, Lenox, *Lords, Attendants.*

Macb. You know your own Degrees, sit down.

Seyt. Thanks to your Majesty.

Macb. Our Self will keep you company,
And Play the humble Host to entertain you:
Our Lady keeps her State; but you shall have
Her welcome too.

　　La. Macb. Pronounce it for me Sir, to all our Friends.

Enter first Murtherer.

Macb. Both sides are even; be free in Mirth, anon
Wee'l drink a measure about the Table.
There's blood upon thy face.　　　　　[*To the Murtherer.*

　　Mur.　　　　　Tis *Banquo's* then.　　　　　10

Macb. Is he dispatch'd?

Mur. My Lord, his Throat is cut: that I did for him.

Macb. Thou art the best of Cut-throats;
Yet he is good that did the like for *Flean.*

Mur. Most Royal Sir, he scap'd.

Macb. Then comes my fit again, I had else been Perfect,
Firm as a Pillar founded on a Rock!
As unconfin'd as the free spreading Air.
But now I'm check'd with sawcy Doubts and Fears.
But *Banquo's* safe?

　　Mur.　　　　Safe in a Ditch he lies,　　　　20
With twenty gaping wounds on his head,
The least of which was Mortal.

Macb. There the grown Serpent lies; the worm that's fled
Hath Nature, that in time will Venom breed,
Though at present it wants a Sting. To morrow,
You shall hear further.   [*Exit Murtherer.*
  La. Macb. My Royal Lord, you spoil the Feast,
The Sauce to Meat is chearfulness.

        Enter the Ghost of Banquo *and sits in* Macbeth's *place.*

  Macb. Let good digestion wait on Appetite,
And Health on both.
  Len.   May it please your Highness to sit.   30
  Macb. Had we but here our Countrys honor;
Were the grac'd person of our *Banquo* present,
Whom we may justly challenge for unkindness.
  Seyt. His absence Sir,
Lays blame upon his promise; will it please
Your Highness to grace us with your Company?
  Macb. Yes, I'le sit down. The Table's full.
  Len. Here is a place reserv'd Sir.
  Macb.   Where Sir?
  Len. Here. What is't that moves your Highness?
  Macb. Which of you have done this?
  Lords.   Done what?   40
  Macb. Thou can'st not say I did it; never shake
Thy goary Locks at me.
  Seyt. Gentlemen rise, his Highness is not well.
  La. Macb. Sit worthy Friends, my Lord is often thus,
And hath been from his youth: pray keep your Seats,
The fit is ever sudden, if you take notice of it,
You shall offend him, and provoke his passion.
In a moment he'l be well again.
Are you a Man?
  Macb. Ay, and a bold one; that dare look on that   50
Which wou'd distract the Devil.
  La. Macb.   O proper stuff:
This is the very painting of your fear:
This is the Air-drawn Dagger, which you said
Led you to *Duncan.* O these Fits and Starts,
(Impostors to true fear) wou'd well become
A womans story, authoriz'd by her Grandam,

Why do you stare thus? when all's done
You look but on a Chair.
   Macb. Prethee see there, how say you now!
Why, what care I, if thou can'st nod; speak too.   60
If Charnel-houses and our Graves must send
Those that we bury, back; our Monuments
Shall be the maws of Kites.
   La. Macb. What, quite unman'd in folly?   *[The Ghost descends.*
   Macb. If I stand here, I saw it.
   La. Macb.   Fye, for shame.
   Macb. Tis not the first of Murders; blood was shed
E're humane Law decreed it for a sin.
Ay, and since Murthers too have been committed
[Too horrid] for the Ear. The times have been,
That when the brains were out, the man wou'd dye;   70
And there lye still; but now they rise again
And thrust us from our seats.
   La. Macb. Sir, your noble Friends do lack you.
   Macb. Wonder not at me my most worthy Friends,
I have a strange Infirmity; tis nothing
To those that know me. Give me some Wine,
Here's to the general Joy of all the Table,
And to our dear friend *Banquo,* whom we miss,
Wou'd he were here: to him, and all, we drink.
   Lords. Our Duties are to pledge it.   80
                  [The Ghost of Banquo *rises at his feet.*
   Macb. [Begone.] Let the Earth hide thee: thy blood is cold,
Thou hast no use now of thy glaring Eyes.
   La. Macb. Think of this good my Lords, but as a thing
Of Custom: tis no other,
Only it spoils the pleasure of the time.
   Macb. What Man can dare, I dare:
Approach thou like the rugged *Russian* Bear,
The Armd *Rhinoceros,* or the *Hircanian* Tigre:
Take any shape but that; and my firm Nerves
Shall never tremble; Or revive a while,   90
And dare me to the Desart with thy Sword,
If any Sinew shrink, proclaim me then
The Baby of a Girl. Hence horrible shadow.   *[Exit Ghost.*

So, now I am a man again: pray you sit still.
   La. Macb. You have disturb'd the Mirth;
Broke the glad Meeting with your wild disorder.
   Macb. Can such things be without Astonishment.
You make me strange,
Even to the disposition that I owe,
When now I think you can behold such sights,   100
And keep the Natural colour of your Cheeks,
Whilst mine grew pale with fear.
   Seyt. What sights [do you mean]?
   La. Macb. I pray you speak not [to him;] he grows worse and
    worse;
Question enrages him, at once good night:
Stand not upon the Order of your going.
   Len. Good night, and better health attend his Majesty.
   La. Macb. A kind good night to all.   [*Exeunt Lords.*
   Macb. It will have Blood they say. Blood will have blood.
Stones have been known to move, and Trees to speak.   110
Augures well read in Languages of Birds
By *Magpyes, Rooks,* and *Dawes,* have reveal'd
The secret Murther. How goes the night?
   La. Macb. Almost at odds with morning, which is which.
   Macb. Why did *Macduff* after a solemn Invitation,
Deny his presence at our Feast?
   La. Macb. Did you send to him Sir?
   Macb. I did; But I'le send again.
There's not one great *Thane* in all *Scotland,*
But in his house I keep a Servant,   120
He and *Banquo* must embrace the same fate.
I will to morrow to the Weyward Sisters,
They shall tell me more; for now I am bent to know
By the worst means, the worst that can befall me:
All Causes shall give way; I am in Blood
Stept in so far, that should I wade no more,
Returning were as bad, as to go o're.
   La. Macb. You lack the season of all Natures, sleep.
   Macb. Well I'le in
And rest; if sleeping I repose can have,   130
When the Dead rise and want it in the Grave.   [*Exeunt.*

[ACT III, SCENE VI]

Enter Macduff *and Lady* Macduff.

La. Macd. Are you resolv'd then to be gone?

Macd.   I am:

I know my Answer cannot but inflame

The Tyrants fury to pronounce my death,

My life will soon be blasted by his breath.

   La. Macd. But why so far as *England* must you fly?

   Macd. The farthest part of *Scotland* is too nigh.

   La. Macd. Can you leave me, your Daughter and your Son,

To perish by that Tempest which you shun.

When Birds of stronger Wing are fled away,

The Ravenous *Kite* do's on the weaker Prey.   10

   Macd. He will not injure you, he cannot be

Possest with such unmanly cruelty:

You will your safety to your weakness owe

As Grass escapes the Syth by being low.

Together we shall be too slow to fly:

Single, we may outride the Enemy.

I'le from the *English* King such Succours crave,

As shall revenge the Dead, and Living save.

My greatest misery is to remove,

With all the wings of haste from what I love.   20

   La. Macd. If to be gone seems misery to you,

Good Sir, let us be miserable too.

   Macd. Your Sex which here is your security,

Will by the toyls of flight your Danger be.

                   Enter Messenger.

What fatal News do's bring thee out of breath?

   Mess. Sir, *Banquo's* kill'd.

   Macd.   Then I am warn'd of Death.

Farewell; our safety, Us, a while must sever.

   La. Macd. Fly, fly, or we may bid farewell for ever.

   Macd. Flying from Death, I am to Life unkind,

For leaving you, I leave my Life behind.   [*Exit.*

    La. Macd. Oh my dear Lord, I find now thou art gone,   31

I am more Valiant when unsafe alone.

My heart feels man-hood, it does Death despise,

Yet I am still a Woman in my eyes.

And of my Tears thy absence is the cause,

So falls the Dew when the bright Sun withdraws.   [*Exeunt.*

[ACT III, SCENE VII]

Enter Lenox *and* Seyton.

  Len. My former speeches have but hit your thoughts

Which can interpret further; Only I say

Things have been strangely carry'd.

Duncan was pitti'd, but he first was dead.

And the right Valiant *Banquo* walk'd too late:

Men must not walk so late: who can want ~~Sence~~

To know how Monstrous it was in Nature,

For *Malcolm* and *Donalbain,* to kill

Their Royal Father; ~~horrid Fact~~! how did   10

It grieve *Macbeth,* did he not straight

In Pious rage the two *Delinquents* kill,

That were the slaves of Drunkenness and Sleep.

Was not that Nobly done?

  Seyt. Ay, and wisely too:

For 'twou'd have anger'd any Loyal heart

To hear the men deny it.

  Len. So that I say he has born all things well:

And I do think that had he *Duncan's* Sons

Under his power (as may please Heaven he shall not)

They shou'd find what it were to kill a Father.   20

So shou'd *Flean:* but peace; I hear *Macduff*

Deny'd his presence at the Feast; For which

He lives in disgrace. Sir, can you tell
Where he bestowes himself?
    Seyt.   I hear that *Malcolm*
Lives i'th' *English* Court, and is received
Of the most Pious *Edward,* with such Grace,
That the Malevolence of Fortune takes
Nothing from his high Respect; thither
Macduff is gone to beg the Holy King's
Kind aid, to wake *Northumberland* and Warlike   30
Seymour, and by the help of these, to finish
What they have so well begun. This report
Do's so Exasperate the King, that he
Prepares for some attempt of War.
    Len. Sent he to *Macduff?*
    Seyt. He did, his absolute Command.
    Len. Some Angel fly toth' *English* Court, and tell
His Message e're he come; that some quick blessing,
To this afflicted Country, may arrive
Whilst those that merit it, are yet alive.   *[Exeunt.*

[ACT III, SCENE VIII]

    Thunder, Enter three Witches meeting Heccate.
    1. *Witch.* How, *Hecat,* you look angerly?
    Hec. Have I not reason *Beldams?*
Why did you all Traffick with *Macbeth*
'Bout Riddles and affairs of Death,
And cal'd not me; All you have done
Hath been but for a Weyward Son:
Make some amends now: get you gon,
And at the pit of *Achæron*
Meet me i'th' morning: Thither he
Will come to know his Destiny.   10

Dire business will be wrought e're Noon,
For on a corner of the Moon,
A drop my Spectacles have found,
I'le catch it e're it come to ground.
And that distil'd shall yet e're night,
Raise from the Center such a Spright:
As by the strength of his Illusion,
Shall draw *Macbeth* to his Confusion.

Musick and Song.

Heccate, Heccate, Heccate! Oh come away:
Hark, I am call'd, my little Spirit see,   20
Sits in a foggy Cloud, and stays for me.   [*Machine descends.*
    Sing within. Come away *Heccate, Heccate!* Oh come away:
    Hec. I come, I come, with all the speed I may,
With all the speed I may.
Where's *Stadling?*
    2. Here.
    Hec. Where's *Puckle?*
    3. Here, and *Hopper* too, and *Helway* too.
    1. We want but you, we want but you:
Come away make up the Count.   30
    Hec. I will but Noint, and then I mount,
I will but, *&c.*
    1. Here comes down one to fetch his due, a Kiss,
A Cull, a sip of blood.
And why thou staist so long, I muse,
Since th' Air's so sweet and good.
O art thou come; What News?
    2. All goes fair for our delight,
Either come, or else refuse,
Now I'm furnish'd for the flight   40
Now I go, and now I flye,
Malking my sweet Spirit and I.
    3. O what a dainty pleasure's this,
To sail i'th' Air while the *Moon* shines fair;
To Sing, to Toy, to Dance and Kiss,
Over Woods, high Rocks and Mountains;
Over Hills, and misty Fountains:

Over Steeples, Towers, and Turrets:
We flye by night 'mongst troops of Spirits.
No Ring of Bells to our Ears sounds,   50
No howles of Wolves, nor Yelps of Hounds;
No, nor the noise of Waters breach,
Nor Cannons Throats our Height can reach.
    1. Come let's make hast, she'll soon be back again.
    2. But whilst she moves through the foggy Air,
Let's to the Cave and our dire Charms prepare.   [*Exeunt.*]

ACT IV, SCENE I

Thunder. Enter 3 Witches.

    [3. *Witch.* No milk mayde yet has bin bedued.]
    1. Thrice the brinded Cat hath Mew'd.
    [3.] Thrice, and once the Hedge-Pig whin'd,
Shutting his Eyes against the Wind.
    [2. Up hollow okes now Emitts clim.]
    3. [And *Heccat*] cries, tis time, tis time.
    1. Then round about the *Cauldron* go,
And poyson'd Entrals throw.
This Toad which under Mossy stone,
Has days and nights lain thirty one: 10
And swelter'd Venom sleeping got,
We'l boyl in the Inchanted Pot.
    All. Double double, toyl and trouble;
Fire burn, and *Cauldron* bubble.
    2. The Fillet of a Fenny Snake,
Of Scuttle Fish the vomit black.
The Eye of New't, and Toe of Frog,
The wool of Bat, and tongue of Dog.
An Adders fork and blind Worms sting,
A Lizzard's leg, and Howlets wing,   20

Shall like a Hell-broth boil and bubble.
    All. Double, double, *&c.*
    3. The scale of Dragon, tooth of Wolf,
A Witches mummy: Maw and Gulf
Of Cormorant and the Sea Shark,
The root of Hemlock dig'd i'th' dark.
The liver of blaspheming Jew,
With gall of Goats, and slips of Yew,
Pluckt when the *Moon* was in Eclips,
With a *Turks* nose, and *Tarters* lips;   30
The finger of a strangl'd Babe
Born of a Ditch deliver'd Drab,
Shall make the Greuel thick and slab.
Adding thereto a fat *Dutchman's* Chawdron.
For the ingredients of our Cawdron.
    All. Double, double, *&c.*
    2. I'le cool it with a Baboones blood,
And so the Charm is firm and good.

          Enter Heccate *and the other three Witches.*

    Hec. Oh well done, I commend your pains,
And every one shall share the Gains.   40
And now about the *Cauldron* sing,
Like Elves and Fairies in a ring.

          Musick and Song.

    Hec. Black Spirits, and white,
Red Spirits and gray;
Mingle, mingle, mingle,
You that mingle may.
    1. *Witch. Tiffin, Tiffin,* keep it stiff in.
    2. Fire drake *Puckey,* make it luckey:
    Hec. Lyer *Robin,* you must bob in.
    Chor. A round, a round, a round, about, about,   50
All ill come running in, all good keep out.
    1. Here's the blood of a Bat!
    Hec. O put in that, put in that.
    2. Here's Lizards brain.
    Hec. Put in a grain.
    1. Here's Juice of Toad, here's oyl of Adder
That will make the Charm grow madder.
    2. Put in all these, 'twill raise the stanch.

Hec. Nay here's three ownces of a red-hair'd Wench.
Chor. A round, a round, &c.   60
2. I by the pricking of my Thumbs,
Know somthing Wicked this way comes,
Open Locks, whoever knocks.

Enter Macbeth.

Macb. How now you Secret, black and mid-night Haggs,
What are you doing?
All.   A deed without a name.
Macb. I conjure you by that which you profess.
How e're you come to know it, answer me.
Though you let loose the raging Winds to shake whole Towns,
Though bladed Corn be lodg'd, and Trees blown down.
Though Castles tumble on their Warders heads;   70
Though Palaces and towring Piramids
Are swallowed up in Earth-quakes. Answer me.
1. *Witch.* Speak.
2.   Pronounce.
3.   Demand.
4.   I'le answer thee.
Macb. What Destinie's appointed for my Fate?
Hec. Thou double *Thane* and King; beware *Macduff:*
Avoiding him, *Macbeth* is safe enough.
Macb. What e're thou art for thy kind Caution, Thanks.
Hec. Be bold and bloody, and man's hatred scorn,
Thou shalt be harm'd by none of Woman born.
Macb. Then live *Macduff;* what need I fear thy power: 80
But none can be too sure, thou shalt not live,
That I may tell pale hearted fear it lies,
And sleep in spite of Thunder.
Hec. Be Confident, be Proud, and take no care
Who wages War, or where Conspirers are,
Macbeth shall like a lucky Monarch Raign,
Till *Birnam Wood* shall come to *Dunsinane.*
Macb. Can Forrests move? the Prophesie is good,
If I shall never fall till the great Wood
Of *Birnam* rise; thou may'st presume *Macbeth,*   90
To live out Natures Lease, and pay thy breath
To Time and mortal Custom. Yet my heart
Longs for more Knowledge: Tell me if your Art

Extends so far: shall *Banquo's* Issue o're
This Kingdom raign?
   All.   Enquire no more.
   Macb. I will not be deny'd. Ha!   [*Cauldron sinks.*
An eternal Curse fall on you; let me know
Why sinks that *Cauldron,* and what noise is this.
   1. *Witch.* Appear.
   2.   Appear.
   3.   Appear.
Wound through his Eyes, his harden'd Heart,   100
   Hec. Like Shaddows come, and straigth depart.
               [*A shaddow of eight Kings, and* Ban-
               quo's *Ghost after them pass by.*
   Macb. Thy Crown offends my sight. A second too
Like the first. A third resembles him:
A fourth too like the former: Ye filthy Hags,
Will they succeed each other still till Dooms-day?
Another yet; a seventh? I'll see no more:
And yet the eigth appears.
Ha! the bloody *Banquo* smiles upon me,
And by his smiling on me, seems to say
That they are all Successors of his race.   110
   Hec. Ay, Sir, all this is so: but why
Macbeth, stand'st thou amazedly:
Come Sisters, let us chear his heart,
And shew the pleasures of our Art;
I'le charm the Air to give a sound
While you perform your Antick round.
               [*Musick. The Witches Dance and Vanish.*
               The Cave sinks.
   Macb. Where are they? Gone?
Let this pernicious hour stand
Accurs'd to all eternity. Without there.
               Enter Seyton.
   Seyt. What's your Graces will?   120
   Macb. Saw you the Wayward sisters?
   Seyt.   No my Lord.
   Macb. Came they not by you?
   Seyt.   By me Sir?

Macb. Infected be the Earth in which they sunk,
And Damn'd all those that trust 'em. Just now I heard
The galloping of Horse; who was't came by?
    Seyt. A Messenger from the *English* Court, who
Brings word *Macduff* is fled to *England.*
    Macb. Fled to *England?*
    Seyt.   Ay my Lord.
    Macb. Time thou Anticipat'st all my Designes;
Our Purposes seldom succeed, unless our Deeds   130
Go with them.
My Thoughts shall henceforth into Actions rise,
The Witches made me cruel, but not wise.   *[Exeunt.*

[ACT IV, SCENE II]

    Enter Macduff's *Wife, and* Lenox.
    La. Macd. I then was frighted with the sad alarm
Of *Banquo's* Death, when I did counsel him
To fly, but now alas! I much repent it,
What had he done to leave the Land? *Macbeth*
Did know him Innocent.
    Len. You must have patience Madam.
    La. Macd.   He had none.
His flight was madness. When our Actions do not,
Our fears oft make us Traytors.
    Len. You know not whether it was his Wisdom or his Fear.
    La. Macd. Wisdom? to leave his Wife and Children in a place   10
From whence himself did fly; he loves us not.
He wants the natural touch: For the poor *Wren*
(The most diminutive of Birds) will with
The Ravenous *Owl,* fight stoutly for her young ones.
    Len. Your Husband, Madam,
Is Noble, Wise, Judicious, and best knows
The fits o'th' Season. I dare not speak much further,
But cruel are the Times; when we are Traytors,

And do not know our selves: when we hold Rumor,
From what we fear, yet know not what we fear;   20
But float upon a wild and violent Sea
Each way, and move. I take my leave of you:
'T shall not be long but I'll be here again.
Things at the worst will cease, or else climb upwards
To what they were before. Heaven protect you.
    La. Macd. Farewell Sir.

Enter a Woman.

Wom. Madam, a Gentleman in haste desires
To speak with you.
    La. Macd.   A Gentleman, admit him.

Enter Seyton.

    Seyt. Though I have not the honour to be known
To you, Yet I was well acquainted with   30
The Lord *Macduff* which brings me here to tell you
There's danger near you, be not found here,
Fly with your little ones; Heaven preserve you,
I dare stay no longer.   [*Exit* Seyton.
    La. Macd. Where shall I go, and whither shall I fly?
I've done no harm; But I remember now
I'm in a vicious world, where to do harm
Is often prosperous, and to do good
Accounted dangerous folly; Why do I then
Make use of this so womanly defence?   40
I'le boldly in, and dare this new Alarm:
What need they fear whom Innocense doth arm?   [*Exit.*

[ACT IV, SCENE III]

The Scene Birnam Wood
Enter Malcolm and Macduff.

Macd. In these close shades of *Birnam Wood* let us

Weep our sad Bosoms empty.

    Mal. You'l think my Fortunes desperate,
That I dare meet you here upon your summons.

    Macd. You should now
Take Arms to save your Country. Each new day
New Widows mourn, new Orphans cry, and still
Changes of sorrow reach attentive Heaven.

    Mal. This Tirant whose foul Name blisters our Tongues,
Was once thought honest. You have lov'd him well.   10
He has not toucht you yet.

    Macd. I am not treacherous.

    Mal. But *Macbeth* is. And yet *Macduff* may be
What I did always think him, just, and good.

    Macd. I've lost my hopes.

    Mal. Perhaps even there where I did find my doubts;
But let not Jealousies be your Dishonours,
But my own safeties.

    Macd.   Bleed, Bleed, poor Country.
Great Tiranny, lay thy Foundation sure,
Villains are safe when good men are suspected.   20
I'le say no more. Fare thee well young Prince,
I would not be that Traytor which thou thinkst me
For twice *Macbeths* reward of Treachery.

    Mal. Be not offended:
I speak not as in absolute fear of you:
I think our Countrey sinks beneath the Yoak,
It weeps, it bleeds, and each new day a gash
Is added to her wounds. I think withall
That many hands would in my Cause be active.
And here from gracious *England* have I offer   30
Of goodly Thousands. But for all this,
When I shall tread upon the Tirants head,
Or wear it on my Sword; yet my poor Country
Will suffer under greater Tiranny
Than what it suffers now.

    Macd.   It cannot be.

    Mal. Alas I find my Nature so inclin'd
To Vice, that foul *Macbeth* when I shall rule,
Will seem as white as Snow.

Macd. There cannot in all ransackt Hell be found
A Devil equal to *Macbeth.*   40
 Mal. I grant him bloody, false, deceiptful, malitious,
And participating in some sins too horrid to name;
But there's no bottom, no depths in my ill appetite,
If such a one be fit to govern, speak?
 Macd. O *Scotland, Scotland,* when shalt thou see day again?
Since that the truest Issue of thy Throne,
Disclaims his Virtue to avoid the Crown?
Your Royal Father was a most Saint-like King;
The Queen that bore thee, Oftner upon her Knees,
Than on her Feet, Dy'd every day she liv'd.   50
Fare thee well, these Evils thou repeat'st
Upon thy self, hath banisht me from *Scotland.*
O my breast! Thy hope ends here.
 Mal. Macduff this Noble Passion,
Child of Integrity hath from my Soul
Wip'd the black scruples, reconcil'd my Thoughts
To thy good truth and honour. *Macbeth*
By many of these Trains hath sought to win me
Into his Power: And modest wisdom plucks me
From over-credulous haste. But now   60
I put my self to thy direction, and
Unspeak my own Detraction. I abjure
The taunts and blames I laid upon my self,
For strangers to my Nature. What I am truly
Is thine, and my poor Countreys to command.
The gracious *Edward* has lent us *Seymour,*
And ten thousand Men. Why are you silent?
 Macd. Such welcom and unwelcom things at once
Are Subjects for my Wonder not my Speech,
My grief and Joy contesting in my bosom,   70
I find that I can scarce my tongue command,
When two Streams meet the Water's at a stand.
 Mal. Assistance granted by that pious King
Must be successful, he who by his touch,
Can cure our Bodies of a foul Disease,
Can by just force subdue a Traitors Mind,
Power supernatural is unconfin'd.

Macd. If his Compassion does on Men Diseas'd
Effect such Cures; What Wonders will he do,
When to Compassion he ads Justice too?   [*Exeunt.*

[ACT IV, SCENE IV]

Enter Macbeth *and* Seyton.

Macb. Seyton, go bid the Army March.
Seyt. The posture of Affairs requires your Presence.
Macb. But the Indosposition of my Wife
Detains me here.
Seyt. Th'Enemy is upon our borders, *Scotland's* in danger.
Macb. So is my Wife, and I am doubly so.
I am sick in her, and in my Kingdom too.
Seyton.
Seyt. Sir.
Macb. The Spur of my Ambition prompts me to go
And make my Kingdom safe, but Love which softens   10
Me to pity her in her distress,
Curbs my Resolves.
Seyt.   He's strangely disorder'd.
Macb. Yet why should Love since confin'd, desire
To controul Ambition, for whose spreading hopes
The world's too narrow, It shall not; Great Fires
Put out the Less; *Seyton* go bid my Grooms
Make ready; Ile not delay my going.
Seyt. I go.
Macb. Stay *Seyton,* stay, Compassion calls me back.
Seyt. He looks and moves disorderly.
Macb.   I'le not go yet.   20
Enter a Servant, who whispers Macbeth.
Seyt. Well Sir.
Macb.   Is the Queen asleep?

Seyt. What makes 'em whisper and his countenance change?
Perhaps some new design has had ill success.
    Macb. Seyton, Go see what posture our Affairs are in.
    Seyt. I shall, and give you notice Sir.   [*Exit* Seyton.

                  Enter Lady Macbeth.

    Macb. How does my Gentle Love?
    La. Macb.   *Duncan* is dead.
    Macb. No words of that.
    La. Macb.   And yet to Me he Lives.
His fatal Ghost is now my shadow, and pursues me
Where e're I go.
    Macb.   It cannot be My Dear,
Your Fears have misinform'd your eyes.   30
    La. Macb. See there; Believe your own.
Why do you follow Me? I did not do it.
    Macb. Methinks there's nothing.
    La. Macb. If you have Valour force him hence.
Hold, hold, he's gone. Now you look strangely.
    Macb. 'Tis the strange error of your Eyes.
    La. Macb. But the strange error of my Eyes
Proceeds from the strange Actions of your Hands.
Distraction does by fits possess my head,
Because a Crown unjustly covers it.   40
I stand so high that I am giddy grown.
A Mist does cover me, as Clouds the tops
Of Hills. Let us get down apace.
    Macb. If by your high ascent you giddy grow,
'Tis when you cast your Eyes on things below.
    La. Macb. You may in Peace resign the ill gain'd Crown.
Why should you labour still to be unjust?
There has been too much Blood already spilt.
Make not the Subjects Victims to your guilt.
    Macb. Can you think that a crime, which you did once   50
Provoke me to commit? had not your breath
Blown my Ambition up into a Flame
Duncan had yet been living.
    La. Macb.   You were a Man.
And by the Charter of your Sex you shou'd
Have govern'd me, there was more crime in you

When you obey'd my Councels, then I contracted
By my giving it. Resign your Kingdom now,
And with your Crown put off your guilt.
   Macb. Resign the Crown, and with it both our Lives.
I must have better Councellors.   60
   La. Macb. What, your Witches?
Curse on your Messengers of Hell. Their Breath
Infected first my Breast: See me no more.
As King your Crown sits heavy on your Head,
But heavier on my Heart: I have had too much
Of Kings already. See the Ghost again.   *[Ghost appears.*
   Macb. Now she relapses.
   La. Macb.   Speak to him if thou canst.
Thou look'st on me, and shew'st thy wounded breast.
Shew it the Murderer.
   Macb.   Within there, Ho.

                 Enter Women.

   La. Macb. Am I ta'ne Prisoner? then the Battle's lost.   70
              [Exit. Lady Macbeth *led out by Women.*
   Macb. She does from *Duncans* death to sickness grieve,
And shall from *Malcolms* death her health receive.
[But her minds weakness cannot now Endure
To take the proper medicine for the Cure.]
When by a Viper bitten, nothing's good
To cure the venom but the Vipers blood.   *[Exit.*

[ACT IV, SCENE V]

   Enter Malcolm, Macduff; *and* Lenox, *Meeting them.*
   Macd. See who comes here!
   Mal. My Countrey-man; but yet I know him not.
   Macd. My ever Gentle Couzin! Welcom.
   Mal. I know him now. Kind Heaven remove

The Means that makes us strangers.
    Len.   Amen.
    Macd. What looks does *Scotland* bear?
    Len.   Alas poor Countrey,
Almost afraid to know it self. It can't
Be call'd our Mother but our Grave; where nothing,
But who knows nothing is once seen to smile?
Where sighs, and groans, and shrieks that rend the air,   10
Are made, not mark'd, where violent sorrow seems
A Modern Extasie: there Bells
Are always ringing, and no Man asks for whom;
There good Mens lives expire, Dying e're they sicken.
[Though what I have related, Sir, seems strange,
My feare does make it probable.]
    Macd. Oh Relation! too nice, and yet too true.
    Mal. What's the newest grief?
    Len. That of an hours age is out of date,
Each Minute brings a new one.   20
    Macd. How does my Wife?
    Len.   Why well.
    Macd. And all my Children?
    Len.   Well too.
    Macd. The Tirant has not quarrell'd at their peace?
    Len. No, they were well at peace when I left 'em.
    Macd. Be not so sparing of your speech. How goe'st?
    Len. When I came hither to transport the tidings,
Which I have heavily born, there ran a rumour
Of many Worthy Men that rose into a head,
Which was to my Belief; witness the rather,
For that I saw the Tirants Power a foot.   30
Now, is the time of help; your Eye in *Scotland*
Would create Soldiers, and make Women fight.
    Mal. Be't their Comfort,
We are coming thither: Gracious *England*
Hath lent us good *Seymour,* and ten thousand Men.
    Len. Wou'd I cou'd answer this comfort with the like;
But I have words,
That would be utter'd in the desart air,
Where no Mans ear should hear'em.

Macd. What concern they? the general cause,   40
Or is't a grief due to some single breast?
   Len. All honest Minds must share in't;
But the main part pertains to you alone.
   Macd. If it be mine, keep it not from Me.
   Len. Let not your ears condemn my tongue for ever,
When it shall possess them with the heaviest sound
That ever yet they heard.
   Macd. At once I guess, yet am afraid to know.
   Len. Your Castle is surpriz'd, your Wife and Children
Savagely Murder'd: to relate the Manner,   50
Were to increase the Butchery of them,
By adding to their fall the Death of You.
   Mal. Merciful Heaven! Noble *Macduff*
Give sorrow words; the grief that does not speak,
Whispers the o're charg'd heart, and bids it break.
   Macd. My Children too?
   Len. Your Wife, and both your Children.
   Macd. And I not with them dead? Both my Children
Did you say; my Wife too?
     Len.   I have said.
   Mal. Be comforted;   60
Let's make us Cordials of our great revenge,
To cure this deadly Grief.
   Macd. He has no Children, nor can he feel
A fathers Grief: Did you say all my Children?
Oh hellish ravenous Kite! all three at one swoop!
   Mal. Dispute it like a Man.
   Macd.   I shall.
But I must first too feel it as a Man.
I cannot but remember such things were,
And were most precious to me: Did Heaven look on,
And would not take their part? sinful *Macduff,*   70
They were all struck for thee; for thee they fell:
Not for their own offences; but for thine.
   Mal. Let this give Edges to our Swords; let griefe
Convert to anger, let your tears become
Oyl to our kindled Rage.
   Macd. Oh I could play the Woman with my Eyes,

And brag[gart] with my tongue; kind Heavens
Bring this Dire Fiend of *Scotland,* and my self
[But] face to face, and set him within the reach
Of my keen Sword. And if he outlives that [minute]   80
May Heaven forgive his sins, and punish Me
For his escape.
    Mal. Let's hasten to the Army, since *Macbeth*
Is ripe for fall.
    Macd. Heaven give our quarrel but as good success
As it hath Justice in't: Kind Powers above
Grant Peace to us, whilst we take his away;
The Night is long that never finds a Day.   *[Exeunt.*

ACT V, SCENE I

Enter Seyton, *and a Lady.*
    [*Lady.* Most strangely, Sir, She walks now in her sleepe.
    Seyt. I am sent at this dead time of night to know
Her health but now Ide have a sight of her.
When walkt she last?
    Lady. Ere since the knights wente to the feild]
I have seen her rise from her bed, throw
Her Night-Gown ore her, unlock her Closet,
Take forth Paper, fold it, write upon't, read it,
Afterwards Seal it, and again return to Bed,
Yet all this while in a most fast sleep.   10
    Seyt. 'Tis strange she should receive the Benefit
Of sleep, and do the Effects of waking.
In this disorder what at any time
Have you heard her say?
    Lady. That Sir, which I will not report after her.
    Seyt. You may to Me; and 'tis most meet you shou'd.
    Lady. Neither to You, nor any one living;
Having no witness to confirm my Speech.

Enter Lady Macbeth.

See here she comes: observe her, and stand close.

    Seyt. You see her eyes are open.   20

    Lady. Ay, But her Sense is shut.

    Seyt. What is't she does now? look how she rubs her hands.

    Lady. It is an accustom'd action with her to seem

Thus washing her hands: I have known

Her continue in this a quarter of an hour.

    La. Macb. Yet out, out, here's a spot.

    Seyt.   Heark, she speaks.

    La. Macb. Out, out, I say. One, two: Nay then 'tis time

To do't: Fy my Lord, fy, a Soldier, and affraid?

What need we fear? who knows it?

There's none dares call our Power to account: 30

Yet who would have thought the old Man had

So much Blood in him.

    Seyt.   Do you mark that?

    La. Macb. Macduff had once a Wife; where is she now?

What, will these Hands n'ere be clean? Fy my Lord,

You spoil all with this starting: Yet here's

The smell of blood; not all the perfumes of *Arabia*

Will sweeten this little Hand. Oh, Oh, Oh.   [*Exeunt.*

ACT V, SCENE II

Enter Donalbain *and* Fleance, *met by* Lenox.

    Len. Is not that *Donalbain* and young *Flean, Banquo's* Son.

    Donal. Who is this my worthy Friend?

    Len. I by your presence feel my hopes full blown,

Which hitherto have been but in the Bud.

What happy gale has brought you here to see

Your Fathers Death Reveng'd?

    Donal. Hearing of aid sent by the *English* King,

To check the Tirants Insolence; I'm come

From *Ireland.*

Flea. And I from *France,* we are but newly met.   10
Donal. Where's my Brother?
Len. He and the Good *Macduff* are with the Army
Behind the Wood.
   Donal.   What do's the Tyrant now?
   Len. He strongly Fortifies in *Dunsinane;*
Some say he's Mad, others who Love him less,
Call it a Valiant Fury; but what e're
The matter is, there is a Civil War
Within his Bosom; [which will hinder him
From waging this successfully. None can
Resist a forreign foe, who alwayes has   20
An enemy within him. For each murder
He weares a dagger In his Breast.
   Flea. We heard that his owne men diserted him.
   Len. Those he Commands move only in Command
And not in love.] He finds his Crown sit loose:
His power grows less, his [Feares grow] greater still.
[Ambition is a tree whose Roots are small,
Whose growth is high: whose shadow ever is
The blackness of the deed attending it,
Under which nothing prospers. All the fruit   30
It beares are doubts and troubles, with whose crowne
The over burdend tree at last falls downe.]
   Donal. Let's haste and meet my Brother, my Interest
Is Grafted into his, and cannot Grow
Without it.
   Len. So may you both Out-grow unlucky Chance,
And may the Tyrant's Fall that Growth Advance.   [*Exeunt.*

ACT V, SCENE III

Enter Macbeth, Seyton *and Attendants.*
   Macb. Bring me no more Reports: Let 'em flie all
Till *Birnam Wood* remove to *Dunsinane*

I cannot fear. What's the Boy *Malcolm?* What
Are all the *English?* Are they not of Women
Born? And t'all such I am Invincible.
Then flie false *Thanes,*
By your Revolt you have inflam'd my Rage,
And now have Borrowed *English* Blood to quench it.

Enter a Messenger.

Now Friend, what means thy change of Countenance?
  Mess. There are Ten Thousand, Sir.
  Macb.   What, Ghosts?   10
  Mess. No, Armed men.
  Macb. But such as shall be Ghosts e're it be Night.
Art thou turn'd Coward, since I made thee Captain:
Go Blush away thy Paleness, I am sure
Thy Hands are of another Colour; thou hast Hands
Of Blood, but Looks of Milk.
  Mess. The *English* Forces so please you [with armd men] ——
  Macb. Take thy Face hence.
He has Infected me with Fear:
I am sure to die by none of Woman born.   20
And yet the *English* Drums beat an Alarm,
As fatal to my Life as are the Crokes
Of *Ravens,* when they Flutter about the Windows
Of departing men. My hopes are great, and yet
Me-thinks I fear; My Subjects cry out Curses
On my Name, which like a North-wind seems
To blast my Hopes.
  Seyt. That Wind is a contagious Vapour exhal'd from Blood.

Enter Second Messenger.

  Macb. What News more?
  2. Mess. All's confirm'd my Leige, that was Reported.   30
  Macb. And my Resolves in spite of Fate shall be as firm.
Send out more Horse; and Scour the Country round.
How do's my Wife?
  Seyt. Not so Sick, my Lord, as She is Troubled
With disturbing Fancies, that keep Her from Her rest.
  Macb. And I, me-thinks, am Sick of her Disease:
Seyton send out; Captain, the *Thanes* flie from thee:
Wou'd she were well, I'de quickly win the Field.

Stay *Seyton,* stay, I'le bear you company,
The *English* cannot long maintain the Fight;   40
They come not here to Kill, but to be Slain;
Send out our Scouts.
    Seyt.   Sir, I am gone.
Aside] Not to Obey your Orders, but the Call of Justice.
I'le to the *English* Train whose Hopes are built
Upon their Cause, and not on Witches Prophesies.   [*Exit.*
    Macb. Poor *Thanes,* you vainly hope for Victory:
You'l find *Macbeth* Invincible; or if
He can be O'recome, it must be then
By *Birnam Oaks,* and not by English-men.   [*Exit.*

ACT V, SCENE IV

Enter Malcolm, Donalbain, Seymour, Macduff, Lenox,
Fleance, *Souldiers.*
    Mal. The Sun shall see us Drain the Tyrants Blood
And Dry up *Scotlands* Tears: How much we are
Oblig'd to *England,* which like a kind Neighbour
Lift's us up when we are Fall'n below
Our own Recovery.
    Seym. What Wood is this before us?
    Mal.   The Wood of *Birnam.*
    Seym. Let every Souldier hew him down a Bough,
And bear't before him: By that we may
Keep the Number of our Forces undiscover'd
By the Enemy.   10
    Mal. It shall be done. We Learn no more then that
The Confident Tyrant keeps still in *Dunsinane,*
And will endure a Seige.
He is of late grown Conscious of his Guilt,
Which makes him make that City his Place of Refuge.

Macd. He'l find even there but little Safety;
His very Subjects will aginst him Rise.
So Travellers Flie to an Aged Barn
For Shelter from the Rain; when the next Shock
Of Wind throws Down that Roof upon their Heads,   20
From which they hop'd for Succour.
    Len. The wretched Kernes which now like Boughs are ty'd
To forc'd Obedience; will when our Swords
Have Cut those Bonds, like boughs start from Obedience.
    Mal. May the Event make good our Guess.
    Macd. It must, unless our Resolutions fail;
They'l kindle, Sir, their just Revenge at ours:
Which double Flame will Singe the Wings of all
Thy Tyrants hopes; depriv'd of those Supports,
He'l quickly Fall.   30
    Seym. Let's all Retire to our Commands; our Breath
Spent in Discourse does but defer his Death,
And but delays our Vengeance.
    Macd. Come let's go.
The swiftest hast is for Revenge too slow.   [*Exeunt.*

[ACT V, SCENE V]

Enter Macbeth, *and Souldier.*

    Macb. Hang out our Banners proudly o're the Wall,
The Cry is still, they Come: Our Castles Strength
Will Laugh a Siege to Scorn: Here let them lie
Till Famine eat them up: Had *Seyton* still
Been ours, and others who now Increase the Number
Of our Enemies, we might have met 'em
Face to Face.   [*Noise within.*
What Noise is that?
    Sol.   It seems the Cry of Women.
    Macb. I have almost forgot the Taste of Fears,

The time has been that Dangers have been my Familiars.   10
Wherefore was that cry?

   Sol. Great Sir, the Queen is Dead.

   Macb. She should have Di'd hereafter, I brought
Her here, to see my Victimes, and not to Die.
To Morrow, and to Morrow, and to Morrow,
Creeps in a stealing pace from Day to Day,
To the last Minute of Recorded Time:
And all our Yesterdays have lighted Fools
To their Eternal [night]: Out, out [short] Candle,
Life's but a Walking Shaddow, a poor Player   20
That Struts and Frets his Hour upon the Stage,
And then is Heard no more. It is a Tale
Told by an Ideot, full of Sound and Fury
Signifying Nothing.

Enter a Messenger.

Thou comest to use thy Tongue: Thy Story quickly.

   Mess. Let my Eyes speak what they have seen,
For my Tongue cannot.

   Macb. Thy Eyes speak Terror, let thy Tongue expound
Their Language, or be for ever Dumb.

   Mess. As I did stand my Watch upon the Hill,   30
I lookt towards *Birnam,* and anon methought
The Wood began to move.

   Macb.   Lyar and Slave.

   Mess. Let me endure your Wrath if't be not so:
Within this three Mile may you see it coming,
I say, a moving Grove.

   Macb. If thou speakst False, I'll send thy Soul
To th'other World to meet with moving Woods,
And walking Forrests;
There to Possess what it but Dreamt before.
If thy Speech be true, I care not if thou doest   40
The same for me. I now begin
To doubt the Equivocation of the Fiend,
They bid me not to fear till *Birnam Wood*
Should come to *Dunsinane:* And now a Wood
Is on its March this way; Arm, Arm.
Since thus a Wood do's in a March appear,

There is no Flying hence, nor staying here:
Methinks I now grow weary of the Sun,
And wish the Worlds great Glass of Life were run.   [*Exeunt.*

ACT V, SCENE VI

Enter Malcolm, Seymour, Macduff, Lenox, Fleance, Seyton,
Donalbain, *and their Army with Boughs.*

Mal. Here we are near enough;
Throw down your Leafie Skreens
And shew like those you are. You worthy Uncle
Shall with my Brother and the Noble *Lenox,*
March in the Van, whilst Valiant *Seymour*
And my Self, make up the Gross of the Army,
And follow you with speed.

Seym. Fare well; the Monster has forsook his hold
And comes to offer Battle.

Macd. Let him come on; his Title now sits loose   10
About him, like a Giants Robe upon
A Dwarfish Thief.   [*Exeunt.*

[ACT V, SCENE VII]

Enter Macbeth.

Macb. 'Tis too Ignoble, and too base to Flie;
Who's he that is not of a Woman Born,
For such a one I am to fear, or none.

Enter Lenox.

Len. Kind Heavens, I thank thee I have found thee here;

Oh *Scotland! Scotland!* mayst thou owe thy just
Revenge to this sharp Sword, or this blest Minute.
    Macb. Retire fond Man, I wou'd not Kill thee.
Why should *Faulcons* prey on Flies?
It is below *Macbeth* to Fight with Men.
    Len. But not to Murder Women.   10
    Macb. Lenox, I pitty thee, thy Arm's too weak.
    Len. This Arm has hitherto found good Success
On your Ministers of Blood, who Murder'd
Macduffs Lady, and brave *Banquo:* Art thou
Less Mortal then they were? Or more exempt
From Punishment? Because thou most deserv'st it.
Have at thy Life.
    Macb. Since then thou art in Love with Death, I will
Vouchsafe it thee.   [*They fight,* Lenox *falls.*
Thou art of Woman Born, I'm sure.   [*Exit* Macbeth.
    Len. Oh my dear Country, Pardon me that I,   21
Do in a Cause so great, so quickly Die.   [*Dies.*

          Enter Macduff.

    Macd. This way the Noise is, Tyrant shew thy Face,
If thou be'st Slain and by no hand of Mine,
My Wife and Childrens Ghosts will haunt me for't.
I cannot Strike at wretched Slaves, who sell
Their Lives for Pay;
No, my Revenge shall seek a Nobler Prey.
Through all the Paths of Death, I'le search him out:
Let me but find him, *Fortune.*   [*Exit.*

        Enter Malcolm, *and* Seymour.

    Seym. This way, Great Sir, the Tyrants People Fight   31
With Fear as great as is his Guilt.
    Mal. See who Lies here; the Noble *Lenox* slain,
What Storm has brought this Cloud over our
Rising hopes.
    Seym. Restrain your Passion, Sir, let's to our Men,
Those who in Noble Causes fall, deserve
Our Pitty, not our Sorrow.
I'le bid some bear the Body further hence.   [*Exeunt.*

[ACT V, SCENE VIII]

Enter Macbeth.

Macb. Why should I play the *Roman* Fool and Fall
On my own Sword, while I have living Foes
To Conquer; my Wounds shew better upon them.

Enter Macduff.

Macd. Turn Hell-Hound, Turn.

Macb. Of all Men else, I have avoided Thee;
But get thee back, my Soul is too much clog'd
With Blood of thine already.

Macd. I'le have no Words, thy Villanies are worse
Then ever yet were Punisht with a Curse.

Macb. Thou mayst as well attempt to Wound the Air,   10
As me; my Destiny's reserv'd for some Immortal Power,
And I must fall by Miracle; I cannot Bleed.

Macd. Have thy black Deeds then turn'd thee to a Devil.

Macb. Thou wouldst but share the Fate of *Lenox.*

Macd. Is *Lenox* slain? and by a Hand that would
Damn all it kills, but that their Cause preserves'em.

Macb. I have a Prophecy secures my Life.

Macd. I have another which tells me I shall have his Blood,
Who first shed mine.

Macb. None of a Woman born can spill my Blood.   20

Macd. Then let the Devil tell thee, *Macduff*
Was from his Mothers Womb untimely Ript.

Macb. Curst be the Tongue that tells me so,
And double Damn'd be they who with a double sence
Make Promise to our Ears, and Break at last
That Promise to our sight: I will not Fight with thee.

Macd. Then yield thy self a Prisoner to be Led
About the World, and Gaz'd on as a Monster,
More Deform'd then ever Ambition Fram'd,
Or Tyrannie could shape.

Macb.   I scorn to Yield.   30

I will in spite of Witchcraft fight with thee,
Though *Birnam Wood* be come to *Dunsinane:*
And thou art of no Woman Born, I'le try,
If by a Man it be thy Fate to Die.

      [They Fight, Macbeth *falls. They shout within.*
 Macd. This for my Royal Master *Duncan,*
This for my dearest Friend my Wife,
This for those Pledges of our Loves, my Children.
Hark I hear a Noise, sure there are more   *[Shout within.*
Reserves to Conquer. I'le as a Trophy bear   39
Away his Sword, to witness my Revenge.   *[Exit* Macduff.
 Macb. Farewell vain World, and what's most vain in it, Ambition.
                 [Dies.

[ACT V, SCENE IX]

Enter Malcolm, Seymour, Donalbain, Fleance, Seyton, *and Souldiers.*
 Mal. I wish *Macduff* were safe Arriv'd, I am
In doubt for him; for *Lenox* I'me in grief.
 Seym. Consider *Lenox,* Sir, is nobly Slain:
They who in Noble Causes fall, deserve
Our Pity, not our Sorrow. Look where the Tyrant is.
 Seyt. Those Witches, Sir, with all the Power of Hell,
Could not preserve him from the Hand of Heaven.

      Enter Macduff *with* Macbeths *Sword.*

 Macd. Long Live *Malcolm,* King of *Scotland,*
So you are; and though I should not Boast,
That one whom Guilt might easily weigh down,   10
Fell by my Hand; yet here I present you with
The Tyrants Sword, to shew that Heaven appointed
Me to take Revenge for you, and all
That Suffered by his Power.
 Mal. Macduff, we have more Ancient Records
Then this of your successful Courage.

Macd. Now *Scotland,* thou shalt see bright Day again,
That Cloud's remov'd that did Ecclipse thy Sun,
And Rain down Blood upon thee: As your Arms
Did all contribute to this Victory;   20
So let your Voices all concur to give
One joyful Acclamation.
Long Live Malcolm, King of Scotland.
   Mal. We shall not make a large Expence of time
Before we Reckon with your several Loves,
And make all even with you: *Thanes* and Kinsmen,
Henceforth be Earls, the first that ever *Scotland*
Saw Honour'd with that Title: And may they still Flourish
On your Families; though like the Laurels
You have Won to Day; they Spring from a Field of Blood.   30
Drag his Body hence, and let it Hang upon
A Pinnacle in *Dunsinane,* to shew
To future Ages what to those is due,
Who others Right, by Lawless Power pursue.
[Ile haste to *Scone* to be invested.]
   Macd. [We'll all attend you thither.]
So may kind Fortune Crown your Raign with Peace,
As it has Crown'd your Armies with Success;
And may the Peoples Prayers still wait on you,
As all their Curses did *Macbeth* pursue: 40
His Vice shall make your Virtue shine more Bright,
As a Fair Day succeeds a Stormy Night.   [*Exeunt.*

THE
TEMPEST,
OR THE
Enchanted Island.
A
COMEDY

As it is now Acted at His Highnefs the Duke of *York's*
THEATRE.

LONDON,
Printed by *T. N.* for *Henry Herringman*, at the *Blew*
Anchor in the *Lower Walk* of the *New-Exchange.*
MDCLXXIV.

PREFACE
TO THE ENCHANTED ISLAND.

The writing of Prefaces to Plays, was probably invented by some very ambitious Poet, who never thought he had done enough: Perhaps by some Ape of the French Eloquence, which uses to make a business of a Letter of Gallantry, an examen of a Farce; and, in short, a great pomp and ostentation of words on every trifle. This is certainly the Talent of that Nation, and ought not to be invaded by any other. They do that out of gaiety, which would be an imposition upon us.

We may satisfie our selves with surmounting them in the Scene, and safely leave them those trappings of writing, and flourishes of 10
the Pen, with which they adorn the borders of their Plays, and which are indeed no more than good Landskips to a very indifferent Picture. I must proceed no farther in this argument, lest I run my self beyond my excuse for writing this. Give me leave therefore to tell you, Reader, that I do it not to set a value on any thing I have written in this Play, but out of gratitude to the memory of Sir William Davenant, *who did me the honour to joyn me with him in the alteration of it.*

It was originally Shakespear's: *a Poet for whom he had particularly a high veneration, and whom he first taught me to admire.* 20
The Play it self had formerly been acted with success in the Black-Friers: *and our excellent* Fletcher *had so great a value for it, that he thought fit to make use of the same Design, not much varied, a second time. Those who have seen his Sea-Voyage, may easily discern that it was a Copy of* Shakespear's Tempest: *the Storm, the Desart Island, and the Woman who had never seen a Man, are all sufficient Testimonies of it. But* Fletcher *was not the onely Poet who made use of* Shakespear's *Plot: Sir* John Suckling, *a profess'd admirer of our Authour, has follow'd his footsteps in his* Goblins; *his* Regmella *being an open imitation of* Shakespear's 30
Miranda; *and his Spirits, though counterfeit, yet are copied from*

111

Ariel. *But Sir* William Davenant, *as he was a man of quick and piercing imagination, soon found that somewhat might be added to the design of* Shakespear, *of which neither* Fletcher *nor* Suckling *had ever thought: and therefore to put the last hand to it, he design'd the Counter-part to* Shakespear's *Plot, namely, that of a Man who had never seen a Woman; that by this means those two Characters of Innocence and Love might the more illustrate and commend each other. This excellent Contrivance he was pleas'd to communicate to me, and to desire my assistance in it. I con-* 40 *fess, that from the very first moment it so pleas'd me, that I never writ anything with more delight. I must likewise do him that justice to acknowledge, that my writing received daily his amendments, and that is the reason why it is not so faulty, as the rest which I have done, without the help or correction of so judicious a Friend. The Comical parts of the Saylers were also of his invention, and for the most part his writing, as you will easily discover by the Style. In the time I writ with him, I had the opportunity to observe somewhat more nearly of him than I had formerly done, when I had onely a bare acquaintance with him: I found him* 50 *then of so quick a fancy, that nothing was propos'd to him, on which he could not suddenly produce a thought extreamly pleasant and surprising: and those first thoughts of his, contrary to the old Latine Proverb, were not always the least happy. And as his fancy was quick, so likewise were the products of it remote and new. He borrowed not of any other; and his imaginations were such as could not easily enter into any other man. His Corrections were sober and judicious: and he corrected his own writings much more severely than those of another man, bestowing twice the time and labour in polishing, which he us'd in invention. It had per-* 60 *haps been easie enough for me to have arrogated more to my self than was my due, in the writing of this Play, and to have pass'd by his name with silence in the Publication of it, with the same ingratitude which others have us'd to him, whose writings he hath not onely corrected, as he hath done this, but has had a greater inspection over them, and sometimes added whole Scenes together, which may as easily be distinguish'd from the rest, as true Gold from counterfeit by the weight. But besides the unworthiness of the Action which deterred me from it (there being nothing so base as to rob the dead of his reputation) I am satisfi'd I could* 70 *never have receiv'd so much honour, in being thought the Authour of any Poem, how excellent soever, as I shall from the joyning my imperfections with the merit and name of* Shakespear *and Sir* William Davenant.

Decemb. 1.
1669.

JOHN DRIDEN.

PROLOGUE

to the *Tempest,* or the *Enchanted Island.*

As when a Tree's cut down, the secret Root
Lives under ground, and thence new branches shoot;
So, from old Shakespear's *honour'd dust, this day*
Springs up and buds a new reviving Play.
Shakespear, *who (taught by none) did first impart*
To Fletcher *Wit, to labouring* Johnson *Art.*
He, Monarch-like, gave those his Subjects Law,
And is that Nature which they paint and draw.
Fletcher *reach'd that which on his heights did grow,*
Whilst Johnson *crept and gather'd all below.*   10
This did his Love, and this his Mirth digest:
One imitates him most, the other best.
If they have since out-writ all other Men,
'Tis with the drops which fell from Shakespear's *Pen.*
The Storm which vanish'd on the neighb'ring shore,
Was taught by Shakespear's *Tempest first to roar.*
That Innocence and Beauty which did smile
In Fletcher, *grew on this* Enchanted *Isle.*
But Shakespear's *Magick could not copy'd be,*
Within that Circle none durst walk but he.   20
I must confess 'twas bold, nor would you now
That liberty to vulgar Wits allow,
Which works by Magick supernatural things:
But Shakespear's *pow'r is Sacred as a King's.*
Those Legends from old Priesthood were receiv'd,
And he then writ, as People then believ'd.
But, if for Shakespear *we your grace implore,*
We for our Theatre shall want it more:
Who by our dearth of Youths are forc'd t' employ
One of our Women to present a Boy.   30
And that's a transformation, you will say,

114

Exceeding all the Magick in the Play.
Let none expect in the last Act to find,
Her Sex transform'd from Man to Woman-kind.
What e'r she was before the Play began,
All you shall see of her is perfect Man.
Or if your fancy will be farther led
To find her Woman, it must be abed.

DRAMATIS PERSONÆ.

Alonzo Duke of *Savoy,* and Usurper of the Dukedom of *Mantua.*
Ferdinand his Son.
Prospero right Duke of *Millain.*
Antonio his Brother, Usurper of the Dukedom.
Gonzalo, a Nobleman of *Savoy.*
Hippolito, one that never saw Woman, right Heir of the Dukedom
 of *Mantua.*
Stephano Master of the Ship.
Mustacho his Mate.
Trincalo Boatswain.
Ventoso a Marriner.
Several Marriners.
A Cabbin-Boy.
Miranda and ⎫
  ⎬ (Daughters to *Prospero*) that never saw Man.
Dorinda ⎭
Ariel an aiery Spirit, attendant on *Prospero.*
Several Spirits, Guards to *Prospero.*
Caliban ⎫
  ⎬ Two Monsters of the Isle.
Sycorax his Sister. ⎭

*The Front of the Stage is open'd, and the Band of 24 Violins,
with the Harpsicals and Theorbo's which accompany the Voices,
are plac'd between the Pit and the Stage. While the Overture is
playing, the Curtain rises, and discovers a new Frontispiece, joyn'd
to the great Pylasters, on each side of the Stage. This Frontispiece
is a noble Arch, supported by large wreathed Columns of the
Corinthian Order; the wreathings of the Columns are beautifi'd
with Roses wound round them, and several Cupids flying about
them. On the Cornice, just over the Capitals, sits on either side a
Figure, with a Trumpet in one hand, and a Palm in the other, rep-* 10
*resenting Fame. A little farther on the same Cornice, on each side
of a Compass-pediment, lie a Lion and a Unicorn, the Supporters
of the Royal Arms of England. In the middle of the Arch are
several Angels, holding the Kings Arms, as if they were placing
them in the midst of that Compass-pediment. Behind this is the
Scene, which represents a thick Cloudy Sky, a very Rocky Coast,
and a Tempestuous Sea in perpetual Agitation. This Tempest
(suppos'd to be rais'd by Magick) has many dreadful Objects in
it, as several Spirits in horrid shapes flying down amongst the
Sailers, then rising and crossing in the Air. And when the Ship is* 20
*sinking, the whole House is darken'd, and a shower of Fire falls
upon 'em. This is accompanied with Lightning, and several Claps
of Thunder, to the end of the Storm.*

ACT I, [SCENE I]

Enter Mustacho *and* Ventoso.

Vent. What a Sea comes in?

Must. A hoaming Sea! we shall have foul weather.

Enter Trincalo.

117

Trinc. The Scud comes against the Wind, 'twill blow hard.

Enter Stephano.

Steph. Bosen!

Trinc. Here, Master, what say you?

Steph. Ill weather! let's off to Sea.

Must. Let's have Sea-room enough, and then let it blow the Devils head off.

Steph. Boy! Boy!

Enter Cabin boy.

Boy. Yaw, yaw, here, Master.   10

Steph. Give the Pilot a dram of the Bottle.

[*Exeunt* Stephano *and Boy.*

Enter Marriners, and pass over the Stage.

Trinc. Bring the Cable to the Capstorm.

Enter Alonzo, Antonio, Gonzalo.

Alon. Good Bosen have a care; where's the Master? Play the men.

Trinc. Pray keep below.

Anto. Where's the Master, Bosen?

Trinc. Do you not hear him? you hinder us: keep your Cabins, you help the storm.

Gonz. Nay, good friend be patient.

Trinc. I, when the Sea is: hence; what care these roarers for   20 the name of Duke? to Cabin; silence; trouble us not.

Gonz. Good friend, remember whom thou hast aboard.

Trinc. None that I love more than my self: you are a Coun-seller, if you can advise these Elements to silence, use your wis-dom: if you cannot, make your self ready in the Cabin for the ill hour. Cheerly good hearts! out of our way, Sirs.

[*Exeunt* Trincalo *and Marriners.*

Gonz. I have great comfort from this fellow; methinks his com-plexion is perfect Gallows; stand fast, good fate, to his hanging; Make the Rope of his Destiny our Cable, for our own does little advantage us; if he be not born to be hang'd, we shall be drown'd.   30

[*Exeunt.*

Enter Trincalo *and* Stephano.

Trinc. Up aloft, Lads. Come, reef both Topsails.

Steph. Make haste, let's weigh, let's weigh, and off to Sea.

[*Exit* Stephano.

Enter two Marriners, and pass over the Stage.

Trinc. Hands down! man your Main-Capstorm.

Enter Mustacho *and* Ventoso *at the other door.*

Must. Up aloft! and man your Seere-Capstorm.

Vent. My Lads, my Hearts of gold, get in your Capstorm Bar:
Hoa up, hoa up, &c.   [*Exeunt* Mustacho *and* Ventoso.

Enter Stephano.

Steph. Hold on well! hold on well! nip well there; Quarter-
Master, get's more Nippers.   [*Exit* Stephano.

Enter two Marriners, and pass over again.

Trinc. Turn out, turn out all hands to Capstorm. You dogs,
is this a time to sleep? lubbord. Heave together, Lads.   40

[Trincalo *whistles.*

[*Exeunt* Mustacho *and* Ventoso.

Must. within. Our Vial's broke.

Vent. within. 'Tis but our Vial-block has given way. Come
heave, Lads! we are fix'd again. Heave together, Bullyes.

Enter Stephano.

Steph. Cut down the Hammocks! cut down the Hammocks!
Come, my Lads: Come, Bullyes, chear up! heave lustily. The
Anchor's a peek.

Trinc. Is the Anchor a Peek?

Steph. Is a weigh! is a weigh.

Trinc. Up aloft, my Lads, upon the Fore-castle! Cut the Anchor,
cut him.   50

All within. Haul Catt, Haul Catt, &c. Haul Catt, haul: haul
Catt, haul. Below.

Steph. Aft, aft, and lose the Misen!

Trinc. Get the Misen-tack aboard. Haul aft Misen-sheet!

Enter Mustacho.

Must. Loose the Main-top-sail!

Steph. Let him alone, there's too much Wind.

Trinc. Loose Fore-sail! Haul aft both sheets! trim her right
afore the Wind. Aft! aft! Lads, and hale up the Misen here.

Must. A Mackrel-gale, Master.

Steph. within. Port hard, port! the Wind veeres forward, bring   60
the Tack aboard Port is. Star-board, star-board, a little steady;
now steady, keep her thus, no nearer you cannot come, till the Sails
are loose.

Enter Ventoso.

Vent. Some hands down: the Guns are loose.   [*Exit* Mustacho.

Trinc. Try the Pump, try the Pump.   [*Exit* Ventoso.

        Enter Mustacho *at the other door.*

Must. O Master! six foot water in Hold.

Steph. Clap the Helm hard aweather! Flat, flat, flat in the Fore-
sheet there.

Trinc. Over-haul your fore-boling.   69

Steph. Brace in the Lar-board.   [*Exit.*

Trinc. A curse upon this houling,   [*A great cry within.*
They are louder than the weather.

        Enter Antonio *and* Gonzalo.

Yet again, what do you here? shall we give o'r, and drown? ha'
you a mind to sink?

Gonz. A pox o' your throat, you bawling, blasphemous, unchar-
itable dog.

Trinc. Work you then and be poxt.

Anto. Hang, Cur, hang, you whorson insolent noise-maker, we
are less afraid to be drown'd then thou art.   79

Trinc. Ease the Fore-Brace a little.   [*Exit.*

Gonz. I'l warrant him for drowning, though the Ship were no
stronger than a Nut-shell, and as leaky as an unstanch'd Wench.

        Enter Alonzo *and* Ferdinand.

Ferd. For my self I care not, but your loss
Brings a thousand Deaths to me.

Alon. O name not me, I am grown old, my Son;
I now am tedious to the world, and that,
By use, is so to me: But, *Ferdinand,*
I grieve my Subjects loss in thee:
Alas, I suffer justly for my crimes,   89
But why thou shouldst —— O Heaven!   [*A cry within.*
Heark, farewel, my Son, a long farewel!   [*Exeunt.*]

        Enter Trincalo, Mustacho, *and* Ventoso.

Trinc. What, must our mouthes be cold then?

Vent. All's lost. To prayers, to prayers.

Gonz. The Duke and Prince are gone within to prayers.
Let's assist them.

Must. Nay, we may e'en pray to; our case is now alike.

Anto. Mercy upon us! we split, we split.

Gonz. Let's all sink with the Duke, and the young Prince. [*Exeunt.*

Enter Stephano, Trincalo.

Trinc. The Ship is sinking. [*A new cry within.*

Steph. Run her ashore! 100

Trinc. Luff! luff! or we are all lost! there's a Rock upon the Starboard-Bow.

Steph. She strikes, she strikes! All shift for themselves. [*Exeunt.*

ACT I, SCENE II

In the midst of the Shower of Fire the Scene changes. The Cloudy Sky, Rocks, and Sea vanish; and when the Lights return, discover that Beautiful part of the Island, which was the habitation of Prospero; *'Tis compos'd of three Walks of Cypress-trees, each Side-walk leads to a Cave, in one of which* Prospero *keeps his Daughters, in the other* Hippolito: *The Middle-Walk is of a great depth, and leads to an open part of the Island.*

Enter Prospero *and* Miranda.

Prosp. Miranda, where's your Sister?

Mir. I left her looking from the pointed Rock,
At the walks end, on the huge beat of Waters.

Prosp. It is a dreadful object.

Mir. If by your Art, my dearest Father, you have
Put them in this roar, allay 'em quickly.

Prosp. I have so order'd, that not one creature
In the ship is lost:
I have done nothing but in care of thee,
My Daughter, and thy pretty Sister: 10
You both are ignorant of what you are,
Not knowing whence I am, nor that I'm more
Than *Prospero,* Master of a narrow Cell,
And thy unhappy Father.

Mir.   I ne'r endeavour'd
To know more then you were pleas'd to tell me.
   Prosp. I should inform thee farther.
   Mir. You often, Sir, began to tell me what I am,
But then you stopt.
   Prosp.   The hour's now come;
Obey, and be attentive. Canst thou remember
A time before we came into this Cell?   20
I do not think thou canst, for then thou wert
Not full three years old.
   Mir.   Certainly I can, Sir.
   Prosp. Tell me the image then of any thing
Which thou dost keep in thy remembrance still.
   Mir. Sir, had I not four or five Women once
That tended me?
   Prosp.   Thou hadst, and more, *Miranda:*
What seest thou else in the dark back-ward,
And abyss of Time?
If thou remembrest ought e'r thou cam'st here,
Then how thou cam'st thou may'st remember too.   30
   Mir. Sir, that I do not.
   Prosp. Fifteen years since, *Miranda,* thy Father was
The Duke of *Millan,* and a Prince of power.
   Mir. Sir, are not you my Father?
   Prosp. Thy Mother was all virtue, and she said,
Thou wast my Daughter, and thy Sister too.
   Mir. O Heavens!
What foul play had we, that we hither
Came, or was't a blessing that we did?
   Prosp. Both, both, my Girl.
   Mir.   But, Sir, I pray proceed.   40
   Prosp. My Brother, and thy Uncle, call'd *Antonio,*
To whom I trusted then the manage of
My State, while I was wrap'd with secret Studies:
That false Uncle having attain'd the craft
Of granting suits, and of denying them;
Whom to advance, or lop, for over-topping,
Soon was grown the Ivy which did hide
My Princely Trunk, and suck'd my verdure out:
Thou attend'st not.

Mir.   O good Sir, I do.
Prosp. I thus neglecting worldly ends, and bent   50
To closeness, and the bettering of my mind,
Wak'd in my false Brother an evil nature:
He did believe he was indeed the Duke,
Because he then did execute the outward
Face of Sovereignty. Do'st thou still mark me?
    Mir. Your story would cure deafness.
    Prosp. This false Duke needs would be Absolute *Millan,*
And Confederates with *Savoy's* Duke,
To give him Tribute, and to do him Homage.
    Mir. False man!   60
    Prosp. This Duke of *Savoy* being an Enemy,
To me inveterate, strait grants my Brother's suit,
And on a night mated to his design,
Antonio opened the gates of *Millan,*
And i'th'dead of darkness, hurri'd me thence
With thy young Sister, and thy crying self.
    Mir. But wherefore did they not that hour destroy us?
    Prosp. They durst not, Girl, in *Millan,* for the love
My people bore me; in short they hurri'd us
Away to *Savoy,* and thence aboard a Bark   70
At *Nissa's* Port: bore us some Leagues to Sea,
Where they prepar'd a rotten carkass of a Boat,
Not rigg'd, no Tackle, Sail, nor Mast;
The very Rats instinctively had quit it.
    Mir. Alack! what trouble was I then to you?
    Prosp. Thou and thy Sister were two Cherubins,
Which did preserve me: you both did smile,
Infus'd with fortitude from Heaven.
    Mir. How came we ashoar?
    Prosp.   By Providence Divine,
Some food we had, and some fresh Water, which   80
A Nobleman of *Savoy,* called *Gonzalo,*
Appointed Master of that black design,
Gave us; with rich Garments, and all necessaries,
Which since have steaded much: and of his gentleness
(Knowing I lov'd my Books) he furnish'd me
From mine own Library, with Volumes which
I prize above my Dukedom.

Mir. Would I might see that man.

Prosp. Here in this Island we arriv'd, and here
Have I your Tutor been. But by my skill   90
I find, that my Mid-heaven doth depend
On a most happy Star, whose influence
If I now court not, but omit, my Fortunes
Will ever after droop: here cease more questions,
Thou art inclin'd to sleep: 'tis a good dulness,
And give it way; I know thou canst not chuse.   [*She falls asleep.*
Come away, my Spirit: I am ready now,
Approach, my *Ariel*, Come.

Enter Ariel.

Ariel. All hail, great Master, grave Sir, hail, I come
To answer thy best pleasure, be it to fly,   100
To swim, to shoot into the fire, to ride
On the curl'd Clouds; to thy strong bidding, task
Ariel and all his Qualities.

Prosp. Hast thou, Spirit, perform'd to point the Tempest
That I bad thee?

Ariel.   To every Article.
I boarded the Dukes Ship, now on the Beak,
Now in the Waste, the Deck, in every Cabin,
I flam'd amazement; and sometimes I seem'd
To burn in many places on the Top-mast,
The Yards, and Bore-sprit; I did flame distinctly.   110
Nay once I rain'd a shower of Fire upon 'em.

Prosp. My brave Spirit!
Who was so firm, so constant, that this coil
Did not infect his Reason?

Ariel.   Not a Soul
But felt a Feaver of the mind, and plaid
Some tricks of desperation; all, but Marriners,
Plung'd in the foaming brine, and quit the Vessel:
The Dukes Son, *Ferdinand*,
With hair upstairing (more like Reeds then Hair)
Was the first man that leap'd; cry'd, Hell is empty,   120
And all the Devils are here.

Prosp.   Why that's my Spirit;
But was not this nigh Shore?

Ariel.   Close by my Master.
Prosp. But, *Ariel,* are they safe?
Ariel.   Not a hair perish'd.
In Troops I have dispers'd them round this Isle.
The Duke's Son I have landed by himself,
Whom I have left warming the Air with sighs,
In an odd angle of the Isle, and sitting,
His arms he folded in this sad knot.
   Prosp. Say how thou hast dispos'd the Marriners
Of the Duke's Ship, and all the rest of the Fleet?   130
   Ariel. Safely in harbour
Is the Dukes Ship, in the deep Nook, where once
Thou called'st me up at midnight to fetch Dew
From the still vex'd *Bermoothes,* there she's hid,
The Marriners all under hatches stow'd,
Whom, with a charm, joyn'd to their suffer'd labour,
I have left asleep; and for the rest o' th' Fleet,
(Which I disperst) they all have met again,
And are upon the *Mediterranean* Float,
Bound sadly home for *Italy;*   140
Supposing that they saw the Duke's Ship wrack'd,
And his great person perish.
   Prosp.   *Ariel,* thy charge
Exactly is perform'd, but there's more work:
What is the time o'th'day?
   Ariel.   Past the mid-season.
   Prosp. At least two Glasses: the time 'tween six and now
Must by us both be spent most preciously.
   Ariel. Is there more toyl? since thou dost give me pains,
Let me remember thee what thou hast promis'd,
Which is not yet perform'd me.
   Prosp.   How now, *Moodie?*
What is't thou canst demand?
   Ariel.   My liberty.   150
   Prosp. Before the time be out? no more.
   Ariel.   I prethee!
Remember I have done thee faithful service,
Told thee no lies, made thee no mistakings,
Serv'd without or grudge, or grumblings:

Thou didst promise to bate me a full year.
   Prosp. Dost thou forget
From what a torment I did free thee?
   Ariel.   No.
   Prosp. Thou dost, and think'st it much to tread the Ooze
Of the salt deep:
To run against the sharp wind of the North,   160
To do my business in the veins of the Earth,
When it is bak'd with Frost.
   Ariel.   I do not, Sir.
   Prosp. Thou ly'st, malignant thing! hast thou forgot
The foul Witch *Sycorax,* who with age and envy
Was grown into a Hoop? hast thou forgot her?
   Ariel. No, Sir.
   Prosp. Thou hast; where was she born? speak, tell me.
   Ariel. Sir, in *Argier.*
   Prosp.   Oh, was she so! I must
Once every month recount what thou hast been,
Which thou forgettest. This damn'd Witch *Sycorax*   170
For mischiefs manifold, and Sorceries
Too terrible to enter humane hearing,
From *Argier* thou know'st was banish'd:
But for one thing she did, they would not take
Her life: is not this true?
   Ariel.   I, Sir.
   Prosp. This blew-ey'd Hag was hither brought with child,
And here was left by th'Sailers, thou, my slave,
As thou report'st thy self, wast then her servant,
And 'cause thou wast a spirit too delicate
To act her earthy and abhor'd commands;   180
Refusing her grand Hests, she did confine thee,
By help of her more potent Ministers,
(In her unmitigable rage) into a cloven Pine,
Within whose rift imprison'd, thou didst painfully
Remain a dozen years; within which space she dy'd,
And left thee there; where thou didst vent thy Groans,
As fast as Mill-wheels strike. Then was this Isle
(Save for two Brats, which she did Litter here,
The brutish *Caliban,* and his twin-sister,

Two freckel'd hag-born Whelps) not honour'd with   190
A humane shape.
    Ariel. Yes! *Caliban* her son, and *Sycorax* his sister.
    Prosp. Dull thing, I say so; he, that *Caliban,*
And she that *Sycorax,* whom I now keep
In service. Thou best know'st what torment
I did find thee in, thy groans did make
Wolves houl, and penetrate the breasts
Of ever angry Bears, it was a torment
To lay upon the damn'd, which *Sycorax*
Could ne'r again undo: It was my Art,   200
When I arriv'd, and heard thee, that made the Pine
To gape, and let thee out.
    Ariel.   I thank thee, Master.
    Prosp. If thou more murmurest, I will rend an Oak,
And peg thee in his knotty entrails, till thou
Hast houl'd away twelve Winters more.
    Ariel. Pardon, Master,
I will be correspondent to command,
And be a gentle spirit.
    Prosp. Do so, and after two days I'l discharge thee.
    Ariel. Thanks, my great Master. But I have yet one request.   210
    Prosp. What's that, my spirit.
    Ariel. I know that this days business is important,
Requiring too much toyl for one alone.
I have a gentle spirit for my Love,
Who twice seven years has waited for my freedom:
Let it appear, it will assist me much,
And we with mutual joy shall entertain
Each other. This I beseech you grant me.
    Prosp. You shall have your desire.
    Ariel. That's my noble Master. *Milcha!*   220
                Milcha *flies down to his assistance.*
    Milc. I am here, my Love.
    Ariel. Thou art free! welcome, my dear! what shall we do?
Say, say, what shall we do?
    Prosp. Be subject to no sight but mine, invisible
To every Eyeball else. Hence with diligence,
Anon thou shalt know more.   [*They both fly up and cross in the air.*

Thou hast slept well my child.   [*To* Miranda.

    Mir. The sadness of your story put heaviness in me.

    Prosp. Shake it off; come on, I'l now call *Caliban,*

My slave, who never yields us a kind answer.   230

    Mir. 'Tis a creature, Sir, I do not love to look on.

    Prosp. But as 'tis, we cannot miss him; he does make

Our Fire, fetch in our Wood, and serve in Offices

That profit us: what hoa! Slave! *Caliban!*

Thou Earth thou, speak.

    Calib. within.   There's Wood enough within.

    Prosp. Thou poisonous slave, got by the Devil himself

Upon thy wicked Dam, come forth.

Enter Caliban.

    Calib. As wicked Dew, as e'r my Mother brush'd

With Raven's feather from unwholesome Fens,

Drop on you both: A Southwest blow on you,   240

And blister you all o'r.

    Prosp. For this be sure, to night thou shalt have cramps,

Sidestiches, that shall pen thy breath up; Urchins

Shall prick thee till thou bleed'st: thou shalt be pinch'd

As thick as Honeycombs, each pinch more stinging

Than the Bees which made 'em.

    Calib.   I must eat my dinner:

This Island's mine by *Sycorax* my Mother,

Which thou took'st from me. When thou cam'st first,

Thou stroak'st me, and mad'st much of me, wouldst give me

Water with Berries in't, and teach me how   250

To name the Bigger Light, and how the Less,

That burn by day and night; and then I lov'd thee,

And shew'd thee all the qualities of the Isle,

The Fresh-springs, Brine-pits, barren places and fertile.

Curs'd be I that I did so: All the Charms

Of *Sycorax,* Toads, Beetles, Bats, light on thee,

For I am all the Subjects that thou hast.

I first was mine own Lord; and here thou stay'st me

In this hard Rock, whiles thou dost keep from me

The rest o'th' Island.

    Prosp.   Thou most lying Slave,   260

Whom stripes may move, not kindness: I have us'd thee

(Filth that thou art) with humane care, and lodg'd thee
In mine own Cell, till thou didst seek to violate
The honour of my Children.
   Calib. Oh ho, Oh ho, would't had been done:
Thou didst prevent me, I had peopl'd else
This Isle with *Calibans.*
   Prosp.   Abhor'd Slave!
Who ne'r would any print of goodness take,
Being capable of all ill: I pity'd thee,
Took pains to make thee speak, taught thee each hour   270
One thing or other; when thou didst not (Savage)
Know thy own meaning, but wouldst gabble, like
A thing most brutish, I endow'd thy purposes
With words, which made them known: But thy wild race
(Though thou didst learn) had that in't, which good Natures
Could not abide to be with: therefore wast thou
Deservedly pent up into this Rock.
   Calib. You taught me language, and my profit by it
Is, that I know to curse: the red botch rid you
For learning me your language.
   Prosp.   Hag-seed hence!   280
Fetch us in fewel, and be quick
To answer other business: shrugst thou (malice)
If thou neglectest, or dost unwillingly what I command,
I'l wrack thee with old Cramps, fill all thy bones with
Aches, make thee roar, that Beasts shall tremble
At thy Din.
   Calib.   No prethee!
I must obey. His Art is of such power,
It would control my Dam's God, *Setebos,*
And make a Vassal of him.
   Prosp.   So Slave, hence.
                 [*Exeunt* Prospero *and* Caliban *severally.*
             Enter Dorinda.
   Dor. Oh, Sister! what have I beheld?   290
   Mir. What is it moves you so?
   Dor.   From yonder Rock,
As I my eyes cast down upon the Seas,
The whistling winds blew rudely on my face,

And the waves roar'd; at first I thought the War
Had been between themselves, but strait I spy'd
A huge great Creature.
    Mir.   O you mean the Ship.
    Dor. Is't not a Creature then? it seem'd alive.
    Mir. But what of it?
    Dor. This floating Ram did bear his Horns above,
All ty'd with Ribbands ruffling in the wind;   300
Sometimes he nodded down his head awhile,
And then the waves did heave him to the Moon;
He clamb'ring to the top of all the Billows,
And then again he curtsi'd down so low,
I could not see him: till, at last, all side-long
With a great crack his belly burst in pieces.
    Mir. There all had perish'd,
Had not my Father's Magick Art reliev'd them.
But, Sister, I have stranger news to tell you;
In this great Creature there were other Creatures,   310
And shortly we may chance to see that thing,
Which you have heard my Father call, a Man.
    Dor. But what is that? for yet he never told me.
    Mir. I know no more than you: but I have heard
My Father say, we Women were made for him.
    Dor. What, that he should eat us, Sister?
    Mir. No sure, you see my Father is a Man, and yet
He does us good. I would he were not old.
    Dor. Me thinks indeed it would be finer, if
We two had two young Fathers.   320
    Mir. No, Sister, no, if they were young, my Father
Said, that we must call them Brothers.
    Dor. But pray how does it come, that we two are not
Brothers then, and have not Beards like him?
    Mir. Now I confess you pose me.
    Dor. How did he come to be our Father too?
    Mir. I think he found us when we both were little,
And grew within the ground.
    Dor. Why could he not find more of us? pray, Sister,
Let you and I look up and down one day,   330
To find some little ones for us to play with.

Mir. Agreed; but now we must go in. This is
The hour wherein my Father's Charm will work,
Which seizes all who are in open air:
Th' effect of his great Art I long to see,
Which will perform as much as Magick can.
    Dor. And I, methinks, more long to see a Man.   [*Exeunt.*

ACT II, SCENE I

*The Scene changes to the wilder part of the Island, 'tis compos'd
of divers sorts of Trees, and barren places, with a prospect of the
Sea at a great distance.*

Enter Stephano, Mustacho, Ventoso.

Vent. The Runlet of Brandy was a loving Runlet, and floated
after us out of pure pity.

Must. This kind Bottle, like an old acquaintance, swam after
it. And this Scollop-shell is all our Plate now.

Vent. 'Tis well we have found something since we landed. I
prethee fill a soop, and let it go round. Where hast thou laid the
Runlet?

Must. I'th'hollow of an old Tree.

Vent. Fill apace, we cannot live long in this barren Island, and
we may take a soop before death, as well as others drink at our   10
Funerals.

Must. This is Prize-Brandy, we steal Custom, and it costs
nothing. Let's have two rounds more.

Vent. Master, what have you sav'd?

Steph. Just nothing but my self.

Vent. This works comfortably on a cold stomach.

Steph. Fill's another round.

Vent. Look! *Mustacho* weeps. Hang losses, as long as we have
Brandy left. Prithee leave weeping.

Steph. He sheds his Brandy out of his eyes: he shall drink no   20
more.

Must. This will be a doleful day with old *Bess.* She gave me a gilt Nutmeg at parting. That's lost too. But, as you say, hang losses. Prethee fill again.

Vent. Beshrew thy heart for putting me in mind of thy Wife, I had not thought of mine else, Nature will shew it self, I must melt. I prithee fill again, my Wife's a good old Jade, and has but one eye left: but she'll weep out that too, when she hears that I am dead.

Steph. Would you were both hang'd for putting me in thought 30
of mine.

Vent. But come, Master, sorrow is dry! there's for you agen.

Steph. A Marriner had e'en as good be a Fish as a Man, but for the comfort we get ashore: O for an old dry Wench now I am wet.

Must. Poor heart! that would soon make you dry agen: but all is barren in this Isle: Here we may lie at Hull till the Wind blow Nore and by South, ere we can cry, A Sail, a Sail, at sight of a white Apron. And therefore here's another soop to comfort us.

Vent. This Isle's our own, that's our comfort, for the Duke, the Prince, and all their train, are perished. 40

Must. Our Ship is sunk, and we can never get home agen: we must e'en turn Salvages, and the next that catches his fellow may eat him.

Vent. No, no, let us have a Government; for if we live well and orderly, Heav'n will drive Shipwracks ashoar to make us all rich; therefore let us carry good Consciences, and not eat one another.

Steph. Whoever eats any of my Subjects, I'll break out his teeth with my Scepter: for I was Master at Sea, and will be Duke on Land: you *Mustacho* have been my Mate, and shall be my Vice- 50
Roy.

Vent. When you are Duke, you may choose your Vice-Roy; but I am a free Subject in a new Plantation, and will have no Duke without my voice. And so fill me the other soop.

Steph. whispering. Ventoso, dost thou hear, I will advance thee, prithee give me thy voice.

Vent. I'l have no whisperings to corrupt the Election; and to show that I have no private ends, I declare aloud that I will be Vice-Roy, or I'l keep my voice for my self.

Must. Stephano, hear me, I will speak for the people, because 60 there are few, or rather none in the Isle to speak for themselves. Know then, that to prevent the farther shedding of Christian bloud, we are all content *Ventoso* shall be Vice-Roy, upon condition I may be Vice-Roy over him. Speak, good people, are you well agreed? what, no man answer? well, you may take their silence for consent.

Vent. You speak for the people, *Mustacho?* I'l speak for 'em, and declare generally with one voice, one and all; That there shall be no Vice-Roy but the Duke, unless I be he.

Must. You declare for the people, who never saw your face!   70 Cold Iron shall decide it.   [*Both draw.*

Steph. Hold, loving Subjects: we will have no Civil War during our Reign: I do hereby appoint you both to be my Vice-Roys over the whole Island.

Both. Agreed! agreed!

        Enter Trincalo, *with a great Bottle, half drunk.*

Vent. How! *Trincalo* our brave Bosen!

Must. He reels: can he be drunk with Sea-water?

Trinc. sings. I shall no more to Sea, to Sea,
                Here I shall die ashore.

This is a very scurvy tune to sing at a man's funeral, but here's my   80 comfort.   [*Drinks.*

Sings. The Master, the Swabber, the Gunner, and I,
        The Surgeon and his Mate,
     Lov'd *Mall, Meg,* and *Marrian,* and *Margery,*
        But none of us car'd for *Kate.*
     For she had a tongue with a tang,
     Wou'd cry to a Sailor, Go hang:
     She lov'd not the savour of Tar nor of Pitch,
     Yet a Tailor might scratch her where ere she did itch.

This is a scurvy Tune too, but here's my comfort agen.   [*Drinks.*

Steph. We have got another Subject now; Welcome, Welcome   91 into our Dominions!

Trinc. What Subject, or what Dominions? here's old Sack, Boys: the King of good-fellows can be no subject. I will be old *Simon* the King.

Must. Hah, old Boy! how didst thou scape?

Trinc. Upon a Butt of Sack, Boys, which the Sailors threw over-board: but are you alive, hoa! for I will tipple with no Ghosts

till I'm dead: thy hand, *Mustacho,* and thine, *Ventoso;* the Storm
has done its worst: *Stephano* alive too! give thy Bosen thy hand, 100
Master.

Vent. You must kiss it then, for, I must tell you, we have chosen
him Duke in a full Assembly.

Trinc. A Duke! where? what's he Duke of?

Must. Of this Island, man. Oh *Trincalo,* we are all made, the
Island's empty; all's our own, Boy; and we will speak to his Grace
for thee, that thou may'st be as great as we are.

Trinc. You great? what the Devil are you?

Vent. We two are Vice-Roys over all the Island; and when we
are weary of Governing, thou shalt succeed us.   110

Trinc. Do you hear, *Ventoso,* I will succeed you in both your
places before you enter into 'em.

Steph. *Trincalo,* sleep and be sober; and make no more uproars
in my Countrey.

Trinc. Why, what are you, Sir, what are you?

Steph. What I am, I am by free Election, and you, *Trincalo,*
are not your self; but we pardon your first fault, because it is the
first day of Our Reign.

Trinc. Umph, were matters carried so swimmingly against me,
whilst I was swimming, and saving my self for the good of the 120
people of this Island.

Must. Art thou mad, *Trincalo*? wilt thou disturb a setled Government, where thou art a meer stranger to the Laws of the
Countrey?

Trinc. I'l have no Laws.

Vent. Then Civil-war begins.   [*Vent., Must. draw.*

Steph. Hold, hold, I'l have no bloudshed, my Subjects are but
few: let him make a rebellion by himself; and a Rebel, I Duke
Stephano declare him: Vice-Roys, come away.

Trinc. And Duke *Trincalo* declares, that he will make open 130
War where ever he meets thee or thy Vice-Roys.

[*Exeunt* Steph., Must., Vent.

Enter Caliban *with wood upon his back.*

Hah! who have we here?

Calib. All the infections that the Sun sucks up

From Fogs, Fens, Flats, on *Prospero* fall, and make him
By inch-meal a Disease: his spirits hear me,
And yet I needs must curse, but they'l not pinch,
Fright me with Urchin shows, pitch me i'th'mire,
Nor lead me in the dark out of my way,
Unless he bid 'em: but for every trifle
He sets them on me; sometimes like Baboons   140
They mow and chatter at me, and often bite me;
Like Hedge-hogs then they mount their prickles at me,
Tumbling before me in my barefoot way.
Sometimes I am all wound about with Adders,
Who with their cloven tongues hiss me to madness.
Hah! yonder stands one of his spirits sent
To torment me.

   Trinc. What have we here, a Man, or a Fish? This is some
Monster of the Isle; were I in *England,* as once I was, and had
him painted, not a Holy-day fool there but would give me six- 150
pence for the sight of him; well, if I could make him tame, he
were a present for an Emperour. Come hither, pretty Monster,
I'l do thee no harm. Come hither!

   Calib. Torment me not; I'l bring thee Wood home faster.

   Trinc. He talks none of the wisest, but I'l give him a dram o'
th'Bottle, that will clear his understanding. Come on your ways,
Master Monster, open your mouth. How now, you perverse
Moon-calf! what, I think you cannot tell who is your friend!
Open your chops, I say.   [*Pours Wine down his throat.*

   Calib. This is a brave God, and bears Coelestial Liquor; I'll 160
kneel to him.

   Trinc. He is a very hopeful Monster; Monster, what sayst thou,
art thou content to turn civil and sober, as I am? for then thou
shalt be my subject.

   Calib. I'l swear upon that Bottle to be true; for the liquor is
not Earthly: did'st thou not drop from Heaven?

   Trinc. Onely out of the Moon, I was the man in her when time
was. By this light, a very shallow Monster.

   Calib. I'l shew thee every fertile inch i' th' Isle, and kiss thy
foot: I prithee be my God, and let me drink.   [*Drinks agen.*

   Trinc. Well drawn Monster, in good faith.   171

Calib. I'l shew thee the best springs, I'l pluck thee Berries,
I'l fish for thee, and get thee wood enough:
A curse upon the Tyrant whom I serve,
I'l bear him no more sticks, but follow thee.
    Trinc. The poor Monster is loving in his drink.
    Calib. I prithee let me bring thee where Crabs grow,
And I with my long nails will dig thee Pig-nuts,
Shew thee a Jays-nest, and instruct thee how
To snare the Marmazete; I'l bring thee   180
To cluster'd Filberds; Wilt thou go with me?
    Trinc. This Monster comes of a good natur'd race;
Is there no more of thy kin in this Island?
    Calib. Divine, here is but one besides my self;
My lovely Sister, beautiful and bright
As the Full Moon.
    Trinc.   Where is she?
    Calib. I left her clambring up a hollow Oak,
And plucking thence the dropping Honey-combs.
Say, my King, shall I call her to thee?
    Trinc. She shall swear upon the Bottle too.   190
If she proves handsome she is mine:
Here, Monster, drink agen for thy good news;
Thou shalt speak a good word for me.   *[Gives him the Bottle.*
    Calib. sings. Farewel, old Master, farewel, farewel.
                No more Dams I'l make for fish,
                Nor fetch in firing at requiring,
                Nor scrape Trencher, nor wash Dish,
                Ban, Ban, *Cackaliban*
                Has a new Master, get a new man.
                Heigh-day! Freedom, freedom!   200
    Trinc. Here's two subjects got already, the Monster,
And his Sister: well, Duke *Stephano,*
I say, and say agen, wars will ensue,
And so I drink.   *[Drinks.*
From this Worshipful Monster, and Mistris Monster his Sister,
I'l lay claim to this Island by alliance:
Monster, I say thy Sister shall be my Spouse:
Come away, Brother Monster, I'l lead thee to my Butt,
And drink her health.   *[Exeunt.*

[ACT II, SCENE II]

Scene Cypress Trees and Cave.
Enter Prospero *alone.*

Prosp. 'Tis not yet fit to let my Daughters know
I kept the Infant Duke of *Mantua*
So near them in this Isle, whose Father dying,
Bequeath'd him to my care; Till my false Brother
(When he design'd t'usurp my Dukedome from me)
Expos'd him to that fate he meant for me.
By calculation of his birth I saw
Death threat'ning him, if, till some time were past,
He should behold the face of any Woman:
And now the danger's nigh: *Hippolito*!   10

Enter Hippolito.

Hip. Sir, I attend your pleasure.
Prosp. How I have lov'd thee from thy infancy,
Heav'n knows, and thou thy self canst bear me witness,
Therefore accuse not me for thy restraint.
Hip. Since I knew life, you've kept me in a Rock,
And you this day have hurri'd me from thence,
Onely to change my Prison, not to free me.
I murmur not, but I may wonder at it.
Prosp. O gentle Youth, Fate waits for thee abroad,
A black Star threatens thee, and death unseen   20
Stands ready to devour thee.
Hip.   You taught me
Not to fear him in any of his shapes:
Let me meet death rather then be a prisoner.
Prosp. 'Tis pity he should seize thy tender youth.
Hip. Sir, I have often heard you say, no creature liv'd
Within this Isle, but those which Man was Lord of;
Why then should I fear?
Prosp. But here are creatures which I nam'd not to thee,
Who share Mans Sovereignty by Nature's Laws,

And oft depose him from it.   30

    Hip. What are those Creatures, Sir?

    Prosp. Those dangerous enemies of men call'd Women.

    Hip. Women! I never heard of them before.

What are Women like?

    Prosp. Imagine something between young Men and Angels:

Fatally beauteous, and have killing Eyes,

Their voices charm beyond the Nightingales,

They are all enchantment, those who once behold 'em,

Are made their slaves for ever.

    Hip. Then I will wink and fight with 'em.   40

    Prosp. 'Tis but in vain,

They'l haunt you in your very sleep.

    Hip. Then I'l revenge it on 'em when I wake.

    Prosp. You are without all possibility of revenge,

They are so beautiful, that you can ne'r attempt,

Nor wish to hurt them.

    Hip.   Are they so beautiful?

    Prosp. Calm sleep is not so soft, nor Winter Suns,

Nor Summer shades so pleasant.

    Hip. Can they be fairer then the Plumes of Swans?

Or more delightful then the Peacocks Feathers?   50

Or than the gloss upon the necks of Doves?

Or have more various beauty then the Rainbow?

These I have seen, and without danger wondred at.

    Prosp. All these are far below 'em: Nature made

Nothing but Woman dangerous and fair:

Therefore if you should chance to see 'em,

Avoid 'em streight I charge you.

    Hip. Well, since you say they are so dangerous,

I'l so far shun 'em as I may with safety

Of the unblemish'd honour which you taught me.   60

But let 'em not provoke me, for I'm sure

I shall not then forbear them.

    Prosp. Go in and read the Book I gave you last.

To morrow I may bring you better news.

    Hip. I shall obey you, Sir.   [*Exit* Hippolito.

    Prosp. So, so; I hope this Lesson has secur'd him,

For I have been constrain'd to change his lodging

From yonder Rock where first I bred him up,
And here have brought him home to my own Cell,
Because the Shipwrack happen'd near his Mansion.   70
I hope he will not stir beyond his limits,
For hitherto he hath been all obedience:
The Planets seem to smile on my designs,
And yet there is one sullen cloud behind,
I would it were disperst.

Enter Miranda and Dorinda.

How, my Daughters! I thought I had instructed
Them enough: Children! retire;
Why do you walk this way?
   Mir. It is within our bounds, Sir.
   Prosp. But both take heed, that path is very dangerous.   80
Remember what I told you.
   Dor. Is the man that way, Sir?
   Prosp. All that you can imagine ill is there,
The curled Lion, and the rugged Bear,
Are not so dreadful as that man.
   Mir. Oh me, why stay we here then?
   Dor. I'l keep far enough from his Den, I warrant him.
   Mir. But you have told me, Sir, you are a man;
And yet you are not dreadful.
   Prosp. I Child! but I am a tame man;   90
Old men are tame by Nature, but all the danger
Lies in a wild young man.
   Dor. Do they run wild about the Woods?
   Prosp. No, they are wild within doors, in Chambers,
And in Closets.
   Dor.   But, Father, I would stroak 'em,
And make 'em gentle, then sure they would not hurt me.
   Prosp. You must not trust them, Child: no Woman can
Come near 'em, but she feels a pain, full nine moneths.
Well, I must in; for new affairs require
My presence: be you, *Miranda,* your Sisters Guardian. [*Exit* Prospero.
   Dor. Come, Sister, shall we walk the other way?   101
The Man will catch us else: we have but two legs,
And he perhaps has four.
   Mir. Well, Sister, though he have; yet look about you,

And we shall spy him ere he comes too near us.

 Dor. Come back, that way is towards his Den.

 Mir. Let me alone; I'l venture first, for sure
He can devour but one of us at once.

 Dor. How dare you venture?

 Mir. We'l find him sitting like a Hare in's Form,   110
And he shall not see us.

 Dor. I, but you know my Father charg'd us both.

 Mir. But who shall tell him on't? we'l keep each
Others counsel.

 Dor.   I dare not for the world.

 Mir. But how shall we hereafter shun him, if we do not
Know him first?

 Dor.   Nay, I confess I would
Fain see him too. I find it in my Nature,
Because my Father has forbidden me.

 Mir. I, there's it, Sister, if he had said nothing,
I had been quiet. Go softly, and if you see him   120
First, be quick, and becken me away.

 Dor. Well, if he does catch me, I'l humble my self to him,
And ask him pardon, as I do my Father,
When I have done a fault.

 Mir. And if I can but scape with life, I had rather
Be in pain nine moneths, as my Father threatn'd,
Then lose my longing.   [*Exeunt.*

[ACT II, SCENE III]

The Scene continues.

Enter Hippolito.

 Hip. Prospero has often said, that Nature makes
Nothing in vain: why then are women made?
Are they to suck the poison of the Earth,

As gaudy colour'd Serpents are? I'l ask
That Question, when next I see him here.

          Enter Miranda *and* Dorinda *peeping.*

  Dor. O Sister, there it is, it walks about like one of us.
  Mir. I, just so, and has legs as we have too.
  Hip. It strangely puzzles me: yet 'tis most likely
Women are somewhat between men and spirits.
  Dor. Heark! it talks, sure this is not it my Father   10
Meant, for this is just like one of us:
Methinks I am not half so much afraid on't
As I was; see, now it turns this way.
  Mir. Heaven! what a goodly thing it is?
  Dor. I'l go nearer it.
  Mir. O no, 'tis dangerous, Sister! I'l go to it.
I would not for the world that you should venture.
My Father charg'd me to secure you from it.
  Dor. I warrant you this is a tame man, dear Sister,
He'll not hurt me, I see it by his looks.   20
  Mir. Indeed he will! but go back, and he shall eat
Me first: Fie, are you not asham'd to be
So much inquisitive?
  Dor. You chide me for't, and wou'd give your self.
  Mir. Come back, or I will tell my Father.
Observe how he begins to stare already.
I'l meet the danger first, and then call you.
  Dor. Nay, Sister, you shall never vanquish me in kindness.
I'l venture you no more then you will me.
  Prosp. within. Miranda, Child, where are you!   30
  Mir. Do you not hear my Father call? go in.
  Dor. 'Twas you he nam'd, not me; I will but say
My prayers, and follow you immediately.
  Mir. Well, Sister, you'l repent it.   [*Exit* Miranda.
  Dor. Though I die for't, I must have th'other peep.
  Hip. seeing her. What thing is that? sure 'tis some Infant of
The Sun, dress'd in his Fathers gayest Beams,
And comes to play with Birds: my sight is dazl'd,
And yet I find I'm loth to shut my Eyes.
I must go nearer it —— but stay a while;   40
May it not be that beauteous Murderer, Woman,

Which I was charg'd to shun? Speak, what art thou?
Thou shining Vision!
  Dor. Alas, I know not; but I'm told I am a Woman;
Do not hurt me, pray, fair thing.
  Hip. I'd sooner tear my eyes out, then consent
To do you any harm; though I was told
A Woman was my Enemy.
  Dor. I never knew what 'twas to be an Enemy,
Nor can I e'r prove so to that which looks   50
Like you: for though I have been charg'd by him
(Whom yet I never disobey'd) to shun
Your presence, yet I'd rather die then lose it;
Therefore I hope you will not have the heart
To hurt me: though I fear you are a Man,
That dangerous thing of which I have been warn'd.
Pray tell me what you are?
  Hip. I must confess, I was inform'd I am a Man,
But if I fright you, I shall wish I were
Some other Creature. I was bid to fear you too.   60
  Dor. Ay me! Heav'n grant we be not poison to each other!
Alas, can we not meet but we must die?
  Hip. I hope not so! for when two poisonous Creatures,
Both of the same kind, meet, yet neither dies.
I've seen two Serpents harmless to each other,
Though they have twin'd into a mutual knot:
If we have any venome in us, sure, we cannot be
More poisonous, when we meet, then Serpents are.
You have a hand like mine, may I not gently touch it?

                                 [Takes her hand.
  Dor. I've touch'd my Father's and my Sister's hands,   70
And felt no pain; but now, alas! there's something,
When I touch yours, which makes me sigh: just so
I've seen two Turtles mourning when they met;
Yet mine's a pleasing grief; and so me thought
Was theirs: For still they mourn'd, and still they seem'd
To murmur too, and yet they often met.
  Hip. Oh Heavens! I have the same sense too: your hand
Methink goes through me; I feel at my heart,
And find it pleases, though it pains me.
  Prosp. within.   *Dorinda!*

Dor. My Father calls again; ah, I must leave you.   80
Hip. Alas, I'm subject to the same command.
Dor. This is my first offence against my Father,
Which he, by severing us, too cruelly does punish.
    Hip. And this is my first trespass too: but he
Hath more offended truth than we have him:
He said our meeting would destructive be,
But I no death but in our parting see.   *[Exeunt several ways.*

ACT II, SCENE [IV]

A wild Island.

Enter Alonzo, Antonio, Gonzalo.

    Gonz. 'Beseech your Grace be merry: you have cause,
So have we all, of joy, for our strange 'scape;
Then wisely, good Sir, weigh our sorrow with our comfort.
    Alon. Prithee peace, you cram these words into my ears,
Against my stomach; how can I rejoyce,
When my dear Son, perhaps this very moment,
Is made a meal to some strange Fish?
    Anto. Sir, he may live, I saw him beat the Billows
Under him, and ride upon their backs;
I do not doubt he came alive to Land.   10
    Alon. No, no, he's gone; and you and I, *Antonio,*
Were those who caus'd his death.
    Anto. How could we help it?
    Alon.   Then, then we should have help'd
    it,
When thou betrai'dst thy Brother *Prospero,*
And *Mantua's* Infant Sovereign, to my power;
And when I, too ambitious, took by force
Another's right: Then lost we *Ferdinand;*
Then forfeited our Navy to this Tempest.
    Anto. Indeed we first broke Truce with Heaven;

You to the waves an Infant Prince expos'd,   20
And on the waves have lost an onely Son.
I did usurp my Brother's fertile Lands,
And now am cast upon this Desart-Isle.
   Gonz. These, Sirs, 'tis true, were crimes of a black die;
But both of you have made amends to Heav'n
By your late Voyage into *Portugal;*
Where, in defence of Christianity,
Your valour has repuls'd the Moors of *Spain.*
   Alon. O name it not, *Gonzalo;*
No act but penitence can expiate guilt!   30
Must we teach Heav'n what price to set on Murder!
What rate on lawless Power and wild Ambition!
Or dare we traffick with the Powers above,
And sell by weight a good deed for a bad?   [*A flourish of Musick.*
   Gonz. Musick! and in the air! sure we are Shipwrack'd
On the Dominions of some merry Devil!
   Anto. This Isle's Inchanted ground; for I have heard
Swift voices flying by my ear, and groans
Of lamenting ghosts.
   Alon. I pull'd a Tree, and bloud pursu'd my hand.   40
Heav'n deliver me from this dire place,
And all the after-actions of my life
Shall mark my penitence and my bounty.   [*Musick agen lowder.*
Hark, the sounds approach us!   [*The Stage opens in several places.*
   Anto. Lo the Earth opens to devour us quick.
These dreadful horrors, and the guilty sense
Of my foul Treason, have unmann'd me quite.
   Alon. We on the brink of swift destruction stand;
No means of our escape is left.
                  [*Another flourish of Voyces under the Stage.*
   Anto. Ah! what amazing sounds are these we hear!   50
   Gonz. What horrid Masque will the dire Fiends present?
                Sung under the Stage.
  1. *Dev. Where does the black Fiend Ambition reside,*
        With the mischievous Devil of Pride?
  2. *Dev. In the lowest and darkest Caverns of Hell*
        Both Pride and Ambition does dwell.
  1. *Dev. Who are the chief Leaders of the damned Host?*
  3. *Dev.   Proud Monarchs, who tyrannize most.*

1. *Dev.*   *Damned Princes there*
          The worst of torments bear.
3. *Dev. Who in Earth all others in pleasures excel,*   60
        Must feel the worst torments of Hell.
                     [They rise singing this Chorus.
Anto. Oh Heav'ns! what horrid Vision's this?
How they upbraid us with our crimes!
    Alon. What fearful vengeance is in store for us!
1. *Dev. Tyrants by whom their Subjects bleed,*
        Should in pains all others exceed.
2. *Dev. And barb'rous Monarchs who their Neighbours invade,*
        And their Crowns unjustly get;
        And such who their Brothers to death have betrai'd,
          In Hell upon burning Thrones shall be set.   70
3. *Dev.* ⎱ —— *In Hell, in Hell with flames they shall reign,*
Chor. ⎰ *And forever, for ever shall suffer the pain.*
Anto. Oh my Soul; for ever, for ever shall suffer the pain.
    Alon. Has Heav'n in all its infinite stock of mercy
No overflowings for us? poor, miserable, guilty men!
    Gonz. Nothing but horrors do encompass us!
For ever, for ever must we suffer!
    Alon. For ever we shall perish! O dismal words, for ever!
1. *Dev. Who are the Pillars of the Tyrants Court?*
2. *Dev. Rapine and Murder his Crown must support!*   80
3. *Dev.* —— *His cruelty does tread*
        On Orphans tender breasts, and Brothers dead!
2. *Dev. Can Heav'n permit such crimes should be*
        Attended with felicity?
3. *Dev. No, Tyrants their Scepters uneasily bear,*
        In the midst of their Guards they their Consciences
        fear.
2. *Dev.* ⎱ *Care their minds when they wake unquiet will keep,*
Chor. ⎰ *And we with dire visions disturb all their sleep.*
Anto. Oh horrid sight! how they stare upon us!
The Fiends will hurry us to the dark Mansion.   90
Sweet Heav'n, have mercy on us!
1. *Dev. Say, Say, shall we bear these bold Mortals from hence?*
2. *Dev. No, no, let us show their degrees of offence.*
3. *Dev. Let's muster their crimes up on every side,*
        And first let's discover their pride.

Enter *Pride*.

Pride.   *Lo here is Pride, who first led them astray,*
          And did to Ambition their minds then betray.

Enter *Fraud*.

Fraud.   *And Fraud does next appear,*
              Their wandring steps who led,
              When they from vertue fled,   100
          They in my crooked paths their course did steer.

Enter *Rapine*.

Rapine. *From Fraud to Force they soon arrive,*
        Where Rapine did their actions drive.

Enter *Murder*.

Murder. *There long they could not stay;*
            Down the steep hill they run,
        And to perfect the mischief which they had begun,
            To Murder they bent all their way.
                Around, around we pace,
Chorus of all.   *About this cursed place;*
                 While thus we compass in   110
                 These Mortals and their sin.   [*Devils vanish.*
    Anto. Heav'n has heard me, they are vanish'd!
    Alon. But they have left me all unmann'd.
I feel my sinews slacken with the fright;
And a cold sweat trills down o'r all my Limbs,
As if I were dissolving into water.
Oh *Prospero*, my crimes 'gainst thee sit heavy on my heart!
    Anto. And mine 'gainst him and young *Hippolito*.
    Gonz. Heav'n have mercy on the penitent.
    Alon. Lead from this cursed ground;   120
The Seas in all their rage are not so dreadful.
This is the Region of despair and death.
    Anto. Shall we not seek some Fruit?
    Alon. Beware all fruit, but what the Birds have peck'd.
The shadows of the Trees are poisonous too:
A secret venom slides from every branch!
My Conscience does distract me! O my Son!
Why do I speak of eating or repose,

146

Before I know thy fortune?
> [*As they are going out, a Devil rises just before*
> *them, at which they start, and are frighted.*

O Heavens! yet more Apparitions!   130

Devil sings. *Arise, arise! ye subterranean winds,*
  More to disturb their guilty minds.
  And all ye filthy damps and vapours rise,
  Which use t' infect the Earth, and trouble all the
    Skies;
  Rise you, from whom devouring plagues have birth:
  You that i' th' vast and hollow womb of Earth,
  Engender Earthquakes, make whole Countreys shake,
  And stately Cities into Desarts turn;
  And you who feed the flames by which Earths entrals
    burn.
  Ye raging winds, whose rapid force can make   140
  All but the fix'd and solid Centre shake:
  Come drive these Wretches to that part o' th' Isle,
    Where Nature never yet did smile:
  Cause Fogs and Storms, Whirlwinds and Earthquakes
    there:
  There let 'em houl and languish in despair.
  Rise and obey the pow'rful Prince o'th' Air.

  Two Winds rise, Ten more enter and dance:
At the end of the Dance, Three winds sink, the rest drive
  Alon. Anto. Gonz. *off.*

ACT III, SCENE I

Scene, A wild Island.
Enter Ferdinand, *and* Ariel *and* Milcha *invisible.*

Ariel. Come unto these yellow sands,
  And then take hands,
Curtsi'd when you have, and kiss'd;
  The wild waves whist.

Foot it featly here and there,
  And sweet sprights the burthen bear.
Hark! hark!
  Bow waugh, the Watch-dogs bark.
Bow waugh. Hark! hark! I hear
The Strain of strutting Chanticleer,   10
  Cry, Cock a doodle do.
  Ferd. Where should this Musick be? i'th'air, or earth?
It sounds no more, and sure it waits upon
Some God i'th'Island; sitting on a bank,
Weeping against the Duke my Father's wrack;
This Musick hover'd on the waters, allaying both
Their fury and my passion with charming Aires.
Thence I have follow'd it, (or it has drawn me rather)
But 'tis gone: No, it begins again.
  Milcha sings. Full fathom five thy Father lies,   20
      Of his bones is Coral made:
    Those are Pearls that were his Eyes,
      Nothing of him that does fade
    But does suffer a Sea-change
    Into something rich and strange:
    Sea-Nymphs hourly ring his knell;
    Hark! now I hear 'em, ding dong Bell.
  Ferd. This mournful Ditty mentions my drown'd Father.
This is no mortal business, nor a sound
Which the Earth owns —— I hear it now before me;   30
However I will on and follow it.   [*Exit* Ferdinand *following* Ariel.

ACT III, SCENE II

The Cypress-trees and Cave.
Enter Prospero *and* Miranda.
  Prosp. Excuse it not, *Miranda,* for to you

(The elder, and I thought the more discreet)
I gave the conduct of your Sisters actions.
    Mir. Sir, when you call'd me thence, I did not fail
To mind her of her duty to depart.
    Prosp. How can I think you did remember hers,
When you forgot your own? did you not see
The man whom I commanded you to shun?
    Mir. I must confess I saw him at a distance.
    Prosp. Did not his Eyes infect and poison you?   10
What alteration found you in your self?
    Mir. I onely wondred at a sight so new.
    Prosp. But have you no desire once more to see him?
Come, tell me truly what you think of him?
    Mir. As of the gayest thing I ever saw,
So fine, that it appear'd more fit to be
Belov'd than feard, and seem'd so near my kind,
That I did think I might have call'd it Sister.
    Prosp. You do not love it?
    Mir. How is it likely that I should,   20
Except the thing had first lov'd me?
    Prosp. Cherish those thoughts: you have a gen'rous soul;
And since I see your mind not apt to take
The light Impressions of a sudden love,
I will unfold a secret to your knowledge.
That Creature which you saw, is of a kind
Which Nature made a prop and guide to yours.
    Mir. Why did you then propose him as an object
Of terrour to my mind? you never us'd
To teach me any thing but God-like truths,   30
And what you said, I did believe as sacred.
    Prosp. I fear'd the pleasing form of this young man
Might unawares possess your tender breast,
Which for a nobler guest I had design'd;
For shortly, my *Miranda,* you shall see
Another of this kind, the full-blown Flower,
Of which this Youth was but the Op'ning Bud.
Go in, and send your Sister to me.
    Mir. Heav'n still preserve you, Sir.   [*Exit* Miranda.
    Prosp. And make thee fortunate.   40

Enter Dorinda.

O Come hither, you have seen a man to day,
Against my strict command.
   Dor. Who I? indeed I saw him but a little, Sir.
   Prosp. Come, come, be clear. Your Sister told me all.
   Dor. Did she? truly she would have seen him more
Then I, but that I would not let her.
   Prosp.   Why so?
   Dor. Because, methought, he would have hurt me less
Then he would her. But if I knew you'd not be angry
With me, I could tell you, Sir, that he
Was much to blame.
   Prosp.   Hah! was he to blame?   50
Tell me, with that sincerity I taught you,
How you became so bold to see the man?
   Dor. I hope you will forgive me, Sir, because
I did not see him much till he saw me.
Sir, he would needs come in my way, and star'd,
And star'd upon my face; and so I thought
I would be reveng'd of him, and therefore I gaz'd
On him as long; but if I e'r come near
A man again ——
   Prosp.   I told you he was dangerous;
But you would not be warn'd.
   Dor.   Pray be not angry,   60
Sir, if I tell you, you are mistaken
In him; for he did me no great hurt.
   Prosp. But he may do you more harm hereafter.
   Dor. No, Sir, I'm as well as e'r I was in all my life,
But that I cannot eat nor drink for thought of him.
That dangerous man runs ever in my mind.
   Prosp. The way to cure you, is no more to see him.
   Dor. Nay pray, Sir, say not so, I promis'd him
To see him once agen; and you know, Sir,
You charg'd me I should never break my promise.   70
   Prosp. Wou'd you see him who did you so much mischief?
   Dor. I warrant you I did him as much harm
As he did me; for when I left him, Sir,
He sigh'd so, as it griev'd my heart to hear him.
   Prosp. Those sighs were poisonous, they infected you:

You say, they griev'd you to the heart.

    Dor. 'Tis true; but yet his looks and words were gentle.

    Prosp. These are the Day-dreams of a Maid in Love.

But still I fear the worst.

    Dor. O fear not him, Sir.   80

    Prosp. You speak of him with too much passion; tell me

(And on your duty tell me true, *Dorinda*)

What past betwixt you and that horrid creature?

    Dor. How, horrid, Sir? if any else but you

Should call it so, indeed I should be angry.

    Prosp. Go too! you are a foolish Girl; but answer

To what I ask, what thought you when you saw it?

    Dor. At first it star'd upon me, and seem'd wild,

And then I trembled, yet it look'd so lovely,

That when I would have fled away, my feet   90

Seem'd fasten'd to the ground, then it drew near,

And with amazement ask'd to touch my hand;

Which, as a ransome for my life, I gave:

But when he had it, with a furious gripe

He put it to his mouth so eagerly,

I was afraid he would have swallow'd it.

    Prosp. Well, what was his behaviour afterwards?

    Dor. He on a sudden grew so tame and gentle,

That he became more kind to me than you are;

Then, Sir, I grew I know not how, and touching   100

His hand agen, my heart did beat so strong,

As I lack'd breath to answer what he ask'd.

    Prosp. You have been too fond, and I should chide you for it.

    Dor. Then send me to that Creature to be punish'd.

    Prosp. Poor Child! thy passion, like a lazy Ague,

Has seiz'd thy bloud, instead of striving, thou humour'st

And feed'st thy languishing disease: thou fight'st

The Battels of thy Enemy, and 'tis one part of what

I threatn'd thee, not to perceive thy danger.

    Dor. Danger, Sir?   110

If he would hurt me, yet he knows not how:

He hath no Claws, nor Teeth, nor Horns to hurt me,

But looks about him like a Callow-bird,

Just straggl'd from the Nest: pray trust me, Sir,

To go to him agen.

Prosp.   Since you will venture,
I charge you bear your self reserv'dly to him,
Let him not dare to touch your naked hand,
But keep at distance from him.
    Dor.   This is hard.
Prosp. It is the way to make him love you more;
He will despise you if you grow too kind.   120
    Dor. I'l struggle with my heart to follow this,
But if I lose him by it, will you promise
To bring him back agen?
    Prosp.   Fear not, *Dorinda;*
But use him ill, and he'l be yours for ever.
    Dor. I hope you have not couzen'd me agen.   [*Exit* Dorinda.
    Prosp. Now my designs are gathering to a head.
My spirits are obedient to my charms.
What, *Ariel!* my servant *Ariel,* where art thou?
                    Enter Ariel.
    Ariel. What wou'd my potent Master? Here I am.
    Prosp. Thou and thy meaner fellows your last service   130
Did worthily perform, and I must use you
In such another Work: how goes the day?
    Ariel. On the fourth, my Lord, and on the sixth,
You said our work should cease.
    Prosp.   And so it shall;
And thou shalt have the open air at freedom.
    Ariel. Thanks, my great Lord.
    Prosp.   But tell me first, my Spirit,
How fares the Duke, my Brother, and their followers?
    Ariel. Confin'd together, as you gave me order,
In the Lime-grove, which weather-fends your Cell;
Within that Circuit up and down they wander,   140
But cannot stir one step beyond their compass.
    Prosp. How do they bear their sorrows?
    Ariel. The two Dukes appear like men distracted, their
Attendants brim full of sorrow mourning over 'em;
But chiefly, he you term'd the good *Gonzalo:*
His Tears run down his Beard, like Winter-drops
From Eaves of Reeds, your Vision did so work 'em,
That if you now beheld 'em, your affections
Would become tender.

Prosp.　　　　　Do'st thou think so, Spirit?
Ariel.　Mine would, Sir, were I humane.
Prosp.　　　　　　　　And mine shall:　　　150
Hast thou, who art but air, a touch, a feeling
Of their Afflictions, and shall not I (a man
Like them, one who as sharply rellish passions
As they) be kindlier mov'd then thou art?
Though they have pierc'd me to the quick with injuries,
Yet with my nobler Reason 'gainst my fury
I will take part; the rarer action is
In vertue than in vengeance. Go, my *Ariel,*
Refresh with needful food their famish'd bodies.
With shows and cheerful Musick comfort 'em.　　　160
　Ariel.　Presently, Master.
　Prosp.　With a twinkle, *Ariel.* But stay, my Spirit;
What is become of my Slave *Caliban,*
And *Sycorax* his Sister?
　Ariel.　　　　　Potent Sir!
They have cast off your service, and revolted
To the wrack'd Marriners, who have already
Parcell'd your Island into Governments.
　Prosp.　No matter, I have now no need of 'em.
But, Spirit, now I stay thee on the Wing;
Hast to perform what I have given in charge:　　　170
But see they keep within the bounds I set 'em.
　Ariel.　I'l keep 'em in with Walls of Adamant,
Invisible as air to mortal eyes,
But yet unpassable.
　Prosp.　　　Make hast then.　　　[*Exeunt severally.*

ACT III, SCENE III

Wild Island.
Enter Alonzo, Antonio, Gonzalo.
Gonz.　I am weary, and can go no further Sir.

Alon. Old Lord, I cannot blame thee, who am my self seiz'd
With a weariness, to the dulling of my spirits: *[They sit.*
Even here I will put off my hope,
And keep it no longer for my flatterers:
He is drown'd whom thus we stray to find.
I'm faint with hunger, and must despair of food.   *[Musick without.*
What! Harmony agen, my good friends, heark!
    Anto. I fear some other horrid apparition.
Give us kind Keepers, Heaven I beseech thee!   10
    Gonz. 'Tis chearful Musick this, unlike the first.

Ariel and Milcha invisible, sings.

    Dry those eyes which are o'rflowing,
    All your storms are overblowing:
    While you in this Isle are biding,
    You shall feast without providing:
    Every dainty you can think of,
    Ev'ry Wine which you would drink of,
    Shall be yours; all want shall shun you,
    Ceres *blessing so is on you.*

    Alon. This voice speaks comfort to us.   20
    Anto. Wou'd 'twere come; there is no Musick in a Song
To me, my stomack being empty.
    Gonz. O for a heavenly vision of Boyl'd,
Bak'd, and Roasted!
        [Dance of fantastick Spirits, after the Dance, a Table fur-
           nish'd with Meat and Fruit is brought in by two Spirits.
    Anto. My Lord, the Duke, see yonder.
A Table, as I live, set out and furnish'd
With all varieties of Meats and fruits.
    Alon. 'Tis so indeed; but who dares taste this feast
Which Fiends provide, perhaps to poison us?   30
    Gonz. Why that dare I; if the black Gentleman
Be so ill-natur'd, he may do his pleasure.
    Anto. 'Tis certain we must either eat or famish;
I will encounter it, and feed.
    Alon. If both resolve, I will adventure too.
    Gonz. The Devil may fright me, yet he shall not starve me.
        [Two Spirits descend, and flie away with the Table.
    Alon. Heav'n! behold, it is as you suspected: 'tis vanish'd.

Shall we be always haunted with these Fiends?

    Anto. Here we shall wander till we famish.

    Gonz. Certainly one of you was so wicked as to say Grace: 40
This comes on't, when men will be godly out of season.

    Anto. Yonders another Table, let's try that ———   [*Exeunt.*

[ACT III, SCENE IV]

Enter Trincalo *and* Caliban.

    Trinc. Brother Monster, welcome to my private Palace. But
where's thy Sister, is she so brave a Lass?

    Calib. In all this Isle there are but two more, the Daughters of
the Tyrant *Prospero;* and she is bigger then 'em both. O here she
comes; now thou may'st judge thy self, my Lord.

Enter Sycorax.

    Trinc. She's monstrous fair indeed. Is this to be my Spouse?
well, she's heir of all this Isle (for I will geld Monster). The
Trincalo's, like other wise men, have antiently us'd to marry for
Estate more then for beauty.

    Syc. I prithee let me have the gay thing about thy neck, and   10
that which dangles at thy wrist.

[Sycorax *points to his Bosens Whistle and his Bottle.*

    Trinc. My dear Blobber-lips; this, observe my Chuck, is a badge
of my Sea-office; my fair Fuss, thou dost not know it.

    Syc. No, my dread Lord.

    Trinc. It shall be a Whistle for our first Babe, and when the
next Shipwrack puts me again to swimming, I'l dive to get a Coral
to it.

    Syc. I'l be thy pretty Child, and wear it first.

    Trinc. I prithee, sweet Baby, do not play the Wanton, and cry
for my goods e'r I'm dead. When thou art my Widow, thou shalt   20
have the Devil and all.

    Syc. May I not have the other fine thing?

    Trinc. This is a Sucking-bottle for young *Trincalo.*

Calib. Shall she not taste of that immortal Liquor?

Trinc. Umph! that's another question: for if she be thus flipant in her Water, what will she be in her Wine?

    Enter Ariel *(invisible) and changes the Bottle which stands upon the ground.*

Ariel. There's Water for your Wine.   [*Exit* Ariel.

Trinc. Well! since it must be so.   [*Gives her the Bottle.*
How do you like it now, my Queen that must be?   [*She drinks.*

Syc. Is this your heavenly Liquor? I'l bring you to a River of   30 the same.

Trinc. Wilt thou so, Madam Monster? what a mighty Prince shall I be then? I would not change my Dukedom to be great Turk *Trincalo.*

Syc. This is the drink of Frogs.

Trinc. Nay, if the Frogs of this Island drink such, they are the merriest Frogs in Christendom.

Calib. She does not know the virtue of this Liquor: I prithee let me drink for her.

Trinc. Well said, Subject Monster.   [Caliban *drinks.*

Calib. My Lord, this is meer Water.   41

Trinc. 'Tis thou hast chang'd the Wine then, and drunk it up, like a debauch'd Fish as thou art. Let me see't, I'l taste it my self. Element! meer Element! as I live. It was a cold gulph, such as this, which kill'd my famous predecessor, old *Simon* the King.

Calib. How does thy honour? prithee be not angry, and I will lick thy shoe.

Trinc. I could find in my heart to turn thee out of my Dominions for a Liquorish Monster.

Calib. O my Lord, I have found it out; this must be done by   50 one of *Prospero's* Spirits.

Trinc. There's nothing but malice in these Devils, I would it had been Holy-water for their sakes.

Syc. 'Tis no matter, I will cleave to thee.

Trinc. Lovingly said, in troth: now cannot I hold out against her. This Wife-like virtue of hers has overcome me.

Syc. Shall I have thee in my arms?

Trinc. Thou shalt have Duke *Trincalo* in thy arms:
But prithee be not too boistrous with me at first;
Do not discourage a young beginner.   [*They embrace.*
Stand to your Arms, my Spouse, and subject Monster.   61

Enter Stephano, Mustacho, Ventoso.

The Enemy is come to surprise us in our Quarters.
You shall know, Rebels, that I am marri'd to a Witch,
And we have a thousand Spirits of our party.
   Steph. Hold! I ask a Truce; I and my Vice-Roys
(Finding no food, and but a small remainder of Brandy)
Are come to treat a Peace betwixt us,
Which may be for the good of both Armies,
Therefore *Trincalo* disband.
   Trinc. Plain *Trincalo,* methinks I might have been   70
A Duke in your mouth; I'l not accept of your
Embassie without my Title.
   Steph. A Title shall break no squares betwixt us:
Vice-Roys, give him his style of Duke, and treat
With him, whilst I walk by in state.
                        [Ventoso *and* Mustacho bow, whilst
                        Trincalo *puts on his Cap.*
   Must. Our Lord and Master, Duke *Stephano,* has sent us
In the first place to demand of you, upon what
Ground you make War against him, having no right
To govern here, as being elected onely by
Your own voice.   80
   Trinc. To this I answer, That having in the face of the world
Espous'd the lawful Inheritrix of this Island,
Queen *Blouze* the first, and having homage done me,
By this Hectoring Spark her Brother, from these two
I claim a lawful Title to this Island.
   Must. Who that Monster? he a Hector?
   Calib. Lo! how he mocks me, wilt thou let him, my Lord?
   Trinc. Vice-Roys! keep good tungs in your heads,
I advise you, and proceed to your business.
   Must. First and foremost, as to your claim that you have an-
     swer'd.
   Vent. But second and foremost, we demand of you,   91
That if we make a peace, the Butt also may be
Comprehended in the Treaty.
   Trinc. I cannot treat with my honour, without your submission.
   Steph. I understand, being present, from my Embassadors, what
your resolution is, and ask an hours time of deliberation, and so I
take our leave; but first I desire to be entertain'd at your Butt, as

becomes a Prince, and his Embassadors.

 Trinc. That I refuse, till acts of hostility be ceas'd.
These Rogues are rather Spies then Embassadors;   100
I must take heed of my Butt. They come to pry
Into the secrets of my Dukedom.

 Vent. Trincalo, you are a barbarous Prince, and so farewel.

             [*Exeunt* Steph., Must., Vent.

 Trinc. Subject Monster! stand you Centry before my Cellar; my
Queen and I will enter, and feast our selves within.   [*Exeunt.*

[ACT III, SCENE V]

    Enter Ferdinand, Ariel *and* Milcha (*invisible*).

 Ferd. How far will this invisible Musician
Conduct my steps? he hovers still about me,
Whether for good or ill, I cannot tell,
Nor care I much; for I have been so long
A slave to chance, that I'm as weary of
Her flatteries as her frowns, but here I am ——

 Ariel.   Here I am.

 Ferd. Hah! art thou so? the Spirit's turn'd an Eccho:
This might seem pleasant, could the burthen of
My Griefs accord with any thing but sighs.
And my last words, like those of dying men,   10
Need no reply. Fain I would go to shades,
Where few would wish to follow me.

 Ariel.   Follow me.

 Ferd. This evil Spirit grows importunate,
But I'l not take his counsel.

 Ariel.   Take his counsel.

 Ferd. It may be the Devil's counsel, I'l never take it.

 Ariel. Take it.

 Ferd. I will discourse no more with thee,
Nor follow one step further.

Ariel.   One step further.
Ferd. This must have more importance then an Eccho.
Some Spirit tempts to a precipice.   20
I'l try if it will answer when I sing
My sorrows to the murmur of this Brook.
                              He sings.
                                        Go thy way.
Ariel.   *Go thy way.*
Ferd.   *Why should'st thou stay?*
Ariel.   *Why shouldst thou stay?*
Ferd. Where the winds whistle, and where the streams creep,
    Under yond Willow-tree, fain would I sleep.
                              Then let me alone,
                              For 'tis time to be
                                  gone,   30
Ariel.   *For 'tis time to be*
                                  gone.
Ferd. What cares or pleasures can be in this Isle?
        Within this desart place
        There lives no humane race;
    Fate cannot frown here, nor kind fortune smile.
Ariel. Kind Fortune smiles, and she
    Has yet in store for thee
    Some strange felicity.
    Follow me, follow me,
    And thou shalt see.   40
Ferd. I'l take thy word for once;
Lead on Musician.   [*Exeunt and return.*

ACT III, SCENE [VI]

The Cypress-trees and Caves.
Scene changes, and discovers Prospero *and* Miranda.
Prosp. Advance the fringed Curtains of thine Eyes,

159

And say what thou seest yonder.

    Mir.   Is it a Spirit?

Lord! how it looks about! Sir, I confess

It carries a brave form. But 'tis a Spirit.

    Prosp. No, Girl, it eats, and sleeps, and has such sences

As we have. This young Gallant, whom thou seest,

Was in the wrack; were he not somewhat stain'd

With grief (beauty's worst cancker) thou might'st

Call him a goodly person; he has lost

His company, and strays about to find 'em.   10

    Mir. I might call him a thing Divine, for nothing

Natural I ever saw so noble.

    Prosp. It goes on as my soul prompts it: Spirit, fine spirit.

I'l free thee within two days for this.

    Ferd. She's sure the Mistris on whom these Airs attend.

Fair Excellence, if, as your form declares,

You are Divine, be pleas'd to instruct me

How you will be worship'd; so bright a beauty

Cannot sure belong to humane kind.

    Mir. I am, like you, a Mortal, if such you are.   20

    Ferd. My language too! O Heavens! I am the best

Of them who speak this speech when I'm in

My own Countrey.

    Prosp. How, the best? What wert thou if the Duke

Of *Savoy* heard thee?

    Ferd. As I am now, who wonders to hear thee speak of *Savoy:*

He does hear me, and that he does I weep,

My self am *Savoy,* whose fatal eyes (e'r since

At ebb) beheld the Duke my Father wrack'd.

    Mir. Alack! for pity.   30

    Prosp. At the first sight they have chang'd eyes, dear *Ariel,*

I'l set thee free for this —— young Sir, a word.

With hazard of your self you do me wrong.

    Mir. Why speaks my Father so urgently?

This is the third man that e'r I saw, the first whom

E'r I sigh'd for, sweet Heaven move my Father

To be inclin'd my way.

    Ferd. O! if a Virgin! and your affections not gone forth,

I'l make you Mistris of *Savoy.*

Prosp. Soft, Sir! one word more.   40
They are in each others powers, but this swift
Bus'ness I must uneasie make, lest too light
Winning make the prize light —— one word more.
Thou usurp'st the name not due to thee, and hast
Put thy self upon this Island as a spy to get the
Government from me the Lord of it.
    Ferd. No, as I'm a man.
    Mir. There's nothing ill can dwell in such a Temple,
If th' evil Spirit hath so fair a house,
Good things will strive to dwell with it.   50
    Prosp. No more. Speak not for him, he's a Traitor.
Come! thou art my pris'ner, and shalt be in
Bonds. Sea-water shalt thou drink, thy food
Shall be the fresh-Brook-Muscles, wither'd Roots,
And Husks, wherein the Acorn crawl'd; follow.
    Ferd. No, I will resist such entertainment,
Till my Enemy has more power.

                    [He draws, and is charm'd from moving.
    Mir. O dear Father! make not too rash a trial
Of him, for he's gentle, and not fearful.
    Prosp. My child my Tutor! put thy Sword up, Traitor,   60
Who mak'st a show, but dar'st not strike: thy
Conscience is possess'd with guilt. Come from
Thy Ward, for I can here disarm thee with
This Wand, and make thy Weapon drop.
    Mir. 'Beseech you, Father.
    Prosp. Hence: hang not on my Garment.
    Mir.   Sir, have pity,
I'l be his Surety.
    Prosp. Silence! one word more shall make me chide thee,
If not hate thee: what, an advocate for an
Impostor? sure thou think'st there are no more   70
Such shapes as his?
To the most of men this is a *Caliban,*
And they to him are Angels.
    Mir. My affections are then most humble,
I have no ambition to see a goodlier man.
    Prosp. Come on, obey:

Thy Nerves are in their infancy again, and have
No vigour in them.
    Ferd.   So they are:
My spirits, as in a Dream, are all bound up:
My Father's loss, the weakness which I feel,   80
The wrack of all my friends, and this man's threats,
To whom I am subdu'd, would seem light to me,
Might I but once a day through my prison
Behold this Maid: all corners else o'th'earth
Let liberty make use of: I have space
Enough in such a prison.
    Prosp.   It works: come on:
Thou hast done well, fine *Ariel:* follow me.
Heark what thou shalt more do for me.   [*Whispers* Ariel.
    Mir. Be of comfort!
My Father's of a better nature, Sir,   90
Then he appears by speech: this is unwonted
Which now came from him.
    [*Prosp.*] Thou shalt be as free as Mountain Winds:
But then exactly do all points of my command.
    Ariel. To a syllable.   [*Exit* Ariel.
    Prosp. to Mir. Go in that way, speak not a word for him:
I'l separate you.   [*Exit* Miranda.
    Ferd. As soon thou may'st divide the waters
When thou strik'st 'em, which pursue thy bootless blow,
And meet when 'tis past.   100
    Prosp. Go practise your Philosophy within,
And if you are the same you speak your self,
Bear your afflictions like a Prince —— That door
Shews you your Lodging.
    Ferd. 'Tis in vain to strive, I must obey.   [*Exit* Ferdinand.
    Prosp. This goes as I would wish it.
Now for my second care, *Hippolito.*
I shall not need to chide him for his fault,
His passion is become his punishment.
Come forth, *Hippolito.*   110
    Hip. entring. 'Tis *Prospero's* voice.
    Prosp. Hippolito! I know you now expect
I should severely chide you: you have seen

A Woman in contempt of my commands.

    Hip. But, Sir, you see I am come off unharm'd;
I told you, that you need not doubt my courage.

    Prosp. You think you have receiv'd no hurt?

    Hip. No, none, Sir.
Try me agen, whene'r you please I'm ready:
I think I cannot fear an Army of 'em.   120

    Prosp. How much in vain it is to bridle Nature!   [*Aside.*
Well! what was the success of your encounter?

    Hip. Sir, we had none, we yielded both at first,
For I took her to mercy, and she me.

    Prosp. But are you not much chang'd from what you were?

    Hip. Methinks I wish and wish! for what I know not,
But still I wish —— yet if I had that woman,
She, I believe could tell me what I wish for.

    Prosp. What wou'd you do to make that Woman yours?

    Hip. I'd quit the rest o'th'world, that I might live   130
Alone with her, she never should be from me.
We two would sit and look till our eyes ak'd.

    Prosp. You'd soon be weary of her.

    Hip.   O, Sir, never.

    Prosp. But you'l grow old and wrinkl'd, as you see me now,
And then you will not care for her.

    Hip. You may do what you please, but, Sir,
We two can never possibly grow old.

    Prosp. You must, *Hippolito.*

    Hip. Whether we will or no, Sir, who shall make us?

    Prosp. Nature, which made me so.   140

    Hip. But you have told me her works are various;
She made you old, but she has made us young.

    Prosp. Time will convince you,
Mean while be sure you tread in honours paths,
That you may merit her, and that you may
Not want fit occasions to employ your virtue,
In this next Cave there is a stranger lodg'd,
One of your kind, young, of a noble presence,
And, as he says himself, of Princely birth,
He is my Pris'ner, and in deep Affliction: 150
Visit, and comfort him; it will become you.

Hip. It is my duty, Sir.   [*Exit* Hippolito.

Prosp. True, he has seen a Woman, yet he lives;
Perhaps I took the moment of his birth
Amiss, perhaps my Art it self is false:
On what strange grounds we build our hopes and fears,
Man's life is all a mist, and in the dark,
Our fortunes meet us.
If fate be not, then what can we foresee?
Or how can we avoid it, if it be?   160
If by free-will in our own paths we move,
How are we bounded by Decrees above?
Whether we drive, or whether we are driven,
If ill, 'tis ours; if good, the act of Heaven.   [*Exit* Prospero.

[ACT III, SCENE VII]

Scene, a Cave.

Enter Hippolito *and* Ferdinand.

Ferd. Your pity, noble youth, doth much oblige me,
Indeed 'twas sad to lose a Father so.

Hip. I, and an onely Father too, for sure you said
You had but one.

Ferd. But one Father! he's wondrous simple!   [*Aside.*

Hip. Are such misfortunes frequent in your world,
Where many men live?

Ferd.   Such are we born to.
But, gentle Youth, as you have question'd me,
So give me leave to ask you, what you are?

Hip. Do not you know?

Ferd.   How should I?   10

Hip. I well hop'd I was a Man, but by your ignorance
Of what I am, I fear it is not so:
Well, *Prospero!* this is now the second time
You have deceiv'd me.

Ferd. Sir, there is no doubt you are a man:
But I would know of whence?
  Hip. Why, of this world, I never was in yours.
  Ferd. Have you a Father?
  Hip. I was told I had one, and that he was
A man, yet I have bin so much deceived,   20
I dare not tell't you for a truth; but I
Have still been kept a Prisoner for fear of women.
  Ferd. They indeed are dangerous, for since I came,
I have beheld one here, whose beauty pierc'd my heart.
  Hip. How did she pierce, you seem not hurt.
  Ferd. Alas! the wound was made by her bright eyes,
And festers by her absence.
But, to speak plainer to you, Sir, I love her.
  Hip. Now I suspect that love's the very thing,
That I feel too! pray tell me, truly, Sir,   30
Are you not grown unquiet since you saw her?
  Ferd. I take no rest.
  Hip.   Just, just my disease.
Do you not wish you do not know for what?
  Ferd. O no! I know too well for what I wish.
  Hip. There, I confess, I differ from you, Sir:
But you desire she may be always with you?
  Ferd. I can have no felicity without her.
  Hip. Just my condition! alas, gentle Sir,
I'l pity you, and you shall pity me.
  Ferd. I love so much, that if I have her not,   40
I find I cannot live.
  Hip. How! do you love her?
And would you have her too? that must not be:
For none but I must have her.
  Ferd. But perhaps we do not love the same:
All beauties are not pleasing alike to all.
  Hip. Why are there more fair Women, Sir,
Besides that one I love?
  Ferd. That's a strange question. There are many
More besides that beauty which you love.   50
  Hip. I will have all of that kind, if there be a hundred of 'em.
  Ferd. But, noble Youth, you know not what you say.

Hip. Sir, they are things I love, I cannot be
Without 'em: O, how I rejoyce! more women!
   Ferd. Sir, if you love, you must be ty'd to one.
   Hip. Ty'd! how ty'd to her?
   Ferd. To love none but her.
   Hip. But, Sir, I find it is against my nature.
I must love where I like, and I believe I may like all,
All that are fair: come! bring me to this woman,   60
For I must have her.
   Ferd.   His simplicity   [*Aside.*
Is such, that I can scarce be angry with him.
Perhaps, sweet Youth, when you behold her,
You will find you do not love her.
   Hip. I find already I love, because she is another woman.
   Ferd. You cannot love two women both at once.
   Hip. Sure 'tis my duty to love all who do resemble
Her whom I've already seen. I'l have as many
As I can, that are so good, and Angel-like,
As she I love. And will have yours.   70
   Ferd. Pretty Youth, you cannot.
   Hip. I can do any thing for that I love.
   Ferd. I may, perhaps, by force restrain you from it.
   Hip. Why do so if you can. But either promise me
To love no woman, or you must try your force.
   Ferd. I cannot help it, I must love.
   Hip. Well you may love, for *Prospero* taught me friendship
Too: you shall love me and other men
If you can find 'em, but all the Angel-women
Shall be mine.   80
   Ferd. I must break off this conference, or he
Will urge me else beyond what I can bear.
Sweet Youth! some other time we will speak
Farther concerning both our loves; at present
I am indispos'd with weariness and grief,
And would, if you are pleas'd, retire a while.
   Hip. Some other time be it; but, Sir, remember
That I both seek and much intreat your friendship,
For next to Women, I find I can love you.
   Ferd. I thank you, Sir, I will consider of it.   [*Exit* Ferdinand.

Hip. This stranger does insult, and comes into my   91
World to take those heavenly beauties from me,
Which I believe I am inspir'd to love,
And yet he said he did desire but one.
He would be poor in love, but I'l be rich:
I now perceive that *Prospero* was cunning;
For when he frighted me from Woman-kind,
Those precious things he for himself design'd.   [*Exit.*

ACT IV, SCENE I

Cypress Trees and Cave.
Enter Prospero *and* Miranda.

Prosp. Your suit has pity in't, and has prevail'd.
Within this Cave he lies, and you may see him:
But yet take heed; let Prudence be your Guide;
You must not stay, your visit must be short.   [*She's going.*
One thing I had forgot; insinuate into his mind
A kindness to that Youth, whom first you saw;
I would have friendship grow betwixt 'em.
     Mir. You shall be obey'd in all things.
     Prosp. Be earnest to unite their very souls.
     Mir. I shall endeavour it.
     Prosp.   This may secure   10
Hippolito from that dark danger which
My Art forebodes; for friendship does provide
A double strength t' oppose the assaults of fortune.   [*Exit* Prospero.

Enter Ferdinand.

     Ferd. To be a Pris'ner where I dearly love,
Is but a double tye, a Link of Fortune
Joyn'd to the Chain of Love; but not to see her,
And yet to be so near her, there's the hardship:
I feel my self as on a Rack, stretch'd out,

And nigh the ground, on which I might have ease,
Yet cannot reach it.

    Mir.   Sir! my Lord! where are you?   20

    Ferd. Is it your voice, my Love? or do I dream?

    Mir. Speak softly, it is I.

    Ferd. O heavenly Creature! ten times more gentle then
Your Father's cruel, how, on a sudden, all
My griefs are vanish'd!

    Mir.   How do you bear your Prison?

    Ferd. 'Tis my Palace while you are here, and love
And silence wait upon our wishes; do but think
We chuse it, and 'tis what we would chuse.

    Mir. I'm sure what I would.
But how can I be certain that you love me?   30
Look to't; for I will die when you are false.
I've heard my Father tell of Maids, who dy'd,
And haunted their false Lovers with their Ghosts.

    Ferd. Your Ghost must take another form to fright me,
This shape will be too pleasing: do I love you?
O Heaven! O Earth! bear witness to this sound,
If I prove false ——————

    Mir.   Oh hold, you shall not swear;
For Heav'n will hate you if you prove forsworn.

    Ferd. Did I not love, I could no more endure
This undeserv'd captivity, then I   40
Could wish to gain my freedom with the loss of you.

    Mir. I am a fool to weep at what I'm glad of:
But I have a suit to you, and that, Sir, shall
Be now the onely trial of your love.

    Ferd. Y'ave said enough, never to be deny'd,
Were it my life; for you have far o'rbid
The price of all that humane life is worth.

    Mir. Sir, 'tis to love one for my sake, who for
His own deserves all the respect which you
Can ever pay him.   50

    Ferd. You mean your Father: do not think his usage
Can make me hate him; when he gave you being,
He then did that which cancell'd all these wrongs.

    Mir. I meant not him, for that was a request,

Which if you love, I should not need to urge.
   Ferd. Is there another whom I ought to love?
And love him for your sake?
   Mir. Yes such a one, who, for his sweetness and
His goodly shape, (if I, who am unskill'd
In forms, may judge) I think can scarce be equall'd: 60
'Tis a Youth, a Stranger too as you are.
   Ferd. Of such a graceful feature, and must I
For your sake love?
   Mir. Yes, Sir, do you scruple to grant the first
Request I ever made? he's wholly unacquainted
With the world, and wants your conversation.
You should have compassion on so meer a stranger.
   Ferd. Those need compassion whom you discommend,
Not whom you praise.
   Mir. Come, you must love him for my sake: you shall.   70
   Ferd. Must I for yours, and cannot for my own?
Either you do not love, or think that I do not:
But when you bid me love him, I must hate him.
   Mir. Have I so far offended you already,
That he offends you onely for my sake?
Yet sure you would not hate him, if you saw
Him as I have done, so full of youth and beauty.
   Ferd. O poison to my hopes!   *[Aside.*
When he did visit me, and I did mention this
Beauteous Creature to him, he did then tell me   80
He would have her.
   Mir.   Alas, what mean you?
   Ferd. It is too plain: like most of her frail Sex,
She's false, but has not learn'd the art to hide it;
Nature has done her part, she loves variety:
Why did I think that any Woman could
Be innocent, because she's young? No, no,
Their Nurses teach them Change, when with two Nipples
They divide their Liking.
   Mir. I fear I have offended you, and yet
I meant no harm: But if you please to hear me———— *[A noise within.*
Heark, Sir! now I am sure my Father comes,   91
I know his steps; dear Love, retire a while,

I fear I've staid too long.

   Ferd. Too long indeed, and yet not long enough:
Oh jealousie! Oh Love! how you distract me?   [*Exit* Ferdinand.

   Mir. He appears displeas'd with that young man, I know
Not why: but, till I find from whence his hate proceeds,
I must conceal it from my Father's knowledge,
For he will think that guiltless I have caus'd it;
And suffer me no more to see my Love.   100

Enter Prospero.

   Prosp. Now I have been indulgent to your wish,
You have seen the Prisoner.

   Mir.   Yes.

   Prosp. And he spake to you?

   Mir. He spoke; but he receiv'd short answers from me.

   Prosp. How like you his converse?

   Mir.   At second sight
A man does not appear so rare a Creature.

   Prosp. aside. I find she loves him much because she hides it.
Love teaches cunning even to innocence. Well go in.

   Mir. aside. Forgive me, truth, for thus disguising thee;
If I can make him think I do not love   110
The stranger much, he'l let me see him oftner.   [*Exit* Miranda.

   Prosp. Stay! stay —— I had forgot to ask her
What she has said of young *Hippolito:*
Oh! here he comes! and with him my *Dorinda.*

Enter Hippolito and Dorinda.

I'l not be seen, let their loves grow in secret.   [*Exit* Prospero.

   Hip. But why are you so sad?

   Dor. But why are you so joyful?

   Hip. I have within me all, all the various Musick of
The Woods. Since last I saw you, I have heard brave news!
I'l tell you, and make you joyful for me.   120

   Dor. Sir, when I saw you first, I, through my eyes,
Drew something in, I know not what it is;
But still it entertains me with such thoughts,
As makes me doubtful whether joy becomes me.

   Hip. Pray believe me;
As I'm a man, I'll tell you blessed news,

I have heard there are more Women in the world,
As fair as you are too.
 Dor. Is this your news? you see it moves not me.
 Hip. And I'll have 'em all.   130
 Dor. What will become of me then?
 Hip. I'll have you too.
But are not you acquainted with these Women?
 Dor. I never saw but one.
 Hip. Is there but one here?
This is a base poor world, I'll go to th' other;
I've heard men have abundance of 'em there.
But pray where is that one Woman?
 Dor. Who, my Sister?
 Hip. Is she your Sister? I'm glad o'that: you shall 140
Help me to her, and I'l love you for't. [*Offers to take her hand.*
 Dor. Away! I will not have you touch my hand.
My Father's counsel which enjoyn'd reservedness,   [*Aside.*
Was not in vain, I see.
 Hip. What makes you shun me?
 Dor. You need not care, you'l have my Sister's hand.
 Hip. Why, must not he who touches hers, touch yours?
 Dor. You mean to love her too.
 Hip.   Do not you love her?
Then why should not I do so?
 Dor. She is my Sister, and therefore I must love her: 150
But you cannot love both of us.
 Hip. I warrant you I can:
Oh that you had more Sisters!
 Dor. You may love her, but then I'l not love you.
 Hip. O but you must;
One is enough for you, but not for me.
 Dor. My Sister told me she had seen another;
A man like you, and she lik'd onely him;
Therefore if one must be enough for her,
He is that one, and then you cannot have her.   160
 Hip. If she like him, she may like both of us.
 Dor. But how if I should change and like that man?
Would you be willing to permit that change?
 Hip. No, for you lik'd me first.

Dor.   So you did me.

Hip. But I would never have you see that man;
I cannot bear it.

Dor.   I'l see neither of you.

Hip. Yes, me you may, for we are now acquainted;
But he's the man of whom your Father warn'd you:
O! he's a terrible, huge, monstrous creature,
I am but a Woman to him.

Dor.   I will see him,   170
Except you'l promise not to see my Sister.

Hip. Yes, for your sake I needs must see your Sister.

Dor. But she's a terrible, huge creature too;
If I were not her Sister, she would eat me;
Therefore take heed.

Hip. I heard that she was fair, and like you.

Dor. No, indeed, she's like my Father, with a great Beard,
'Twould fright you to look on her,
Therefore that man and she may go together,
They are fit for no body, but one another.   180

Hip. looking in. Yonder he comes with glaring eyes, fly! fly!
Before he sees you.

Dor.   Must we part so soon?

Hip. Y'are a lost woman if you see him.

Dor. I would not willingly be lost, for fear you
Should not find me. I'l avoid him.   [*Exit* Dorinda.

Hip. She fain would have deceived me, but I know her
Sister must be fair, for she's a Woman;
All of a kind that I have seen are like to one
Another: all the Creatures of the Rivers and
The Woods are so.   190

Enter Ferdinand.

Ferd. O! well encounter'd, you are the happy man!
Y'have got the hearts of both the beauteous Women.

Hip. How! Sir? pray, are you sure on't?

Ferd. One of 'em charg'd me to love you for her sake.

Hip. Then I must have her.

Ferd.   No, not till I am dead.

Hip. How dead? what's that? but whatsoe'r it be,
I long to have her.

Ferd. Time and my grief may make me die.

   Hip. But for a friend you should make haste;
I ne'r ask'd any thing of you before.   200

   Ferd. I see your ignorance;
And therefore will instruct you in my meaning.
The Woman, whom I love, saw you, and lov'd you.
Now, Sir, if you love her, you'l cause my death.

   Hip. Be sure I'l do't then.

   Ferd.   But I am your friend;
And I request you that you would not love her.

   Hip. When friends request unreasonable things,
Sure th'are to be deny'd: you say she's fair,
And I must love all who are fair; for, to tell
You a secret, Sir, which I have lately found   210
Within my self; they're all made for me.

   Ferd. That's but a fond conceit: you are made for one,
And one for you.

   Hip.   You cannot tell me, Sir,
I know I'm made for twenty hundred Women.
(I mean if there so many be i' th' world)
So that if once I see her, I shall love her.

   Ferd. Then do not see her.

   Hip.   Yes, Sir, I must see her.
For I wou'd fain have my heart beat again,
Just as it did when I first saw her Sister.

   Ferd. I find I must not let you see her then.   220

   Hip. How will you hinder me?

   Ferd.   By force of Arms.

   Hip. By force of Arms?
My Arms perhaps may be as strong as yours.

   Ferd. He's still so ignorant that I pity him,
And fain would avoid force: pray do not see her,
She was mine first; you have no right to her.

   Hip. I have not yet consider'd what is right,
But, Sir, I know my inclinations are
To love all Women: And I have been taught,
That to dissemble what I think, is base.   230
In honour then of truth, I must declare
That I do love, and I will see your Woman.

Ferd. Wou'd you be willing I should see and love
Your Woman, and endeavour to seduce
Her from that Affection which she vow'd to you?

Hip. I wou'd not you should do it, but if she should
Love you best, I cannot hinder her.
But, Sir, for fear she shou'd, I will provide
Against the worst, and try to get your Woman.

Ferd. But I pretend no claim at all to yours;   240
Besides you are more beautiful then I,
And fitter to allure unpractis'd hearts.
Therefore I once more beg you will not see her.

Hip. I'm glad you let me know I have such beauty,
If that will get me Women, they shall have it
As far as e'r 'twill go: I'l never want 'em.

Ferd. Then since you have refus'd this act of friendship,
Provide your self a sword, for we must fight.

Hip. A sword, what's that?

Ferd.   Why such a thing as this.

Hip. What should I do with it?   250

Ferd. You must stand thus, and push against me,
While I push at you, till one of us fall dead.

Hip. This is brave sport;
But we have no Swords growing in our world.

Ferd. What shall we do then to decide our quarrel?

Hip. We'l take the Sword by turns, and fight with it.

Ferd. Strange ignorance! you must defend your life,
And so must I: but since you have no Sword,
Take this; for in a corner of my Cave   [*Gives him his Sword.*
I found a rusty one; perhaps 'twas his   260
Who keeps me Pris'ner here: that I will fit:
When next we meet, prepare your self to fight.

Hip. Make haste then, this shall ne'r be yours agen.
I mean to fight with all the men I meet, and
When they are dead, their Women shall be mine.

Ferd. I see you are unskilful; I desire not to take
Your life, but, if you please, we'l fight on
These conditions; He who first draws bloud,
Or who can take the others Weapon from him,
Shall be acknowledg'd as the Conquerour,   270

And both the Women shall be his.
    Hip.   Agreed,
And ev'ry day I'l fight for two more with you.
    Ferd. But win these first.
    Hip. I'll warrant you I'll push you.   [*Exeunt severally.*

ACT IV, SCENE II

The Wild Island.
Enter Trincalo, Caliban, Sycorax.

    Calib. My Lord, I see 'em coming yonder.
    Trinc. Whom?
    Calib. The starv'd Prince, and his two thirsty Subjects, that would have our Liquor.
    Trinc. If thou wert a Monster of parts, I would make thee my Master of Ceremonies, to conduct 'em in. The Devil take all Dunces, thou hast lost a brave Employment by not being a Linguist, and for want of behaviour.
    Syc. My Lord, shall I go meet 'em? I'll be kind to all of 'em, just as I am to thee.   10
    Trinc. No, that's against the fundamental Laws of my Dukedom: you are in a high place, Spouse, and must give good Example. Here they come, we'll put on the gravity of Statesmen, and be very dull, that we may be held wise.
    Enter Stephano, Ventoso, Mustacho.
    Vent. Duke *Trincalo,* we have consider'd.
    Trinc. Peace or War?
    Must. Peace, and the Butt.
    Steph. I come now as a private person, and promise to live peaceably under your Government.
    Trinc. You shall enjoy the benefits of Peace; and the first fruits 20 of it, amongst all Civil Nations, is to be drunk for joy: *Caliban,* skink about.

175

Steph. I long to have a Rowse to her Graces health, and to the *Haunse in Kelder,* or rather Haddock in *Kelder,* for I ghess it will be half Fish. [*Aside.*

Trinc. Subject *Stephano,* here's to thee; and let old quarrels be drown'd in this draught. [*Drinks.*

Steph. Great Magistrate, here's thy Sisters health to thee.
[*Drinks to* Caliban.

Syc. He shall not drink of that immortal Liquor, my Lord, let him drink Water. 30

Trinc. O Sweet-heart, you must not shame your self to day. Gentlemen Subjects, pray bear with her good Huswifry: she wants a little breeding, but she's hearty.

Must. Ventoso, here's to thee. Is it not better to pierce the Butt, then to quarrel and pierce one another's bellies?

Vent. Let it come, Boy.

Trinc. Now wou'd I lay greatness aside, and shake my heels, if I had but Musick.

Calib. O my Lord! my Mother left us in her Will a hundred Spirits to attend us, Devils of all sorts, some great roaring Devils, 40 and some little singing Sprights.

Syc. Shall we call? and thou shalt hear them in the air.

Trinc. I accept the motion: let us have our Mother-in-law's Legacy immediately.

Calib. sings. We want Musick, we want Mirth,
   Up, Dam, and cleave the Earth:
   We have now no Lords that wrong us,
   Send thy merry Sprights among us.

Trinc. What a merry Tyrant am I, to have my Musick, and pay nothing for't? 50
  [*A Table rises, and four Spirits with Wine and Meat enter,*
  placing it, as they dance, on the Table: The Dance ended,
  the Bottles vanish, and the Table sinks agen.

Vent. The Bottle's drunk.

Must. Then the Bottle's a weak shallow fellow, if it be drunk first.

Trinc. Stephano, give me thy hand, thou hast been a Rebel, but here's to thee: [*Drinks.*] Prithee why should we quarrel? Shall I swear two Oaths? By Bottle, and by Butt I love thee: In witness whereof I drink soundly.

Steph. Your Grace shall find there's no love lost, for I will pledge you soundly.

Trinc. Thou hast been a false Rebel, but that's all one; Pledge   60
my Grace faithfully. *Caliban,* Go to the Butt, and tell me how it sounds: Peer *Stephano,* dost thou love me?   [*Exit* Caliban.]

Steph. I love your Grace, and all your Princely Family.

Trinc. 'Tis no matter if thou lov'st me; hang my Family: Thou art my friend, prithee tell me what thou think'st of my Princess?

Steph. I look on her, as on a very noble Princess.

Trinc. Noble? indeed she had a Witch to her Mother, and the Witches are of great Families in *Lapland,* but the Devil was her Father, and I have heard of the Mounsor *De-Viles* in *France;* but look on her beauty, is she a fit Wife for Duke *Trincalo?* mark her   70
behaviour too, shee's tipling yonder with the Serving-men.

Steph. An't please your Grace, she's somewhat homely, but that's no blemish in a Princess. She is virtuous.

Trinc. Umph! virtuous! I am loath to disparage her; but thou art my friend, canst thou be close?

Steph. As a stopt Bottle, an't please your Grace.

Enter Caliban *agen with a bottle.*

Trinc. Why then I'll tell thee, I found her an hour ago under an Elder-tree, upon a sweet Bed of Nettles, singing Tory, Rory, and Ranthum, Scantum, with her own Natural Brother.

Steph. O Jew! make love in her own Tribe?   80

Trinc. But 'tis no matter, to tell thee true, I marri'd her to be a great man and so forth: but make no words on't, for I care not who knows it, and so here's to thee agen, give me the Bottle, *Caliban!* did you knock the Butt? how does it sound?

Calib. It sounds as though it had a noise within.

Trinc. I fear the Butt begins to rattle in the throat and is departing: give me the Bottle.   [*Drinks.*

Must. A short life and a merry, I say.   [Steph. *whispers* Sycorax.

Syc. But did he tell you so?

Steph. He said you were as ugly as your Mother, and that he   90
Marri'd you onely to get possession of the Island.

Syc. My Mothers Devils fetch him for't.

Steph. And your Fathers too, hem! skink about his Graces health agen. O if you will but cast an eye of pity upon me ———

Syc. I will cast two eyes of pity on thee, I love thee more then

Haws, or Black-berries, I have a hoard of Wildings in the Moss, my Brother knows not of 'em; but I'll bring thee where they are.

Steph. Trincalo was but my Man when time was.

Syc. Wert thou his God, and didst thou give him Liquor?

Steph. I gave him Brandy, and drunk Sack my self; wilt thou 100 leave him, and thou shalt be my Princess?

Syc. If thou canst make me glad with this Liquor.

Steph. I'll warrant thee we'll ride into the Countrey where it grows.

Syc. How wilt thou carry me thither?

Steph. Upon a Hackney-Devil of thy Mothers.

Trinc. What's that you will do? hah! I hope you have not be-tray'd me? how does my Pigs-nye?   [*To* Sycorax.

Syc. Be gone! thou shalt not be my Lord, thou say'st I'm ugly.

Trinc. Did you tell her so ——— hah! he's a Rogue, do not 110 believe him, Chuck.

Steph. The foul words were yours: I will not eat 'em for you.

Trinc. I see if once a Rebel, then ever a Rebel. Did I receive thee into Grace for this? I will correct thee with my Royal Hand.

[*Strikes* Stephano.

Syc. Dost thou hurt my Love?   [*Flies at Trincalo.*

Trinc. Where are our Guards? Treason! Treason!

[*Vent. Must. Calib. run betwixt.*

Vent. Who took up Arms first, the Prince or the People?

Trinc. This false Traitor has corrupted the Wife of my bosom.

[*Whispers* Mustacho *hastily.*

Mustacho, strike on my side, and thou shalt be my Vice-Roy.

Must. I'm against Rebels! *Ventoso,* obey your Vice-Roy.   120

Vent. You a Vice-Roy?   [*They two fight off from the rest.*

Steph. Hah! Hector Monster! do you stand neuter?

Calib. Thou would'st drink my Liquor, I will not help thee.

Syc. 'Twas his doing that I had such a Husband, but Ill claw him.   [Syc. *and* Calib. *fight,* Syc. *beating him off the Stage.*

Trinc. The whole Nation is up in arms, and shall I stand idle?

[*Trincalo beats off* Stephano *to the door. Exit* Stephano.

I'll not pursue too far, for fear the Enemy should rally agen, and surprise my Butt in the Cittadel; well, I must be rid of my Lady *Trincalo,* she will be in the fashion else; first, Cuckold her Hus-band, and then sue for a separation, to get Alimony.   [*Exit.*

ACT IV, SCENE III

The Cypress-trees and Cave.

Enter Ferdinand, Hippolito (*with their swords drawn.*)

Ferd. Come, Sir, our Cave affords no choice of place,
But the ground's firm and even: are you ready?
Hip. As ready as your self, Sir.
Ferd. You remember on what conditions we must fight?
Who first receives a wound is to submit.
Hip. Come, come, this loses time; now for the Women, Sir.

     [*They fight a little,* Ferdinand *hurts him.*

Ferd. Sir, you are wounded.
Hip.   No.
Ferd.   Believe your bloud.
Hip. I feel no hurt, no matter for my bloud.
Ferd. Remember our Conditions.
Hip. I'll not leave, till my Sword hits you too.   10

    [Hip. *presses on,* Ferd. *retires and wards.*

Ferd. I'm loth to kill you, you are unskilful, Sir.
Hip. You beat aside my Sword, but let it come
As near as yours, and you shall see my skill.
Ferd. You faint for loss of bloud, I see you stagger,
Pray, Sir, retire.
Hip.   No! I will ne'r go back ——
Methink the Cave turns round, I cannot find ——
Ferd. Your eyes begin to dazle.
Hip. Why do you swim so, and dance about me?
Stand but still till I have made one thrust. [Hippolito *thrusts and falls.*
Ferd. O help, help, help!   20
Unhappy man! what have I done?
Hip. I'm going to a cold sleep, but when I wake,
I'll fight agen. Pray stay for me.   [*Swounds.*
Ferd. He's gone! he's gone! O stay, sweet lovely Youth!
Help! help!

Enter Prospero.

Prosp. What dismal noise is that?

Ferd.   O see, Sir, see!

What mischief my unhappy hand has wrought.

   Prosp. Alas! how much in vain doth feeble Art

Endeavour to resist the will of Heaven?   [*Rubs* Hippolito.

He's gone for ever; O thou cruel Son   30

Of an inhumane Father! all my designs

Are ruin'd and unravell'd by this blow.

No pleasure now is left me but revenge.

   Ferd. Sir, if you knew my innocence ———

   Prosp.   Peace, peace,

Can thy excuses give me back his life?

What *Ariel?* sluggish Spirit, where art thou?

Enter Ariel.

   Ariel. Here, at thy beck, my Lord.

   Prosp.   I, now thou com'st,

When Fate is past and not to be recall'd.

Look there, and glut the malice of thy Nature,

For as thou art thy self, thou canst not but be   40

Glad to see young Virtue nipt i'th' Blossom.

   Ariel. My Lord, the *Being* high above can witness

I am not glad; we Airy Spirits are not

Of a temper so malicious as the Earthy,

But of a Nature more approaching good.

For which we meet in swarms, and often combat

Betwixt the Confines of the Air and Earth.

   Prosp. Why did'st thou not prevent, at least foretel,

This fatal action then?

   Ariel.   Pardon, great Sir,

I meant to do it, but I was forbidden   50

By the ill Genius of *Hippolito,*

Who came and threaten'd me, if I disclos'd it,

To bind me in the bottom of the Sea,

Far from the lightsome Regions of the Air,

(My Native fields) above a hundred years.

   Prosp. I'll chain thee in the North for thy neglect,

Within the burning bowels of Mount *Hecla;*

I'll singe thy airy wings with sulph'rous flames,

And choak thy tender nostrils with blew smoak,

At ev'ry Hick-up of the belching Mountain,   60
Thou shalt be lifted up to taste fresh air,
And then fall down agen.
    Ariel.   Pardon, dread Lord.
    Prosp. No more of pardon then just Heav'n intends thee
Shalt thou e'r find from me: hence! fly with speed,
Unbind the Charms which hold this Murtherer's
Father, and bring him, with my Brother, streight
Before me.
    Ariel. Mercy, my potent Lord, I'll outfly thy thought.   [*Exit* Ariel.
    Ferd. O Heavens! what words are those I heard?
Yet cannot see who spoke 'em: sure the Woman   70
Whom I lov'd was like this, some aiery Vision.
    Prosp. No, Murd'rer, she's, like thee, of mortal mould,
But much too pure to mix with thy black Crimes;
Yet she had faults, and must be punish'd for 'em.
Miranda and *Dorinda*! where are ye?
The will of Heaven's accomplish'd: I have now
No more to fear, and nothing left to hope,
Now you may enter.
               Enter Miranda *and* Dorinda.

    Mir. My Love! is it permitted me to see
You once agen?   80
    Prosp. You come to look your last; I will
For ever take him from your eyes.
But, on my blessing, speak not, nor approach him.
    Dor. Pray, Father, is not this my Sister's Man?
He has a noble form; but yet he's not
So excellent as my *Hippolito*.
    Prosp. Alas, poor Girl, thou hast no Man: look yonder;
There's all of him that's left.
    Dor. Why, was there ever any more of him?
He lies asleep, Sir, shall I waken him?   90
               [*She kneels by* Hippolito, *and jogs him.*
    Ferd. Alas! he's never to be wak'd agen.
    Dor. My Love, my Love! will you not speak to me?
I fear you have displeas'd him, Sir, and now
He will not answer me, he's dumb and cold too;

But I ll run streight, and make a fire to warm him.

[*Exit* Dorinda *running.*
Enter Alonzo, Gonzalo, Antonio, Ariel (*invisible.*)
Alon. Never were Beasts so hunted into Toils,
As we have been pursu'd by dreadful shapes.
But is not that my Son? O *Ferdinand!*
If thou art not a Ghost, let me embrace thee.
    Ferd. My Father! O sinister happiness! Is it   100
Decreed I should recover you alive,
Just in that fatal hour when this brave Youth
Is lost in Death, and by my hand?
    Anto. Heaven! what new wonder's this?
    Gonz. This Isle is full of nothing else.
    Prosp. You stare upon me as
You ne'r had seen me; have fifteen years
So lost me to your knowledge, that you retain
No memory of *Prospero?*
    Gonz. The good old Duke of *Millain!*   110
    Prosp. I wonder less, that thou, *Antonio,* know'st
Me not, because thou didst long since forget
I was thy Brother, else I never had been here.
    Anto. Shame choaks my words.
    Alon.   And wonder mine.
    Prosp. For you, usurping Prince.   [*To* Alonzo.
Know, by my Art, you were shipwrack'd on this Isle,
Where, after I a while had punish'd you,
My vengeance wou'd have ended, I design'd
To match that Son of yours, with this my Daughter.
    Alon. Pursue it still, I am most willing to't.   120
    Prosp. So am not I. No Marriages can prosper
Which are with Murderers made; Look on that Corps,
This, whilst he liv'd, was young *Hippolito,*
That infant Duke of *Mantua,* Sir, whom you
Expos'd with me; and here I bred him up,
Till that bloud-thirsty Man, that *Ferdinand* ————
But why do I exclaim on him, when Justice
Calls to unsheath her Sword against his guilt?
    Alon. What do you mean?
    Prosp.   To execute Heav'ns Laws.

Here I am plac'd by Heav'n, here I am Prince,   130
Though you have dispossess'd me of my *Millain.*
Bloud calls for bloud; your *Ferdinand* shall die,
And I, in bitterness, have sent for you,
To have the sudden joy of seeing him alive,
And then the greater grief to him die.

    Alon. And think'st thou I, or these, will tamely stand,
To view the Execution?   [*Lays hand upon his Sword.*

    Ferd. Hold, dear Father! I cannot suffer you
T' attempt against his life, who gave her being
Whom I love.   140

    Prosp. Nay then appear my Guards —— I thought no more to
Use their aid; (I'm curs'd because I us'd it).

                  [*He stamps, and many Spirits appear.*
But they are now the Ministers of Heaven,
Whilst I revenge this Murder.

    Alon. Have I for this found thee, my Son, so soon agen,
To lose thee? *Antonio, Gonzalo,* speak for pity.

    Ferd. to Mir. Adieu, my fairest Mistris.

    Mir. Now I can hold no longer; I must speak.
Though I am loth to disobey you, Sir,
Be not so cruel to the Man I love,   150
Or be so kind to let me suffer with him.

    Ferd. Recall that Pray'r, or I shall wish to live,
Though death be all the mends that I can make.

    Prosp. This night I will allow you, *Ferdinand,* to fit
You for your death, that Cave's your prison.

    Alon. Ah, *Prospero!* hear me speak. You are a Father,
Look on my Age, and look upon his Youth.

    Prosp. No more! all you can say is urg'd in vain,
I have no room for pity left within me.
Do you refuse! help, *Ariel,* with your Fellows   160
To drive 'em in; *Alonzo* and his Son
Bestow in yonder Cave, and here *Gonzalo*
Shall with *Antonio* lodge. [*Spirits drive 'em in, as they are appointed.*
                 Enter Dorinda.

    Dor. Sir, I have made a fire, shall he be warm'd?

    Prosp. He's dead, and vital warmth will ne'r return.

    Dor. Dead, Sir, what's that?

Prosp.   His Soul has left his Body.
Dor. When will it come agen?
Prosp.   O never, never!
He must be laid in Earth, and there consume.
    Dor. He shall not lie in Earth, you do not know
How well he loves me: indeed he'l come agen;   170
He told me he would go a little while,
But promis'd me he would not tarry long.
    Prosp. He's murder'd by the man who lov'd your Sister.
Now both of you may see what 'tis to break
A Father's Precept; you would needs see men,
And by that sight are made for ever wretched.
Hippolito is dead, and *Ferdinand*
Must die for murdering him.
    Mir.   Have you no pity?
    Prosp. Your disobedience has so much incens'd me,
That I this night can leave no blessing with you.   180
Help to convey the Body to my Couch,
Then leave me to mourn over it alone.
                    [*They bear off the Body of* Hippolito.
        Enter Miranda *and* Dorinda *again.* Ariel *behind 'em.*
    Ariel. I've been so chid for my neglect by *Prospero,*
That I must now watch all, and be unseen.
    Mir. Sister, I say agen, 'twas long of you
That all this mischief happen'd.
    Dor. Blame not me for your own fault, your
Curiosity brought me to see the Man.
    Mir. You safely might have seen him, and retir'd,
But you wou'd needs go near him, and converse,   190
You may remember my Father call'd me thence,
And I call'd you.
    Dor.   That was your envy, Sister,
Not your love; you call'd me thence, because
You could not be alone with him your self;
But I am sure my Man had never gone
To Heaven so soon, but that yours made him go.   [*Crying.*
    Mir. Sister, I could not wish that either of 'em shou'd
Go to Heaven without us, but it was his fortune,
And you must be satisfi'd.

184

Dor. I'll not be satisfi'd: my Father says   200
He'll make your Man as cold as mine is now,
And when he is made cold, my Father will
Not let you strive to make him warm agen.
   Mir. In spite of you mine never shall be cold.
   Dor. I'm sure 'twas he that made me miserable,
And I will be reveng'd. Perhaps you think
'Tis nothing to lose a Man.
   Mir. Yes, but there is some difference betwixt
My *Ferdinand,* and your *Hippolito.*
   Dor. I, there's your judgment. Your's is the oldest   210
Man I ever saw, except it were my Father.
   Mir. Sister, no more. It is not comely in a Daughter,
When she says her Father's old.
   Dor. But why do I stay here, whilst my cold Love
Perhaps may want me?
I'll pray my father to make yours cold too.
   Mir. Sister, I'l never sleep with you again.
   Dor. I'll never more meet in a Bed with you,
But lodge on the bare ground, and watch my Love.
   Mir. And at the entrance of that Cave I'll lie,   220
And eccho to each blast of wind a sigh.
            [Exeunt severally, looking discontentedly on one another.
   Ariel. Harsh discord reigns throughout this fatal Isle,
At which good Angels mourn, ill spirits smile;
Old *Prospero* by his Daughters robb'd of rest,
Has in displeasure left 'em both unblest.
Unkindly they abjure each others bed,
To save the living, and revenge the dead.
Alonzo and his Son are pris'ners made,
And good *Gonzalo* does their crimes upbraid.
Antonio and *Gonzalo* disagree,   230
And wou'd, though in one Cave, at distance be.
The Seamen all that cursed Wine have spent,
Which still renew'd their thirst of Government;
And wanting subjects for the food of Pow'r,
Each wou'd to rule alone the rest devour.
The Monsters *Sycorax* and *Caliban,*
More monstrous grow by passions learn'd from Man.

Even I not fram'd of warring Elements,
Partake and suffer in these discontents.
Why shou'd a Mortal by Enchantments hold   240
In Chains a Spirit of Ætherial mold?
Accursed Magick we our selves have taught,
And our own pow'r has our subjection wrought!   [*Exit.*

ACT V, [SCENE I]

Enter Prospero *and* Miranda.

Prosp. You beg in vain; I cannot pardon him,
He has offended Heaven.
   Mir. Then let Heaven punish him.
   Prosp.   It will by me.
   Mir. Grant him at least some respite for my sake.
   Prosp. I by deferring Justice should incense
The Deity against my self and you.
   Mir. Yet I have heard you say, The Powers above
Are slow in punishing, and shou'd not you
Resemble them?
   Prosp.   The Argument is weak,
But I want time to let you see your errours;   10
Retire, and, if you love him, pray for him.   [*He's going.*
   Mir. And can you be his Judge and Executioner?
   Prosp. I cannot force *Gonzalo* or my Brother,
Much less the Father to destroy the Son;
It must be then the Monster *Caliban*,
And he's not here; but *Ariel* strait shall fetch him.
                  Enter Ariel.
   Ariel. My Potent Lord, before thou call'st, I come,
To serve thy will.
   Prosp. Then, Spirit, fetch me here my salvage Slave.
   Ariel. My Lord, it does not need.   20

Prosp. Art thou then prone to mischief, wilt thou be
Thy self the Executioner?

Ariel. Think better of thy Aiery Minister, who,
For thy sake, unbidden, this night has flown
O'r almost all the habitable World.

    Prosp. But to what purpose was all thy diligence?

    Ariel. When I was chidden by my mighty Lord
For my Neglect of young *Hippolito,*
I went to view his Body, and soon found
His Soul was but retir'd, not sally'd out: 30
Then I collected the best of Simples underneath
The Moon, the best of Balms, and to the wound
Apply'd the healing juice of vulnerary Herbs.
His onely danger was his loss of bloud,
But now he's wak'd, my Lord, and just this hour
He must be dress'd again, as I have done it.
Anoint the Sword which pierc'd him with this
Weapon-Salve, and wrap it close from Air
Till I have time to visit him again.

    Prosp. Thou art my faithful Servant,   40
It shall be done, be it your task, *Miranda,*
Because your Sister is not present here,
While I go visit your dear *Ferdinand,*
From whom I will a while conceal this news,
That it may be more welcome.

    Mir. I obey you, and with a double duty, Sir:
For now you twice have given me life.

    Prosp. My *Ariel,* follow me.   [*Exeunt severally.*

[ACT V, SCENE II]

Hippolito *discover'd on a Couch,* Dorinda *by him.*

    Dor. How do you find your self?

Hip. I'm somewhat cold, can you not draw me nearer
To the Sun? I am too weak to walk.
    Dor. My Love, I'll try.   [*She draws the Chair nearer the Audience.*
I thought you never would have walk'd agen,
They told me you were gone away to Heaven;
Have you been there?
    Hip.   I know not where I was.
    Dor. I will not leave till you promise me
You will not die agen.
    Hip.   Indeed I will not.
    Dor. You must not go to Heav'n, unless we go   10
Together; For I've heard my Father say,
That we must strive to be each others guide,
The way to it will else be difficult,
Especially to those who are so young.
But I much wonder what it is to die.
    Hip. Sure 'tis to dream, a kind of breathless sleep,
When once the Soul's gone out.
    Dor.   What is the Soul?
    Hip. A small blew thing, that runs about within us.
    Dor. Then I have seen it in a frosty morning run
Smoaking from my mouth.
    Hip.   But, dear *Dorinda,*   20
What is become of him who fought with me?
    Dor. O, I can tell you joyful news of him,
My Father means to make him die to day,
For what he did to you.
    Hip. That must not be, my dear *Dorinda;* go
And beg your Father, he may not die; it was
My fault he hurt me, I urg'd him to it first.
    Dor. But if he live, he'll never leave killing you.
    Hip. O no! I just remember when I fell asleep,
I heard him calling me a great way off,   30
And crying over me as you wou'd do;
Besides we have no cause of quarrel now.
    Dor. Pray how began your difference first?
    Hip. I fought with him for all the Women in the World.
    Dor. That hurt you had was justly sent from Heaven,
For wishing to have any more but me.

Hip. Indeed I think it was, but I repent it,
The fault was onely in my bloud, for now
'Tis gone, I find I do not love so many.
    Dor. In confidence of this, I'l beg my Father,   40
That he may live; I'm glad the naughty bloud,
That made you love so many, is gone out.
    Hip. My dear, go quickly, lest you come too late.   [*Exit* Dorinda.

      Enter Miranda *at the other door, with* [Ferdinand's]
                Sword wrapt up.

Who's this who looks so fair and beautiful,
As nothing but *Dorinda* can surpass her?
O! I believe it is that Angel-Woman,
Whom she calls Sister.
    Mir. Sir, I am sent hither to dress your wound;
How do you find your strength?
    Hip. Fair Creature, I am faint with loss of bloud.   50
    Mir. I'm sorry for't.
    Hip.   Indeed and so am I,
For if I had that bloud, I then should find
A great delight in loving you.
    Mir. But, Sir, I am another's, and your love
Is given already to my Sister.
    Hip. Yet I find that, if you please, I can love still a little.
    Mir. I cannot be unconstant, nor shou'd you.
    Hip. O my wound pains me.
    Mir. I am come to ease you.   [*She unwraps the Sword.*
    Hip. Alas! I feel the cold Air come to me,   60
My wound shoots worse then ever.   [*She wipes and anoints the Sword.*
    Mir. Does it still grieve you?
    Hip. Now methinks there's something laid just upon it.
    Mir. Do you find no ease?
    Hip. Yes, yes, upon the sudden all the pain
Is leaving me: Sweet Heaven, how I am eas'd!

        Enter Ferdinand *and* Dorinda *to them.*

    Ferd. to Dor. Madam, I must confess my life is yours,
I owe it to your generosity.
    Dor. I am o'rjoy'd my Father lets you live,
And proud of my good fortune, that he gave   70
Your life to me.

Mir. How? gave his life to her!

Hip. Alas! I think she said so, and he said
He ow'd it to her generosity.

Ferd. But is not that your Sister with *Hippolito*?

Dor. So kind already?

Ferd. I came to welcome life, and I have met the
Cruellest of deaths.

Hip. My dear *Dorinda* with another man?

Dor. Sister, what bus'ness have you here?

Mir. You see I dress *Hippolito*.　　　　　　　　　　　　80

Dor. Y'are very charitable to a Stranger.

Mir. You are not much behind in charity,
To beg a pardon for a man, whom you
Scarce ever saw before.

Dor. Henceforward let your Surgery alone,
For I had rather he should die, than you
Should cure his wound.

Mir. And I wish *Ferdinand* had dy'd before
He ow'd his life to your entreaty.

Ferd. to Hip. Sir, I'm glad you are so well recover'd,　　90
You keep your humour still to have all Women.

Hip. Not all, Sir, you except one of the number,
Your new Love there, *Dorinda*.

Mir. Ah *Ferdinand*! can you become inconstant?
If I must lose you, I had rather death
Should take you from me, than you take your self.

Ferd. And if I might have chosen, I would have wish'd
That death from *Prospero,* and not this from you.

Dor. I, now I find why I was sent away,
That you might have my Sisters company.　　　　　　100

Hip. *Dorinda,* kill me not with your unkindness,
This is too much, first to be false your self,
And then accuse me too.

Ferd. We all accuse each other, and each one
Denies their guilt, I should be glad it were
A mutual errour. And therefore first to clear
My self from fault, Madam, I beg your pardon,
While I say I onely love your Sister.　　　　　　[*To* Dorinda.

Mir. O blest word!

I'm sure I love no man but *Ferdinand.*   110

 Dor. Nor I, Heaven knows, but my *Hippolito.*

 Hip. I never knew I lov'd so much; before

I fear'd *Dorinda's* constancy, but now

I am convinc'd that I lov'd none but her,

Because none else can recompense her loss.

 Ferd. 'Twas happy then we had this little trial.

But how we all so much mistook, I know not.

 Mir. I have onely this to say in my defence:

My Father sent me hither, to attend

The wounded Stranger.   120

 Dor. And *Hippolito* sent me to beg the life of *Ferdinand.*

 Ferd. From such small errours left at first unheeded,

Have often sprung sad accidents in love:

But see, our Fathers and our Friends are come

To mix their joys with ours.

    Enter Prospero, Alonzo, Antonio, Gonzalo.

 Alon. to Prosp. Let it no more be thought of, your purpose,

Though it was severe, was just. In losing *Ferdinand*

I should have mourn'd, but could not have complain'd.

 Prosp. Sir, I am glad kind Heaven decreed it otherwise.

 Dor. O wonder! How many goodly Creatures 130

Are there here! How beauteous Mankind is!

 Hip. O brave new world, that has such People in't!

 Alon. to Ferd. Now all the blessings of a glad Father

Compass thee about, and make thee happy

In thy beauteous choice.

 Gonz. I've inward wept, or should have spoken ere this.

Look down, sweet Heaven, and on this Couple drop

A blessed Crown, For it is you chalk'd out the

Way which brought us hither.

 Anto. Though penitence forc'd by necessity can scarce 140

Seem real, yet, dearest Brother, I have hope

My bloud may plead for pardon with you; I resign

Dominion, which, 'tis true, I could not keep,

But Heaven knows too, I would not.

 Prosp. All past crimes I bury in the joy

Of this blessed day.

 Alon. And, that I may not be behind in Justice,

To this young Prince I render back his Dukedom,
And as the Duke of *Mantua* thus salute him.
   Hip. What is it that you render back, methinks   150
You give me nothing.
   Prosp. You are to be Lord of a great People,
And o're Towns and Cities.
   Hip. And shall these People be all Men and Women?
   Gonz. Yes, and shall call you Lord.
   Hip. Why then I'll live no longer in a Prison,
But have a whole Cave to my self hereafter.
   Prosp. And that your happiness may be compleat,
I give you my *Dorinda* for your Wife,
She shall be yours for ever, when the Priest   160
Has made you one.
   Hip. How can he make us one? shall I grow to her?
   Prosp. By saying holy words you shall be joyn'd
In Marriage to each other.
   Dor. I warrant you those holy words are charms.
My Father means to conjure us together.
   Prosp. to his Daughters. My *Ariel* told me, when last night you
     quarrell'd,
You said you would for ever part your beds;
But what you threaten'd in your anger, Heaven
Has turn'd to Prophecy.   170
For you, *Miranda,* must with *Ferdinand,*
And you, *Dorinda,* with *Hippolito*
Lie in one Bed hereafter.
   Alon. And Heaven make those Beds still fruitful in
Producing Children, to bless their Parents Youth,
And Grandsires age.
   Mir. to Dor. If Children come by lying in a Bed,
I wonder you and I had none between us.
   Dor. Sister, it was our fault, we meant like fools
To look 'em in the fields, and they, it seems,   180
Are onely found in Beds.
   Hip. I am o'rjoy'd that I shall have *Dorinda*
In a Bed, we'll lie all night and day
Together there, and never rise again.
   Ferd. aside to him. Hippolito! you yet are ignorant

Of your great Happiness, but there is somewhat,
Which for your own and fair *Dorinda's* sake,
I must instruct you in.
    Hip. Pray teach me quickly how Men and Women
In your World make love, I shall soon learn,   190
I warrant you.
          Enter Ariel, *driving in* Stephano, Trincalo, Mustacho,
                Ventoso, Caliban, Sycorax.
    Prosp. Why that's my dainty *Ariel,* I shall miss thee,
But yet thou shalt have freedom.
    Gonz. O look, Sir, look the Master and the Saylors ——
The Bosen too —— my Prophecy is out,
That if a Gallows were on land, that man
Could ne'r be drown'd.
    Alon. to Trinc. Now, Blasphemy, what not one Oath ashore?
Hast thou no mouth by Land? why star'st thou so?
    Trinc. What, more Dukes yet? I must resign my Dukedom;   200
But 'tis no matter, I was almost starv'd in't.
    Must. Here's nothing but wild Sallads, without Oyl or Vinegar.
    Steph. The Duke and Prince alive! would I had now
Our gallant Ship agen, and were her Master,
I'd willingly give all my Island for her.
    Vent. And I my Vice-Roy-ship.
    Trinc. I shall need no Hangman, for I shall e'n hang
My self, now my friend Butt has shed his last
Drop of life. Poor Butt is quite departed.
    Anto. They talk like mad-men.   210
    Prosp. No matter, time will bring 'em to themselves,
And now their Wine is gone, they will not quarrel.
Your Ship is safe and tight, and bravely rigg'd,
As when you first set Sail.
    Alon.   This news is wonderful.
    Ariel. Was it well done, my Lord?
    Prosp.   Rarely, my Diligence.
    Gonz. But pray, Sir, what are those mishapen Creatures?
    Prosp. Their Mother was a Witch, and one so strong,
She would controul the Moon, make Flows and Ebbs,
And deal in her command without her power.
    Syc. O *Setebos!* these be brave Sprights indeed.   220

Prosp. to Calib. Go, Sirrah, to my Cell, and as you hope
For Pardon, trim it up.
   Calib. Most carefully. I will be wise hereafter.
What a dull Fool was I, to take those Drunkards
For Gods, when such as these were in the world?
   Prosp. Sir, I invite your Highness and your Train
To my poor Cave this night; a part of which
I will employ, in telling you my story.
   Alon. No doubt it must be strangely taking, Sir.
   Prosp. When the morn draws, I'l bring you to your Ship,   230
And promise you calm Seas, and happy Gales.
My *Ariel,* that's thy charge: then to the Elements
Be free, and fare thee well.
   Ariel.   I'll do it, Master.
   Prosp. Now to make amends
For the rough treatment you have found to day,
I'll entertain you with my Magick Art:
I'll, by my power, transform this place, and call
Up those that shall make good my promise to you.
                [*Scene changes to the Rocks, with the Arch of Rocks,*
                   and calm Sea. Musick playing on the Rocks.
   Prosp. Neptune, and your fair *Amphitrite,* rise;
Oceanus, with your *Tethys* too, appear;   240
All ye Sea-Gods, and Goddesses, appear!
Come, all ye *Trytons;* all ye *Nereides,* come,
And teach your sawcy Element to obey:
For you have Princes now to entertain,
And unsoil'd Beauties, with fresh youthful Lovers.
              [Neptune, Amphitrite, Oceanus *and* Tethys *appear in a*
              Chariot drawn with Sea-horses; on each side of the
              Chariot, Sea-gods and Goddesses, Tritons and Nereides.
   Alon. This is prodigious.
   Anto. Ah! what amazing Objects do we see?
   Gonz. This Art doth much exceed all humane skill.
                    SONG.
Amph.   *My Lord: Great* Neptune, *for my sake,*
              Of these bright Beauties pity take: 250
                And to the rest allow
                Your mercy too.

     Let this inraged Element be still,
      Let Æolus obey my will:
     Let him his boystrous Prisoners safely keep
      In their dark Caverns, and no more
     Let 'em disturb the bosome of the Deep,
      Till these arrive upon their wish'd-for Shore.

Neptune.   *So much my* Amphitrite's *love I prize,*
     That no commands of hers I can despise.   260
      Tethys *no furrows now shall wear,*
     Oceanus *no wrinkles on his brow,*
      Let your serenest looks appear!
       Be calm and gentle now.

Nept. & ⎤
Amph. ⎦ *Be calm, ye great Parents of the Flouds and the Springs,*
     While each Nereide *and* Triton *Plays, Revels, and Sings.*

Oceanus. *Confine the roaring Winds, and we*
      Will soon obey you cheerfully.

Chorus of ⎤ *Tie up the Winds, and we'll obey,* ⎡*Here the Dan-*
Tritons ⎬ *Upon the Flouds we'll sing and play,* ⎨*cers mingle with*
and Ner. ⎦ *And celebrate a* Halcyon *day.*   ⎣*the Singers.*

                 [Dance.

Nept.   *Great Nephew* Æolus *make no noise,*   272
     Muzle your roaring Boys, *[*Æolus *appears.*

Amph.   *Let 'em not bluster to disturb our ears,*
     Or strike these Noble Passengers with fears.

Nept.   *Afford 'em onely such an easie Gale,*
     As pleasantly may swell each Sail.

Amph.   *While fell Sea-monsters cause intestine jars,*
     This Empire you invade with foreign Wars.

Nept.   *But you shall now be still,*   280
     And shall obey my Amphitrites *will.*

Æolus descends. You I'll obey, who at one stroke can make,
     With your dread Trident, the whole Earth to
      quake.
     Come down, my Blusterers, swell no more,
      Your stormy rage give o'r.   ⎡*Winds from*
      Let all black Tempests cease — ⎨*the four cor-*
     And let the troubled Ocean rest: ⎣*ners appear.*
     Let all the Sea enjoy as calm a peace,
     As where the Halcyon *builds her quiet Nest.*

To your *Prisons below,*   290
Down, down you must go:
You in the Earths Entrals your Revels may keep;
But no more till I call shall you trouble the Deep.
　　　　　　　　　　　　　[Winds fly down.
Now they are gone, all stormy Wars shall cease:
Then let your Trumpeters proclaim a Peace.

Amph.　　　Tritons, *my Sons, your Trumpets sound,*
And let the noise from Neighbouring Shores
　　rebound.

Chorus.　　$\begin{cases} \textit{Sound a Calm.} \\ \textit{Sound a Calm.} \\ \textit{Sound a Calm.} \\ \textit{[Sound] a Calm.} \\ \textit{Sound a Calm.} \end{cases}$ 300

[Here the Trytons, *at every repeat of* Sound a Calm,
*changing their Figure and Postures, seem to sound
their wreathed Trumpets made of Shells.*

A Symphony of Musick, like Trumpets, to which
four *Trytons* Dance.

Nept.　　*See, see, the Heavens smile, all your troubles are*
　　past,
Your joys by black Clouds shall no more be
　　o'rcast.

Amph.　　*On this barren Isle ye shall lose all your fears*
Leave behind all your sorrows, and banish your
　　cares.

Both.　　*And your Loves and your Lives shall in safety*
　　enjoy;
No influence of Stars shall your quiet destroy.

Chor. of all.　　*And your Loves, &c.*
No influence, &c.　*[Here the Dancers mingle* 310
with the Singers.

Oceanus.　*We'll safely convey you to your own happy Shore,*
And yours and your Countrey's soft peace we'll
　　restore.

Tethys.　*To treat you blest Lovers, as you sail on the Deep,*
The Trytons *and* Sea-Nymphs *their Revels shall*
　　keep.

196

Both.   *On the swift Dolphins backs they shall sing and*
                shall play;
                They shall guard you by night, and delight you by
                day.
Chorus of all.   *On the swift, &c.*
                And shall guard, &c.
                   [Here the Dancers mingle with the Singers.
                      [A Dance of twelve Tritons.

  Mir. What charming things are these?
  Dor. What heavenly power is this?   320
  Prosp. Now, my *Ariel,* be visible
And let the rest of your Aerial Train
Appear, and entertain 'em with a Song;
            [Scene changes to the Rising Sun, and a number of Aerial
             Spirits in the Air, Ariel *flying from the Sun, advances*
             towards the Pit.
And then farewell my long lov'd *Ariel.*
  Alon. Heav'n! what are these we see?
  Prosp. They are Spirits, with which the Air abounds
In swarms, but that they are not subject to
Poor feeble mortal Eyes.
  Anto. O wondrous skill!
  Gonz.   O power Divine!
        Ariel *and the rest sing the following Song.*
  Ariel.   *Where the Bee sucks, there suck I,*   330
        In a Cowslips Bed I lie;
        There I couch when Owls do cry.
        On the Swallows wings I fly
        After Summer merrily.
      Merrily, merrily shall I live now,
      Under the Blossom that hangs on the Bow.
             [Song ended, Ariel *speaks, hovering in the Air.*
  Ariel. My Noble Master!
May theirs and your blest Joys never impair.
And for the freedom I enjoy in Air,
I will be still your *Ariel,* and wait   340
On Aiery accidents that work for Fate.
What ever shall your happiness concern,
From your still faithful *Ariel* you shall learn.

Prosp. Thou hast been always diligent and kind!
Farewell, my long lov'd *Ariel,* thou shalt find,
I will preserve thee ever in my mind.
Henceforth this Isle to the afflicted be
A place of Refuge, as it was to me:
The promises of blooming Spring live here,
And all the blessings of the ripening Year.   350
On my retreat, let Heav'n and Nature smile,
And ever flourish the *Enchanted Isle.*   [*Exeunt.*

EPILOGUE.

Gallants, by all good signs it does appear,
That Sixty seven's a very damning year,
For Knaves abroad, and for ill Poets here.

Among the Muses there's a gen'ral rot,
The Rhyming Monsieur, and the Spanish Plot:
Defie or Court, all's one, they go to Pot.

The Ghosts of Poets walk within this place,
And haunt us Actors wheresoe'r we pass,
In Visions bloudier then King Richard's was.

For this poor Wretch, he has not much to say.   10
But quietly brings in his part o' th' Play,
And begs the favour to be damn'd to day.

He sends me onely like a Sh'riff's man here,
To let you know the Malefactor's near,
And that he means to die, en Cavalier.

For if you shou'd be gracious to his Pen,
Th' Example will prove ill to other men,
And you'll be troubl'd with 'em all agen.

THE
HISTORY
OF
KING
LEAR.

Acted at the

Duke's Theatre.

Reviv'd with Alterations.

By *N. TATE.*

LONDON,
Printed for *E. Flesher*, and are to be sold by *R. Bentley*, and *M. Magnes* in *Russel-street* near *Covent-Garden*, **1681**.

TO

My Esteemed FRIEND

Thomas Boteler, Esq;

SIR,

*You have a natural Right to this Piece, since, by your Advice, I
attempted the Revival of it with Alterations. Nothing but the
Power of your Perswasion, and my Zeal for all the Remains of*
Shakespear, *cou'd have wrought me to so bold an Undertaking.
I found that the Newmodelling of this Story, wou'd force me
sometimes on the difficult Task of making the chiefest Persons
speak something like their Character, on Matter whereof I had no
Ground in my Author.* Lear's *real, and* Edgar's *pretended Madness have so much of extravagant* Nature (*I know not how else to
express it*) *as cou'd never have started but from our* Shakespear's   10
*Creating Fancy. The Images and Language are so odd and sur-
prizing, and yet so agreeable and proper, that whilst we grant that
none but* Shakespear *cou'd have form'd such Conceptions, yet we
are satisfied that they were the only Things in the World that
ought to be said on those Occasions. I found the whole to answer
your Account of it, a Heap of Jewels, unstrung and unpolisht; yet
so dazling in their Disorder, that I soon perceiv'd I had seiz'd a
Treasure. 'Twas my good Fortune to light on one Expedient to
rectifie what was wanting in the Regularity and Probability of the
Tale, which was to run through the whole, A* Love *betwixt* Edgar   20
and Cordelia, *that never chang'd word with each other in the
Original. This renders* Cordelia's *Indifference and her Father's
Passion in the first Scene probable. It likewise gives Countenance
to* Edgar's *Disguise, making that a generous Design that was before
a poor Shift to save his Life. The Distress of the Story is evidently
heightned by it; and it particularly gave Occasion of a New Scene
or Two, of more Success (perhaps) than Merit. This Method
necessarily threw me on making the Tale conclude in a Success to
the innocent distrest Persons: Otherwise I must have incumbred*

203

the Stage with dead Bodies, which Conduct makes many Tragedies   30
conclude with unseasonable Jests. Yet was I Rackt with no small
Fears for so bold a Change, till I found it well receiv'd by my
Audience; and if this will not satisfie the Reader, I can produce
an Authority that questionless will. Neither is it   *Mr.* Dryd.
of so Trivial an Undertaking to make a Tragedy   *Pref. to the*
end happily, for 'tis more difficult to Save than   Span. Fryar.
'tis to Kill: The Dagger and Cup of Poyson are alwaies in Readiness; but to bring the Action to the last Extremity, and then by
probable Means to recover All, will require the Art and Judgment
of a Writer, and cost him many a Pang in the Performance.   40

I have one thing more to Apologize for, which is, that I have
us'd less Quaintness of Expression even in the newest Parts of this
Play. I confess 'twas Design in me, partly to comply with my
Author's Style to make the Scenes of a Piece, and partly to give
it some Resemblance of the Time and Persons here Represented.
This, Sir, I submit wholly to you, who are both a Judge and
Master of Style. Nature had exempted you before you went
Abroad from the Morose Saturnine Humour of our Country, and
you brought home the Refinedness of Travel without the Affecta-
tion. Many Faults I see in the following Pages, and question not   50
but you will discover more; yet I will presume so far on your
Friendship, as to make the Whole a Present to you, and Subscribe
my self

Your obliged Friend
and humble Servant,

N. Tate.

PROLOGUE.

Since by Mistakes your best Delights are made,
(For ev'n your Wives can please in Masquerade)
'Twere worth our While t' have drawn you in this day
By a new Name to our old honest Play;
But he that did this Evenings Treat prepare ⎤
Bluntly resolv'd before-hand to declare ⎬
Your Entertainment should be most old Fare. ⎦
Yet hopes, since in rich Shakespear's soil it grew, ⎤
'Twill relish yet with those whose Tasts are True, ⎬
And his Ambition is to please a Few. ⎦   10
If then this Heap of Flow'rs shall chance to wear
Fresh Beauty in the Order they now bear,
Ev'n this Shakespear's Praise; each Rustick knows
'Mongst plenteous Flow'rs a Garland to Compose,
Which strung by his course Hand may fairer Show,
But 'twas a Pow'r Divine first made 'em Grow.
Why shou'd these Scenes lie hid, in which we find
What may at Once divert and teach the Mind?
Morals were alwaies proper for the Stage,
But are ev'n necessary in this Age.   20
Poets must take the Churches Teaching Trade,
Since Priests their Province of Intrigue invade;
But We the worst in this Exchange have got,
In vain our Poets Preach, whilst Church-men Plot.

THE PERSONS.

King *Lear,*	Mr. *Betterton.*
Gloster,	Mr. *Gillo.*
Kent,	Mr. *Wiltshire.*
Edgar,	Mr. *Smith.*
Bastard,	Mr. *Jo. Williams.*
Cornwall,	Mr. *Norris.*
Albany,	Mr. *Bowman.*
[*Burgundy,*]	
Gentleman-Usher,	Mr. *Jevon.*
[*An Old Man,*]	
[*Physician,*]	
Gonerill,	Mrs. *Shadwell.*
Regan,	Lady *Slingsby.*
Cordelia,	Mrs. *Barry.*
[*Arante,*]	

Guards, Officers, Messengers, [*Two Ruffians,*] *Attendants.*

ACT I, [SCENE I]

Enter Bastard *solus.*

Bast. Thou Nature art my Goddess, to thy Law
My Services are bound, why am I then
Depriv'd of a Son's Right because I came not
In the dull Road that custom has prescrib'd?
Why Bastard, wherefore Base, when I can boast
A Mind as gen'rous and a Shape as true
As honest Madam's Issue? why are we
Held Base, who in the lusty stealth of Nature
Take fiercer Qualities than what compound
The scanted Births of the stale Marriage-bed?   10
Well then, legitimate *Edgar,* to thy right
Of Law I will oppose a Bastard's Cunning.
Our Father's Love is to the Bastard *Edmund*
As to Legitimate *Edgar:* with success
I've practis'd yet on both their easie Natures:
Here comes the old Man chaf't with th' Information
Which last I forg'd against my Brother *Edgar,*
A Tale so plausible, so boldly utter'd
And heightned by such lucky Accidents,
That now the slightest circumstance confirms him,   20
And Base-born *Edmund* spight of Law inherits.

Enter Kent *and* Gloster.

Glost. Nay, good my Lord, your Charity
O'reshoots it self to plead in his behalf;
You are your self a Father, and may feel
The sting of disobedience from a Son
First-born and best Belov'd: Oh Villain *Edgar*!

Kent. Be not too rash, all may be forgery,
And time yet clear the Duty of your Son.

Glost. Plead with the Seas, and reason down the Winds,
Yet shalt thou ne're convince me, I have seen   30
His foul Designs through all a Father's fondness:
But be this Light and Thou my Witnesses
That I discard him here from my Possessions,
Divorce him from my Heart, my Blood and Name.
  Bast. It works as I cou'd wish; I'll shew my self.
  Glost. Ha *Edmund*! welcome Boy; O *Kent* see here
Inverted Nature, *Gloster's* Shame and Glory,
This By-born, the wild sally of my Youth,
Pursues me with all filial Offices,
Whilst *Edgar,* begg'd of Heaven and born in Honour,   40
Draws plagues on my white head that urge me still
To curse in Age the pleasure of my Youth.
Nay weep not, *Edmund,* for thy Brother's crimes;
O gen'rous Boy, thou shar'st but half his blood,
Yet lov'st beyond the kindness of a Brother.
But I'll reward thy Vertue. Follow me.
My Lord, you wait the King who comes resolv'd
To quit the Toils of Empire, and divide
His Realms amongst his Daughters, Heaven succeed it,
But much I fear the Change.
  Kent.   I grieve to see him   50
With such wild starts of passion hourly seiz'd,
As renders Majesty beneath it self.
  Glost. Alas! 'tis the Infirmity of his Age,
Yet has his Temper ever been unfixt,
Chol'rick and suddain; hark, They approach.
                              [*Exeunt* Gloster *and* Bastard.
  Flourish. Enter Lear, Cornwall, Albany, Burgundy, Edgar,
      Goneril, Regan, Cordelia, Edgar *speaking to* Cordelia *at
      Entrance.*
  Edg. Cordelia, royal Fair, turn yet once more,
And e're successfull *Burgundy* receive
The treasure of thy Beauties from the King,
E're happy *Burgundy* for ever fold Thee,
Cast back one pitying Look on wretched *Edgar.*   60
  Cord. Alas what wou'd the wretched *Edgar* with
The more Unfortunate *Cordelia;*

Who in obedience to a Father's will
Flys from her *Edgar's* Arms to *Burgundy's*?
  Lear. Attend my Lords of *Albany* and *Cornwall*
With Princely *Burgundy.*
  Alb.   We do, my Liege.
  Lear. Give me the Mapp —— know, Lords, We have divided
In Three our Kingdom, having now resolved
To disengage from Our long Toil of State,
Conferring All upon your younger years;   70
You, *Burgundy, Cornwall* and *Albany,*
Long in Our Court have made your amorous sojourn
And now are to be answer'd —— tell me my Daughters
Which of you Loves Us most, that We may place
Our largest Bounty with the largest Merit.
Gonerill, Our Eldest-born, speak first.
  Gon. Sir, I do love You more than words can utter,
Beyond what can be valu'd, Rich or Rare,
Nor Liberty, nor Sight, Health, Fame, or Beauty
Are half so dear, my Life for you were vile,   80
As much as Child can love the best of Fathers.
  Lear. Of all these Bounds, ev'n from this Line to this
With shady Forests and wide-skirted Meads,
We make Thee Lady, to thine and *Albany's* Issue
Be this perpetual —— What says Our Second Daughter?
  Reg. My Sister, Sir, in part exprest my Love,
For such as Hers, is mine, though more extended;
Sense has no other Joy that I can relish,
I have my All in my dear Lieges Love!
  Lear. Therefore to thee and thine Hereditary   90
Remain this ample Third of our fair Kingdom.
  Cord. Now comes my Trial, how am I distrest,   [*Aside.*
That must with cold speech tempt the chol'rick King
Rather to leave me Dowerless, than condemn me
To loath'd Embraces!
  Lear. Speak now Our last, not least in Our dear Love,
So ends my Task of State, —— *Cordelia* speak,
What canst Thou say to win a richer Third
Than what thy Sisters gain'd?
  Cord. Now must my Love in words fall short of theirs   100

As much as it exceeds in Truth —— Nothing my Lord.

 Lear. Nothing can come of Nothing, speak agen.

 Cord. Unhappy am I that I can't dissemble,
Sir, as I ought, I love your Majesty,
No more nor less.

 Lear.   Take heed *Cordelia,*
Thy Fortunes are at stake, think better on't
And mend thy Speech a little.

 Cord.   O my Liege,
You gave me Being, Bred me, dearly Love me,
And I return my Duty as I ought,
Obey you, Love you, and most Honour you!   110
Why have my Sisters Husbands, if they love you All?
Happ'ly when I shall Wed, the Lord whose Hand
Shall take my Plight, will carry half my Love,
For I shall never marry, like my Sisters,
To Love my Father All.

 Lear. And goes thy Heart with this?
'Tis said that I am Chol'rick, judge me Gods,
Is there not cause? now Minion I perceive
The Truth of what has been suggested to Us,
Thy Fondness for the Rebel Son of *Gloster,*   120
False to his Father, as Thou art to my Hopes:
And oh take heed, rash Girl, lest We comply
With thy fond wishes, which thou wilt too late
Repent, for know Our nature cannot brook
A Child so young and so Ungentle.

 Cord. So young my Lord and True.

 Lear. Thy Truth then be thy Dow'r,
For by the sacred Sun and solemn Night
I here disclaim all my paternal Care,
And from this minute hold thee as a Stranger   130
Both to my Blood and Favour.

 Kent.   This is Frenzy.
Consider, good my Liege ——

 Lear.   Peace *Kent.*
Come not between a Dragon and his Rage.
I lov'd her most, and in her tender Trust
Design'd to have bestow'd my Age at Ease!

So be my Grave my Peace as here I give
My Heart from her, and with it all my Wealth:
My Lords of *Cornwall* and of *Albany,*
I do invest you jointly with full Right
In this fair Third, *Cordelia's* forfeit Dow'r.   140
Mark me, My Lords, observe Our last Resolve,
Our Self attended with an hundred Knights
Will make Aboad with you in monthly Course,
The Name alone of King remain with me,
Yours be the Execution and Revenues,
This is Our final Will, and to confirm it
This Coronet part between you.
    Kent.   Royal *Lear,*
Whom I have ever honour'd as my King,
Lov'd as my Father, as my Master follow'd,
And as my Patron thought on in my Pray'rs ———   150
    Lear. Away, the Bow is bent, make from the Shaft.
    Kent. No, let it fall and drench within my Heart,
Be *Kent* unmannerly when *Lear* is mad:
Thy youngest Daughter ——
    Lear.   On thy Life no more.
    Kent. What wilt thou doe, old Man?
    Lear.   Out of my sight!
    Kent. See better first.
    Lear.   Now by the gods ——
    Kent. Now by the gods, rash King, thou swear'st in vain.
    Lear. Ha Traytour ——
    Kent.   Do, kill thy Physician, *Lear,*
Strike through my Throat, yet with my latest Breath
I'll Thunder in thine Ear my just Complaint,   160
And tell Thee to thy Face that Thou dost ill.
    Lear. Hear me rash Man, on thy Allegiance hear me;
Since thou hast striv'n to make Us break our Vow
And prest between our Sentence and our Pow'r,
Which nor our Nature nor our Place can bear,
We banish thee for ever from our Sight
And Kingdom; if when Three days are expir'd
Thy hated Trunk be found in our Dominions
That moment is thy Death; Away.

Kent. Why fare thee well, King, since thou art resolv'd,   170
I take thee at thy word, and will not stay
To see thy Fall: the gods protect the Maid
That truly thinks, and has most justly said.
Thus to new Climates my old Truth I bear,
Friendship lives Hence, and Banishment is Here.   [*Exit.*
  Lear. Now *Burgundy,* you see her Price is faln,
Yet if the fondness of your Passion still
Affects her as she stands, Dow'rless, and lost
In our Esteem, she's yours, take her or leave her.
  Burg. Pardon me, Royal *Lear,* I but demand   180
The Dow'r your Self propos'd, and here I take
Cordelia by the Hand Dutchess of *Burgundy.*
  Lear. Then leave her Sir, for by a Father's rage
I tell you all her Wealth. Away.
  Burg. Then Sir be pleas'd to charge the breach
Of our Alliance on your own Will
Not my Inconstancy.   [*Exeunt. Manent* Edgar *and* Cordelia.
  Edg. Has Heaven then weigh'd the merit of my Love,
Or is't the raving of my sickly Thought?
Cou'd *Burgundy* forgoe so rich a Prize   190
And leave her to despairing *Edgar's* Arms?
Have I thy Hand *Cordelia,* do I clasp it,
The Hand that was this minute to have join'd
My hated Rivals? do I kneel before thee
And offer at thy feet my panting Heart?
Smile, Princess, and convince me, for as yet
I doubt, and dare not trust the dazling Joy.
  Cord. Some Comfort yet that 'twas no vicious Blot
That has depriv'd me of a Father's Grace,
But meerly want of that that makes me rich   200
In wanting it, a smooth professing Tongue:
O Sisters, I am loth to call your fault
As it deserves; but use our Father well,
And wrong'd *Cordelia* never shall repine.
  Edg. O heav'nly Maid that are thy self thy Dow'r,
Richer in Vertue than the Stars in Light,
If *Edgar's* humble fortunes may be grac't
With thy Acceptance, at thy feet he lays 'em.

Ha my *Cordelia!* dost thou turn away?
What have I done t'offend Thee?
 Cord.   Talk't of Love.   210
 Edg. Then I've offended oft, *Cordelia* too
Has oft permitted me so to offend.
 Cord. When, *Edgar,* I permitted your Addresses,
I was the darling Daughter of a King,
Nor can I now forget my royal Birth,
And live dependent on my Lover's Fortune.
I cannot to so low a fate submit,
And therefore study to forget your Passion,
And trouble me upon this Theam no more.
 Edg. Thus Majesty takes most State in Distress!   220
How are we tost on Fortune's fickle flood!
The Wave that with surprising kindness brought
The dear Wreck to my Arms, has snatcht it back,
And left me mourning on the barren Shore.
 Cord. This Baseness of th' ignoble *Burgundy*   [*Aside.*
Draws just suspicion on the Race of Men,
His Love was Int'rest, so may *Edgar's* be
And He but with more Complement dissemble;
If so, I shall oblige him by Denying:
But if his Love be fixt, such Constant flame   230
As warms our Breasts, if such I find his Passion,
My Heart as gratefull to his Truth shall be,
And Cold *Cordelia* prove as Kind as He.   [*Exit.*
      Enter Bastard *hastily.*
 Bast. Brother, I've found you in a lucky minute,
Fly and be safe, some Villain has incens'd
Our Father against your Life.
 Edg. Distrest *Cordelia*! but oh! more Cruel!
 Bast. Hear me Sir, your Life, your Life's in Danger.
 Edg. A Resolve so sudden
And of such black Importance!
 Bast.   'Twas not sudden,   240
Some Villain has of long time laid the Train.
 Edg. And yet perhaps 'twas but pretended Coldness,
To try how far my passion would pursue.
 Bast. He hears me not; wake, wake Sir.

Edg. Say ye Brother? ——
No Tears good *Edmund,* if thou bringst me tidings
To strike me dead, for Charity delay not,
That present will befit so kind a Hand.
    Bast. Your danger Sir comes on so fast
That I want time t'inform you, but retire   250
Whilst I take care to turn the pressing Stream.
O gods! for Heav'ns sake Sir.
    Edg. Pardon me Sir, a serious Thought
Had seiz'd me, but I think you talkt of danger
And wisht me to Retire; must all our Vows
End thus! —— Friend I obey you —— O *Cordelia!*   *[Exit.*
    Bast. Ha! ha! fond Man, such credulous Honesty
Lessens the Glory of my Artifice,
His Nature is so far from doing wrongs
That he suspects none: if this Letter speed   260
And pass for *Edgar's,* as himself wou'd own
The Counterfeit but for the foul Contents,
Then my designs are perfect —— here comes *Gloster.*
              Enter Gloster.
    Glost. Stay *Edmund,* turn, what paper were you reading?
    Bast. A Trifle Sir.
    Glost. What needed then that terrible dispatch of it
Into your Pocket, come produce it Sir.
    Bast. A Letter from my Brother Sir, I had
Just broke the Seal but knew not the Contents,
Yet fearing they might prove to blame   270
Endeavour'd to conceal it from your sight.
    Glost. 'Tis *Edgar's* Character.   *[Reads.*
   *This Policy of Fathers is intollerable that keeps our Fortunes
     from us till Age will not suffer us to enjoy 'em; I am weary
     of the Tyranny: Come to me that of this I may speak more:
     if our Father would sleep till I wak't him, you shou'd enjoy
     half his Possessions, and live beloved of your Brother*
                            Edgar
Slept till I wake him, you shou'd enjoy
Half his possessions —— *Edgar* to write this
'Gainst his indulgent Father! Death and Hell!   280
Fly, *Edmund,* seek him out, wind me into him
That I may bite the Traytor's heart, and fold

His bleeding Entrals on my vengefull Arm.

   Bast. Perhaps 'twas writ, my Lord, to prove my Vertue.

   Glost. These late Eclipses of the Sun and Moon
Can bode no less; Love cools, and friendship fails,
In Cities mutiny, in Countrys discord,
The bond of Nature crack't 'twixt Son and Father:
Find out the Villain, do it carefully
And it shall lose thee nothing.   *[Exit.*

   Bast. So, now my project's firm, but to make sure   291
I'll throw in one proof more and that a bold one;
I'll place old *Gloster* where he shall o're-hear us
Confer of this design, whilst to his thinking,
Deluded *Edgar* shall accuse himself.
Be Honesty my Int'rest and I can
Be honest too, and what Saint so Divine
That will successfull Villany decline!   *[Exit.*

[ACT I, SCENE II]

Enter Kent *disguis'd.*

   Kent. Now banisht *Kent,* if thou canst pay thy duty
In this disguise where thou dost stand condemn'd,
Thy Master *Lear* shall find thee full of Labours.

Enter Lear *attended.*

   Lear. In there, and tell our Daughter we are here
Now; What are Thou?

   Kent.   A Man, Sir.

   Lear. What dost thou profess, or wou'dst with us?

   Kent. I do profess to be no less then I seem, to serve him truly
that puts me in Trust, to love him that's Honest, to converse with
him that's wise and speaks little, to fight when I can't choose; and
to eat no Fish.   10

   Lear. I say, what are Thou?

   Kent. A very honest-hearted fellow, and as poor as the King.

Lear. Then art thou poor indeed —— What can'st thou do?

Kent. I can keep honest Counsel, marr a curious Tale in the telling, deliver a plain Message bluntly, that which ordinary Men are fit for I am qualify'd in, and the best of me is Diligence.

Lear. Follow me, thou shalt serve me.

Enter one of Gonerill's *Gentlemen.*

Now Sir?

Gent. Sir ——————   [*Exit;* Kent [*and Servant*] *run after him.*

Lear. What says the fellow? Call the Clatpole back.

Att. My Lord, I know not, but methinks your Highness is en-   20
tertain'd with slender Ceremony.

[*Enter Servant.*]

Serv. He says, my Lord, your Daughter is not well.

Lear. Why came not the Slave back when I call'd him?

Serv. My Lord, he answer'd me i'th' surliest manner,
That he wou'd not.

Re-enter Gentleman brought in by Kent.

Lear. I hope our Daughter did not so instruct him:
Now, who am I Sir?

Gent.   My Ladies Father.

Lear. My Lord's Knave ——   [*Strikes him.*

Gonerill *at the Entrance.*

I'll not be struck my Lord.

Kent. Nor tript neither, thou vile Civet-box.   [*Strikes up his heels.*

Gon. By Day and Night this is insufferable,   30
I will not bear it.

Lear. Now, Daughter, why that frontlet on?
Speak, do's that Frown become our Presence?

Gon. Sir, this licentious Insolence of your Servants
Is most unseemly, hourly they break out
In quarrels bred by their unbounded Riots,
I had fair hope by making this known to you
T'have had a quick Redress, but find too late
That you protect and countenance their out-rage;
And therefore, Sir, I take this freedom, which   40
Necessity makes Discreet.

Lear.   Are you our Daughter?

Gon. Come, Sir, let me entreat you to make use
Of your discretion, and put off betimes

This Disposition that of late transforms you
From what you rightly are.

    Lear. Do's any here know me? why this is not *Lear.*
Do's *Lear* walk thus? speak thus? where are his Eyes?
Who is it that can tell me who I am?

    Gon. Come, Sir, this Admiration's much o'th' savour
Of other your new humours, I beseech you   50
To understand my purposes aright;
As you are old, you shou'd be staid and wise,
Here do you keep an hundred Knights and Squires,
Men so debaucht and bold that this our Palace
Shews like a riotous Inn, a Tavern, Brothel;
Be then advised by her that else will take
That she beggs, to lessen your Attendance,
Take half away, and see that the remainder
Be such as may befit your Age, and know
Themselves and you.

    Lear.   Darkness and Devils!   60
Saddle my Horses, call my Train together;
Degenerate Viper, I'll not stay with Thee;
I yet have left a Daughter —— Serpent, Monster,
Lessen my Train, and call 'em riotous?
All men approv'd of choice and rarest Parts,
That each particular of duty know ——
How small, *Cordelia,* was thy Fault? O *Lear,*
Beat at this Gate that let thy Folly in,
And thy dear Judgment out; Go, go, my People.

            Going off meets Albany *entring.*
Ingratefull Duke, was this your will?

    Alb.   What Sir?   70

    Lear. Death! fifty of my Followers at a clap!

    Alb. The matter Madam?

    Gon. Never afflict your self to know the Cause,
But give his Dotage way.

    Lear.   Blasts upon thee,
Th' untented woundings of a Father's Curse
Pierce ev'ry Sense about Thee; old fond Eyes
Lament this Cause again, I'll pluck ye out
And cast ye with the Waters that ye lose
To temper Clay —— No, *Gorgon,* thou shalt find

That I'll resume the Shape which thou dost think   80
I have cast off for ever.
   Gon.   Mark ye that.
   Lear. Hear Nature!
Dear Goddess hear, and if thou dost intend
To make that Creature fruitfull, change thy purpose;
Pronounce upon her Womb the barren Curse,
That from her blasted Body never spring
A Babe to honour her —— but if she must bring forth,
Defeat her Joy with some distorted Birth,
Or monstrous Form, the Prodigy o'th' Time,
And so perverse of spirit, that it may Live   90
Her Torment as 'twas Born, to fret her Cheeks
With constant Tears, and wrinkle her young Brow.
Turn all her Mother's Pains to Shame and Scorn,
That she may curse her Crime too late, and feel
How sharper than a Serpent's Tooth it is
To have a Thankless Child! Away, away.   [*Exit cum suis.*
   Gon. Presuming thus upon his numerous Train
He thinks to play the Tyrant here, and hold
Our Lives at will.
   Alb.   Well, you may bear too far.   [*Exeunt.*

ACT II, [SCENE I]

Scene, Gloster's *House.*
Enter Bastard.

   Bast. The Duke comes here to night, I'll take advantage
Of his Arrival to compleat my project,
Brother a Word, come forth, 'tis I your Friend,
              Enter Edgar.
My Father watches for you, fly this place,
Intelligence is giv'n where you are hid,
Take the advantage of the Night, bethink ye
Have you not spoke against the Duke of *Cornwall*

218

Something might shew you a favourer of
Duke *Albany's* Party?
    Edg.   Nothing, why ask you?
    Bast. Because he's coming here to Night in haste   10
And *Regan* with him —— heark! the Guards, Away.
    Edg. Let 'em come on, I'll stay and clear my self.
    Bast. Your Innocence at leisure may be heard,
But *Gloster's* storming Rage as yet is deaf,
And you may perish e're allow'd the hearing.   [*Exit* Edgar.
Gloster comes yonder: now to my feign'd scuffle ——
Yield, come before my Father! Lights here, Lights!
Some Blood drawn on me wou'd beget opinion   [*Stabs his Arm.*
Of our more fierce Encounter —— I have seen
Drunkards do more than this in sport.   20
             Enter Gloster *and Servants.*

    Glost. Now, *Edmund,* where's the Traytour?
    Bast.   That Name, Sir,
Strikes Horrour through me, but my Brother, Sir,
Stood here i'th' Dark.
    Glost. Thou bleed'st, pursue the Villain
And bring him piece-meal to me.
    Bast.   Sir, he's fled.
    Glost. Let him fly far, this Kingdom shall not hide him:
The noble Duke, my Patron, comes to Night,
By his Authority I will proclaim
Rewards for him that brings him to the Stake,
And Death for the Concealer.   30
Then of my Lands, loyal and natural Boy,
I'll work the means to make thee capable.   [*Exeunt.*

[ACT II, SCENE II]

Enter Kent *(disguis'd still) and* Goneril's *Gentleman, severally.*
    Gent. Good morrow Friend, belong'st thou to this House?

Kent. Ask them will answer thee.

Gent. Where may we set our Horses?

Kent. I'th' Mire.

Gent. I am in haste, prethee an' thou lov'st me, tell me.

Kent. I love thee not.

Gent. Why then I care not for Thee.

Kent. An' I had thee in *Lipsbury* Pinfold, I'd make thee care for me.

Gent. What dost thou mean? I know thee not.   10

Kent. But, Minion, I know Thee.

Gent. What dost thou know me for?

Kent. For a base, proud, beggarly, white-liver'd, Glass-gazing, superserviceable finical Rogue; one that wou'd be a Pimp in way of good Service, and art nothing but a composition of Knave, Beggar, Coward, Pandar ——

Gent. What a monstrous Fellow art thou to rail at one that is neither known of thee nor knows thee?

Kent. Impudent Slave, not know me, who but two days since tript up thy heels before the King: draw, Miscreant, or I'll make   20 the Moon shine through thee.

Gent. What means the Fellow? —— Why prethee, prethee; I tell thee I have nothing to do with thee.

Kent. I know your Rogueship's Office, you come with Letters against the King, taking my young Lady *Vanity's* part against her royal Father; draw Rascal.

Gent. Murther, murther, help Ho!

Kent. Dost thou scream Peacock, strike Puppet, stand dappar Slave.

Gent. Help Hea'! Murther, help.   [*Exit.* Kent *after him.*
Flourish. Enter Duke of Cornwal, Regan, *attended,* Gloster, Bastard.

Glost. All Welcome to your Graces, you do me honour.   31

Duke. *Gloster* w'ave heard with sorrow that your Life
Has been attempted by your impious Son,
But *Edmund* here has paid you strictest Duty.

Glost. He did betray his Practice, and receiv'd
The Hurt you see, striving to apprehend him.

Duke. Is He pursu'd?

Glost.   He is, my Lord.

Reg. Use our Authority to apprehend

The Traytour and do Justice on his Head;
For you, *Edmund,* that have so signaliz'd   40
Your Vertue, you from henceforth shall be ours;
Natures of such firm Trust we much shall need.
A charming Youth and worth my further Thought.   [*Aside.*
   Duke. Lay comforts, noble *Gloster,* to your Breast,
As we to ours, This Night be spent in Revels,
We choose you, *Gloster,* for our Host to Night,
A troublesome expression of our Love.
On, to the Sports before us — who are These?

        Enter the Gentleman pursu'd by Kent.

   Glost. Now, what's the matter?
   Duke. Keep peace upon your Lives, he dies that strikes.   50
Whence and what are ye?
   Att. Sir, they are Messengers, the one from your Sister,
The other from the King.
   Duke. Your Difference? speak.
   Gent.   I'm scarce in breath, my Lord.
   Kent. No marvel, you have so bestirr'd your Valour.
Nature disclaims the Dastard, a Taylor made him.
   Duke. Speak yet, how grew your Quarrel?
   Gent. Sir this old Ruffian here, whose Life I spar'd
In pity to his Beard ——
   Kent.   Thou Essence Bottle!
In pity to my Beard? —— Your leave, my Lord,   60
And I will tread the Muss-cat into Mortar.
   Duke. Know'st thou our Presence?
   Kent. Yes, Sir, but Anger has a Privilege.
   Duke. Why art thou angry?
   Kent. That such a Slave as this shou'd wear a Sword
And have no Courage, Office and no Honesty.
Not Frost and Fire hold more Antipathy
Than I and such a Knave.
   Glost. Why dost thou call him Knave?
   Kent. His Countenance likes me not.   70
   Duke. No more perhaps does Mine, nor His or Hers.
   Kent. Plain-dealing is my Trade, and to be plain, Sir,
I have seen better Faces in my time
Than stands on any Shoulders now before me.

Reg. This is some Fellow that having once been prais'd,
For Bluntness, since affects a sawcy Rudeness,
But I have known one of these surly Knaves
That in his Plainness harbour'd more Design
Than twenty cringing complementing Minions.
    Duke. What's the offence you gave him?   80
    Gent. Never any, Sir.
It pleas'd the King his Master lately
To strike me on a slender misconstruction,
Whilst watching his Advantage this old Lurcher
Tript me behind, for which the King extold him;
And, flusht with th' honour of this bold exploit,
Drew on me here agen.
    Duke. Bring forth the Stocks, we'll teach you.
    Kent. Sir I'm too old to learn;
Call not the Stocks for me, I serve the King,   90
On whose Employment I was sent to you,
You'll shew too small Respect, and too bold Malice
Against the Person of my royal Master,
Stocking his Messenger.
    Duke. Bring forth the Stocks, as I have Life and Honour,
There shall he sit till Noon.
    Reg. Till Noon, my Lord? till Night, and all Night too.
    Kent. Why, Madam, if I were your Father's Dog
You wou'd not use me so.
    Reg. Sir, being his Knave I will.   100
    Glost. Let me beseech your Graces to forbear him,
His fault is much, and the good King his Master
Will check him for't, but needs must take it ill
To be thus slighted in his Messenger.
    Duke. Wee'l answer that;
Our Sister may receive it worse to have
Her Gentleman assaulted: to our business lead.   [*Exit.*
    Glost. I am sorry for thee, Friend, 'tis the Duke's pleasure
Whose Disposition will not be controll'd,
But I'll entreat for thee.
    Kent.   Pray do not, Sir —   110
I have watcht and travell'd hard,
Some time I shall sleep out, the rest I'll whistle:

Fare-well t'ye, Sir.   *[Exit* Gloster.
All weary and o're-watcht,
I feel the drowzy Guest steal on me; take
Advantage heavy Eyes of this kind Slumber,
Not to behold this vile and shamefull Lodging.   *[Sleeps.*

Enter Edgar.

   Edg. I heard my self proclaim'd,
And by the friendly Hollow of a Tree
Escapt the Hunt, no Port is free, no place   120
Where Guards and most unusual Vigilance
Do not attend to take me —— how easie now
'Twere to defeat the malice of my Trale,
And leave my Griefs on my Sword's reeking point;
But Love detains me from Death's peacefull Cell,
Still whispering me *Cordelia's* in distress;
Unkinde as she is I cannot see her wretched,
But must be neer to wait upon her Fortune.
Who knows but the white minute yet may come
When *Edgar* may do service to *Cordelia,*   130
That charming Hope still ties me to the Oar
Of painfull Life, and makes me too, submit
To th' humblest shifts to keep that Life a foot;
My Face I will besmear and knit my Locks,
The Country gives me proof and president
Of Bedlam Beggars, who with roaring Voices
Strike in their numm'd and mortify'd bare Arms
Pins, Iron-spikes, Thorns, sprigs of Rosemary,
And thus from Sheep-coats Villages and Mills,
Sometimes with Prayers, sometimes with Lunatick Banns   140
Enforce their Charity, poor *Tyrligod,* poor *Tom*
That's something yet, *Edgar* I am no more.   *[Exit.*

Kent *in the Stocks still; Enter* Lear *attended.*

   Lear. 'Tis strange that they shou'd so depart from home
And not send back our Messenger.
   Kent. Hail, noble Master.
   Lear. How? mak'st thou this Shame thy Pastime?
What's he that has so much mistook thy Place
To set thee here?

Kent. It is both He and She, Sir, your Son and Daughter.
Lear. No.
Kent.   Yes.
Lear.   No I say.
Kent.   I say yea.   150
Lear. By *Jupiter* I swear no.
Kent. By *Juno* I swear, I swear I.
  Lear.   They durst not do't
They cou'd not, wou'd not do't, 'tis worse then Murder
To doe upon Respect such violent out-rage.
Resolve me with all modest haste which way
Thou mayst deserve, or they impose this usage?
  Kent. My Lord, when at their Home
I did commend your Highness Letters to them,
E'er I was Ris'n, arriv'd another Post
Steer'd in his haste, breathless and panting forth   160
From *Gonerill* his Mistress Salutations,
Whose Message being deliver'd, they took Horse,
Commanding me to follow and attend
The leisure of their Answer; which I did,
But meeting that other Messenger
Whose welcome I perceiv'd had poison'd mine,
Being the very Fellow that of late
Had shew'n such rudeness to Your Highness, I
Having more Man than Wit about me, Drew,
On which he rais'd the House with Coward cries: 170
This was the Trespass which your Son and Daughter
Thought worth the shame you see it suffer here.
  Lear. Oh! how this Spleen swells upward to my Heart
And heaves for passage —— down thou climing Rage
Thy Element's below; where is this Daughter?
  Kent. Within, Sir, at a Masque.

Enter Gloster.

  Lear. Now Gloster? —— ha!
Deny to speak with me? th'are sick, th'are weary,
They have travell'd hard to Night —— meer fetches;
Bring me a better Answer.
  Glost.   My dear Lord,   180
You know the fiery Quality of the Duke ——

Lear. Vengeance! Death, Plague, Confusion,
Fiery? what Quality — why *Gloster, Gloster,*
I'd speak with the Duke of *Cornwal* and his Wife.
   Glost. I have inform'd 'em so.
   Lear. Inform'd 'em! dost thou understand me, Man,
I tell thee *Gloster* ——
   Glost.   I, my good Lord.
   Lear. The King wou'd speak with *Cornwal,* the dear Father
Wou'd with his Daughter speak, commands her Service.
Are they inform'd of this? my Breath and Blood!   190
Fiery! the fiery Duke! tell the hot Duke ——
No, but not yet, may be he is not well:
Infirmity do's still neglect all Office;
I beg his Pardon, and I'll chide my Rashness
That took the indispos'd and sickly Fit
For the sound Man — but wherefore sits he there?
Death on my State, this Act convinces me
That this Retiredness of the Duke and her
Is plain Contempt; give me my Servant forth,
Go tell the Duke and's Wife I'd speak with 'em.   200
Now, instantly, bid 'em come forth and hear me,
Or at their Chamber door I'll beat the Drum
Till it cry sleep to Death ——
              Enter Cornwall *and* Regan.
                  Oh! are ye come?
   Duke. Health to the King.
   Reg. I am glad to see your Highness.
   Lear. Regan, I think you are, I know what cause
I have to think so; shoud'st thou not be glad
I wou'd divorce me from thy Mother's Tomb.
Beloved *Regan,* thou wilt shake to hear
What I shall utter: Thou coud'st ne'r ha' thought it,   210
Thy Sister's naught, O *Regan,* she has ty'd   [Kent *here set at liberty.*
Ingratitude like a keen Vulture here,
I scarce can speak to thee.
   Reg. I pray you, Sir, take patience; I have hope
That you know less to value her Desert,
Then she to slack her Duty.
   Lear   Ha! how's that?

Reg. I cannot think my Sister in the least
Would fail in her respects, but if perchance
She has restrain'd the Riots of your Followers
'Tis on such Grounds, and to such wholsome Ends   220
As clears her from all Blame.
    Lear.   My Curses on her.
    Reg. O Sir, you are old
And shou'd content you to be rul'd and led
By some discretion that discerns your State
Better than you yourself, therefore, Sir,
Return to our Sister, and say you have wrong'd her.
    Lear. Ha! ask her Forgiveness?
No, no, 'twas my mistake thou didst not mean so,
Dear Daughter, I confess that I am old;
Age is unnecessary, but thou art good,   230
And wilt dispense with my Infirmity.
    Reg. Good Sir, no more of these unsightly passions,
Return back to our Sister.
    Lear.   Never, *Regan,*
She has abated me of half of my Train,
Lookt black upon me, stabb'd me with her Tongue;
All the stor'd Vengeances of Heav'n fall
On her Ingratefull Head; strike her young Bones
Ye taking Ayrs with Lameness.
    Reg. O the blest Gods! Thus will you wish on me
When the rash mood ——   240
    Lear. No, *Regan,* Thou shalt never have my Curse,
Thy tender Nature cannot give thee o're
To such Impiety; Thou better know'st
The Offices of Nature, bond of Child-hood,
And dues of Gratitude: Thou bear'st in mind
The half o'th' Kingdom which our love conferr'd
On thee and thine.
    Reg.   Good Sir, toth' purpose.
    Lear. Who put my Man i'th' Stocks?
    Duke. What Trumpet's that?
    Reg. I know't, my Sister's, this confirms her Letters.   250
Sir, is your Lady come?
              Enter Gonerill's *Gentleman.*

Lear.　　　　　　More Torture still?
This is a Slave whose easie borrow'd pride
Dwells in the fickle Grace of her he follows;
A Fashion-fop that spends the day in Dressing,
And all to bear his Ladie's flatt'ring Message,
That can deliver with a Grace her Lie,
And with as bold a face bring back a greater.
Out Varlet from my sight.
　　Duke.　　　　　　What means your Grace?
　　Lear. Who stockt my Servant? *Regan,* I have hope
Thou didst not know it.

　　　　　　　　Enter Gonerill.

　　　　　　Who comes here! oh Heavens!　　　　　260
If you do love Old men, if your sweet sway
Allow Obedience; if your selves are Old,
Make it your Cause, send down and take my part;
Why, *Gorgon,* dost thou come to haunt me here?
Art not asham'd to look upon this Beard?
Darkness upon my Eyes they play me false,
O *Regan,* wilt thou take her by the Hand?
　　Gon. Why not by th' Hand, Sir, how have I offended?
All's not Offence that indiscretion finds,
And Dotage terms so.
　　Lear.　　　　　Heart thou art too tough.　　　　270
　　Reg. I pray you, Sir, being old confess you are so,
If till the expiration of your Month
You will return and sojourn with our Sister,
Dismissing half your Train, come then to me,
I am now from Home, and out of that Provision
That shall be needfull for your Entertainment.
　　Lear. Return with her and fifty Knights dismist?
No, rather I'll forswear all Roofs, and chuse
To be Companion to the Midnight Wolf,
My naked Head expos'd to th' merciless Air　　　280
Then have my smallest wants suppli'd by her.
　　Gon. At your choice, Sir.
　　Lear. Now I prithee Daughter do not make me mad;
I will not trouble thee, my Child, farewell,
Wee'l meet no more, no more see one another;

Let shame come when it will, I do not call it,
I do not bid the Thunder-bearer strike,
Nor tell Tales of thee to avenging Heav'n;
Mend when thou canst, be better at thy leisure,
I can be patient, I can stay with *Regan,*   290
I, and my hundred Knights.
   Reg.   Your Pardon, Sir.
I lookt not for you yet, nor am provided
For your fit welcome.
   Lear.   Is this well spoken now?
   Reg. My Sister treats you fair; what! fifty Followers;
Is it not well? what shou'd you need of more?
   Gon. Why might not you, my Lord, receive Attendance
From those whom she calls Servants, or from mine?
   Reg. Why not, my Lord? if then they chance to slack you
We cou'd controll 'em —— if you come to me,
For now I see the Danger, I entreat you   300
To bring but Five and Twenty; to no more
Will I give place.
   Lear. Hold now my Temper, stand this bolt unmov'd
And I am Thunder-proof;
The wicked when compar'd with the more wicked
Seem beautifull, and not to be the worst,
Stands in some rank of Praise; now, *Gonerill,*
Thou art innocent agen, I'll go with thee;
Thy Fifty yet, do's double Five and Twenty,
And thou art twice her Love.
   Gon.   Hear me, my Lord,   310
What need you Five and Twenty, Ten, or Five,
To follow in a House where twice so many
Have a Command t'attend you?
   Reg.   What need one?
   Lear. Blood, Fire! hear —— Leaprosies and bluest Plagues!
Room, room for Hell to belch her Horrors up
And drench the *Circes* in a stream of Fire;
Heark how th' Infernals eccho to my Rage
Their Whips and Snakes ——
   Reg.   How lewd a thing is Passion!
   Gon. So old and stomachfull.   *[Lightning and Thunder.*
   Lear. Heav'ns drop your Patience down;   320

228

You see me here, ye Gods, a poor old Man
As full of Griefs as Age, wretched in both ——
I'll bear no more: no, you unnatural Haggs,
I will have such Revenges on you both,
That all the world shall — I will do such things
What they are yet I know not, but they shall be
The Terrors of the Earth; you think I'll weep,   [*Thunder again.*
This Heart shall break into a thousand pieces
Before I'll weep —— O Gods! I shall go mad.   [*Exit.*
   Duke. 'Tis a wild Night, come out o'th' Storm.   [*Exeunt.*

ACT III, [SCENE I]

Scene, A Desert Heath.
Enter Lear *and* Kent *in the Storm.*

   Lear. Blow Winds and burst your Cheeks, rage louder yet,
Fantastick Lightning singe, singe my white Head;
Spout Cataracts, and Hurricanos fall
Till you have drown'd the Towns and Palaces
Of proud ingratefull Man.
   Kent. Not all my best intreaties can perswade him
Into some needfull shelter, or to 'bide
This poor slight Cov'ring on his aged Head
Expos'd to this wild war of Earth and Heav'n.
   Lear. Rumble thy fill, fight Whirlwind, Rain and Fire: 10
Not Fire, Wind, Rain or Thunder are my Daughters:
I tax not you ye Elements with unkindness;
I never gave you Kingdoms, call'd you Children,
You owe me no Obedience, then let fall
Your horrible pleasure, here I stand your Slave,
A poor, infirm, weak and despis'd old man;
Yet I will call you servile Ministers,
That have with two pernicious Daughters join'd
Their high-engendred Battle against a Head

So Old and White as mine, Oh! oh! 'tis Foul.   20
   Kent. Hard by, Sir, is a Hovel that will lend
Some shelter from this Tempest.
   Lear. I will forget my Nature, what? so kind a Father,
I, there's the point.
   Kent. Consider, good my Liege, Things that love Night
Love not such Nights as this; these wrathfull Skies
Frighten the very wanderers o'th' Dark,
And make 'em keep their Caves; such drenching Rain,
Such Sheets of Fire, such Claps of horrid Thunder,
Such Groans of roaring Winds have ne're been known.   30
   Lear. Let the Great Gods,
That keep this dreadfull pudder o're our Heads
Find out their Enemies now, tremble thou Wretch
That hast within thee undiscover'd Crimes.
Hide, thou bloody Hand,
Thou perjur'd Villain, holy, holy Hypocrite,
That drinkst the Widows Tears, sigh now and cry
These dreadfull Summoners Grace, I am a Man
More sin'd against than sinning.
   Kent. Good Sir, to th' Hovell.
   Lear.   My wit begins to burn,   40
Come on my Boy, how dost my Boy? art Cold?
I'm cold my self; shew me this Straw, my Fellow,
The Art of our Necessity is strange,
And can make vile things precious; my poor Knave,
Cold as I am at Heart, I've one place There   *[Loud Storm.*
That's sorry yet for Thee.   *[Exeunt.*

[ACT III, SCENE II]

Gloster's *Palace.*
Enter Bastard.
   Bast. The Storm is in our louder Rev'lings drown'd.
Thus wou'd I Reign cou'd I but mount a Throne.

The Riots of these proud imperial Sisters
Already have impos'd the galling Yoke
Of Taxes, and hard Impositions on
The drudging Peasants Neck, who bellow out
Their loud Complaints in Vain — Triumphant Queens!
With what Assurance do they tread the Crowd.
O for a Tast of such Majestick Beauty,
Which none but my hot Veins are fit t' engage;   10
Nor are my Wishes desp'rate, for ev'n now
During the Banquet I observed their Glances
Shot thick at me, and as they left the Room
Each cast by stealth a kind inviting Smile,
The happy Earnest —— ha!

Two Servants from several Entrances deliver him each a Letter,
and Exeunt.

Where merit is so Transparent, not to behold it   [*Reads.*
Were Blindness, and not to reward it Ingratitude.
                            Gonerill.
Enough! Blind, and Ingratefull should I be
Not to Obey the Summons of This Oracle.   19
Now for a Second Letter.   [*Opens the other.*
If Modesty be not your Enemy, doubt not to   [*Reads.*
Find me your Friend.
                            Regan.
Excellent *Sybill!* O my glowing Blood!
I am already sick of expectation,
And pant for the Possession —— here *Gloster* comes
With Bus'ness on his Brow; be husht my Joys.

                    [*Enter* Gloster.]

    Glost. I come to seek thee, *Edmund,* to impart
A business of Importance; I knew thy loyal Heart
Is toucht to see the Cruelty of these
Ingratefull Daughters against our royal Master.   30
    Bast. Most Savage and Unnatural.
    Glost. This change in the State sits uneasie. The Commons
Repine aloud at their female Tyrants,
Already they Cry out for the re-installment
Of their good old King, whose Injuries
I fear will inflame 'em into Mutiny.

Bast. 'Tis to be hopt, not fear'd.

Glost. Thou hast it Boy, 'tis to be hopt indeed,
On me they cast their Eyes, and hourly Court me
To lead 'em on, and whilst this Head is Mine   40
I am Theirs, a little covert Craft, my Boy,
And then for open Action, 'twill be Employment
Worthy such honest daring Souls as Thine.
Thou, *Edmund,* art my trusty Emissary,
Haste on the Spur at the first break of day   ⎰ *Gives him*
With these Dispatches to the Duke of *Combray;*   ⎱ *Letters.*
You know what mortal Feuds have alwaies flam'd
Between this Duke of *Cornwall's* Family, and his;
Full Twenty thousand Mountaners
Th' invetrate Prince will send to our Assistance.   50
Dispatch; Commend us to his Grace, and Prosper.

Bast. Yes, credulous old Man,   [*Aside.*
I will commend you to his Grace,
His Grace the Duke of *Cornwall* —— instantly
To shew him these Contents in thy own Character,
And Seal'd with thy own Signet; then forthwith
The Chol'rick Duke gives Sentence on thy Life;
And to my hand thy vast Revenues fall
To glut my Pleasure that till now has starv'd.

   Gloster *going off is met by* Cordelia *entring* [*with* Arante], Bastard
                  observing at a Distance.

Cord. Turn, *Gloster,* Turn, by all the sacred Pow'rs   60
I do conjure you give my Griefs a Hearing,
You must, you shall, nay I am sure you will,
For you were always stil'd the Just and Good.

Glost. What wou'dst thou, Princess? rise and speak thy Griefs.

Cord. Nay, you shall promise to redress 'em too,
Or here I'll kneel for ever; I intreat
Thy succour for a Father and a King,
An injur'd Father and an injur'd King.

Bast. O charming Sorrow! how her Tears adorn her
Like Dew on Flow'rs, but she is Virtuous,   70
And I must quench this hopeless Fire i'th' Kindling.

Glost. Consider, Princess,
For whom thou begg'st, 'tis for the King that wrong'd Thee.

Cord. O name not that; he did not, cou'd not wrong me.
Nay muse not, *Gloster,* for it is too likely
This injur'd King e're this is past your Aid,
And gone Distracted with his savage Wrongs.
    Bast. I'll gaze no more —— and yet my Eyes are Charm'd.
    Cord. Or what if it be Worse? can there be Worse?
As 'tis too probable this furious Night   80
Has pierc'd his tender Body, the bleak Winds
And cold Rain chill'd, or Lightning struck him Dead;
If it be so your Promise is discharg'd,
And I have only one poor Boon to beg,
That you'd Convey me to his breathless Trunk,
With my torn Robes to wrap his hoary Head,
With my torn Hair to bind his Hands and Feet,
Then with a show'r of Tears
To wash his Clay-smear'd Cheeks, and Die beside him.
    Glost. Rise, fair *Cordelia,* thou has Piety   90
Enough t' attone for both thy Sisters Crimes.
I have already plotted to restore
My injur'd Master, and thy Vertue tells me
We shall succeed, and suddenly.   [*Exit.*
    Cord. Dispatch, *Arante,*
Provide me a Disguise, we'll instantly
Go seek the King, and bring him some Relief.
    Ar. How, Madam? are you Ignorant
Of what your impious Sisters have decreed?
Immediate Death for any that relieve him.   100
    Cord. I cannot dread the Furies in this case.
    Ar. In such a Night as This? Consider, Madam,
For many Miles about there's scarce a Bush
To shelter in.
    Cord. Therefore no shelter for the King,
And more our Charity to find him out:
What have not Women dar'd for vicious Love,
And we'll be shining Proofs that they can dare
For Piety as much; blow Winds, and Lightnings fall,
Bold in my Virgin Innocence, I'll flie   110
My Royal Father to Relieve, or Die.   [*Exit* [*with* Arante.]
    Bast. Provide me a Disguise, we'll instantly

Go seek the King: ——— ha! ha! a lucky change,
That Vertue which I fear'd would be my hindrance
Has prov'd the Bond to my Design;
I'll bribe two Ruffians that shall at a distance follow,
And seise 'em in some desert Place, and there
Whilst one retains her t' other shall return
T' inform me where she's Lodg'd; I'll be disguis'd too.
Whilst they are poching for me I'll to the Duke   120
With these Dispatches, then to th' Field
Where like the vig'rous *Jove* I will enjoy
This *Semele* in a Storm, 'twill deaf her Cries
Like Drums in Battle, lest her Groans shou'd pierce
My pittying Ear, and make the amorous Fight less fierce.   [*Exit.*

[ACT III, SCENE III]

Storm still. The Field Scene.
Enter Lear *and* Kent.

Kent. Here is the place, my Lord; good my Lord enter;
The Tyranny of this open Night's too rough
For Nature to endure.
    Lear.   Let me alone.
    Kent. Good my Lord, enter.
    Lear.   Wilt break my Heart?
    Kent. Beseech you, Sir.
    Lear. Thou think'st 'tis much that this contentious Storm
Invades us to the Skin; so 'tis to thee
But where the greater Malady is fixt
The lesser is scarce felt: the Tempest in my Mind
Do's from my Senses take all feeling else   10
Save what beats there. Filial Ingratitude!
Is it not as this Mouth shou'd tear this Hand

For lifting Food to't? —— but I'll punish home.
No, I will weep no more; in such a Night
To shut me out —— pour on, I will endure
In such a Night as this: O *Regan, Gonerill,*
Your old kind Father whose frank heart gave All,
O that way madness lies, let me shun that,
No more of that.

    Kent. See, my Lord, here's the Entrance.   20
    Lear. Well, I'll go in
And pass it all, I'll pray and then I'll sleep:
Poor naked Wretches wheresoe're you are,
That 'bide the pelting of this pittiless Storm,
How shall your houseless Heads and unfed Sides
Sustain this Shock? your raggedness defend you
From Seasons such as These. O I have ta'ne
Too little Care of this, take Physick, Pomp,
Expose thy self to feel what Wretches feel,
That thou may'st cast the superflux to them,   30
And shew the Heav'ns more Just.

    Edg. in the Hovell. Five Fathom and a half, poor *Tom.*
    Kent. What art thou that dost grumble there i'th' Straw?
Come forth.

        [*Enter* Edgar *disguis'd as a madman.*]
    Edg. Away! The foul Fiend follows me —— through the sharp
Haw-thorn blows the cold Wind —— Mum, Go to thy Bed and
warm Thee.——
Ha! what do I see?
By all my Griefs the poor old King bareheaded,   [*Aside.*
And drencht in this fow Storm, professing *Syren,*   40
Are all your Protestations come to this?
    Lear. Tell me, Fellow, didst thou give all to thy Daughters?
    Edg. Who gives any thing to poor *Tom,* whom the foul Fiend
has led through Fire and through Flame, through Bushes and
Boggs, that has laid Knives under his Pillow, and Halters in his
Pue, that has made him proud of Heart to ride on a Bay-trotting
Horse over four inch'd Bridges, to course his own Shadow for a
Traytor. —— bless thy five Wits, *Tom's* a cold. [*Shivers.*] Bless thee
from Whirlwinds, Star-blasting and Taking: do poor *Tom* some
Charity, whom the foul Fiend vexes —— Sa, sa, there I could have   50

him now, and there, and there agen.

Lear. Have his Daughters brought him to this pass?
Cou'dst thou save Nothing? didst thou give 'em All?

Kent. He has no Daughters, Sir.

Lear. Death, Traytor, nothing cou'd have subdu'd Nature
To such a Lowness but his unkind Daughters.

Edg. Pillicock sat upon Pillicock Hill; Hallo, hallo, hallo.

Lear. Is it the fashion that discarded Fathers
Should have such little Mercy on their Flesh?
Judicious punishment, 'twas this Flesh begot   60
Those Pelican Daughters.

Edg. Take heed of the fow Fiend, obey thy Parents, keep thy
Word justly, Swear not, commit not with Man's sworn Spouse, set
not thy sweet Heart on proud Array: *Tom's* a Cold.

Lear. What hast thou been?

Edg. A Serving-man proud of Heart, that curl'd my Hair, us'd
Perfume and Washes, that serv'd the Lust of my Mistresses Heart,
and did the Act of Darkness with her. Swore as many Oaths as I
spoke Words, and broke 'em all in the sweet Face of Heaven:
Let not the Paint, nor the Patch, nor the rushing of Silks betray   70
thy poor Heart to Woman, keep thy Foot out of Brothels, thy
Hand out of Plackets, thy Pen from Creditors Books, and defie
the foul Fiend —— still through the Hawthorn blows the cold
Wind —— Sess, Suum, Mun, Nonny, Dolphin my Boy —— hist! the
Boy, Sesey! soft let him Trot by.

Lear. Death, thou wert better in thy Grave, than thus to answer
with thy uncover'd Body this Extremity of the Sky. And yet consider him well, and Man's no more than This; Thou art indebted
to the Worm for no Silk, to the Beast for no Hide, to the Cat for
no Perfume —— ha! here's Two of us are Sophisticated; Thou art   80
the Thing it self, unaccommodated Man is no more than such a
poor bare forkt Animal as thou art.
Off, Off, ye vain Disguises, empty Lendings,
I'll be my Original Self, quick, quick, Uncase me.

Kent. Defend his Wits, good Heaven!

Lear. One point I had forgot; what's your Name?

Edg. Poor *Tom* that eats the swimming Frog, the Wall-nut, and
the Water-nut; that in the fury of his Heart when the foul Fiend
rages eats Cow-dung for Sallets, swallows the old Rat and the

Ditch-dog, that drinks the green Mantle of the standing Pool, 90
that's whipt from Tithing to Tithing; that has Three Suits to his
Back, Six Shirts to his Body,

>Horse to Ride, and Weapon to wear,
>But Rats and Mice, and such small Deer
>Have been *Tom's* Food for Seven long Year.

Beware, my Follower; Peace, Smulkin; Peace, thou foul Fiend.

Lear. One word more, but be sure true Councel; tell me, is a
Madman a Gentleman, or a Yeoman?

Kent. I fear'd 't wou'd come to This, his Wits are gone.

Edg. Fraterreto calls me, and tells me, *Nero* is an Angler in 100
the Lake of Darkness. Pray, Innocent, and beware the foul Fiend.

Lear. Right, ha! ha! was it not pleasant to have a Thousand
with red hot Spits come hizzing in upon 'em?

Edg. My Tears begin to take his part so much
They marr my Counterfeiting.

Lear. The little Dogs and all, Trey, Blanch and Sweet-heart,
see they Bark at me.

Edg. Tom will throw his Head at 'em; Avaunt ye Curs.

>Be thy Mouth or black or white,
>Tooth that poysons if it bite,   110
>Mastiff, Grey-hound, Mungrill, Grim,
>Hound or Spanniel, Brach or Hym,
>Bob-tail, Tight, or Trundle-tail,
>*Tom* will make 'em weep and wail,
>For with throwing thus my Head
>Dogs leap the Hatch, and All are fled.

Ud, de, de, de. Se, se, se. Come march to Wakes, and Fairs, and
Market-Towns, —— poor *Tom,* thy Horn is dry.

Lear. You Sir, I entertain you for One of my Hundred, only I
do not like the fashion of your Garments, you'll say they're *Persian,* 120
but no matter, let 'em be chang'd.

Enter Gloster.

Edg. This is the foul *Flibertigibet,* he begins at Curfew and
walks at first Cock, he gives the Web and the Pin, knits the Elflock,
squints the Eye, and makes the Hair-lip, mildews the white Wheat,
and hurts the poor Creature of the Earth;

>*Swithin* footed Thrice the Cold,
>He met the Night-mare and her Nine-fold,

'Twas there he did appoint her;
He bid her alight and her Troth plight,
And arroynt the Witch arroynt her.   130

Glost. What, has your Grace no better Company?

Edg. The Prince of Darkness is a Gentleman; *Modo* he is call'd, and *Mahu.*

Glost. Go with me, Sir, hard by I have a Tenant.
My Duty cannot suffer me to obey
In all your Daughters hard Commands,
Who have enjoyn'd me to make fast my Doors,
And let this Tyrannous Night take hold upon you.
Yet have I ventur'd to come seek you out,
And bring you where both Fire and Food is ready.   140

Kent. Good my Lord, take his offer.

Lear. First let me talk with this Philosopher,
Say, *Stagirite,* what is the Cause of Thunder.

Glost. Beseech you, Sir, go with me.

Lear. I'll talk a Word with this same Learned *Theban.* What is your Study?

Edg. How to prevent the Fiend, and to kill Vermin.

Lear. Let me ask you a Word in private.

Kent. His Wits are quite unsetled; Good Sir, let's force him hence.   150

Glost. Canst blame him? his Daughters seek his Death; This Bedlam
But disturbs him the more. Fellow, be gone.

Edg. Child *Rowland* to the dark Tow'r came,
His Word was still Fie, Fo, and Fum,
I smell the Bloud of a British Man. —— Oh Torture!   [*Exit.*

Glost. Now, I prethee Friend, let's take him in our Arms,
And carry him where he shall meet both Welcome,
And Protection. Good Sir, along with us.

Lear. You say right, let 'em Anatomize *Regan,* see what breeds about her Heart; is there any Cause in Nature for these hard 160 Hearts?

Kent. Beseech your Grace.

Lear. Hist! —— Make no Noise, make no Noise —— so so; we'll to Supper i' th' Morning.   [*Exeunt.*

238

[ACT III, SCENE IV]

Enter Cordelia *and* Arante.

Ar. Dear Madam, rest ye here, our search is Vain,
Look here's a shed, beseech ye, enter here.

Cord. Prethee go in thy self, seek thy own Ease,
Where the Mind's free, the Body's Delicate:
This Tempest but diverts me from the Thought
Of what wou'd hurt me more.

Enter Two Ruffians.

1. Ruff. We have dog'd 'em far enough, this Place is private,
I'll keep 'em Prisoners here within this Hovell,
Whilst you return and bring Lord *Edmund* Hither;
But help me first to House 'em.   10

2. Ruff. Nothing but this dear Devil   [*Shows Gold.*
Shou'd have drawn me through all this Tempest;
But to our Work.

               [*They seize* Cordelia *and* Arante, *who Shriek out.*
Soft, Madam, we are Friends, dispatch, I say.

Cord. Help, Murder, help! Gods! some kind Thunderbolt
To strike me Dead.

Enter Edgar.

Edg. What Cry was That? —— ha, Women seiz'd by Ruffians?
Is this a Place and Time for Villany?
Avaunt ye Bloud-hounds.   [*Drives 'em with his Quarter-staff.*

Both. The Devil, the Devil!   [*Run off.*

Edg. O speak, what are ye that appear to be   21
O' th' tender Sex, and yet unguarded Wander
Through the dead Mazes of this dreadfull Night,
Where (tho' at full) the Clouded Moon scarce darts
Imperfect Glimmerings.

Cord. First say what art thou
Our Guardian Angel, that wer't pleas'd t' assume
That horrid shape to fright the Ravishers?
We'll kneel to Thee.

Edg.   O my tumultuous Bloud!
By all my trembling Veins *Cordelia's* Voice!   30
'Tis she her self! —— My Senses sure conform
To my wild Garb, and I am Mad indeed.
   Cord. Whate're thou art, befriend a wretched Virgin,
And if thou canst direct our weary search.
   Edg. Who relieves poor *Tom,* that sleeps on the Nettle, with
the Hedge-pig for his Pillow.
                    Whilst Smug ply'd the Bellows
                    She truckt with her Fellows,
                       The Freckle-fac't Mab
                       Was a Blouze and a Drab,   40
Yet *Swithin* made *Oberon* jealous —— Oh! Torture.
   Ar. Alack, Madam, a poor wandring Lunatick.
   Cord. And yet his Language seem'd but now well temper'd.
Speak, Friend, to one more wretched than thy self,
And if thou hast one Interval of sense,
Inform us if thou canst where we may find
A poor old Man, who through this Heath has stray'd
The tedious Night —— Speak, sawest thou such a One?
   Edg. The King, her Father, whom she's come to seek   [*Aside.*
Through all the Terrors of this Night. O Gods!   50
That such amazing Piety, such Tenderness
Shou'd yet to me be Cruel ——
Yes, Fair One, such a One was lately here,
And is convey'd by some that came to seek him,
T' a Neighb'ring Cottage; but distinctly where,
I know not.
   Cord.   Blessings on 'em,
Let's find him out, *Arante,* for thou seest
We are in Heavens Protection.   [*Going off.*
   Edg. O *Cordelia!*
   Cord.   Ha! —— Thou knowst my Name.
   Edg. As you did once know *Edgar's.*
   Cord.   *Edgar!*   60
   Edg. The poor Remains of *Edgar,* what your Scorn
Has left him.
   Cord.   Do we wake, *Arante?*
   Edg. My Father seeks my Life, which I preserv'd

In hopes of some blest Minute to oblidge
Distrest *Cordelia,* and the Gods have giv'n it;
That Thought alone prevail'd with me to take
This Frantick Dress, to make the Earth my Bed,
With these bare Limbs all change of Seasons bide,
Noons scorching Heat, and Midnights piercing Cold,
To feed on Offals, and to drink with Herds,   70
To Combat with the Winds, and be the Sport
Of Clowns, or what's more wretched yet, their Pity.
  Ar. Was ever Tale so full of Misery!
  Edg. But such a Fall as this I grant was due
To my aspiring Love, for 'twas presumptuous,
Though not presumptuously persu'd;
For well you know I wore my Flames conceal'd,
And silent as the Lamps that Burn in Tombs,
'Till you perceiv'd my Grief, with modest Grace
Drew forth the Secret, and then seal'd my Pardon.   80
  Cord. You had your Pardon, nor can you Challenge more.
  Edg. What do I Challenge more?
Such Vanity agrees not with these Rags;
When in my prosp'rous State rich *Gloster's* Heir,
You silenc'd my Pretences, and enjoyn'd me
To trouble you upon that Theam no more;
Then what Reception must Love's Language find
From these bare Limbs and Beggers humble Weeds?
  Cord. Such as the Voice of Pardon to a Wretch
Condemn'd; such as the Shouts of succ'ring Forces   90
To a Town besieg'd.
  Edg. Ah! what new Method now of Cruelty?
  Cord. Come to my Arms, thou dearest, best of Men,
And take the kindest Vows that e're were spoke
By a protesting Maid.
  Edg.   Is't possible?
  Cord. By the dear Vital Stream that baths my Heart,
These hallow'd Rags of Thine, and naked Vertue,
These abject Tassels, these fantastick Shreds,
(Ridiculous ev'n to the meanest Clown)
To me are dearer than the richest Pomp   100
Of purple Monarchs.

Edg.   Generous charming Maid,
The Gods alone that made, can rate thy Worth!
This most amazing Excellence shall be
Fame's Triumph, in succeeding Ages, when
Thy bright Example shall adorn the Scene,
And teach the World Perfection.
    Cord.   Cold and weary,
We'll rest a while, *Arante,* on that Straw,
Then forward to find out the poor Old King.
    Edg. Look I have Flint and Steel, the Implements
Of wandring Lunaticks, I'll strike a Light,   110
And make a Fire beneath this Shed, to dry
Thy Storm-drencht Garments, e're thou Lie to rest thee;
Then Fierce and Wakefull as th' *Hesperian* Dragon,
I'll watch beside thee to protect thy Sleep;
Mean while, the Stars shall dart their kindest Beams,
And Angels Visit my *Cordelia's* Dreams.   [*Exeunt.*

[ACT III, SCENE V]

Scene, The Palace.
Enter Cornwall, Regan, Bastard, *Servants.* Cornwall
with Gloster's *Letters.*

    Duke. I will have my Revenge e're I depart his house.
Regan, see here, a Plot upon our State,
'Tis *Gloster's* Character, that has betray'd
His double Trust of Subject, and of Ost.
    Reg. Then double be our Vengeance, this confirms
Th' Intelligence that we now receiv'd,
That he has been this Night to seek the King;
But who, Sir, was the kind Discoverer?
    Duke. Our Eagle, quick to spy, and fierce to seize,
Our trusty *Edmund.*

Reg.   'Twas a noble Service;   10
O *Cornwall,* take him to thy deepest Trust,
And wear him as a Jewel at thy Heart.
   Bast. Think, Sir, how hard a Fortune I sustain,
That makes me thus repent of serving you!   [*Weeps.*
O that this Treason had not been, or I
Not the Discoverer.
   Duke. Edmund, Thou shalt find
A Father in our Love, and from this Minute
We call thee Earl of *Gloster;* but there yet
Remains another Justice to be done,   20
And that's to punish this discarded Traytor;
But least thy tender Nature shou'd relent
At his just Sufferings, nor brooke the Sight,
We wish thee to withdraw.
   Reg. The *Grotto,* Sir, within the lower Grove,   [*To* Edmund *aside.*
Has Privacy to suit a Mourner's Thought.
   Bast. And there I may expect a Comforter,
Ha, Madam?
   Reg.   What may happen, Sir, I know not,
But 'twas a Friends Advice.   [*Exit* Bastard.
   Duke.   Bring in the Traytour.
                Gloster *brought in.*
Bind fast his Arms.
   Glost.   What mean your Graces?   30
You are my Guests, pray do me no foul Play.
   Duke. Bind him, I say, hard, harder yet.
   Reg. Now, Traytor, thou shalt find ———
   Duke. Speak, Rebel, where hast thou sent the King?
Whom spight of our Decree thou saw'st last Night.
   Glost. I'm tide to th' Stake, and I must stand the Course.
   Reg. Say where, and why thou hast conceal'd him.
   Glost. Because I wou'd not see thy cruel Hands
Tear out his poor old Eyes, nor thy fierce Sister
Carve his anointed Flesh; but I shall see   40
The swift wing'd Vengeance overtake such Children.
   Duke. See't shalt thou never, Slaves perform your Work,
Out with those treacherous Eyes, dispatch, I say,
If thou seest Vengeance ————

Glost. He that will think to live 'till he be old,
Give me some help —— O cruel! oh! ye Gods.   [*They put out his Eyes.*
 Serv. Hold, hold, my Lord, I bar your Cruelty,
I cannot love your safety and give way
To such a barbarous Practise.
 Duke.   Ha, my Villain.
 Serv. I have been your Servant from my Infancy,   50
But better Service have I never done you
Then with this Boldness ——
 Duke.   Take thy Death, Slave.
 Serv. Nay, then Revenge whilst yet my Bloud is Warm.   [*Fight.*
 Reg. Help here —— are you not hurt, my Lord?
 Glost. *Edmund,* enkindle all the sparks of Nature
To quit this horrid Act.
 Reg. Out, treacherous Villain,
Thou call'st on him that Hates thee, it was He
That broacht thy Treason, shew'd us thy Dispatches;
There —— read, and save the *Cambrian* Prince a Labour,   60
If thy Eyes fail thee call for Spectacles.
 Glost. O my Folly!
Then *Edgar* was abus'd, kind Gods forgive me that.
 Reg. How is't, my Lord?
 Duke. Turn out that Eye-less Villain, let him smell
His way to *Cambray,* throw this Slave upon a Dunghill.
Regan, I Bleed apace, give me your Arm.   [*Exeunt.*
 Glost. All Dark and Comfortless!
Where are those various Objects that but now
Employ'd my busie Eyes? where those Eyes?   70
Dead are their piercing Rays that lately shot
O're flowry Vales to distant Sunny Hills,
And drew with Joy the vast Horizon in.
These groping Hands are now my only Guids,
And Feeling all my Sight.
O Misery! what words can sound my Grief?
Shut from the Living whilst among the Living;
Dark as the Grave amidst the bustling World.
At once from Business and from Pleasure bar'd;
No more to view the Beauty of the Spring,   80
Nor see the Face of Kindred, or of Friend.

Yet still one way th' extreamest Fate affords,
And ev'n the Blind can find the Way to Death.
Must I then tamely Die, and unreveng'd?
So *Lear* may fall: No, with these bleeding Rings
I will present me to the pittying Crowd,
And with the Rhetorick of these dropping Veins
Enflame 'em to Revenge their King and me;
Then when the Glorious Mischief is on Wing,
This Lumber from some Precipice I'll throw,   90
And dash it on the ragged Flint below;
Whence my freed Soul to her bright Sphear shall fly,⎫
Through boundless Orbs, eternal Regions spy,   ⎬
And like the Sun, be All one glorious Eye.   ⎭   [*Exit.*

ACT IV, [SCENE I]

A Grotto.

Edmund *and* Regan *amorously Seated, Listning to Musick.*

Bast. Why were those Beauties made Another's Right
Which None can prize like Me? charming Queen
Take all my blooming Youth, for ever fold me
In those soft Arms, Lull me in endless Sleep
That I may dream of pleasures too transporting
For Life to bear.
    Reg.   Live, live, my *Gloster,*
And feel no Death but that of swooning joy,
I yield thee Blisses on no harder Terms
Than that thou continue to be Happy.
    Bast. This Jealousie is yet more kind, is't possible   10
That I should wander from a Paradise
To feed on sickly Weeds? such Sweets live here
That Constancy will no Vertue in me,

And yet must I forthwith go meet her Sister,   *[Aside.*
To whom I must protest as much ——
Suppose it be the same; why best of all,
And I have then my Lesson ready conn'd.
 Reg. Wear this Remembrance of me ——I dare now
         [Gives him a Ring.
Absent my self no longer from the Duke
Whose Wound grows Dangerous —— I hope Mortal. 20
 Bast. And let this happy Image of your *Gloster,*
    [Pulling out a Picture drops a Note.
Lodge in that Breast where all his Treasure lies. *[Exit.*
 Reg. To this brave Youth a Womans blooming beauties
Are due: my Fool usurps my Bed —— What's here?
Confusion on my Eyes.   *[Reads.*
Where Merit is so Transparent, not to behold it were Blindness,
and not to reward it, Ingratitude.
      Gonerill.
Vexatious Accident! yet Fortunate too,
My Jealousie's confirm'd, and I am taught
To cast for my Defence ——   *[Enter an Officer.*
Now, what mean those Shouts? and what thy hasty Entrance? 31
 Off. A most surprizing and a sudden Change,
The Peasants are all up in Mutiny,
And only want a Chief to lead 'em on
To Storm your Palace.
 Reg.   On what Provocation?
 Off. At last day's publick Festival, to which
The Yeomen from all Quarters had repair'd,
Old *Gloster,* whom you late depriv'd of Sight,
(His Veins yet Streaming fresh) presents himself,
Proclaims your Cruelty, and their Oppression, 40
With the King's Injuries; which so enrag'd 'em,
That now that Mutiny which long had crept
Takes Wing, and threatens your Best Pow'rs.
 Reg. White-liver'd Slave!
Our Forces rais'd and led by Valiant *Edmund,*
Shall drive this Monster of Rebellion back
To her dark Cell; young *Gloster's* Arm allays
The Storm, his Father's feeble Breath did Raise. *[Exeunt.*

[ACT IV, SCENE II]

The Field Scene
Enter Edgar.

Edg. The lowest and most abject Thing of Fortune
Stands still in Hope, and is secure from Fear,
The lamentable Change is from the Best,
The Worst returns to Better —— who comes here?

Enter Gloster, *led by an old Man.*

My Father poorly led? depriv'd of Sight,
The precious Stones torn from their bleeding Rings!
Some-thing I heard of this inhumane Deed
But disbeliev'd it, as an Act too horrid
For the hot Hell of a curst Woman's fury,
When will the measure of my woes be full?   10

Glost. Revenge, thou art afoot, Success attend Thee.
Well have I sold my Eyes, if the Event
Prove happy for the injur'd King.

Old M. O, my good Lord, I have been your Tenant, and your
Father's Tenant these Fourscore years.

Glost. Away, get thee Away, good Friend, be gone,
Thy Comforts can do me no good at All,
Thee they may hurt.

Old M.   You cannot see your Way.

Glost. I have no Way, and therefore want no Eyes,
I stumbled when I saw: O dear Son *Edgar,*   20
The Food of thy abused Father's Wrath,
Might I but live to see thee in my Touch
I'd say, I had Eyes agen.

Edg. Alas, he's sensible that I was wrong'd,
And shou'd I own my Self, his tender Heart
Would break betwixt th' extreams of Grief and Joy.

Old M. How now, who's There?

Edg. A Charity for poor *Tom.* Play fair, and defie the foul
    Fiend.

O Gods! and must I still persue this Trade,   [*Aside.*
Trifling beneath such Loads of Misery?   30
    Old M. 'Tis poor mad *Tom.*
    Glost. In the late Storm I such a Fellow saw,
Which made me think a Man a Worm,
Where is the Lunatick?
    Old M.   Here, my Lord.
    Glost. Get thee now away, if for my sake
Thou wilt o're-take us hence a Mile or Two
I' th' way tow'rd *Dover,* do't for ancient Love,
And bring some cov'ring for this naked Wretch
Whom I'll intreat to lead me.
    Old M. Alack, my Lord, He's Mad.   40
    Glost. 'Tis the Time's Plague when Mad-men lead the Blind.
Do as I bid thee.
    Old M. I'll bring him the best 'Parrel that I have
Come on't what will.   [*Exit.*
    Glost.   Sirrah, naked Fellow.
    Edg. Poor *Tom's* a cold; —— I cannot fool it longer,
And yet I must —— bless thy sweet Eyes they Bleed,
Believe't poor *Tom* ev'n weeps his Blind to see 'em.
    Glost. Know'st thou the way to *Dover?*
    Edg. Both Stile and Gate, Horse-way and Foot-path, poor *Tom*
has been scar'd out of his good Wits; bless every true Man's Son   50
from the foul Fiend.
    Glost. Here, take this Purse, that I am wretched
Makes thee the Happier, Heav'n deal so still.
Thus let the griping Userers Hoard be Scatter'd,
So Distribution shall undo Excess,
And each Man have enough. Dost thou know *Dover?*
    Edg. I, Master.
    Glost. There is a Cliff, whose high and bending Head
Looks dreadfully down on the roaring Deep.
Bring me but to the very Brink of it,   60
And I'll repair the Poverty thou bearst
With something Rich about me, from that Place
I shall no leading need.
    Edg. Give me thy Arm: poor *Tom* shall guid thee.
    Glost. Soft, for I hear the Tread of Passengers.

Enter Kent *and* Cordelia.

Cord. Ah me! your Fear's too true, it was the King;
I spoke but now with some that met him
As Mad as the vext Sea, Singing aloud,
Crown'd with rank Femiter and furrow Weeds,
With Berries, Burdocks, Violets, Dazies, Poppies,   70
And all the idle Flow'rs that grow
In our sustaining Corn, conduct me to him
To prove my last Endeavours to restore him,
And Heav'n so prosper thee.
   Kent.   I will, good Lady.
Ha, *Gloster* here! ——— turn, poor dark Man, and hear
A Friend's Condolement, who at Sight of thine
Forgets his own Distress, thy old true *Kent.*
   Glost. How, *Kent*? from whence return'd?
   Kent. I have not since my Banishment been absent,
But in Disguise follow'd the abandon'd King;   80
'Twas me thou saw'st with him in the late Storm.
   Glost. Let me embrace thee, had I Eyes I now
Should weep for Joy, but let this trickling Blood
Suffice instead of Tears.
   Cord.   O misery!
To whom shall I complain, or in what Language?
Forgive, O wretched Man, the Piety
That brought thee to this pass, 'twas I that caus'd it,
I cast me at thy Feet, and beg of thee
To crush these weeping Eyes to equal Darkness,
If that will give thee any Recompence.   90
   Edg. Was ever Season so distrest as This?   [*Aside.*
   Glost. I think *Cordelia's* Voice! rise, pious Princess,
And take a dark Man's Blessing.
   Cord.   O, my *Edgar,*
My Vertue's now grown Guilty, works the Bane
Of those that do befriend me, Heav'n forsakes me,
And when you look that Way, it is but Just
That you shou'd hate me too.
   Edg. O wave this cutting Speech, and spare to wound
A Heart that's on the Rack.
   Glost. No longer cloud thee, *Kent,* in that Disguise,   100

There's business for thee and of noblest weight;
Our injur'd Country is at length in Arms,
Urg'd by the King's inhumane Wrongs and Mine,
And only want a Chief to lead 'em on.
That Task be Thine.
    Edg. Brave *Britains* then there's Life in't yet.   *[Aside.*
    Kent. Then have we one cast for our Fortune yet.
Come, Princess, I'll bestow you with the King,
Then on the Spur to Head these Forces.
Farewell, good *Gloster,* to our Conduct trust.   110
    Glost. And be your Cause as Prosp'rous as tis Just.   *[Exeunt.*

[ACT IV, SCENE III]

Gonerill's *Palace.*

Enter Gonerill, *Attendants.*

    Gon. It was great Ignorance *Gloster's* Eyes being out
To let him live, where he arrives he moves
All Hearts against us, *Edmund* I think is gone
In pity to his Misery to dispatch him.
    Gent. No, Madam, he's return'd on speedy Summons
Back to your Sister.
    Gon.   Ha! I like not That,
Such speed must have the Wings of Love; where's *Albany*?
    Gent. Madam, within, but never Man so chang'd;
I told him of the uproar of the Peasants,
He smil'd at it, when I inform'd him   10
Of *Gloster's* Treason ——
    Gon.   Trouble him no further,
It is his coward Spirit, back to our Sister,
Hasten her Musters, and let her know I have giv'n
The Distaff into my Husband's Hands. That done,
With special Care deliver these Dispatches
In private to young *Gloster.*

Enter a Messenger.

Mess. O Madam, most unseasonable News,
The Duke of *Cornwall's* Dead of his late Wound,
Whose loss your Sister has in part supply'd,
Making brave *Edmund* General of her Forces.   20
    Gon. One way I like this well;
But being Widow and my *Gloster* with her
May blast the promis'd Harvest of our Love.
A word more, Sir, — add Speed to your Journey,
And if you chance to meet with that blind Traytor,
Preferment falls on him that cuts him off.   *[Exeunt.*

[ACT IV, SCENE IV]

Field Scene.

[Enter] Gloster *and* Edgar.

Glost. When shall we come to th' Top of that same Hill?
Edg. We climb it now, mark how we Labour.
Glost. Methinks the Ground is even.
Edg. Horrible Steep; heark, do you hear the Sea?
Glost. No truly.
Edg. Why then your other Senses grow imperfect,
By your Eyes Anguish.
    Glost.   So may it be indeed.
Methinks thy Voice is alter'd, and thou speak'st
In better Phrase and Matter than thou did'st.
    Edg. You are much deceiv'd, in nothing am I Alter'd   10
But in my Garments.
    Glost.   Methinks y'are better Spoken.
    Edg. Come on, Sir, here's the Place, how fearfull
And dizy 'tis to cast one's Eyes so Low.
The Crows and Choughs that wing the Mid-way Air
Shew scarce so big as Beetles, half way down

Hangs one that gathers Sampire, dreadfull Trade!
The Fisher-men that walk upon the Beach
Appear like Mice, and yon tall Anch'ring Barque
Seems lessen'd to her Cock, her Cock a Buoy
Almost too small for Sight; the murmuring Surge   20
Cannot be heard so high, I'll look no more
Lest my Brain turn, and the disorder make me
Tumble down head long.
   Glost. Set me where you stand.
   Edg. You are now within a Foot of th' extream Verge.
For all beneath the Moon I wou'd not now
Leap forward.
   Glost.   Let go my Hand,
Here, Friend, is another Purse, in it a Jewel
Well worth a poor Man's taking; get thee further,
Bid me Farewell, and let me hear thee going.   30
   Edg. Fare you well, Sir, —— that I do Trifle thus
With this his Despair is with Design to cure it.
   Glost. Thus, mighty Gods, this World I do renounce,
And in your Sight shake my Afflictions off;
If I cou'd bear 'em longer and not fall
To quarrel with your great opposeless Wills,
My Snuff and feebler Part of Nature shou'd
Burn it self out; if *Edgar* Live, O Bless him.
Now, Fellow, fare thee well.
   Edg.   Gone, Sir! Farewell.
And yet I know not how Conceit may rob   40
The Treasury of Life, had he been where
He thought, by this had Thought been past —— Alive,
Or Dead? Hoa Sir, Friend; hear you, Sir, speak ——
Thus might he pass indeed —— yet he revives.
What are you, Sir?
   Glost.   Away, and let me Die.
   Edg. Hadst thou been ought but Gosmore, Feathers, Air,
Falling so many Fathom down thou hadst Shiver'd like an Egg;
But thou dost breath, hast heavy Substance, bleedst not,
Speak'st, art sound; Thy Live's a Miracle.
   Glost. But have I faln or no?   50
   Edg. From the dread Summet of this chalky Bourn:

Look up an Height, the Shrill-tun'd Lark so high
Cannot be seen, or heard; do but look up.
   Glost. Alack, I have no Eyes.
Is wretchedness depriv'd that Benefit
To End it self by Death?
   Edg.   Give me your Arm.
Up, so, how is't? feel you your Legs? you stand.
   Glost. Too well, too well.
   Edg. Upon the Crown o'th' Cliff, what Thing was that
Which parted from you?
   Glost.   A poor unfortunate Begger.   60
   Edg. As I stood here below, me-thought his Eyes
Were two Full Moons, wide Nostrils breathing Fire.
It was some Fiend, therefore thou happy Father,
Think that th'all-powerfull Gods who make them Honours
Of Mens Impossibilities have preserv'd thee.
   Glost. 'Tis wonderfull; henceforth I'll bear Affliction
Till it expire; the Goblin which you speak of,
I took it for a Man: oft-times 'twould say,
The Fiend, the Fiend: He led me to that Place.
   Edg. Bear free and patient Thoughts: but who comes here?   70

      Enter Lear, *a Coronet of Flowers on his Head. Wreaths*
              and Garlands about him.

   Lear. No, no, they cannot touch me for Coyning, I am the
King Himself.
   Edg. O piercing Sight.
   Lear. Nature's above Art in that Respect; There's your Press-
money: that Fellow handles his Bow like a Cow-keeper,————
draw me a Clothier's yard. A mouse, a Mouse; peace hoa: there's
my Gauntlet, I'll prove it on a Giant: bring up the brown Bills:
O well flown Bird; i'th' White, i'th' White —— Hewgh! give the
Word.
   Edg. Sweet *Marjorum.*   80
   Lear. Pass.
   Glost. I know that Voice.
   Lear. Ha! *Gonerill* with a white Beard! they flatter'd me like a
Dog, and told me I had white Hairs on my Chin, before the Black
ones were there; to say I and No to every thing that I said, I and
No too was no good Divinity. When the Rain came once to wet

me, and the Winds to make me Chatter; when the Thunder wou'd
not Peace at my Bidding. There I found 'em, there I smelt 'em
out; go too, they are not men of their words, They told me I was
a King, 'tis a Lie, I am not Ague proof.   90

    Glost. That Voice I well remember, is't not the King's?

    Lear. I, every Inch a King, when I do Stare
See how the Subject quakes.
I pardon that Man's Life, what was the Cause?
Adultery? Thou shalt not Die. Die for Adultery!
The Wren goes to't, and the small gilded Flie
Engenders in my Sight: Let Copulation thrive,
For *Gloster's* Bastard Son was kinder to his Father
Than were my Daughters got i'th'lawfull Bed.
To't Luxury, pell mell, for I lack Souldiers.   100

    Glost. Not all my Sorrows past so deep have toucht me,
As the sad Accents: Sight were now a Torment ——

    Lear. Behold that simp'ring Lady, she that starts
At Pleasure's Name, and thinks her Ear profan'd
With the least wanton Word, wou'd you believe it,
The Fitcher nor the pamper'd Steed goes to't
With such a riotous Appetite: down from the Wast they are
Centaurs, tho Women all Above; but to the Girdle do the Gods
inherit, beneath is all the Fiends; There's Hell, there's Darkness,
the Sulphurous unfathom'd —— Fie! fie! pah! —— an Ounce of 110
Civet, good Apothecary, to sweeten my Imagination —— There's
Money for thee.

    Glost. Let me kiss that Hand.

    Lear. Let me wipe it first; it smells of Mortality.

    Glost. Speak, Sir; do you know me?

    Lear. I remember thy Eyes well enough: Nay, do thy worst,
blind *Cupid,* I'll not Love —— read me this Challenge, mark but
the penning of it.

    Glost. Were all the Letters Suns I cou'd not see.

    Edg. I wou'd not take this from Report: wretched *Cordelia,* 120
What will thy Vertue do when thou shalt find
This fresh Affliction added to the Tale
Of thy unparrallel'd Griefs.

    Lear. Read.

    Glost. What! with this Case of Eyes?

Lear. O ho! are you there with me? no Eyes in your Head, and no money in your Purse? yet you see how this World goes.

Glost. I see it Feelingly.

Lear. What? art Mad? a Man may see how this World goes with no Eyes. Look with thy Ears, see how yon Justice rails on 130 that simple Thief; shake 'em together, and the first that drops, be it Thief or Justice, is a Villain. —— Thou hast seen a Farmer's Dog bark at a Beggar.

Glost. I, Sir.

Lear. And the Man ran from the Curr; there thou mightst behold the great Image of Authority, a Dog's obey'd in Office. Thou Rascal, Beadle, hold thy bloody Hand, why dost thou Lash that Strumpet? thou hotly Lust'st to enjoy her in that kind for which thou whipst her, do, do, the Judge that sentenc'd her has been before-hand with thee.   140

Glost. How stiff is my vile Sense that yields not yet?

Lear. I tell thee the Usurer hangs the Couz'ner, through tatter'd Robes small Vices do appear, Robes and Fur-gowns hide All: Place Sins with Gold, why there 'tis for thee, my Friend, make much of it, it has the Pow'r to seal the Accuser's Lips. Get thee glass Eyes, and like a scurvy Politician, seem to see the Things thou dost not. Pull, pull off my Boots, hard, harder, so, so.

Glost. O Matter and Impertinency mixt!
Reason in Madness.

Lear. If thou wilt weep my Fortunes take my Eyes,   150
I know thee well enough, thy Name is *Gloster.*
Thou must be patient, we came Crying hither
Thou knowst, the first time that We tast the Air
We Wail and Cry —— I'll preach to thee, Mark.

Edg. Break lab'ring Heart.

Lear. When we are Born we Cry that we are come
To this great Stage of Fools. ——

Enter Two or Three Gentlemen.

Gent. O here he is, lay hand upon him, Sir,
Your dearest Daughter sends ——

Lear. No Rescue? what, a Prisoner? I am even the natural 160 Fool of Fortune: Use me well, you shall have Ransome —— let me have Surgeons, Oh I am cut to th' Brains.

Gent. You shall have any Thing.

Lear. No Second's? all my Self? I will Die bravely like a smug Bridegroom, flusht and pamper'd as a Priest's Whore. I am a King, my Masters, know ye that?

Gent. You are a Royal one, and we Obey you.

Lear. It were an excellent Stratagem to Shoe a Troop of Horse with Felt, I'll put in proof —— no Noise, no Noise —— now will we steal upon these Sons in Law, and then —— Kill, kill, kill, kill!   170

[Exit Running.

Glost. A Sight most moving in the meanest Wretch,
Past speaking in a King. Now, good Sir, what are you?

Edg. A most poor Man made tame to Fortune's strokes,
And prone to Pity by experienc'd Sorrows; give me your Hand.

Glost. You ever gentle Gods take my Breath from me,
And let not my ill Genius tempt me more
To Die before you please.

Enter Gonerill's *Gentleman-Usher.*

Gent. A proclaim'd Prize, O most happily met,
That Eye-less Head of thine was first fram'd Flesh
To raise my Fortunes; Thou old unhappy Traytor,   180
The Sword is out that must Destroy thee.

Glost. Now let thy friendly Hand put Strength enough to't.

Gent. Wherefore, bold Peasant,
Darst thou support a publisht Traytor, hence,
Lest I destroy Thee too. Let go his Arm.

Edg. 'Chill not Let go Zir, without 'vurther 'Casion.

Gent. Let go Slave, or thou Dyest.

Edg. Good Gentleman go your Gate, and let poor Volk pass, and 'Chu'd ha' bin Zwagger'd out of my Life it wou'd not a bin zo long as 'tis by a Vort-night —— Nay, an' thou com'st near th' old   190
Man, I'ce try whether your Costard or my Ballow be th' harder.

Gent. Out, Dunghill.

Edg. 'Chill pick your Teeth, Zir; Come, no matter vor your Voines.   *[They fight.]*

Gent. Slave, thou hast Slain me; oh untimely Death.

Edg. I know thee well, a serviceable Villain,
As duteous to the Vices of thy Mistress
As Lust cou'd wish.

Glost. What, is he Dead?
Edg.   Sit you, Sir, and rest you.
This is a Letter Carrier, and may have   200
Some Papers of Intelligence that may stand
Our Party in good stead, to know —— what's here?
              [*Takes a Letter out of his Pocket, opens, and reads.*
To *Edmund* Earl of *Gloster.*
  Let our Mutual Loves be remembred, you have many oppor-
  tunities to Cut him off, if he return the Conqueror then I
  am still a Prisoner, and his Bed my Goal, from the loath'd
  Warmth of which deliver me, and supply the Place for your
  Labour.   Gonerill.
A Plot upon her Husband's Life,
And the Exchange my Brother —— here i'th' Sands   210
I'll rake thee up thou Messenger of Lust,
Griev'd only that thou hadst no other Deaths-man.
In Time and Place convenient I'll produce
These Letters to the Sight of th' injur'd Duke
As best shall serve our Purpose; Come, your Hand.
Far off methinks I hear the beaten Drum,
Come, Sir, I will bestow you with a Friend.   [*Exeunt.*

[ACT IV, SCENE V]

A Chamber. Lear *a Sleep on a Couch;* Cordelia, [*Physician,*] *and*
Attendants standing by him.
  Cord. His Sleep is sound, and may have good Effect
To Cure his jarring Senses, and repair
This Breach of Nature.
  Phys. We have employ'd the utmost Pow'r of Art,
And this deep Rest will perfect our Design.
  Cord. O *Regan, Gonerill,* inhumane Sisters,

Had he not been your Father, these white Hairs
Had challeng'd sure some pity, was this a Face
To be expos'd against the jarring Winds?
My Enemy's Dog though he had bit me shou'd   10
Have stood that Night against my Fire —— he wakes,
Speak to him.
  Gent. Madam, do you, 'tis fittest.
  Cord. How do's my royal Lord? how fares your Majesty?
  Lear. You do me wrong to take me out o'th'Grave.
Ha! is this too a World of Cruelty?
I know my Priviledge, think not that I will
Be us'd still like a wretched Mortal, no,
No more of That.
  Cord. Speak to me, Sir, who am I?
  Lear. You are a Soul in Bliss, but I am bound
Upon a wheel of Fire, which my own Tears   20
Do scald like Molten Lead.
  Cord.   Sir, do you know me?
  Lear. You are a Spirit, I know, where did you Die?
  Cord. Still, still, far wide.
  Phys. Madam, he's scarce awake; he'll soon grow more
   compos'd.
  Lear. Where have I been? where am I? fair Day-light!
I am mightily abus'd, I shou'd ev'n Die with pity
To see Another thus. I will not swear
These are my Hands.
  Cord. O look upon me, Sir,
And hold your Hands in Blessing o're me, nay,
You must not kneel.
  Lear. Pray do not mock me.   30
I am a very foolish fond Old Man,
Fourscore and upward, and to deal plainly
With you, I fear I am not in my perfect Mind.
  Cord. Nay, then farewell to patience; witness for me
Ye mighty Pow'rs, I ne're complain'd till now!
  Lear. Methinks I shou'd know you, and know this Man,
Yet I am Doubtfull, for I am mainly Ignorant
What Place this is, and all the skill I have

Remembers not these Garments, nor do I know
Where I did Sleep last Night —— pray do not mock me ——   40
For, as I am a Man, I think that Lady
To be my Child *Cordelia.*
    Cord. O my dear, dear Father!
    Lear. Be your Tears wet? yes faith; pray do not weep,
I know I have giv'n thee Cause, and am so humbled
With Crosses since, that I cou'd ask
Forgiveness of thee were it possible
That thou cou'dst grant it, but I'm well assur'd
Thou canst not; therefore I do stand thy Justice,
If thou hast Poyson for me I will Drink it,   50
Bless thee and Die.
    Cord. O pity, Sir, a bleeding Heart, and cease
This killing Language.
    Lear.   Tell me, Friends, where am I?
    Gent. In your own Kingdom, Sir.
    Lear.   Do not Abuse me.
    Gent. Be comforted, good Madam, for the Violence
Of his Distemper's past; we'll lead him in
Nor trouble him, till he is better Setled.
Wilt please you, Sir, walk into freer Air.
    Lear. You must bear with me, I am Old and Foolish.
                                      [They lead him off.
    Cord. The Gods restore you ——   60
Heark, I hear afar the beaten Drum,
Old *Kent's* a Man of's Word. O for an Arm
Like the fierce Thunderer's, when th' earth-born Sons
Storm'd Heav'n, to fight this injur'd Father's Battle.
That I cou'd shift my Sex, and die me deep
In his Opposer's Blood, but as I may
With Womens Weapons, Piety and Pray'rs,
I'll aid his Cause —— You never-erring Gods
Fight on his side, and Thunder on his Foes
Such Tempest as his poor ag'd Head sustain'd;   70
Your Image suffers when a Monarch bleeds.
'Tis your own Cause, for that your Succours bring,
Revenge your Selves, and right an injur'd King.   *[Exeunt.]*

ACT V, [SCENE I]

Scene, A Camp.
Enter Gonerill *and Attendants.*

Gon. Our Sisters Pow'rs already are arriv'd,
And She her self has promis'd to prevent
The Night with her Approach: have you provided
The Banquet I bespoke for her Reception
At my Tent?
    Att.   So, please your Grace, we have.
    Gon. But thou, my Poysner, must prepare the Bowl
That Crowns this Banquet, when our Mirth is high,
The Trumpets sounding and the Flutes replying,
Then is the Time to give this fatal Draught
To this imperious Sister; if then our Arms succeed,   10
Edmund more dear than Victory is mine.
But if Defeat or Death it self attend me,
'Twill charm my Ghost to think I've left behind me   [*Trumpet.*
No happy Rival: heark, she comes.   [*Exeunt.*

[ACT V, SCENE II]

Enter Bastard *in his Tent.*

    Bast. To both these Sisters have I sworn my Love,
Each jealous of the other, as the Stung
Are of the Adder; neither can be held
If both remain Alive; where shall I fix?
Cornwall is Dead, and *Regan's* empty Bed
Seems cast by Fortune for me, but already

I have enjoy'd her, and bright *Gonerill*
With equal Charms brings dear variety,
And yet untasted Beauty: I will use
Her Husband's Countenance for the Battail, then   10
Usurp at once his Bed and Throne.

> *Enter Officers.*

My trusty Scouts y'are well return'd, have ye descry'd
The Strength and Posture of the Enemy?
    Off. We have, and were surpriz'd to find
The banisht *Kent* return'd, and at their Head;
Your Brother *Edgar* on the Rear; Old *Gloster*
(A moving Spectacle) led through their Ranks,
Whose pow'rfull Tongue, and more prevailing Wrongs,
Have so enrag'd their rustick Spirits, that with
Th'approaching Dawn we must expect their Battle.   20
    Bast. You bring a welcome Hearing; Each to his Charge.
Line well your Ranks and stand on your Award,
To Night repose you, and i'th'Morn we'll give
The Sun a Sight that shall be worth his Rising.   [*Exeunt.*

[ACT V, SCENE III]

> *Scene, A Valley near the Camp.*
> *Enter* Edgar *and* Gloster.

    Edg. Here, Sir, take you the shadow of this Tree
For your good Host, pray that the Right may thrive:
If ever I return to you again
I'll bring you Comfort.   [*Exit.*
    Glost.   Thanks, friendly Sir;
The Fortune your good Cause deserves betide you.

> *An Alarum, after which* Gloster *speaks.*

The Fight grows hot; the whole War's now at Work,
And the goar'd Battle bleeds in every Vein,

Whilst Drums and Trumpets drown loud Slaughter's Roar:
Where's *Gloster* now that us'd to head the Fray,
And scour the Ranks where deadliest Danger lay?   10
Here like a Shepherd in a lonely Shade,
Idle, unarm'd, and listning to the Fight.
Yet the disabled Courser, Maim'd and Blind,
When to his Stall he hears the ratling War,
Foaming with Rage tears up the batter'd Ground,
And tugs for Liberty.
No more of Shelter, thou blind Worm, but forth
To th' open Field; the War may come this way
And crush thee into Rest. —— Here lay thee down
And tear the Earth, that work befits a Mole.   20
O dark Despair! when, *Edgar,* wilt thou come
To pardon and dismiss me to the Grave!   [*A Retreat sounded.*
Heark! a Retreat, the King has Lost or Won.

Re-enter Edgar, *bloody.*

Edg. Away, old Man, give me your Hand, away!
King *Lear* has lost, He and his Daughter tane,
And this, ye Gods, is all that I can save
Of this most precious Wreck: give me your Hand.
    Glost. No farther, Sir, a Man may Rot even here.
    Edg. What? in ill Thoughts again? Men must endure
Their going hence ev'n as their coming hither.   30
    Glost. And that's true too.   [*Exeunt.*

[ACT V, SCENE IV]

Flourish. Enter in Conquest, Albany, Gonerill, Regan, Bastard. ——
Lear, Kent, Cordelia *Prisoners.*

    Alb. It is enough to have Conquer'd, Cruelty
Shou'd ne're survive the Fight, Captain o'th'Guards
Treat well your royal Prisoners till you have

Our further Orders, as you hold our Pleasure.
   Gon. Heark, Sir, not as you hold our Husbands pleasure
                                 [To the Captain aside.
But as you hold your Life, dispatch your Pris'ners.
Our Empire can have no sure Settlement
But in their Death, the Earth that covers them
Binds fast our Throne. Let me hear they are Dead.
   Capt. I shall obey your Orders.   10
   Bast. Sir, I approve it safest to pronounce
Sentence of Death upon this wretched King,
Whose Age has Charms in it, his Title more,
To draw the Commons once more to his Side,
'Twere best prevent ——
   Alb.   Sir, by your Favour,
I hold you but a Subject of this War,
Not as a Brother.
   Reg.   That's as we list to Grace him.
Have you forgot that He did lead our Pow'rs?
Bore the Commission of our Place and Person?
And that Authority may well stand up   20
And call it self your Brother.
   Gon.   Not so hot,
In his own Merits he exalts himself
More than in your Addition.
                 Enter Edgar, *disguised.*
   Alb. What art Thou?
   Edg. Pardon me, Sir, that I presume to stop
A Prince and Conquerour, yet e'er you Triumph,
Give Ear to what a Stranger can deliver
Of what concerns you more than Triumph can.
I do impeach your General there of Treason,
Lord *Edmund,* that usurps the Name of *Gloster,*   30
Of fowlest Practice 'gainst your Life and Honour;
This Charge is True, and wretched though I seem
I can produce a Champion that will prove
In single Combat what I do avouch;
If *Edmund* dares but trust his Cause and Sword.
   Bast. What will not *Edmund* dare, my Lord, I beg

The favour that you'd instantly appoint
The Place where I may meet this Challenger,
Whom I will sacrifice to my wrong'd Fame,
Remember, Sir, that injur'd Honour's nice   40
And cannot brook delay.

    Alb. Anon, before our Tent, i'th' Army's view,
There let the Herald cry.

    Edg. I thank your Highness in my Champion's Name,
He'll wait your Trumpet's call.

    Alb.   Lead.   *[Exeunt.*
               Manent Lear, Kent, Cordelia, *guarded.*
    Lear. O *Kent, Cordelia!*
You are the onely Pair that I e'er wrong'd,
And the just Gods have made you Witnesses
Of my Disgrace, the very shame of Fortune,
To see me chain'd and shackled at these years!   50
Yet were you but Spectatours of my Woes,
Not fellow-sufferers, all were well!

    Cord. This language, Sir, adds yet to our Affliction.

    Lear. Thou, *Kent,* didst head the Troops that fought my Battel,
Expos'd thy Life and Fortunes for a Master
That had (as I remember) banisht Thee.

    Kent. Pardon me, Sir, that once I broke your Orders,
Banisht by you, I kept me here disguis'd
To watch your Fortunes, and protect your Person,
You know you entertain'd a rough blunt Fellow,   60
One *Cajus,* and you thought he did you Service.

    Lear. My trusty *Cajus,* I have lost him too!   *[Weeps.*
'Twas a rough Honesty.

    Kent.   I was that *Cajus,*
Disguis'd in that course Dress to follow you.

    Lear. My *Cajus* too! wer't thou my trusty *Cajus,*
Enough, enough ——

    Cord. Ah me, he faints! his Blood forsakes his Cheek,
Help, *Kent* ——

    Lear.   No, no, they shall not see us weep,
We'll see them rot first, —— Guards lead away
To Prison, come, *Kent, Cordelia* come,   70

We Two will sit alone, like Birds i'th' Cage,
When Thou dost ask me Blessing, I'll kneel down
And ask of Thee Forgiveness; Thus we'll live,
And Pray, and Sing, and tell old Tales, and Laugh
At gilded Butter-flies, hear Sycophants
Talk of Court News, and we'll talk with them too,
Who loses, and who wins, who's in, who's out,
And take upon us the Mystery of Things
As if we were Heav'ns Spies.
   Cord. Upon such Sacrifices   80
The Gods themselves throw Incense.
    Lear.   Have I caught ye?
He that parts us must bring a Brand from Heav'n.
Together we'll out-toil the spight of Hell,
And Die the Wonders of the World; Away.   *[Exeunt, guarded.*

[ACT V, SCENE V]

Flourish: Enter before the Tents, Albany, Gonerill, Regan,
Guards and Attendants; Gonerill *speaking apart to the
Captain of the Guards entring.*

   Gon. Here's Gold for Thee, Thou knowst our late Command
Upon your Pris'ners Lives, about it streight, and at
Our Ev'ning Banquet let it raise our Mirth
To hear that They are Dead.
   Capt. I shall not fail your Orders.   *[Exit.*
               [Albany, Gonerill, Regan take their Seats.
   Alb. Now, *Gloster,* trust to thy single Vertue,
For thy Souldiers, all levied in my Name,
Have in my Name took their Discharge; now let
Our Trumpets speak, and Herald read out This.
                          [Herald Reads.
If any Man of Quality, within the Lists of the Army, will main- 10

tain upon Edmund, *suppos'd Earl of* Gloster, *that he is a manifold Traytour, let him appear by the third sound of the Trumpet; He is bold in his Defence.* —— *Agen, Agen.*

                           [Trumpet Answers from within.

                 Enter Edgar, *Arm'd.*

  Alb. Lord *Edgar!*
  Bast.   Ha! my Brother!
This is the onely Combatant that I cou'd fear;
For in my Breast Guilt Duels on his side,
But, Conscience, what have I to do with Thee?
Awe Thou thy dull Legitimate Slaves, but I
Was born a Libertine, and so I keep me.
  Edg. My noble Prince, a word —— e'er we engage   20
Into your Highness's Hands I give this Paper,
It will the truth of my Impeachment prove
Whatever be my fortune in the Fight.
  Alb. We shall peruse it.
  Edg. Now, *Edmund,* draw thy Sword,
That if my Speech has wrong'd a noble Heart,
Thy Arm may doe thee Justice: here i'th' presence
Of this high Prince, these Queens, and this crown'd List,
I brand thee with the spotted name of Traytour,
False to thy Gods, thy Father and thy Brother,   30
And what is more, thy Friend; false to this Prince:
If then Thou shar'st a spark of *Gloster's* Vertue,
Acquit thy self, or if Thou shar'st his Courage,
Meet this Defiance bravely.
  Bast.   And dares *Edgar,*
The beaten routed *Edgar,* brave his Conquerour?
From all thy Troops and Thee, I forc't the Field,
Thou has lost the gen'ral Stake, and art Thou now
Come with thy petty single Stock to play
This after-Game?
  Edg.   Half-blooded Man,
Thy Father's Sin first, then his Punishment,   40
The dark and vicious Place where he begot thee
Cost him his Eyes: from thy licentious Mother
Thou draw'st thy Villany; but for thy part

Of *Gloster's* Blood, I hold thee worth my Sword.
   Bast. Thou bear'st thee on thy Mother's Piety,
Which I despise; thy Mother being chaste
Thou art assur'd Thou art but *Gloster's* Son,
But mine, disdaining Constancy, leaves me
To hope that I am sprung from nobler Blood,
And possibly a King might be my Sire: 50
But be my Birth's uncertain Chance as 'twill,
Who 'twas that had the hit to Father me
I know not; 'tis enough that I am I:
Of this one thing I'm certain —— that I have
A daring Soul, and so have at thy Heart.
Sound Trumpet.   [*Fight,* Bastard *falls.*
   Gon. and Reg. Save him, save him.
   Gon. This was Practice, *Gloster,*
Thou won'st the Field, and wast not bound to Fight
A vanquisht Enemy, Thou art not Conquer'd   60
But couz'ned and betray'd.
   Alb. Shut your Mouth, Lady,
Or with this Paper I shall stop it —— hold, Sir,
Thou worse than any Name, reade thy own evil,
No Tearing, Lady, I perceive you know it.
   Gon. Say if I do, who shall arraign me for't?
The Laws are Mine, not Thine.
   Alb. Most monstrous! ha, Thou know'st it too?
   Bast. Ask me not what I know,
I have not Breath to Answer idle Questions.   70
   Alb. I have resolv'd —— your Right, brave Sir, has conquer'd,
                           [*To* Edgar.
Along with me, I must consult your Father.
                [*Exeunt* Albany *and* Edgar.
   Reg. Help every Hand to save a noble Life;
My half o'th' Kingdom for a Man of Skill
To stop this precious stream.
   Bast.   Away ye Empericks,
Torment me not with your vain Offices:
The Sword has pierc't too far; *Legitimacy*
At last has got it.

Reg.   The Pride of Nature Dies.

Gon. Away, the minutes are too precious,
Disturb us not with thy impertinent Sorrow.   80

   Reg. Art Thou my Rival then profest?

   Gon. Why, was our Love a Secret? cou'd there be
Beauty like Mine, and Gallantry like His
And not a mutual Love? just Nature then
Had err'd: behold that Copy of Perfection,
That Youth whose Story will have no foul Page
But where it says he stoopt to *Regan's* Arms:
Which yet was but Compliance, not Affection;
A Charity to begging, ruin'd Beauty!

   Reg. Who begg'd when *Gonerill* writ That? expose it   90

                                       [*Throws her a Letter.*

And let it be your Army's mirth, as 'twas
This charming Youth's and mine, when in the Bow'r
He breath'd the warmest ecstasies of Love,
Then panting on my Breast, cry'd matchless *Regan*
That *Gonerill* and Thou shou'd e'er be Kin!

   Gon. Die, *Circe,* for thy Charms are at an End,
Expire before my Face, and let me see
How well that boasted Beauty will become
Congealing Blood and Death's convulsive Pangs.
Die and be husht, for at my Tent last Night   100
Thou drank'st thy Bane, amidst thy rev'ling Bowls:
Ha! dost thou Smile? is then thy Death thy Sport
Or has the trusty Potion made thee Mad?

   Reg. Thou com'st as short of me in thy Revenge
As in my *Gloster's* Love, my Jealousie
Inspir'd me to prevent thy feeble Malice
And Poison Thee at thy own Banquet.

   Gon.   Ha!

   Bast. No more, my Queens, of this untimely Strife,
You both deserv'd my Love and both possest it.
Come, Souldiers, bear me in; and let   110
Your royal Presence grace my last minutes:
Now, *Edgar,* thy proud Conquest I forgive;
Who wou'd not choose, like me, to yield his Breath
T'have Rival Queens contend for him in Death?   [*Exeunt.*

[ACT V, SCENE VI]

Scene, A Prison.

Lear *asleep, with his Head on* Cordelia's *Lap.*

  Cord. What Toils, thou wretched King, hast Thou endur'd
To make thee draw, in Chains, a Sleep so sound?
Thy better Angel charm thy ravisht Mind
With fancy'd Freedom; Peace is us'd to lodge
On Cottage Straw, Thou hast the Begger's Bed,
Therefore shou'dst have the Begger's careless Thought.
And now, my *Edgar,* I remember Thee,
What Fate has seiz'd Thee in this general Wreck
I know not, but I know thou must be wretched
Because *Cordelia* holds Thee Dear. O Gods!   10
A suddain Gloom o'er-whelms me, and the Image
Of Death o'er-spreads the Place. —— ha! who are These?

          Enter Captain *and* Officers *with Cords.*

  Capt. Now, Sirs, dispatch, already you are paid
In part, the best of your Reward's to come.
  Lear. Charge, charge upon their Flank, their last Wing haults;
Push, push the Battel, and the Day's our own.
Their Ranks are broke, down, down with *Albany.*
Who holds my Hands? —— O thou deceiving Sleep,
I was this very Minute on the Chace;
And now a Prisoner here —— What mean the Slaves?   20
You will not Murder me?
  Cord.   Help Earth and Heaven!
For your Souls sake's, dear Sirs, and for the Gods.
  Off. No Tears, good Lady, no pleading against Gold
And Preferment; Come, Sirs, make ready your Cords.
  Cord. You, Sir, I'll seize,
You have a humane Form, and if no Pray'rs
Can touch your Soul to spare a poor King's Life,
If there be any Thing that you hold dear,
By That I beg you to dispatch me First.

Capt. Comply with her Request, dispatch her First.   30
Lear. Off Hell-hounds, by the Gods I charge you spare her;
'Tis my *Cordelia,* my true pious Daughter:
No Pity? ——Nay then take an old Man's Vengeance.

> *Snatches a Partizan, and strikes down two of them; the rest*
> *quit* Cordelia, *and turn upon him. Enter* Edgar *and* Albany

Edg. Death! Hell! Ye Vultures hold your impious Hands,
Or take a speedier Death than you wou'd give.
Capt. By whose Command?
Edg.   Behold the Duke your Lord.
Alb. Guards, seize those Instruments of Cruelty.
Cord. My *Edgar,* Oh!
Edg. My dear *Cordelia,* Lucky was the Minute
Of our Approach, the Gods have weigh'd our Suffrings;   40
W'are past the Fire, and now must shine to Ages.
Gent. Look here, my Lord, see where the generous King
Has slain Two of 'em.
Lear.   Did I not, Fellow?
I've seen the Day, with my good biting Faulchion
I cou'd have made 'em skip; I am Old now,
And these vile Crosses spoil me; Out of Breath!
Fie, Oh! quite out of Breath and spent.
Alb. Bring in old *Kent,* and, *Edgar,* guide you hither
Your Father, whom you said was near,   [*Exit* Edgar.
He may be an Ear-witness at the least   50
Of our Proceedings.

> Kent *brought in here.*

Lear. Who are you?
My Eyes are none o'th' best, I'll tell you streight;
Oh *Albany!* Well, Sir, we are your Captives,
And you are come to see Death pass upon us.
Why this Delay? —— or is't your Highness pleasure
To give us first the Torture? Say ye so?
Why here's old *Kent* and I, as tough a Pair
As e'er bore Tyrant's Stroke: — but my *Cordelia,*
My poor *Cordelia* here, O pitty! ——   60
Alb. Take off their Chains —— Thou injur'd Majesty,
The Wheel of Fortune now has made her Circle,
And Blessings yet stand 'twixt thy Grave and Thee.

Lear. Com'st Thou, inhumane Lord, to sooth us back
To a Fool's Paradise of Hope, to make
Our Doom more wretched? go too, we are too well
Acquainted with Misfortune to be gull'd
With Lying Hope; No, we will hope no more.
    Alb. I have a Tale t' unfold so full of Wonder
As cannot meet an easy Faith;   70
But by that Royal injur'd Head 'tis True.
    Kent. What wou'd your Highness?
    Alb.   Know the noble *Edgar*
Impeacht Lord *Edmund* since the Fight, of Treason,
And dar'd him for the Proof to single Combat,
In which the Gods confirm'd his Charge by Conquest;
I left ev'n now the Traytor wounded Mortally.
    Lear. And whither tends this Story?
    Alb.   E'er they fought
Lord *Edgar* gave into my Hands this Paper,
A blacker Scrowl of Treason, and of Lust
Than can be found in the Records of Hell;   80
There, Sacred Sir, behold the Character
Of *Gonerill* the worst of Daughters, but
More Vicious Wife.
    Cord. Cou'd there be yet Addition to their Guilt?
What will not They that wrong a Father doe?
    Alb. Since then my Injuries, *Lear,* fall in with Thine:
I have resolv'd the same Redress for Both.
    Kent. What says my Lord?
    Cord.   Speak, for me thought I heard
The charming Voice of a descending God.
    Alb. The Troops by *Edmund* rais'd, I have disbanded;   90
Those that remain are under my Command.
What Comfort may be brought to cheer your Age
And heal your savage Wrongs, shall be apply'd;
For to your Majesty we do Resign
Your Kingdom, save what Part your Self conferr'd
On Us in Marriage.
    Kent.   Hear you that, my Liege?
    Cord. Then there are Gods, and Vertue is their Care.
    Lear. Is't Possible?

Let the Spheres stop their Course, the Sun make Hault,
The Winds be husht, the Seas and Fountains Rest;   100
All Nature pause, and listen to the Change.
Where is my *Kent,* my *Cajus?*
    Kent.   Here, my Liege.
    Lear. Why I have News that will recall thy Youth;
Ha! Didst Thou hear't, or did th'inspiring Gods
Whisper to me Alone? Old *Lear* shall be
A King again.
    Kent. The Prince, that like a God has Pow'r, has said it.
    Lear. Cordelia then shall be a Queen, mark that:
Cordelia shall be Queen; Winds catch the Sound
And bear it on your rosie Wings to Heav'n.   110
Cordelia is a Queen.
              Re-enter Edgar *with* Gloster.
    Alb. Look, Sir, where pious *Edgar* comes
Leading his Eye-less Father: O my Liege!
His wondrous Story will deserve your Leisure:
What He has done and suffer'd for your Sake,
What for the Fair *Cordelia's.*
    Glost. Where is my Liege? Conduct me to his Knees to hail
His second Birth of Empire; my dear *Edgar*
Has, with himself, reveal'd the King's blest Restauration.
    Lear. My poor dark *Gloster.*   120
    Glost. O let me kiss that once more sceptred Hand!
    Lear. Hold, Thou mistak'st the Majesty, kneel here;
Cordelia has our Pow'r, *Cordelia's* Queen.
Speak, is not that the noble Suffring *Edgar?*
    Glost. My pious Son, more dear than my lost Eyes.
    Lear. I wrong'd Him too, but here's the fair Amends.
    Edg. Your leave, my Liege, for an unwelcome Message.
Edmund (but that's a Trifle) is expir'd;
What more will touch you, your imperious Daughters
Gonerill and haughty *Regan,* both are Dead,   130
Each by the other poison'd at a Banquet;
This, Dying, they confest.
    Cord. O fatal Period of ill-govern'd Life!
    Lear. Ingratefull as they were, my Heart feels yet
A Pang of Nature for their wretched Fall; ——

But, *Edgar,* I defer thy Joys too long:
Thou serv'dst distrest *Cordelia;* take her Crown'd:
Th'imperial Grace fresh Blooming on her Brow;
Nay, *Gloster,* Thou hast here a Father's Right;
Thy helping Hand t'heap Blessings on their Heads.   140
   Kent. Old *Kent* throws in his hearty Wishes too.
   Edg. The Gods and You too largely recompence
What I have done; the Gift strikes Merit Dumb.
   Cord. Nor do I blush to own my Self o'er-paid
For all my Suffrings past.
   Glost. Now, gentle Gods, give *Gloster* his Discharge.
   Lear. No, *Gloster,* Thou hast Business yet for Life;
Thou, *Kent* and I, retir'd to some cool Cell
Will gently pass our short reserves of Time
In calm Reflections on our Fortunes past,   150
Cheer'd with relation of the prosperous Reign
Of this celestial Pair; Thus our Remains
Shall in an even Course of Thought be past,
Enjoy the present Hour, nor fear the Last.
   Edg. Our drooping Country now erects her Head,
Peace spreads her balmy Wings, and Plenty Blooms.
Divine *Cordelia,* all the Gods can witness
How much thy Love to Empire I prefer!
Thy bright Example shall convince the World
(Whatever Storms of Fortune are decreed)   160
That Truth and Vertue shall at last succeed.   *[Exeunt Omnes.*

EPILOGUE.

Spoken by Mrs. *Barry.*

Inconstancy, the reigning Sin o'th' Age,
Will scarce endure true Lovers on the Stage;
You hardly ev'n in Plays with such dispense,
And Poets kill 'em in their own Defence.
Yet One bold Proof I was resolv'd to give,
That I cou'd three Hours Constancy Out-live.
You fear, perhaps, whilst on the Stage w'are made
Such Saints, we shall indeed take up the Trade;
Sometimes we Threaten —— but our Vertue may
For Truth I fear with your Pit-Valour weigh:　　　　　10
For (not to flatter either) I much doubt
When We are off the Stage, and You are out,
We are not quite so Coy, nor You so Stout.
We talk of Nunn'ries — but to be sincere
Whoever lives to see us Cloyster'd There,
May hope to meet our Critiques at Tangier.
For shame give over this inglorious Trade
Of worrying Poets, and go maule th' Alcade.
Well —— since y'are All for blustring in the Pit,
This Play's Reviver humbly do's admit　　　　　20
Your abs'lute Pow'r to damn his Part of it;
But still so many Master-Touches shine
Of that vast Hand that first laid this Design,
That in great Shakespear's *Right, He's bold to say*
If you like nothing you have seen to Day
The Play your Judgment damns, not you the Play.

THE
𝕿𝖗𝖆𝖌𝖎𝖈𝖆𝖑 𝕳𝖎𝖘𝖙𝖔𝖗𝖞
O F
King Richard III.

As it is Acted at the

THEATRE ROYAL.

By *C. Cibber*.

———*Domestica Facta.*

LONDON,

Printed for *B. Lintott* at the Middle *Temple-Gate,* in *Fleet-street,* and *A. Bettesworth* at the *Red-Lyon* on *London*-Bridge.

The [1700] edition from original in the Harvard College Library.

TO

HENRY BRETT, Jun.

OF

COWLEY, Esq;

*I Was ever Fond and Proud of your good opinion, it has sometimes
recommended me to Men of the first merit; where, without that
umbrage, perhaps, not all the Advantages of Fortune, could have
made me tolerable. You taught me first to know a little of my self,
then shew'd me other Men; and knowing them, taught me to
value You. I know not whether the World will allow there can be
any Gratitude in a Dedication; but I am assur'd you are well
enough acquainted with my sincerity, to believe this comes purely
from an Hearty and Uninterested Inclination. I am loath to remind you of the many handsom Obligations you have laid on me;* 10
*for in being thanked I have observ'd you often in a pain great as
your delight in giving: Which generous softness in your Temper
has made me many times conclude, that were you once Passion-
ately touch'd in Love (as certainly no man was ever so kindly
formed for it) the happy Fair One will at least have this security,
that your Natural Pleasure in obliging will instruct her to preserve
you long, and only Hers. I can't help talking thus, because I am
fond of publishing that ev'n such Qualities are what I have had
several Happy hours of leisure to observe in you. Nay, I freely
confess, I have all the Vanity of a young Lover, and can't really* 20
*think the Fair One absolutely mine, till I have told all the World
of her favours. I wou'd have my Lord, and all the Cheerful Table
know, that the very Gentleman they were so loath to part with,
had out staid his Appointment with* Cibber *for the reading an
Act or two of* Richard III. *I would have my Lady know too, that
ask'd the Civil Gentleman's name in the next Box, that 'twas not
her Ladyships kind advances that kept him there, but a certain
Promise made him behind the Scenes, that a little Extraordinary
Pains should be taken in the Performance of one of* Richard's

Soliloquies; And I wou'd have the Players know, that my so   30
often wishing the Vacation near, is, because Cowley *and your*
Conversation in the Summer to me, perhaps is as Entertaining an
Amusement, as a Family, and Uncertain pay in the Winter. I once
designed to have delay'd this Dedication till I was capable of pre-
fixing it to some piece more worthy your Acceptance: You have
often perswaded me to undertake another Comedy; but, I confess,
your own happy Talent in that kind (you'll excuse my blabbing)
and your common Conversation, have quite discourag'd me: A
Poet ought to be vain enough to suppose himself the best in his
kind, and unless I could believe I were able to write, as you talk,   40
with the same life, and happy turn of Thought, it will be Prudence
in me to let it alone till I am advis'd to it by some body that knows
you, as well as I do: So that I rather chuse to pay this little, while
I have it, than by an Idle Expectation of better success, run the
hazard of being in your debt as long as I live: but that I am afraid
I shall ever be; my long Account will not be easily settled, while
you forget as fast as you confer, and always grant a favour, as if
you were returning one, so 'tis partly your own Fault if I subscribe
my self,

Your eternally obliged
and humble Servant,

Lon. Feb.
1700

Colley Cibber.

THE PREFACE.

This Play came upon the Stage with a very Unusual disadvantage, the whole first Act being Intirely left out in the Presentation; and tho' it had been read by several persons of the first Rank and Integrity, some of which were pleas'd to honour me with an offer of giving it under their hands that the whole was an Inoffensive piece, and free from any bold Paralel, or ill manner'd reflection, yet this was no satisfaction to him, who had the Relentless power of licensing it for the Stage. I did not spare for intreaties; but all the reason I could get for its being refus'd, was, that *Henry* the Sixth being a Character Unfortunate and Pitied, wou'd put the Audience in mind of the late *King James:* Now, I confess, I never thought of him in the Writing it, which possibly might proceed from there not being any likeness between 'em. But however, there was no hazard of offending the Government, though the whole Play had been refus'd, and a man is not obliged to be Just, when he can get as much by doing an Injury. I am only sorry it hapned to be the best Act in the Whole, and leave it to the Impartial Reader how far it is offensive, and whether its being Acted would have been as injurious to good Manners, as the omission of it was to the rest of the Play.

Tho' there was no great danger of the Readers mistaking any of my lines for *Shakespear's;* yet, to satisfie the curious, and unwilling to assume more praise than is really my due, I have caus'd those that are intirely *Shakespear's* to be Printed in this *Italick Character;* and those lines with this mark (') before 'em, are generally his thoughts, in the best dress I could afford 'em: What is not so mark'd, or in a different Character is intirely my own. I have done my best to imitate his Style, and manner of thinking: If I have fail'd, I have still this comfort, that our best living Author in his imitation of *Shakespear's* Style only writ Great and Masterly.

THE PERSONS.

	[1700]	[1718]
King *Henry* the Sixth, designed for	Mr. *Wilks.*	[Wilks]
Edward Prince of *Wales,*		
Richard Duke of *York,* the young Sons	Mrs. *Allison.*	[Norris, Jun.]
of *Edward* the Fourth,	Miss. *Chock.*	[Miss Lindar]
Richard Duke of *Gloucester,*	Mr. *Cibber.*	[Cibber]
afterwards King of *England,*		
Duke of *Buckingham,*	Mr. *Powel.*	[Mills]
Lord *Stanley,*	Mr. *Mills.*	
Duke of *Norfolk,*	Mr. *Simpson.*	[Boman, Sr.]
Ratcliff,	Mr. *Kent.*	[Oates]
Catesby,	Mr. *Thomas.*	[Diggs]
Henry Earl of *Richmond,* afterwards	Mr. *Evans.*	[Ryan]
King of *England,*		
Oxford,	Mr. *Fairbank.*	[Boman, Jun.]
Blunt,	———	[Wright]
[*Tressell,*		Will. Wilks]
[Lieutenant of the *Tower,*		Quin]
[Lord Mayor,		Miller]
[*Tirrel,*		Weller]
[*Forrest,*		Wilson]
[*Dighton,*		Higginson]
[*Rivers*]		
[*Dorset*]		
[*Lovel*]		
Elizabeth, Relict of *Edward* the Fourth,	Mrs. *Knight.*	[Mrs. Porter]

Ann, Relict of *Edward* Prince of *Wales,* Son to *Henry* the Sixth, afterwards married to *Richard* the Third,	Mrs. *Rogers.*	[Mrs.Horton]
Cicely, Dutchess of *York,* Mother to *Richard* the Third,	Mrs. *Powel.*	[Mrs.Baker]
[Gentlemen, Ladies, Guards, and Attendants.]		

ACT I, [SCENE I]

The Scene, A Garden within the Tower.
Enter the Lieutenant with a Servant.

Lieu. Has King *Henry* walk'd forth this Morning?

Ser. No, Sir, but 'tis near his Hour.

Lieu. At any time when you see him here,
Let no Stranger into the Garden:
I wou'd not have him star'd at —— See! Who's that
Now entring at the Gate?   [*Knocking without.*

Ser.   Sir, the Lord *Stanley.*

Lieu. Leave me. ——   [*Exit Servant.*

Enter Lord Stanley.

My Noble Lord you're welcome to the Tower,
I heard last Night you late arriv'd with News
Of *Edward's* Victory to his joyful Queen.   10

Ld. Stan. Yes, Sir; and I am proud to be the Man
That first brought home the last of Civil Broils,
The Houses now of *York,* and *Lancaster,*
Like Bloody Brothers fighting for Birth-right,
No more shall wound the Parent that wou'd part 'em.
Edward now sits secure on *England's* Throne.

Lieu. Near *Tewkesbury,* my Lord I think they fought:
Has the Enemy lost any Men of Note?

Ld. Stan. Sir, I was Posted Home
E're an Account was taken of the Slain,   20
But as I left the Field, a Proclamation
From the King was made in Search of *Edward,*
Son to your Prisoner, King *Henry* the Sixth,
Which gave Reward to those Discover'd him,
And him his Life, if he'd surrender.

Lieu. That Brave Young Prince, I fear's unlike his Father,

Too high of Heart to brook submissive Life:
This will be heavy News to *Henry's* Ear:
For on this Battles cast his All was set.

    Ld. Stan. King *Henry,* and ill Fortune are familiar: 30
He ever threw with an indifferent Hand,
But never yet was known to lose his Patience:
How does he pass the Time in his Confinement?

    Lieu. As one whose Wishes never reacht a Crown,
The King seems Dead in him: But as a Man
He sighs sometimes in want of Liberty.
Sometimes he Reads, and Walks, and wishes
That Fate had blest him with an humbler Birth,
Not to have felt the falling from a Throne.

    Ld. Stan. Were it not possible to see this King?   40
They say he'll freely talk with *Edward's* Friends,
And ever treats them with Respect, and Honour.

    Lieu. This is his usual Time of walking forth,
(For he's allow'd the freedom of the Garden;)
After his Morning-Prayer; he seldom fails:
Behind this Arbor we unseen may stand
A while t'observe him.   [*They retire.*

             Enter King Henry *the Sixth in Mourning.*

    K. Hen. By this time the Decisive Blow is struck,
Either my Queen and Son are blest with Victory,
Or I'm the cause no more of Civil Broils.   50
Wou'd I were Dead if Heavens good Will were so,
'For what is in this World but Grief and Care?
What Noise, and Bustle do Kings make to find it?
When Life's but a short Chace, our Game content
Which most pursued is most compell'd to fly;
And he that mounts him on the swiftest Hope,
Shall often Run his Courser to a stand,
While the poor Peasant from some distant Hill
Undanger'd, and at Ease views all the Sport,
And sees Content take shelter in his Cottage.   60

    Ld. Stan. He seems Extreamly mov'd.
    Lieu.   Does he know you?
    Ld. Stan. No! nor wou'd I have him.   *Aside.*
    Lieu.   We'll show our selves.
                            [*They come forward.*

283

K. Hen. Why, there's another Check to Proud Ambition.
That Man receiv'd his Charge from me, and now
I'm his Prisoner, he lock's me to my Rest:
Such an unlook'd for Change who cou'd suppose,
That saw him kneel to Kiss the Hand that rais'd him?
But that I shou'd not now complain off,
Since I to that, 'tis possible, may owe
His Civil Treatment of me, —— 'Morrow Lieutenant,　　　　70
Is any News arriv'd? —— Who's that with you?
　　Lieu. A Gentleman that came last Night Express
From *Tewkesbury.* We've had a Battle.
　　K. Hen. Comes he to me with Letters or Advice?
　　Lieu. Sir, he's King *Edward's* Officer, your Foe.
　　K. Hen. Then he won't flatter me, you're welcome, Sir;
Not less because you are King *Edward's* Friend;
For I have almost learn'd my self to be so:
Cou'd I but once forget I was a King,
I might be truly Happy, and his Subject.　　　　　　　80
You've gain'd a Battle? Is't not so?
　　Ld. Stan. We have, Sir; How, will reach your Ear too soon.
　　K. Hen. If to my Loss, it can't too soon — Pray speak,
For Fear makes Mischief greater than it is:
My Queen! my Son! say, Sir! are they living!
　　Ld. Stan. Since my Arrival, Sir, another Post
Came in, which brought us word your Queen, and Son
Were Prisoners now at *Tewkesbury.*
　　K. Hen. Heav'ns Will be done! the Hunters have 'em now ——
And I have only Sighs, and Prayers to help 'em!　　　90
　　Ld. Stan. King *Edward,* Sir, depends upon his Sword,
Yet prays heartily, when the Battle's won:
And Soldiers love a Bold and Active Leader,
Fortune like Women will be close pursu'd;
The *English* are high Mettl'd, Sir, and 'tis
No easie part to Sit 'em well. King *Edward*
Feels their Temper, and 'twill be hard to throw him.
　　K. Hen. Alas, I thought 'em Men, and rather hop'd
To win their Hearts by Mildness, than Severity.
My Soul was never form'd for Cruelty,　　　　　　100
In my Eye Justice has seem'd bloody,

When on the City Gates I have beheld
A Traytor's Quarters parching in the Sun,
My Blood has turn'd with Horror at the Sight,
I took 'em down, and Buried with his Limbs
The Memory of the Dead Man's Deeds: Perhaps
That Pity made me look less Terrible,
Giving the mind of weak Rebellion Spirit:
For King's are put in Trust for all Mankind,
And when themselves take Injuries, who is safe?   110
If so I have deserv'd these frowns of Fortune.

           Enter a Servant to the Lieutenant.

   Serv. Sir, here's a Gentleman brings a Warrant
For his Access to King *Henry's* Presence.
   Lieu. I come to him.
   Ld. Stan. His Business may require your Privacy,
I'll leave you, Sir, wishing you all the Good
That can be wish'd, not wronging him I serve.   [*Exeunt.*
   K. Hen. Farewell: Who can this be? A sudden Coldness
Like the Damp Hand of Death has seiz'd my Limbs:
I fear some heavy News! ——   120

           Enter Lieutenant.

Who is it, good Lieutenant?
   Lieu. A Gentleman, Sir, from *Tewkesbury*, he seems
A melancholly Messenger: For when I ask'd
What News? His Answer was a deep faught Sigh:
I wou'd not urge him, but I fear 'tis fatal.   [*Exit.*

           Enter Tressell *in Mourning.*

   K. Hen. Fatal indeed! His Brows the Title Page
That speaks the Nature of a Tragick Volume;
'Say, Friend, how does my Queen, my Son!
Thou tremblest, and the whiteness of thy Cheek
Is apter than thy Tongue to tell the Errand,   130
Ev'n such a Man, so Faint, so Spiritless,
So Dull, so Dead in Look, so Woe be gone,
Drew Priam's *Curtain in the Dead of Night,*
And wou'd have told him half his Troy *was burn'd,*
But Priam *found the Fire, e're he his Tongue,*
And I my poor Son's Death e're thou relatest it;

Now wou'd'st thou say: Your Son did thus and thus,
'And thus your Queen; So fought the Valiant *Oxford,*
Stopping my greedy Ear with their bold Deeds,
But in the End (to stop my Ear indeed,)   140
Thou hast a Sigh to blow away this Praise,
'Ending with Queen and Son, and all are Dead.

    Tress. 'Your Queen yet Lives, and many of your Friends,
'But for my Lord your Son ——

    K. Hen. Why, he is Dead; —— yet speak, I Charge thee!
'Tell thou thy Master his Suspicion lies,
And I will take it as a kind Disgrace,
'And thank thee well, for doing me such wrong.

    Tress. Wou'd it were wrong to say, but, Sir, your Fears are true.

    K. Hen. Yet for all this, say not my Son is Dead.   150

    Tress. Sir, I am sorry I must force you to
Believe, what wou'd to Heav'n I had not seen!
But in this last Battle, near *Tewkesbury,*
'Your Son, whose Active Spirit lent a Fire
'Ev'n to the dullest Peasant in our Camp,
Still made his way, where Danger stood t'oppose him,
A braver Youth of more Couragious Heat,
'Ne'er spurr'd his Courser at the Trumpets sound:
But who can Rule th' uncertain Chance of War,
In Fine, King *Edward* won the Bloody Field,   160
Where both your Queen, and Son were made his Prisoners.

    K. Hen. 'Yet, hold! for oh! this Prologue lets me in
'To a most fatal Tragedy to come. ——
Dy'd he Prisoner, say'st thou? How? By Grief,
Or by the bloody Hands of those, that caught him?

    Tress. After the Fight, *Edward* in Triumph ask'd
To see the Captive Prince; the Prince was brought,
Whom *Edward* roughly Chid for bearing Arms,
Asking what Reparation he cou'd make
For having stirr'd his Subjects to Rebellion?   170
Your Son impatient of such Taunts, reply'd,
'Bow like a Subject, Proud Ambitious *York*!
'While I now speaking with my Father's Mouth,
'Propose the self same Rebel Words to thee,
'Which, Traytor, thou wou'dst have me answer to:

From these, more Words arose, till in the End
King *Edward* swell'd with what th'unhappy Prince
At such a time too freely spoke, his Gauntlet
In his young Face with Indignation struck:
At which Crook'd *Richard, Clarence,* and the rest   180
Buried their fatal Daggers in his Heart:
In Bloody State I saw him on the Earth,
From whence with Life he never more sprung up.
    K. Hen. 'O had'st thou stabb'd at every Words deliverance,
'Sharp Ponyards in my Flesh, while this was told
'Thy Wounds had giv'n less Anguish than thy Words.——
O Heav'ns! methinks I see my tender Lamb
Gasping beneath the Ravenous Wolves fell gripe!
But say, did all? Did they all strike him, say'st thou?
    Tress. All, Sir: But the first Wound Duke *Richard* gave.   190
    K. Hen. There let him stop! be that his last of Ills!
O barbarous Act; Unhospitable Men!
Against the rigid Laws of Arms to kill him!
Was't not enough, his hope of Birth-right gone,
But must your Hate be levell'd at his Life?
Nor cou'd his Father's Wrongs content you?
Nor cou'd a Father's Grief disswade the Deed?
'You have no Children, (Butchers if you had)
'The thought of them wou'd sure have stirr'd Remorse.
    Tress. Take Comfort, Sir; and hope a better Day.   200
    K. Hen. O! who can hold a Fire in his Hand,
By thinking on the Frosty Caucasus?
Or wallow Naked in December's *Snow,*
'By bare remembrance of the Summer's Heat?
Away! by Heav'n, I shall abhor his Sight,
Whoever bids me be of Comfort more:
If thou wilt sooth my Sorrows, then I'll thank thee:
Ay! now thou'rt kind indeed! these Tears oblige me.
    Tress. Alas, my Lord! I fear more Evils toward you.
    K. Hen. Why, let it come! I scarce shall feel it now,   210
My present Woes have beat me to the Ground,
And my hard Fate can make me fall no lower:
What can it be? Give it its ugliest Shape, —— O my poor Boy! ——
    Tress. A word does that; it comes in *Gloucester's* Form.

K. Hen. Frightful indeed! give me the worst that threatens.

Tress. After the Murther of your Son, stern *Richard,*
As if unsated with the Wounds he had giv'n,
With unwash'd Hands went from his Friends in hast,
And being ask'd by *Clarence* of the Cause,
He low'ring cry'd, Brother, I must to the *Tower*!   220
I've Business there, excuse me to the King,
Before you reach the Town, expect some News:
This said, he vanish'd, and I hear's arriv'd.

K. Hen. Why, then the Period of my Woes is set;
For Ills but thought by him are half perform'd.

                Enter Lieutenant with an Order.

Lieu. Forgive me, Sir; what I'm compell'd t'obey
An Order for your close Confinement.

K. Hen. Whence comes it, good Lieutenant?

Lieu. Sir, from the Duke of *Gloucester.*

K. Hen. Good Night to all then: I obey it —   230
And now good Friend suppose me on my Death-bed,
And take of me, thy last, short, Living leave: ——
Nay, keep thy Tears till thou hast seen me Dead:
And when in tedious Winter Nights, with Good
Old Folks, thou sit'st up late
To hear 'em tell thee Dismal Tales
'Of times long past, even now with Woe remember'd;
Before thou bidst good night, to quit their Grief,
Tell thou the lamentable fall of me,
And send thy hearers weeping to their Beds.   [*Exeunt.*

[ACT I, SCENE II]

Enter Richard *Duke of* Gloucester. *Solus.*

Rich. Now are our Brows bound with Victorious wreaths,
Our stern allarms are changed to Merry-meetings,

Our dreadfull marches to delightful measures.
Grim visaged War has smoothed his wrinkled Front,
And now instead of mounting Barbed Steeds
To fright the Souls of fearful Adversaries
He Capers nimbly in a Ladies Chamber
To the Lascivious Pleasing of a Lute;
But I that am not shaped for sportive tricks,
I that am curtailed of Man's fair proportion,   10
Deform'd, Unfinish'd, sent before my time
Into this breathing World scarce half made up,
And that so lamely and unfashionable
That Dogs bark at me as I halt by 'em;
Why I, in this weak, this piping time of Peace,
Have no delight to pass away my hours,
Unless to see my shadow in the Sun,
And descant on my own deformity:
——— Then since this Earth affords no joy to me,
But to Command, to Check, and to Orebear such,   20
'As are of Happier Person than my self,
'Why then to me this restless World's but Hell,
Till this mishapen trunks aspiring head
'Be circled in a glorious Diadem ———
But then 'tis fixt on such an heighth, O! I
Must stretch the utmost reaching of my Soul.
  I'll climb betimes without Remorse or Dread,
  And my first step shall be on *Henry's* Head.   [*Exit.*

[ACT I, SCENE III]

Scene, a Chamber in the Tower: *K.* Henry *sleeping.*
Enter Lieutenant.

  Lieu. Asleep so soon! But sorrow minds no seasons,
The Morning, Noon, and Night with her's the same,
She's fond of any hour that yields Repose.

289

K. Hen. Who's there? Lieutenant! is it you? Come hither.   *[Rising.*
Lieu. You shake, my Lord, and look affrighted.
  K. Hen. O! I have had the fearfull'st Dream; such sights,
That, as I live ——
I would not pass another hour so dreadful
Though 'twere to buy a world of happy days.
Reach me a Book —— I'll try if reading can   10
Divert these melancholy thoughts.

Enter Richard.

  Rich. Good day, my Lord; what, at your Book so hard?
I disturb you.
  K. Hen.   You do indeed ——   *[Sighing.*
  Rich. Go, Friend, leave us to our selves; we must confer.
                     [Exit Lieutenant.
  K. Hen. What Bloody Scene has *Roscius* now to Act?
  Rich. Suspicion always haunts the guilty mind,
The Thief does fear each bush an Officer.
  K. Hen. Where Thieves without Controulment rob and kill,
The Traveller does fear each bush a Thief:
The poor bird that has been already lim'd   20
With trembling Wings misdoubts of every Bush,
And I, the hapless Male to one sweet Bird,
Have now the fatal object in my Eye,
'By whom my young one bled, was caught and kill'd.
  Rich. Why, what a peevish Fool was that of Creet,
That taught his Son the office of a Fowl?
And yet for all his Wings the fool was drown'd:
Thou should'st have taught thy Boy his Prayers alone,
And then he had not broke his neck with Climbing.
  K. Hen. Ah, kill me with thy weapon, not with words,   30
My breast can better brook thy Daggers point,
'Than can my ears that piercing story.
But wherefore dost thou come, is't for my life?
  Rich. Thinkest thou I am an Executioner?
  K. Hen. If Murthering Innocents be Executing
'Then thou'rt the worst of Executioners.
  Rich. Thy Son I kill'd for his Presumption.
  K. Hen. Hadst thou been kill'd when first thou didst Presume,
Thou hadst not liv'd to kill a Son of mine.

But thou wert born to Massacre Mankind.   40
'How many Old Mens sighs, and Widows moans,
'How many Orphans Water standing eyes,
Men, for their Sons, Wives for their Husbands Fate,
And Children, for their Parents timeless death,
Will rue the hour that ever thou wert born?
The Owl shriek'd at thy Birth: An Evil sign.
The night Crow cry'd, foreboding luckless time,
Dogs howl'd, and hideous Tempests shook down Trees;
The Raven rook'd her on the Chimneys top,
And chattering Pies in dismal discords sung.   50
Thy Mother felt more than a Mothers Pain,
And yet brought forth less than a Mothers Hope:
Teeth hadst thou in thy head when thou wert born,
Which plainly said, Thou cam'st to bite Mankind,
And, if the rest be true which I have heard,
Thou cam'st ——
    Rich. I'll hear no more: Dye, Prophet, in thy speech.   [*Stabs him.*
For this, amongst the rest was I ordain'd.
    K. Hen. O! and for much more slaughter after this.
Just Heaven forgive my sins, and pardon thee.   [*Dies.*
    Rich. What, will the aspiring blood of Lancaster   61
Sink in the ground? —— *I thought it would have mounted.*
See how my Sword weeps for the poor King's death;
——— *O, may such purple tears be always shed*
From those that wish the Downfall of our House.
If any spark of Life be yet remaining,
Down, down to Hell! and say, I sent thee thither.
I that have neither Pity, Love nor Fear:
Indeed 'tis true, what Henry *told me of,*
For I have often heard my Mother say,   70
I came into the World with my Legs forward:
The Midwife wonder'd, and the Women cry'd,
Good Heaven bless us, he is born with Teeth;
And so I was, which plainly signified,
That I should snarl and bite, and play the Dog.
Then since the Heavens have shap'd my body so,
Let Hell make crooked my mind to answer it ——
I have no Brother, am like no Brother,

And this word Love, which Gray beards call Divine,
Be resident in Men, like one another,   80
And not in me —— I am —— my self alone.
Clarence, *beware, thou keep'st me from the Light,*
But if I fail not in my deep intent,
Thou'st not another day to live, which done,
Heaven take the weak King Edward *to his Mercy,*
And leave the World for me to bustle in:
But soft —— I'm sharing spoil before the Field is won,
   Clarence still Breaths, *Edward* still Lives and Reigns,
   When they are gone, then I must count my gains.   [*Exit.*

ACT II, [SCENE I]

The Scene, St. Pauls.
Enter Tressel *meeting Lord* Stanley.

Tress. My Lord, your Servant, pray what brought you to *Paul's?*
Ld. Stan. I came amongst the Crowd to see the Corps
Of poor King *Henry.* 'Tis a dismal sight,
But yesterday I saw him in the Tower;
His talk is still so fresh within my memory:
That I could weep to think how Fate has us'd him.
I wonder where's Duke *Richard's* policy
In suffering him to lie exposed to view?
Can he believe that Men will love him for't?
   Tress. O yes, Sir, love him, as he loves his Brothers: 10
When was you with King *Edward,* pray, my Lord?
I hear he leaves his Food, is Melancholy,
And his Physicians fear him mightily.
   Ld. Stan. 'Tis thought he'll scarce recover:
Shall we to Court, and hear more News of him?
   Tress. I am oblig'd to pay Attendance here,
The Lady *Ann* has license to remove

King *Henry's* Corps to be Interr'd at *Chertsey,*
And I am engag'd to follow her.

    Ld. Stan. Mean you King *Henry's* Daughter-in-Law?   20
    Tress. The same, Sir, Widow to the late Prince *Edward,*
Whom *Gloucester* kill'd at *Tewkesbury.*
    Ld. Stan. Alas, poor Lady, she's severely used.
And yet I hear *Richard* attempts her Love:
Methinks the wrongs he's done her should discourage him.
    Tress. Neither those wrongs nor his own shape can fright him;
He sent for leave to visit her this morning,
And she was forc'd to keep her Bed to avoid him.
But see, she is arriv'd: Will you along
To see this doleful Ceremony?
    Ld. Stan.   I'll wait on you.   *[Exeunt.*

            Enter Richard *Solus.*

    Rich. 'Twas her excuse t' avoid me —— Alas!   31
She keeps no Bed ——
She has health enough to progress far as *Chertsey,*
Tho' not to bear the sight of me;
—— I cannot blame her ——
Why Love forswore me in my Mothers Womb,
And for I should not deal in his soft Laws,
He did corrupt frail Nature with some Bribe
To shrink my Arm up like a wither'd Shrub,
To make an envious Mountain on my back,   40
Where sits Deformity to mock my Body,
To shape my Legs of an unequal size,
To disporportion me in every part:
And am I then a man to be belov'd?
O monstrous Thought! more vain my Ambition.

            Enter Lieutenant hastily.

    Lieu. My Lord, I beg your Grace ——
    Rich. Be gone, Fellow —— I'm not at leisure ———
    Lieu. My Lord, the King your Brother's taken ill.
    Rich. I'll wait on him, leave me, Friend ——   *[Exit Lieutenant.]*
Ha! *Edward* ta'en ill! ———   50
Wou'd he were wasted, Marrow, Bones and all,
'That from his loins no more young Brats may rise
'To cross me in the golden time I look for ——

Scene draws and discovers Lady Ann *in Mourning,*
Lord Stanley, Tressel, Guards *and* Bearers, *with King* Henry's *Body.*

But see, my Love appears: Look where she shines,
Darting pale Lustre, like the Silver Moon
Through her dark Veil of Rainy sorrow:
So mourn'd the Dame of *Ephesus* her Love,
And thus the Soldier arm'd with Resolution
Told his soft tale, and was a thriving Woer.
'Tis true, my Form perhaps, will little move her,   60
But I've a Tongue shall wheadle with the Devil.
Yet hold; She mourns the Man whom I have kill'd:
First, let her sorrows take some vent — Stand here;
I'll take her passion in its wain, and turn
This storm of grief to gentle drops of pity
For his Repentant Murderer. ——   [*He retires.*
    Lady A. 'Hung be the Heavens with black, yield day to night,
'Comets importing change of Times and States,
'Brandish your fiery Tresses in the Sky,
'And with 'em scourge the bad revolting Stars   70
'That have consented to King *Henry's* death:
O be Accurst the Hand that shed this Blood;
Accurst the Head that had the Heart to do it,
More direful hap betide that hated Wretch
Than I can wish to Wolves, to Spiders, Toads,
Or any creeping venom'd thing that lives:
If ever he have Wife, let her be made
'More miserable by the Life of him,
'Than I am now by *Edward's* death and thine.
    Rich. Poor Girl! What pains she takes to curse her self?   [*Aside.*
    Lady A. If ever he have Child Abortive be it,   81
Prodigious and Untimely brought to Light,
'Whose hideous Form, whose most unnatural Aspect
May fright the hopeful Mother at her view,
And that be Heir to his unhappiness.
'Now on, to *Chertsey* with your sacred Load.
                    Richard *comes forward.*
    Rich. Stay, you that bear the Coarse, and set it down.
    Lady A. What black Magician Conjures up this Fiend
To stop devoted charitable deeds?

Rich. *Villains, set down the Coarse, or, by St.* Paul,   90
I'll make a Coarse of him that disobeys.
   Guard. *My Lord, stand back, and let the Coffin pass.*
   Rich. 'Unmanner'd Slave! *Stand thou, when I command:*
Advance thy Halbert higher than my Breast,
Or, by St. Paul, *I'll strike thee to my foot,*
And spurn thee, beggar, for this boldness.
   Lady A. Why dost thou haunt him thus, unsated Fiend?
Thou hadst but power over his mortal Body,
His Soul thou canst not reach; therefore be gone.
   Rich. *Sweet Saint, be not so* hard *for Charity.*   100
   Lady A. *If thou delight to view thy heinous deeds,*
Behold this pattern of thy Butcheries.
Why didst thou do this deed? Cou'd not the Laws
Of Man, of Nature, nor of Heavan disswade thee?
No Beast so fierce, but knows some touch of pity.
   Rich. If want of pity be a Crime so hateful,
Whence is it thou, fair Excellence, art guilty?
   Lady A. What means the slanderer?
   Rich. *Vouchsafe, Divine Perfection of a Woman,*
Of these my Crimes suppos'd to give me leave   110
By Circumstance, but to acquit my self.
   Lady A. Then take that Sword, whose bloody point still **reeks**
With *Henry's* Life, with my lov'd Lord's young *Edwards,*
And here let out thy own t' appease their Ghosts.
   Rich. *By such despair I shou'd accuse my self.*
   Lady A. *Why by despairing only canst thou stand excused?*
Didst thou not kill this King?
   Rich.   *I grant ye.*
   Lady A. *O! he was Gentle, Loving, Mild and Vertuous;*
But he's in Heaven, where thou canst never come.
   Rich. Was I not kind to send him thither then?   120
He was much fitter for that place than Earth.
   Lady A. *And thou unfit for any place but Hell.*
   Rich. *Yes, one place else, if you will hear me name it.*
   Lady A. *Some Dungeon.*
   Rich.   *Your Bed Chamber.*
   Lady A. *Ill rest betide the Chamber where thou liest.*
   Rich. *So it will, Madam, till I lie in yours.*
   Lady A. *I hope so.*

Rich. I know so. But gentle Lady Ann,
'To leave this keen encounter of our Tongues,
'And fall to something a more serious method.   130
Is not the causer of th' untimely deaths
Of these Plantagenets, Henry *and* Edward,
As blameful as the Executioner?
   Lady A. Thou wert the cause, and most accurst effect.
   Rich. Your Beauty was the cause of that effect:
Your Beauty that did haunt me in my sleep,
To undertake the Death of all the World,
So I might live one hour in that soft Bosom.
   Lady A. If I thought that, I tell thee, Homicide,
'These Hands shou'd rend that Beauty from my Cheeks.   140
   Rich. These Eyes cou'd not endure that Beauties rack,
You shou'd not blemish it, if I stood by.
'As all the World is nourish'd by the Sun,
So I by that: It is my Day, my Life.
   Lady A. I wou'd it were to be reveng'd on thee.
   Rich. It is a Quarrel most Unnatural
To wish revenge on him that loves thee.
   Lady A. Say rather 'tis my duty,
'To seek revenge on him that kill'd my Husband.
   Rich. Fair Creature, he that kill'd thy Husband   150
'Did it to —— help thee to a better Husband.
   Lady A. His better does not breath upon the Earth.
   Rich. He lives that lov'd thee better, than he could.
   Lady A. Name him.
   Rich.   Plantagenet.
   Lady A.   *Why, that was he.*
   Rich. The self same Name, but one of softer Nature.
   Lady A. Where is he?
   Rich. Ah! take more pity in thy Eyes, and see him —— here.
   Lady A. Wou'd they were Basilisks to strike thee dead.
   Rich. I wou'd they were, that I might die at once,
For now they kill me with a living death,   160
Darting with cruel aim Despair and Love;
I never sued to Friend or Enemy,
My Tongue could never learn sweet smoothing Words,
But now thy Beauty is propos'd my Fee
My proud Heart sues, and prompts my Tongue to speak.

Lady A. Is there a Tongue on Earth can speak for thee?
Why dost thou Court my hate?

 Tress. Where will this end? she frowns upon him yet. ⎫
 Ld. Stan. But yet she hears him in her frowns; I fear him. ⎭   *Aside.*

 Rich. 'O! teach not thy soft lip such cold contempt ——   170
If thy Relentless Heart cannot forgive,
Lo, here I lend thee this sharp pointed Sword,
Which if thou please to hide in this true Breast,
And let the honest Soul out, that adores thee,
I lay it naked to the deadly stroke,
And humbly beg that Death upon my knee.

 Lady A. What shall I say or do? Direct me Heaven; ⎫
When stones weep sure the tears are natural,   ⎬   *Aside.*
And Heaven it self instructs us to forgive,
When they do flow from a sincere Repentance. ⎭   180

 Rich. Nay, do not pause: For I did kill *King* Henry,
But 'twas thy wondrous Beauty did provoke me;
Nay now dispatch: 'Twas I that stab'd young Edward,
But 'twas thy Heavenly face that set me on,
And I might still persist (so stubborn is
My Temper) to rejoice at what I've done,
But that thy powerful Eyes (as roaring Seas
Obey the changes of the Moon) have turn'd
My Heart, and made it flow with Penitence.   [*She lets fall the Sword.*
Take up the Sword agen, or take up me.   190

 Lady A. No, tho' I wish thy Death,
I will not be thy Executioner.

 Rich. Then bid me kill my self, and I will do it.

 Lady A. I have already.

 Rich.   *That was in thy rage:*
Say it again, and even with thy word
'This guilty hand that rob'd thee of thy Love
'Shall for thy Love revenge thee on thy Lover;
To both their deaths shalt thou be Accessary.

 Tress. By Heaven she wants the heart to bid him do't. ⎫
 Ld. Stan. What think you now, Sir?   ⎪   200
 Tress. I'm struck! I scarce can credit what I see. ⎬
 Ld. Stan. Why, you see —— A Woman.   ⎪   *Aside.*
 Tress. When future Chronicles shall speak of this
They will be thought Romance, not History. ⎭

Rich. What, not a word to pardon or condemn me?
But thou art wise —— and canst with silence kill me;
Yet even in death my fleeting Soul pursues thee:
Dash not the tears of Penitence away.
I ask but leave t' indulge my cold despair:
By Heaven, there's Joy in this extravagance   210
Of Woe; 'tis Melting, Soft, 'tis pleasing Ruin.
Oh! 'tis too much, too much for Life to bear
This aching tenderness of thought.
    Lady A. Wou'dst thou not blame me to forgive thy Crimes?
    Rich. They are not to be forgiven: No, not even
Penitence can atone 'em. O misery
Of Thought! that strikes me with at once Repentance
And Despair; tho' unpardon'd, yield me pity.
    Lady A. Wou'd I knew thy heart.
    Rich. 'Tis figur'd in my Tongue.   220
    Lady A. I fear me both are false.
    Rich. Then never Man was true.
    Lady A. Put up thy Sword.
    Rich. Say then, my Peace is made.
    Lady A. That shalt thou know hereafter.
    Rich. But shall I live in hope?
    Lady A. All Men, I hope, live so.
    Rich. I swear, bright Saint, I am not what I was:
Those Eyes have turn'd my stubborn heart to Woman,
Thy goodness makes me soft in Penitence,   230
And my harsh thoughts are tun'd to Peace and Love.
O! if thy poor devoted Servant might
But beg one favour at thy gracious hand,
Thou wouldst confirm his Happiness for ever.
    Lady A. What is it?
    Rich. That it may please thee, leave these sad designs
To him that has most cause to be a Mourner,
And presently repair to Crosby House,
Where, after I have solemnly Interr'd
At Chertsey Monastery, *this Injur'd King,*   240
And wet his Grave with my repentant Tears,
I will with all expedient duty see you:
For divers unknown reasons I beseech you

'Grant me this favour.

    Lady A. I do my Lord, and much it joys me too
To see you are become so Penitent.
Tressel *and* Berkley *go along with me.*
    Rich. Bid me Farewell.
    Lady A.   *'Tis more than you deserve;*
But since you teach me how to flatter you,
Imagine I have said Farewell already.   [*Exit with* Tress. *and* Berk.
    Guard. Towards Chertsey, *my Lord?*   251
    Rich. No, to White-Fryars, *there attend my coming.*
                      [*Exeunt Guards with the Body.*

            Richard *Solus.*

    Rich. (smiling.) Was ever Woman in this humour wooed?
Was ever Woman in this humour won?
I'll have her: But I will not keep her long.
What! I that kill'd her Husband and his Father,
To take her in her Hearts extreamest hate,
With Curses in her mouth, Tears in her Eyes,
The bleeding witness of my hatred by,
Having Heaven, her Conscience, and these Bars against me,   260
And I no Friends to back my suit withal,
But the plain Devil, and dissembling looks?
And yet to win her! All the world to nothing.
Can she abase her Beauteous eyes on me?
Whose all not equals Edward's *moiety?*
On me! that halt and am mishapen Thus!
'My Dukedom to a Widows Chastity
I do mistake my Person all this while!
Upon my life! she finds, altho I cannot,
My self to be a marvellous proper Man,   270
'I'll have my Chambers lin'd with Looking-glass
And entertain a score or two of Taylors
To study fashions to adorn my body.
Since I am crept in favour with my self,
I will maintain it with some little cost.
'But first, I'll turn St. *Harry* to his grave,
And then return lamenting to my Love.
'Shine out fair Sun till I salute my Glass,
That I may see my shadow as I pass.   [*Exit.*

[ACT II, SCENE II]

Scene, the Presence: Enter the Duke of Buckingham
hastily, Lord Stanley *meeting him.*

D. Buck. Did you see the Duke?

Ld. Stan.   What Duke my Lord?

D. Buck. His Grace of *Gloucester,* did you see him?

Ld. Stan. Not lately, my Lord — I hope no ill news.

D. Buck. The worst that heart e're bore, or tongue can utter.
Edward the King! his Royal Brother's Dead.

    Ld. Stan. 'Tis sad indeed —— I wish by your impatience
To acquaint him tho you think it so to him.   [*Aside.*
Did the King, my Lord, make any mention
Of a Protector for his Crown and Children?

    D. Buck. He did, Duke *Richard* has the care of both.   10

    Ld. Stan. That sad news you are afraid to tell him too.   [*Aside.*

    D. Buck. He'll spare no toile, I'm sure to fill his Place!

    Ld. Stan. Pray Heav'n he's not too diligent!   [*Aside.*
My Lord, is not that the Dutchess of *York,*
The King's Mother? coming I fear to visit him.

    D. Buck. 'Tis she! little thinking what has befallen us.

Enter Dutchess of York.

    Dutch. Good day, my Lords! How takes the King his Rest.

    D. Buck. Alas! Madam, too well! he sleeps for ever.

    Dutch. Dead! — Good Heav'n support me!

    D. Buck. Madam, 'twas my unhappy lot to hear   20
His last Departing Groans, and close his eyes.

    Dutch. Another taken from me too! why just Heav'n
Am I still left the last in life and woe?
'First I bemoan'd a noble Husbands death,
'Yet liv'd with looking on his Images.
'But now my last support is gone, First *Clarence,*
Now *Edward* is forever taken from me.
Both Crutches now the unrelenting hand
Of Death has stricken from my feeble Arms

And I must now of force sink down with sorrow.   30
    D. Buck. Your youngest Son, the Noble *Richard* lives.
His love I know will feel his Mothers Cares,
And bring new comfort to your latter days.
    Dutch. 'Twere new indeed! for yet of him I've none,
Unless a churlish disobedience may
Be counted from a Child a Mothers Comfort:
'From his malicious grudge I know my Son,
'His brother *Clarence* death was first contriv'd,
But may his Penitence find Heav'n's mercy.
Where is the Queen, my Lord?   40
    D. Buck. I left her with her kinsmen deep in Sorrow,
Who have with much adoe perswaded her
To leave the Body —— Madam they are here.

      Enter the Queen attended with Rivers *and* Dorset, *and others.*

    Queen. Why do you thus oppose my grief, unless
To make me Rave, and Weep the faster? Ha!
My Mother too in Tears! Fresh Sorrow strikes
My heart, at sight of every Friend, that lov'd
My *Edward* living —— O Mother! He's Dead!
Edward, my Lord, thy Son, our King is Dead.
O that my eyes cou'd weep away my Soul!   50
Then I might follow worthy of his Hearse.
    Ld. Stan. Your Duty, Madam, of a Wife is Dead,
And now the Mother's only claims your care.
Think on the Prince your Son: send for him strait,
And let his Coronation clear your eyes.
Bury your griefs in the dead *Edward's* Grave,
Revive your Joys on living *Edward's* Throne.
    Queen. Alas! That thought, but adds to my Afflictions.
New Tears for *Edward* gone, and fears for *Edward* living,
'An helpless Child, and his Minority   60
'Is in the Trust of his stern Uncle *Gloucester,*
A man that frowns on me, and all of mine.   [*Weeps.*
    D. Buck. Judge not so hardly, Madam, of his love,
Your Son will find in him a Father's Care.

      Enter Richard *behind.*

    Rich. Why ay! — These tears look well! sorrow's the mode,
And every one at Court must wear it now ——

With all my heart, I'll not be out of Fashion.   [*Aside.*
   Queen. My Lord, just Heav'n knows I never hated *Richard,*
But wou'd on any terms embrace his friendship.
   D. Buck. These words would make him weep, —— I know him
      yours.   70
See where he comes in sorrow for our loss.
   Rich. My Lords, — good morrow —— Cousin of *Buckingham,*
I am yours ———   [*Weeping.*
   D. Buck.   Good-morning to your Grace.
   Rich. Methinks ———
We meet, like men, that had forgot to speak.
   D. Buck. We may remember: But our argument
Is now too mournful to admit much talk.
   Rich. It is indeed! Peace be with him has made it so.
'Sister! Take Comfort —— Tis true we've all cause
'To mourn the dimming of our shining Star: 80
But sorrow never cou'd revive the dead ——
— And if it cou'd, hope wou'd prevent our fears,
So we must weep, because we weep in vain.
'Madam, my Mother —— I do cry you mercy:
'My grief was blind —— I did not see your Grace,
Most humbly on my knee I crave your Blessing.
   Dutch. Thou hast it, and may thy charitable
Heart, and Tongue love one another, may Heaven
Indow thy breast with meekness, and obedience.
   Rich. Amen, and make me die a good old man,   90
That's the old Butt-end of a Mother's Blessing;
I marvel that her Grace did leave it out.   [*Aside.*
   D. Buck. My Lords, I think 'twere fit, that now Prince Edward
Forthwith from Ludlow *shou'd be sent for home,*
In order to his Coronation.
   Rich. By all means, my Lords, come let's in to Counsel,
And appoint who shall be the messengers.
Madam, and you my Sister, please you go
'To give your sentiments on this occasion?
   Queen. My Lord, your Wisdom needs no help from me,   100
My glad consent you have in all that's just:
Or for the peoples good, tho I suffer by't.
   Rich. Please you to retire, Madam, we shall propose

What you'd not think the peoples wrong, nor yours.
    Queen. May Heav'n prosper all your good intent.
                      [Exit with all but Buckingham *and* Richard.
    Rich. Amen, with all my Heart. For mine's the Crown.
And is not that a good one? ha! Pray'd she not well, Cousin?
    D. Buck. I hope she prophesied —— You now stand Fair.
    Rich. Now by St. *Paul,* I feel it here! Methinks
The massy weight on't galls my laden Brow.   110
What think'st thou, Cousin, wer't not an easie matter
To get Lord *Stanley's* hand to help it on.
    D. Buck. 'My Lord, I doubt that for his Fathers sake,
'He loves the Prince to well, he'll scarce be won
'To any thing against him.
    Rich. Poverty the reward of Honest Fools
O'retake him for't! what thinkst thou then of *Hastings?*
    D. Buck. He shall be tri'd my Lord: I'll find out *Catesby,*
Who shall at subtle distance sound his thoughts,
But we must still suppose the worst may happen,   120
What if we find him cold in our design?
    Rich. Chop of his head. —— *Something we'll soon determine.*
But haste, and find out *Catesby,*
That done, follow me to the Counsel Chamber;
We'll not be seen together much, nor have
It known that we confer in Private —— Therefore
Away good Cousin.
    D. Buck.   I am gone, My Lord.   *[Exit* Buckingham.
    Rich. Thus far we run before the wind;
My Fortune smiles, and gives me all that I dare ask.
The conquer'd Lady *Ann* is bound in vows,   130
Fast as the priest can make us, we are one.
The King my Brother, sleeps without his Pillow,
And I am left the Guardian of his Infant Heir.
Let me see ——
The Prince will soon be here — let him — the Crown!
O yes! he shall have twenty, Globes, and Scepters too,
New ones made to play withall — But no Coronation!
No! nor no Court flies about him, no Kinsmen ——
—— Hold ye! —— Where shall he keep his Court!
— Ay! — the *Tower.*   *[Exit.*

ACT III, [SCENE I]

Enter Prince Edward, *with the Dukes of* Gloucester, Buckingham,
Lord Stanley, Tressel, *and Attendants.*

 Rich. 'Now, my Royal Cousin, welcome to *London*,
'Welcome to all those honour'd Dignities
'Which by your Father's Will, and by your Birth,
'You stand the undoubted Heir Possess'd of;
And, if my plain simplicity of Heart
May take the liberty to shew it self,
You're farther welcome to your Uncles Care
And Love: Why do you sigh, my Lord?
The weary way has made you melancholy.
 Pr. Ed. No, Uncle, but our crosses on the way   10
Have made it Tedious, Wearisome and Heavy,
I want more Uncles here to welcome me.
 Tress. More Uncles! What means his Highness?
 Ld. Stan. Why, Sir, the careful Duke of *Gloucester* has
Secur'd his Kinsmen on the way: Lord *Rivers, Gray,*
Sir *Thomas Vaughan,* and others of his Friends,   *Aside.*
Are Prisoners now in *Pomfret* Castle;
On what pretence it boots not: There they are;
Let the Devil and the Duke alone to accuse 'em.
 Rich. My Lord, the Mayor of London *comes to greet you.*   20
    Enter Lord Mayor, and Citizens.
 Ld. May. Vouchsafe, most Gracious Sovereign to accept
The general Homage of your Loyal City;
We farther beg your Royal leave to speak
In deep Condolement of your Father's loss:
And, far as our true sorrow will permit
To gratulate your Accession to the Throne.
 Pr. Ed. I thank you, good my Lord, and thank you all.
Alas, my youth is yet unfit to govern,
Therefore the Sword of Justice is in abler hands:
But be assur'd of this, so much already   30

I perceive I love you, that tho' I know not yet
To do you offices of good, yet this I know,
I'll sooner die, than basely do you wrong.
    Rich. So wise, so young, they say do never live long.   [*Aside.*
    Pr. Ed. My Lords,
I thought my Mother and my Brother York
Wou'd long e're this have met us on the way:
Say, Uncle Gloucester, *if our Brother come,*
Where shall we sojourn till our Coronation?
    Rich. Where it shall seem best to your Royal self,   40
May I advise you, Sir, some day or two
Your Highness shall repose you at the Tower,
Then where you please, and shall be thought most fit
For your best Health and Recreation.
    Pr. Ed. Why at the *Tower?* But be it as you please.
    D. Buck. My Lord, your Brother's Grace of *York.*

           Enter Duke and Duchess of York.

    Pr. Ed. Richard *of* York! *How fares our dearest Brother?*
                                     [*Embracing.*
    D. York. 'O! my dear Lord! So I must call you now.
    Pr. Ed. I, Brother, to our grief, as it is yours:
'Too soon he dy'd who might have better worn   50
'That Title, which in me will loose its Majesty.
    Rich. How fares our Cousin, Noble Lord of York?
    D. York. Thank you kindly, dear Uncle. O my Lord,
You said that Idle Weeds were fast in growth,
The King my Brother has out grown me far.
    Rich. He has my Lord.
    D. York.   *And therefore is he Idle?*
    Rich. O pretty Cousin, I must not say so.
    D. York. Nay, Uncle, I don't believe the sayings true,
For if it were, you'd be an Idle Weed.
    Rich. How so, Cousin?   60
    D. York. Because I've heard Folks say you grew so fast
Your Teeth wou'd gnaw a Crust at two hours old,
Now 'twas two years e'er I cou'd get a Tooth.
    Rich. Indeed —— I find the Brat is taught this lesson.   [*Aside.*
Who told thee this, my pretty merry Cousin?
    D. York. Why, your Nurse, Uncle.

Rich. My Nurse, Child, she was dead before thou wert born.
D. York. If 'twas not she, I can't tell who told me.
Rich. So subtle too; 'tis pity thou art short liv'd.   [*Aside.*
Pr. Ed. My Brother, Uncle, will be cross in talk.   70
Rich. O, fear not, my Lord, we shall never Quarrel.
Pr. Ed. I hope your Grace knows how to bear with him?
D. York. You mean to bear me; not to bear With me,
Uncle, *my Brother mocks both you and me,*
Because that I am little, like an Ape,
He thinks that you should bear me on your shoulders.
Pr. Ed. Fie, Brother, I have no such meaning.
Ld. Stan. With what a sharp, provided Wit he reasons,
To mitigate the scorn he gives his Uncle:
He prettily and aptly taunts himself.   *Aside.*
Tress. So cunning, and so young, is wonderful.   80
Rich. My Lord, wilt please you pass along?
My self, and my good Cousin Buckingham
Will to your Mother to entreat of her
To meet and bid you welcome at the Tower.
D. York. What! will you go to the Tower, *my dear Lord?*
Pr. Ed. My Lord Protector will have it so.
D. York. I sha'n't sleep in quiet at the Tower.
Rich. I'll warrant you. King *Henry* lay there,
And he sleeps in quiet.   [*Aside.*
Pr. Ed. What shou'd you fear, Brother?   91
D. York. My Uncle Clarence *Ghost, my Lord.*
My Grandmother told me he was kill'd there.
Pr. Ed. I fear no Uncles dead.
Rich. 'Nor any, Sir, that live, I hope.
Pr. Ed. 'I hope so too. But come, my Lords,
'To the *Tower,* since it must be so.
                    [*Exeunt all but* Richard *and* Buckingham.
D. Buck. Think you, my Lord, this little prating York
Was not instructed by his subtle Mother
To taunt and scorn you thus Opprobriously?   100
Rich. 'No doubt, no doubt. O! 'tis a shrewd young Master:
Stubborn, Bold, Quick, Forward and Capable;
He is all the Mothers from the Top to the Toe.

306

But let them rest: now what says Catesby?
   D. Buck. My Lord, 'tis much as I suspected, and
He's here himself to inform you.

Enter Catesby.

   Rich. So, *Catesby,* hast thou been tampering? What News?
   Cat. My Lord, according to the instruction given me,
With words at distance dropt I sounded *Hastings,*
Piercing how far he did affect your purpose,   110
To which indeed I found him Cold, Unwilling.
The sum is this, he seem'd a while to understand me not.
At length from plainer speaking urg'd to answer,
He said in heat, rather than wrong the Head
To whom the Crown was due, he'd lose his own.
   Rich. Indeed, his own then answer for that saying,
He shall be taken care of: Mean while *Catesby,*
Be thou near me: *Cousin of* Buckingham
Lets lose no time: The Mayor and Citizens
Are now buisie meeting in Guild-Hall,   120
'Thither I'd have you haste immediately,
'And at your meetest 'vantage of the time
'Improve those Hints I gave you late to speak of:
But above all, infer the Bastardy
Of Edward's *Children;*
Nay, for a need, thus far come near my Person,
Tell 'em, when my Mother went with Child of him,
My Princely Father then had Wars in France,
And by true Computation of the time
Found, that the issue was not his begot,   130
Which in his lineaments too plain appear'd,
Being nothing like the Noble York *my Father:*
Yet touch this sparingly, as 'twere far of,
Because, my Lord, you know my Mother lives.
   D. Buck. 'Doubt not, my Lord, I'll play the Orator
'As if my self might wear the Golden Fee,
'For which I Plead.
   Rich. If you thrive well, bring 'em to see me here,
'Where you shall find me seriously employ'd
'With the most Learned Fathers of the Church.   140

D. Buck. I fly, my Lord, to serve you.

Rich. To serve thy self, my Cousin;
For look, when I am King, claim thou of me
The Earldom of Hereford, *and all those Moveables,*
Whereof the King my Brother stood possest.

   D. Buck. I shall remember that your Grace was Bountiful.

   Rich. Cousin, I have said it.

   D. Buck. I am gone, my Lord.   [*Exit* Buckingham.

   Rich. So —— I've secur'd my Cousin here: These Moveables
Will never let his Brains have rest till I am King: 150
Catesby, *go thou with speed to Doctor* Shaw, *and thence*
'To Fryar *Beuker:* Haste, and bid 'em both
'Attend me here, within an hour at farthest: [*Exit* Catesby.
Mean while my private orders shall be given
To lock out all admittance to the Princes.
Now, by St. *Paul,* the work goes bravely on ——
How many frightful stops wou'd Conscience make
In some soft heads to undertake like me:
—— Come; this Conscience is a convenient Scarecrow,
It Guards the fruit which Priests and Wisemen tast,   160
Who never set it up to fright themselves:
They know 'tis rags, and gather in the face on't,
While half-starv'd shallow Daws thro Fear are honest.
Why were Laws made, but that we're Rogues by Nature?
Conscience! 'tis our Coin, we live by parting with it,
And he thrives best that has the most to spare:
The protesting Lover buys hope with it,
And the deluded Virgin short liv'd pleasure.
Old gray beards cram their Avarice with it,
Your Lank-jaw'd hungry Judge will dine upon't,   170
And hang the Guiltless rather than eat his Mutton cold.
The Crown'd Head quits it for Despotick sway,
The stubborn People for unaw'd Rebellion:
There's not a Slave but has his share of Villain;
Why then shall after Ages think my deeds
Inhumane? Since my worst are but Ambition:
   Ev'n all Mankind to some lov'd Ills incline,
   Great Men chuse Greater Sins —— Ambition's mine.   [*Exit.*

[ACT III, SCENE II]

Enter Lady Ann, *Sola.*

Lady A. When, when shall I have rest? Was Marriage made
To be the Scourge of our Offences here?
Oh no! 'Twas meant a Blessing to the Vertuous,
It once was so to me, tho' now my Curse:
The fruit of *Edward's* Love was sweet and pleasing:
But oh! Untimely cropt by cruel *Richard,*
Who rudely having grafted on his stock
Now makes my Life yield only sorrow.
Let me have Musick to compose my thoughts.   [*Soft Musick.*
It will not be: Nought but the grave can close my Eyes.   10
———— How many labouring Wretches take their rest,
While I, night after night, with cares lie waking,
As if the gentle Nurse of Nature, Sleep,
Had vow'd to rock my peevish sense no more.
'O partial sleep! Canst thou in smoaky Cottages
'Stretch out the Peasants Limbs on Beds of Straw,
'And lay him fast, cram'd with distressful Bread?
Yet in the softest breeze of Peaceful Night
'Under the Canopies of costly State,
'Tho' lull'd with sounds of sweetest melody,   20
Refuse one moments slumber to a Princess?
O mockery of Greatness! But see,
He comes! The rude disturber of my Pillow.

Enter Richard, *Aloof.*

Rich. Ha! still in tears; let 'em flow on; they're signs ⎫
Of a substantial grief —— Why don't she die? |
She must: My Interest will not let her live. |
The fair *Elizabeth* hath caught my Eye, |
My Heart's vacant; and she shall fill her place ——   ⎬   *Aside.*
They say that Women have but tender hearts, |
'Tis a mistake, I doubt; I've found 'em tough: | 30
They'll bend, indeed: But he must strain that cracks 'em.|
All I can hope's to throw her into sickness: |
Then I may send her a Physicians help.   ⎭

So, Madam: What, you still take care, I see
To let the World believe I love you not,
This outward Mourning now has malice in't,
So have these sullen disobedient tears:
I'll have you tell the World I doat on you.
    Lady A. I wish I could, but 'twill not be believ'd:
Have I deserv'd this usage?   40
    Rich. You have: You do not please me as at first.
    Lady A. What have I done? What horrid Crime committed?
    Rich. To me the worst of Crimes, out-liv'd my liking.
    Lady A. If that be Criminal, Just Heaven be kind,
And take me while my Penitence is warm:
O Sir, forgive, and kill me.
    Rich. Umh! No, —— The medling World will call it murder,
And I wou'd have 'em think me pitifull:
Now wert thou not afraid of self-Destruction,
Thou hast a fair excuse for't.   50
    Lady A. How fain wou'd I be Friends with Death? O name it.
    Rich. Thy Husband's hate: Nor do I hate thee only
From the dull'd edge of sated Appetite
But from the eager Love I bear another:
Some call me Hypocrite: What think'st thou now,
Do I dissemble?
    Lady A. Thy Vows of Love to me were all dissembled.
    Rich. Not one: For when I told thee so, I lov'd:
Thou art the only Soul I never yet deceiv'd:
And 'tis my honesty that tells thee now   60
With all my heart, I hate thee ——
If this have no Effect, she is immortal.   [*Aside.*
    Lady A. Forgive me Heaven, that I forgave this Man.
O may my story told in after Ages,
Give warning to our easie Sexes ears:
May it Unveil the hearts of Men, and strike
Them deaf to their dissimulated Love.
                  Enter Catesby.
    Cat. My Lord, his Grace of *Buckingham* attends
Your Highness Pleasure.
    Rich. Wait on him; I'll expect him here.   [*Exit* Catesby.
Your Absence, Madam, will be necessary.   71

Lady A. Wou'd my death were so.   [*Exit.*
Rich.   It may be shortly.
                        Enter Buckingham.
So, my Cousin, What say the Citizens?
  D. Buck. 'Now, by our hopes, my Lord, they're senseless stones,
'Their hesitating fear has struck 'em dumb.
  Rich. Touch'd you the Bastardy of Edward's *Children?*
  D. Buck. I did, with his Contract to Lady Lucy.
Nay, his own Bastardy and Tyranny for Trifles;
—— *Laid open all your Victories in* Scotland,
Your Discipline in War, Wisdom in Peace: 80
Your Bounty, Justice, fair Humility.
Indeed left nothing that might gild our Cause
Untouch'd, or slightly handled in my talk,
And when my Oration drew towards an end,
I urg'd of them that lov'd their Countries good
To do you right, and cry, Long live King Richard.
  Rich. And did they so?
  D. Buck. 'Not one, by Heaven: But each like Statues fix'd
'Speechless and Pale, star'd in his fellows Face,
Which when I saw, I reprehended them,   90
And ask'd the Mayor what meant this wilfull silence?
His answer was, the people were not us'd
To be spoken to but by the Recorder,
'Who then took on him to repeat my words.
Thus saith the Duke, thus hath the Duke inferr'd:
But nothing urg'd in Warrant from himself.
When he had done, some Followers of my own
At lower end of th' Hall, hurl'd up their Caps,
And some ten voices cry'd, God save King Richard,
At which I took the 'vantage of those few,   100
And cry'd, Thanks gentle Citizens and Friends,
This general applause and chearful shout
Argues your Wisdom, and your Love to Richard,
And even here broke of, and came away.
  Rich. O Tongueless Blocks! Wou'd they not speak?
Will not the Mayor then and his Brethren come?
  D. Buck. The Mayor is here at hand: Feign you some fear,
And be not spoke with, but by mighty suit:

'A Prayer-Book in your hand, my Lord, were well,
Standing between two Churchmen of Repute,   110
For on that ground I'll make an holy descant:
Yet be not easily won to our Requests,
'Seem, like the Virgin, fearful of your wishes.
  Rich. 'My other self! My Counsel's Consistory!
'My Oracle! my Prophet! My dear Cousin!   [*Embracing.*
'I, as a Child, will go by thy direction.
  D. Buck. Hark! the Lord Mayor's at hand: Away, my Lord;
Nor doubt, but yet we reach our point propos'd.
  Rich. We cannot fail, my Lord, while you are Pilot.
A little flattery sometimes does well.   [*Aside. Exit* Richard.

     Enter Lord Mayor, and Citizens.

  D. Buck. Welcome, my Lord, I dance attendance here;   121
I'm afraid the Duke will not be spoke withal.

     Enter Catesby.

Now, Catesby, *what says your Lord to my request?*
  Cat. My Lord, he humbly does entreat your Grace
To visit him to morrow, or next day.
He's now retir'd with two Right Reverend Fathers
Divinely bent to Meditation,
And in no worldly suits wou'd he be mov'd,
To interrupt his Holy Exercise.
  D. Buck. Return, good Catesby, *to the gracious Duke;*   130
Tell him, my Self, the Mayor, and Citizens,
In deep designs, in matters of great moment,
No less importing than our general good,
Are come to have some Conference with his Grace.
  Cat. My Lord, I'll instantly inform his Highness.
  D. Buck. Ah! my good Lord! This Prince is not an Edward,
He is not lolling on a lewd Love-bed;
But on his knees at Meditation:
Not dallying with a brace of Curtizans,
But with two deep Divines in secret praying.   140
Happy were England *wou'd this Vertuous Prince*
Take on himself the toil of Sovereignty.
  Ld. May. Happy indeed, my Lord.
He will not sure refuse our proffer'd Love?
  D. Buck. Alas my Lord, you know him not, his mind's

Above this World; he's for a Crown Immortal!
Look there! His door opens: Now where's our hope?

   Ld. May. See where his Grace stands 'tween two Clergymen?

   D. Buck. Ay, ay; 'tis there he's caught: There's his Ambition.

   Ld. May. How low he bows to thank 'em for their care!   150
And, see, a Prayer-Book in his hand!

   D. Buck. Wou'd he were King, we'd give him leave to pray.
Methinks I wish it for the love he bears the City.
How have I heard him vow he thought it Hard
The Mayor should lose his Title with his Office?
Well! who knows? he may be won?

   Ld. May. Ah! my Lord!

   D. Buck. See! He comes forth: my Friends be resolute,
I know he's cautious to a fault but do not
Leave him till our honest suit be granted.   160

            Enter Richard *with a Book.*

   Rich. Cousin of Buckingham!
I do beseech your Grace to pardon me,
Who, earnest in my Zealous Meditation,
So long deferr'd the service of my Friends:
Now do I fear I've done some strange offence,
That looks disgracious in the City's Eye;
If so, 'tis Just you shou'd reprove my Ignorance.

   D. Buck. You have, my Lord: We wish your Grace
On our entreaties wou'd amend your fault.

   Rich. Else wherefore breath I in a Christian Land?   170

   D. Buck. Know then it is your fault, that you resign
The Sceptred Office of your Ancestors,
Fair England's *Throne, your own due right of Birth,*
To the Corruption of a blemisht stock,
While in the Mildness of your sleeping thoughts,
(Which here we waken to our Country's good)
This wounded Isle does want her proper Limbs,
'Which to recure, joyn'd with these Loyal Men,
'Your very Worshipful and Loving Friends,
And by their zealous Instigation,   180
In this Just Cause, I come to move your Highness,
That on your gracious self you'd take the Charge
And Kingly Government of this your Land,

Not as Protector, Steward, Substitute,
Or lowly Factor for another's Gain:
But as successively from Blood to Blood,
Your own, by right of Birth, and lineal Glory.
   Rich. I cannot tell, if to depart in silence,
Or bitterly to speak in your reproof,
Fits best with my Degree or your Condition: 190
'Therefore to speak in just refusal of your suit,
And then in speaking not to check my Friends.
Definitively thus I answer you;
Your Love deserves my Thanks, but my desert
Unmeritable shuns your fond Request:
For, Heaven be thanked, there is no need of me;
The Royal stock has left us Royal fruit,
Which mellow'd by the stealing hours of time,
Will well become the seat of Majesty,
And make us (no doubt) happy by his Reign.   200
On him I lay what you wou'd lay on me,
The Right and Fortune of his happier Stars,
'Which Heaven forbid my thoughts shou'd rob him of.
   D. Buck. My Lord, this argues Conscience in your Grace,
But Circumstances well consider'd:
The weak respects thereof are nice and trivial.
You say that Edward *was your Brothers Son*
So say we too, but not by Edward's *Wife:*
'If solemn Contracts are of any force,
'That Title Justice gave to Lady *Lucy:*   210
'Even of his Birth cou'd I severely speak;
Save that for reverence to some alive,
I give a spairing limit to my Tongue.
   Ld. May. Upon our knees, my Lord, we beg your Grace
To wear this precious Robe of Dignity,
Which on a Child must sit too loose and heavy.
'Tis yours; befitting both your Wisdom and your Birth.
   Cat. My Lord, this coldness is unkind,
Nor suits it with such ardent Loyalty.
   D. Buck. O make 'em happy: Grant their Lawful Suit.   220
   Rich. Alas! Why wou'd you heap this care on me?
I am unfit for State and Majesty.

I thank you for your Loves, but must declare
(I do beseech you take it not amiss)
I will not! dare not! must not yield to you.
   D. Buck. If you refuse us through a soft remorse,
Loth to depose the Child, your Brother's Son:
(As well we know your tenderness of Heart)
Yet know, tho' you deny us to the last,
Your Brother's Son shall never Reign our King: 230
But we will plant some other in the Throne,
To the disgrace and downfall of your House.
'And thus resolv'd I bid you, Sir, Farewell.
My Lord, and Gentlemen, I crave your pardon
For this vain trouble: M' intent was good,
I wou'd have serv'd my Country and my King;
But 'twill not be: Farewel! When next we meet ——
   Ld. *May.* Be not too rash, my Lord, his Grace relents.
   D. Buck. Away, you but deceive your selves —— [*Exit* Buckingham.
   Cat. Sweet Prince accept their suit.   240
   Ld. *May.* If you deny us, all the Land will rue it.
   Rich. Call him again —— You will enforce me to
A World of cares; I am not made of stone,
But penetrable to your kind entreaties:
Tho' Heaven knows against my own Inclining.
              Re-enter Buckingham.
Cousin of Buckingham, *and sage grave Men.*
Since you will buckle Fortune on my Back
To bear her burthen whether I will or no,
I must have patience to endure the load:
But if black Scandal or foul-fac'd Reproach   250
Attend the sequel of your Imposition,
Your meer Enforcement shall Acquittance me:
For Heaven knows, as you may all partly see,
How far I am from the desire of this.
   Ld. *May. Heaven guard your Grace: We see it, and will say it.*
   Rich. You will but say the truth, my Lord.
   D. Buck. My heart's so full it scarce has vent for words;
My knee will better speak my duty now.   [*Kneels.*
Long live our Soveraign, *Richard* King of *England.*
   Rich. Indeed your words have touch'd me nearly Cousin: 260

Pray rise. I wish you cou'd recall 'em.
    D. Buck. It wou'd be Treason now, my Lord: To morrow,
'If it so please your Majesty, from Counsel
'Orders shall be given for your Coronation.
    Rich. Even when you please: for you will have it so.
    D. Buck. To morrow then we will attend your Majesty:
And now we take our leaves with joy.
    Rich. Cousin Adieu! my loving Friends farewel:
I must to my Holy Work again.   [*Exeunt* Buckingham *and Citizens.*

Richard. Solus.

Why now my golden dream is out ——   270
Ambition like an early Friend throws back
My Curtains with an eager Hand, o'rejoy'd
To tell me what I dreamt is true —— A Crown!
Thou bright reward of ever daring minds,
O! How thy awful Glory fills my Soul!
Nor can the means that got thee dim thy lustre;
For, not mens Love, Fear pays thee Adoration:
And Fame not more survives from Good than Evil deeds.
Th' aspiring youth that fir'd th' *Ephesian* Dome
Out-lives in Fame the pious Fool that rais'd it: 280
    Conscience, lie still —— More lives must yet be drain'd,
    Crowns got with Blood must be with Blood maintain'd.   [*Exit.*

ACT IV, [SCENE I]

The Scene, The Tower.
Enter the two Princes with the Queen, the Dutchess
of York, and Lady Ann in tears.

    Pr. Ed. Pray, Madam, do not leave me yet,
For I have many more complaints to tell you.
    Queen. And I unable to redress the least:
What wou'dst thou say, my Child?

316

Pr. Ed. O Mother! Since I first have lain i'th' *Tower*
My rest has still been broke with frightful Dreams,
Or shocking News has wak'd me into tears.
I'm scarce allow'd a Friend to visit me:
All my old honest Servants are turn'd off,
And in their rooms are strange ill-natur'd fellows,   10
Who look so bold, as they were all my Masters;
And, I'm afraid, they'll shortly take you from me.
    Dutch. O mournful hearing!
    Lady A.   O unhappy Prince!
    D. York. Dear Brother, why do you weep so?
You make me cry too.
    Queen. Alas, poor Innocence!
    Pr. Ed. Wou'd I but knew at what my Uncle aims;
If 'twere my Crown, I'd freely give it him,
So he'd but let me 'joy my life in quiet.
    D. York. Why! will my Uncle kill us, Brother?   20
    Pr. Ed. I hope he wo'n't: We never injur'd him.
    Queen. I cannot bear to see 'em thus. ——   *[Weeping.*

           Enter to them, Lord Stanley.

    Ld. Stan. Madam, I hope your Majesty will pardon
What I am griev'd to tell, Unwelcome News.
    Queen. Ah me! more sorrow yet! My Lord; we've long
Despair'd of happy Tydings, pray what is't?
    Ld. Stan. On *Tuesday* last, your noble Kinsmen *Rivers,*
Grey, and Sir *Thomas Vaughan* at *Pomfret,*
Were Executed on a publick Scaffold.
    Dutch. O dismal Tydings.   30
    Pr. Ed. O poor Uncles! I doubt my turn is next.
    Lady A. Nor mine, I fear, far off.
    Queen. Why, then let's welcome Blood and Massacre,
Yield all our Throats to the fierce Tygers rage,
And die lamenting one another's wrongs.
O! I foresaw this ruin of our House.   *[Weeps.*

           Enter Catesby *to Lady* Ann.

    Cat. Madam, the King
Has sent me to inform your Majesty
That you prepare (as is advis'd from Counsel)
To morrow for your Royal Coronation.   40

Queen. What do I hear? Support me, Heaven!

Lady A. Despightful Tydings! O unpleasing News!
Alas, I heard of this before, but cou'd not
For my soul take heart to tell you of it.

Cat. The King does further wish your Majesty
Wou'd less employ your visits at the *Tower.*
He gives me leave t' attend you to the Court,
And is impatient, Madam, till he sees you.

Lady A. Farewel to all, and thou, poor injur'd Queen:
Forgive the unfriendly duty I must pay.   50

Queen. Alas, kind Soul, I envy not thy Glory,
Nor think I'm pleas'd thou'rt partner in our sorrow.

Cat. Madam. ——

Lady A.   I come ———

Queen. Farewel, thou woeful welcomer of Glory.

Cat. Shall I attend your Majesty?

Lady A. Attend me! Whither, to be Crown'd?
Let me with deadly Venome be Anointed,
And die e'er Men can say, Long live the Queen.

Queen. Poor grieving heart, I pity thy complaining.

Lady A. No more than with my Soul I mourn for yours: 60
A long farewel to all. ——   [*Exit Lady* Ann *and* Catesby.

Ld. Stan.   Take comfort, Madam.

Queen. Alas, where is it to be found?
Death and Destruction follow us so close,
They shortly must o'retake us.

Ld. Stan.   In *Brittany*
My Son-in-Law the Earl of *Richmond* still
Resides, who with a jealous Eye observes
The lawless actions of aspiring *Richard:*
To him, (wou'd I advise you) Madam, fly
Forthwith for Aid, Protection, and Redress.
He will I'm sure with open arms receive you.   70

Dutch. Delay not Madam,
For 'tis the only hope that Heaven has left us.

Queen. Do with me what you please: For any Change
Must surely better our Condition.

Ld. Stan. I farther wou'd advise you, Madam, this
Instant to remove Princes to some

Remote Abode, where you your self are Mistress.

 Pr. Ed. Dear Madam take me hence: For I shall ne'er
Enjoy a moments quiet here.

 D. York. Nor I: Pray Mother let me go too?   80

 Queen. Come then, my pretty young ones, lets away:
For here you lie within the Falcon's reach,
Who watches but th' unguarded hour to seize you.

Enter the Lieutenant with an Order.

 Lieu. I beg your Majesty will pardon me:
But the young Princes must, on no account,
Have Egress from the *Tower,*
Nor must, without the King's especial License,
Of what degree soever, any Person
Have admittance to 'em. —— All must retire.

 Queen. 'I am their Mother, Sir, who else commands 'em?   90
'If I pass freely, they shall follow me.
'For you —— I'll take the peril of your fault upon my self.

 Lieu. My Inclination, Madam, wou'd oblige you,
'But I am bound by Oath, and must obey.
Nor, Madam, can I now with safety answer
For this continued Visit.
Please you my Lord to read these Orders.   [*Gives 'em Lord* Stanley.

 Queen. O Heavenly powers! Shall I not stay with 'em?

 Lieu. Such are the Kings Commands, Madam.

 Queen.   My Lord!

 Ld. Stan. 'Tis too true, and it were vain t' oppose 'em.   100

 Queen. Support me Heaven!
For life can never bear the pangs of such a parting.
O my poor Children! O distracting thought!
I dare not bid 'em (as I shou'd) farewel,
And then to part in silence stabs my Soul.

 Pr. Ed. What, must you leave us, Mother?

 Queen.   What shall I say? [*Aside.*
But for a time, my Loves —— we shall meet again,
At least in Heaven.   [*To her self.*

 D. York. Won't you take me with you, Mother?
I shall be so 'fraid to stay when you are gone.   110

 Queen. I cannot speak to 'em, and yet we must
Be parted —— Then let these kisses say farewel.   [*Kissing 'em.*

319

Why! O why just Heaven, must these be our last?
  Dutch. Give not your grief such way: be sudden when you part.
  Queen. I will —— since it must be, to Heaven I leave 'em.
Hear me, you Guardian powers of Innocence!
Awake or sleeping: O! protect 'em still,
Still may their helpless youth attract mens pity;
That when the arm of Cruelty is rais'd,
Their looks may drop the lifted Dagger down   120
From the stern murderers relenting hand,
And throw him on his knees in penitence.
  Both Pr. O Mother! Mother!
  Queen.   O my poor Children!
                            [Exeunt parted severally.

[ACT IV, SCENE II]

The Scene changes to the Presence, discovering Richard *seated
with* Buckingham, Catesby, Ratcliff, Lovel, *other Lords
and Attendants.*

  Rich. Stand all apart: Cousin of Buckingham.
  D. Buck. My gracious Sovereign.
  Rich.   *Give me thy hand:*
At length by thy advice and thy assistance
Is Richard *seated on the* English *Throne.*
But say, my Cousin, what,
Shall we wear these Glories for a day?
Or shall they last, and we rejoyce in 'em?
  D. Buck. I hope for Ages, Sir, Long may they Grace you.
  Rich. O Buckingham! *now do I play the touch-stone,*
'To try if thou be current Friend indeed.   10
'Young *Edward* lives: So does his Brother *York.*
'Now think what I wou'd speak!
  D. Buck. 'Say on, my gracious Lord.

320

Rich. I tell thee, Cuz, I've lately had two Spiders
Crawling upon my startled hopes: Now tho'
Thy friendly hand has brush'd 'em from me,
Yet still they Crawl offensive to my Eyes,
I wou'd have some Friend to tread upon 'em.
I wou'd be King, my Cousin ———

    D. Buck. Why so I think you are, my Royal Lord.   20
    Rich. Ha, am I King? 'Tis so — But — Edward lives!
    D. Buck. Most true, my Lord.
    Rich. Cousin, thou wert not wont to be so dull ——
Shall I be plain? I wish the Bastards dead.
And I wou'd have it suddenly perform'd ——
'Now Cousin, canst thou answer me?
    D. Buck. None dare dispute your Highness Pleasure.
    Rich. 'Indeed, methinks thy kindness freezes Cousin;
'Thou dost refuse me then! —— They shall not die?
    D. Buck. 'My Lord, since 'tis an action cannot be   30
'Recall'd, allow me but some pause to think,
'Ill instantly resolve your Highness.   [*Exit* Buckingham.
    Cat. The King seems angry; see he gnaws his lip.
    Rich. I'll henceforth deal with shorter sighted Fools,
None are for me that look into my Deeds,
'With thinking Eyes ——
High reaching Buckingham *grows Circumspect.*
The best on't is it may be done without him,
Tho' not so well perhaps —— had he consented,
Why, then the murther had been his, not mine. ——   40
—— We'll make a shift as 'tis —— Come hither, *Catesby.*
Where's that same *Tirrel* whom thou toldst me of?
Hast thou given him those sums of Gold I order'd?
    Cat. I have, my Liege.
    Rich.   Where is he?
    Cat. He waits your Highness pleasure.
    Rich. Give him this Ring, and say my self
Will bring him farther Orders instantly.   [*Exit* Catesby.
'The deep revolving Duke of *Buckingham*
No more shall be the Neighbour to my Counsels:
Has he so long held out with me untir'd,   50
And stops he now for Breath? Well, be it so. ——

Enter Lord Stanley.

How now, Lord Stanley? *What's the News?*

   Ld. Stan. I hear, my Liege, the Lord Marquess of Dorset
Is fled to Richmond, *now in* Brittany.

   Rich. Why let him go, my Lord, he may be spar'd.
Hark thee, *Ratcliff,* when saw'st thou *Ann,* my Queen?
Is she still weak? Has my Physician seen her?

   Rat. He has, my Lord, and fears her mightily.

   Rich. But he's excelling skillful, she'll mend shortly.

   Rat. I hope she will, my Lord.   60

   Rich. And, if she does, I have mistook my man.   [*Aside.*
I must be married to my Brother's Daughter,
At whom I know the Brittain Richmond aims;
And by that knot looks proudly on the Crown.
But then to stain me with her Brother's Blood:
Is that the way to wooe the Sisters Love?
'—— No matter what's the way —— For while they live
'My goodly Kingdom's on a weak Foundation.
'Tis done: My daring heart's resolv'd —— they're dead.

Re-enter Duke of Buckingham.

   D. Buck. My Lord, I have consider'd in my mind,   70
The late Request that you did sound me in.

   Rich. Well, let that rest: Dorset *is fled to* Richmond.

   D. Buck. I have heard the News, my Lord.

   Rich. Stanley, *he's your near Kinsman —— Well,* look to him.

   D. Buck. My Lord, I claim that gift, my due by promise,
'For which your Honour and your Faith's engag'd;
'The Earldom of *Hereford,* and those Moveables,
'Which you have promis'd I shall possess.

   Rich. Stanley, *look to your Wife; if she convey*
Letters to Richmond, *you shall answer it.*   80

   D. Buck. 'What says your Highness to my Just request?

   Rich. I do remember me, Harry the Sixth
Did Prophecy that Richmond *should be King,*
When Richmond *was a peevish Boy!*
"Tis odd —— A King perhaps.

Enter Catesby.

   Cat. My Lord, I have obey'd your Highness Orders.

   D. Buck. May it please you to resolve me in my Suit?

322

Rich. Lead *Tirrel* to my Closet, I'll meet him.
D. Buck. I beg your Highness ear my Lord ——
Rich. I'm busie: Thou troubl'st me —— I'm not i'th' vein. 90
                                          [*Exit* Richard.
D. Buck. O patience, Heaven! Is't thus he pays my service?
Was it for this I rais'd him to the Throne?
O! if the peaceful dead have any sence
Of those vile injuries they bore, while living:
Then sure the joyful Souls of Blood-suck'd *Edward,*
Henry, Clarence, Hastings, and All that through
His foul corrupted dealings have miscarried,
Will from the Walls of Heav'n in smiles look down ⎤
To see this Tyrant tumbling from his Throne,   ⎬
His Fall unmourn'd, and Bloody as their own.   ⎦   [*Exit.*

[ACT IV, SCENE III]

Scene the Tower: *Enter* Tirrel, Dighton, *and* Forest.
  Tir. Come, Gentlemen:
Have you concluded on the means?
  For. Smothering will make no noise, Sir.
  Tir. Let it be done i'th' dark: For shou'd you see
Their young faces, who knows how far their looks
Of Innocence may tempt you into pity.
  For. 'Tis ease and living well makes Innocence:
I hate a face less guilty than my own:
Were all that now seem Honest deep as we
In trouble and in want they'd all be Rogues.   10
  Tir. Stand back —— Lieutenant, have you brought the Keys?
              Enter Lieutenant.
  Lieu. I have 'em, Sir.
  Tir. Then here's your warrant to deliver 'em.   [*Gives a Ring.*
  Lieu. Your Servant, Sir. ——
What can this mean? Why, at this dead of night

To give 'em too? — 'Tis not for me t' enquire.   [*Exit Lieutenant.*
 Tir. There, Gentlemen: [*Giving them the Keys.*
That way! You have no farther need of me.   [*Exeunt severally.*
       Enter Richard.
 Rich. Wou'd it were done: There is a busie something here,
That foolish Custom has made terrible,   20
To the intent of evil Deeds; And Nature too,
As if she knew me Womanish, and Weak,
Tugs at my Heart-Strings with complaining Cries,
To talk me from my Purpose ——
And then the thought of what Mens Tongues will say,
Of what their Hearts must think; To have no Creature
Love me Living, nor my Memory when Dead.
Shall future Ages, when these Childrens Tale
Is told, drop Tears in pity of their hapless Fate,
And read with Detestation the Misdeeds of *Richard,* 30
The crook-back Tyrant, Cruel, Barbarous,
And Bloody ——— will they not say too,
That to possess the Crown, nor Laws Divine
Nor Human stopt my way —— Why let 'em say it;
They can't but say I had the Crown;
I was not Fool as well as Villain.
Hark! the Murder's doing; Princes farewel,
To me there's Musick in your Passing-Bell.   [*Exit.*
     Enter Tirrel. *Solus.*
 Tir. "Tis done: The barbarous bloody act is done.
Ha! the King: His coming hither at this   40
Late hour, speaks him impatient for the welcome News.
       Enter Richard.
 Rich. Now my *Tirrel,* how are the Brats dispos'd?
Say; am I happy? Hast thou dealt upon 'em?
 Tir. 'If to have done the thing you gave in charge
'Beget your happiness, then, Sir, be happy;
For it is done.
 Rich.   *But didst thou see 'em dead?*
 Tir. I did, my Lord.
 Rich.   *And buried, my good* Tirrel?
 Tir. In that I thought to ask your Grace's Pleasure.

Rich. I have't — I'll have 'em sure — Get me a Coffin
Full of holes, let 'em be both cram'd into't;   50
And, hark thee, in the night-tide throw 'em down
The *Thames;* once in, they'll find the way to th' bottom,
Mean time but think how I may do thee good,
And be Inheritor of thy desire.
   Tir. I humbly thank your Highness.
   Rich. About it strait, good *Tirrel.*
   Tir. Conclude it done, my Lord.   [*Exit* Tirrel.
   Rich. Why then my lowdest fears are husht.
'The Sons of *Edward* have Eternal Rest,
'And *Ann,* my Wife, has bid this World good night,   60
While fair *Elizabeth* my beauteous Neice
Like a New Morn lights onward to my wishes.
Enter Catesby.

   Cat. My Lord!
   Rich. Good News, or bad, that thou comest in so bluntly?
   Cat. Bad News, my Lord, *Morton* is fled to *Richmond,*
And Buckingham, *back'd with the hardy* Welshmen,
Is in the Field, and still his Power increases.
   Rich. Morton *with* Richmond, *touches me more near*
Than Buckingham *and his rash levied numbers.*
'But come, dangers retreat when boldly they're confronted,   70
'And dull delays lead impotence and fear.
'Then fiery Expedition raise my Arm,
And fatal may it fall on crush'd Rebellion.
   Let's muster Men, my Councel is my Shield,
   We must be brief when Traytors brave the Field.   [*Exeunt.*

[ACT IV, SCENE IV]

Enter the Queen and Dutchess of York.

Queen. O my poor Children! O my tender Babes!

My unblown flowers pluck'd by untimely hands:
'If yet your gentle Souls fly in the Air,
'And be not fix'd in doom perpetual;
'Hover about me with your Airy wings,
'And hear your Mothers Lamentation:
Why slept their Guardian Angels, when this deed was done?
   Dutch. 'So many miseries have drain'd my Eyes,
'That my woe-wearied Tongue is still and mute.
'Why should Calamity be full of Words?   10
   Queen. Let's give 'em scope, for tho' they can't remove,
'Yet they do ease Affliction.
   Dutch. Why then let us be loud in Exclamations
To *Richard*! Haste, and pierce him with our cries!
That from henceforth his Conscience may out-Tongue
The close whispers of his relentless heart.
Hark! His Trumpet sounds! This way he must pass.
                         [*Trumpet sounds a march.*
   Queen. Alas, I've not the Daring to confront him.
   Dutch. I have a Mothers right, I'll force him hear me.
Enter Richard *with his Powers, the Dutchess meets and stops him, &c.*
   Rich. Who intercepts me in my Expedition?   20
   Dutch. Dost thou not know me? Art thou not my Son?
   Rich. I cry you mercy, Madam, is it you?
   Dutch. 'Art thou my Son?
   Rich. I, I thank Heaven, my Father and your Self.
   Dutch. 'Then I command thee, hear me.
   Rich. Madam, I have a touch of your condition,
That cannot brook the accent of Reproof.
   Dutch. Stay, I'll be mild and gentle in my Words.
   Rich. And brief, good Mother, for I am in haste.
   Dutch. Why, I have staid for thee (just Heaven knows)   30
In Torment and Agony.
   Rich. And came I not at last to comfort you?
   Dutch. No, on my Soul, too well thou know'st it.
A grievous burthen was thy Birth to me;
Tetchy and way-ward was thy Infancy,
Thy prime of Manhood daring, bold and stubborn:
Thy Age confirm'd most subtle, proud and bloody.
   Rich. If I am so disgracious in your eye,

Let me march on, and not offend you, Madam.
Strike up the Drum.
    Dutch.   Yet stay, I charge thee hear me.   40
    Queen. If not, hear me; for I have wrongs will speak
Without a Tongue: methinks the very sight
Of me shou'd turn thee into stone.
'Where are my Children, *Richard?*
    Dutch. 'Where is thy Brother *Clarence?*
    Queen.   Where *Hastings?*
    Dutch. '*Rivers?*
    Queen.   '*Vaughan?*
    Dutch.   '*Grey?*
    Rich. A Flourish, Trumpets: Strike Allarum, Drums.
Let not the Heavens hear these Tell-tale Women
Rail on the Heavens Anointed. Strike, I say.
                      [Allarum of Drums and Trumpets.
Either be patient and intreat me fair,   50
Or with the Clamorous report of War
Thus will I drown your Exclamations.
    Dutch. Then hear me Heaven, and Heaven at his latest hour
Be Deaf to Him as he is now to me:
'E'er from this War he turn a Conqueror,
Ye Pow'rs, cut off his dangerous thread of Life,
Least his black sins rise higher in Account,
Than Hell has pains to punish ———
Mischance and sorrow wait thee to the Field:
Hearts Discontent, languid and lean Despair   60
With all the Hells of Guilt pursue thy steps for ever.   *[Exit Dutchess.*
    Queen. Tho' far more cause, yet much less power to curse
Abides in me: I say *Amen* to her.
    Rich. Stay, Madam, I wou'd beg some words with you?
    Queen. 'What canst thou ask, that I have now to grant?
'Is't another Son? *Richard* I have none.
    Rich. You have a Beauteous Daughter call'd Elizabeth.
    Queen. 'Must she die too?
    Rich. For whose fair sake I'll bring more Good to you,
Than ever You or Yours from me had Harm;   70
So in the Lethe *of thy angry Soul*
Thou'lt drown the sad remembrance of those wrongs

'Which thou supposest me the cruel cause of.
    Queen. Be brief, least that the process of thy Kindness
Last longer telling than thy kindness Date.
    Rich. 'Know then, that from my Soul I love the fair
'*Elizabeth,* and will, with your permission,
'Seat her on the Throne of *England.*
    Queen. 'Alas, vain man, how canst thou wooe her?
    Rich. That would I learn of you,   80
As one being best acquainted with her humour.
    Queen. If thou wilt learn of me, then wooe her thus,
Send to her, by the man that kill'd her Brothers,
'A pair of bleeding Hearts; thereon Engrave
'*Edward* and *York*: Then haply will she weep.
'On this present her with an Handkerchief
'Stain'd in their Blood, to wipe her woeful Eyes.
If this Inducement move her not to Love,
Read o'er the History of thy Noble Deeds;
'Tell her, thy Policy took off her Uncle   90
Clarence, Rivers, Grey; nay, and for her sake,
Made quick conveyance with her dear Aunt Ann.
    Rich. You mock me, Madam; this is not the way
To win your Daughter.
    Queen.   *There is no other way,*
Unless thou couldst put on some other form,
And not be Richard *that has done all this.*
    Rich. As I intend to prosper and Repent,
So thrive I in my dangerous Affairs
Of Hostile Arms: My self, my self confound,
Heaven and Fortune bar me happy hours: 100
Day yield me not thy light, nor Night thy Rest;
Be opposite all Planets of good luck,
To my Proceeding, if with dear Hearts Love,
Immaculate Devotion, Holy Thoughts,
I tender not the fair Elizabeth,
In her consists thy happiness and mine:
Without her follows to my self and thee,
Her self, the Land, and many a Christian Soul,
Death, Desolation, Ruin and Decay.
'It cannot, will not be avoided, but by this.   110

Queen. What shall I say? still to affront his love,
I fear will but incense him to Revenge.
And to consent I shou'd abhor my self,
Yet I may seemingly comply, and thus   *Aside.*
By sending *Richmond* Word of his Intent,
Shall gain some time to let my Child escape him.
It shall be so,
I have consider'd, Sir, of your important wishes,
And cou'd I but believe you real ——
   Rich. Now by the sacred Hosts of Saints above ——   120
   Queen. O do not swear, my Lord, I ask no Oath;
Unless my Daughter doubts you more than I.
   Rich. O my kind Mother (I must call you so)
Be thou to her my loves soft Orator;
Plead what I Will be, not what I Have been;
Not my deserts, but what I Will deserve:
'And when this Warlike arm shall have chastis'd
'Th' audacious Rebel hot-brain'd *Buckingham:*
Bound with Triumphant Garlands will I come,
And lead thy Daughter to a Conqueror's Bed.   130
   Queen. My Lord, farewel: in some few days expect
To hear how fair a progress I have made.
Till when be Happy, as you're Penitent.
   Rich. My heart goes with you to my Love, farewel.   [*Exit Queen.*
'Relenting, Shallow-thoughted Woman.

Enter Ratcliff.

How now! the News?
   Rat. Most gracious Sovereign, on the Western Coasts
Rides a most powerful Navy and our fears
Inform us Richmond *is their Admiral,*
There do they Hull expecting but the aid,   140
Of Buckingham *to welcome them a shore.*   [*Exit.*
   Rich. 'We must prevent him then. Come hither *Catesby.*
   Cat. 'My Lord, your pleasure?
   Rich. Post to the Duke of Norfolk *instantly;*
Bid him strait levy all the strength and power
That he can make, and meet me suddenly
At *Salisbury:* Commend me to his Grace: away!   [*Exit* Catesby.

Enter Lord Stanley.

329

Well, my Lord, What News have you gather'd?

    Ld. Stan. Richmond *is on the Seas, my Lord.*

    Rich. There let him sink, and be the Seas on Him: 150

White Liver'd Runnagade, what does he there?

    Ld. Stan. I know not, mighty Sovereign, but by guess.

    Rich. Well, as you guess?

    Ld. Stan. Stir'd up by Dorset, Buckingham, *and* Morton,

He makes for England *here to claim the Crown.*

    Rich. Traytor, the Crown: Where is thy power then

To beat him back?

Where be thy Tenants, and thy Followers?

'The Foe upon our Coast, and thou no Friends to meet 'em?

Or hast thou marched 'em to the Western shore,   160

To give the Rebels Conduct from their Ships?

    Ld. Stan. My Lord, my Friends are ready all, i'th' North.

    Rich. The North! Why, what do they do in the North,

When they shou'd serve their Sovereign in the West?

    Ld. Stan. They yet have had no Orders, Sir, to move:

If 'tis your Royal Pleasure they should march,

'I'll lead 'em on with utmost haste to joyn you,

'Where, and what Time your Majesty shall please.

    Rich. What, thou wou'dst be gone, to joyn with Richmond?

    Ld. Stan. 'Sir, you've no Cause to doubt my Loyalty;   170

'I ne'er yet was, nor ever will be false.

    Rich. Away then, to thy Friends, and lead 'em on

'To meet me — Hold! Come back! I will not trust thee,

I've thought a way to make thee sure: Your Son

George Stanley, *Sir, I'll have him left behind;*

And look your Heart be Firm,

Or else his heads Assurance is but Frail.

    Ld. Stan. As I prove true, my Lord, so deal with him. [*Exit* Stanley.

Enter Ratcliff.

    Rat. My Lord, the Army of Great Buckingham

By sudden Floods, and fall of Waters,   180

Is half lost and scatter'd,

And he himself wander'd away alone;

No man knows whither.

    Rich. 'Has any careful Officer proclaim'd

Reward to him that brings the Traytor in?

330

Rat. Such Proclamation has been made, my Lord.

Enter Catesby.

Cat. My Liege, the Duke of Buckingham *is taken.*
Rich. Off with his head. So much for Buckingham.
Cat. My Lord, I'm sorry I must tell more News.
Rich. Out with it.   190
Cat. The Earl of Richmond *with a mighty power*
Is Landed, Sir, at Milford:
And, to confirm the News, Lord Marquess Dorset,
And Sir Thomas Lovewel *are up in* Yorkshire.
Rich. Why ay, this looks Rebellion. Ho! my Horse!
By Heaven the News allarms my stirring Soul.
'And as the Wretch, whose fever-weakned joynts,
'Like strengthless hinges buckle under Life;
'Impatient of his fit, breaks like a fire
'From his fond Keeper's Arms, and starts away: 200
'Even so these War-worn Limbs grown weak
'From Wars disuse, being now inrag'd with War,
'Feel a new Fury, and are thrice themselves.
Come forth my Honest Sword, which here I vow,
By my Souls hope, shall ne'er again be sheath'd,
Ne'er shall these watching Eyes have needful rest,
Till Death has clos'd 'em in a glorious Grave,
Or Fortune given me Measure of Revenge.   [*Exeunt.*

ACT V, [SCENE I]

Scene, The Field.

Enter Richmond, Oxford, Blunt, Herbert, *and others, marching.*

Richm. Thus far into the bowels of the Land
Have we march'd on without Impediment.
'*Richard,* the bloody and devouring Boar,
'Whose Ravenous Appetite has spoil'd your Fields;

331

'Laid this rich Country waste, and rudely crop'd
'Its ripned hopes of fair Posterity,
Is now ev'n in the center of the Isle,
As we're inform'd, near to the Town of Leicester:
From Tamworth *thither, is but one days march,*
And, here receive we from our Father Stanley,   10
Lines of fair Comfort and Encouragement,
Such as will help and animate our cause,
On which lets Cheerly on, Couragious Friends,
To reap the harvest of a lasting Peace;
Or Fame more lasting from a well fought War.
    Ox. Your words have fire, my Lord, and warm our men,
Who look'd methought but cold before, disheartned
With the unequal numbers of the Foe.
    Richm. Why, double 'em still, our Cause wou'd Conquer 'em.
Thrice is he arm'd that has his Quarrel Just,   20
And he but naked, tho' lock'd up in Steel,
Whose Conscience with Injustice is Corrupted:
The very weight of *Richard's* guilt shall crush him.
    Blunt. His best of Friends, no doubt will soon be ours.
    Ox. He has no Friends but what are such thro' fear.
    Richm. And we no Foes but what are such to Heaven;
Then doubt not, Heaven's for us. Let's on, my Friends:
    True hope ne'er tires, but mounts with Eagles wings,
    Kings it makes Gods, and meaner Creatures Kings.   [*Exeunt.*

[ACT V, SCENE II]

The Scene, Bosworth *Field: Enter* Richard *in Arms, with*
Norfolk, Ratcliff, Surrey, *&c.*
    Rich. Here pitch our Tent, ev'n in Bosworth *Field:*
My good Lord of *Norfolk,* the cheerful speed
Of your supply, has merited my thanks.
    D. Nor. I am rewarded, Sir, in having power

To serve your Majesty.
   Rich. You have our thanks, my Lord. *Up with my Tent:*
Here will I lie to night — But where to morrow? Well,
No matter where —— Has any careful Friend
Discover'd yet the number of the Rebels?
   D. Nor. 'My Lord, as I from certain Spies am well   10
'Inform'd, six or seven thousand is their
'Utmost Power.
   Rich. Why, our Battalions treble that account;
Beside, the Kings name is a Tower of strength,
Which they upon the adverse Faction want.
   D. Nor. Their wants are greater yet, my Lord: Those ev'n
Of Motion, Life, and Spirit —— Did you but know
How wretchedly their Men disgrace the Field.
O! such a tatter'd Host of mounted Scare-crows,
'So poor, so famish'd; their Executors,   20
'The greedy Crows, fly hovering o'er their heads,
Impatient for their lean Inheritance.
   Rich. 'Now, by St. *Paul,* we'll send 'em Dinners and Apparel;
'Nay, give their fasting Horses Provender,
'And after fight 'em. How long must we stay,
My Lords, before these desp'rate Fools will give
Us time to lay 'em with their Faces upwards?
   D. Nor. Unless their Famine saves our Swords that labour,
To morrows Sun will light 'em to their ruin,
So soon, I hear, they mean to give us Battle.   30
   Rich. The sooner still the better. —— *Come, my Lords,*
Now let's survey, the 'vantage of the Ground:
Call me some men of sound direction.
   D. Nor. My Gracious Lord. ——
   Rich.   What say'st thou, *Norfolk?*
   D. Nor. Might I advise your Majesty, you yet
Shall save the blood that may be shed to morrow.
   Rich. How so, my Lord?
   D. Nor. The poor Condition of the Rebels tells me,
That on a Pardon offer'd to the lives
Of those who instantly shall quit their Arms,   40
Young *Richmond,* e'er to morrows dawn, were Friendless.
   Rich. Why, that indeed was our Sixth *Harry's* way,
Which made his Reign one Scene of rude Commotion.

I'll be in mens despite a Monarch: No,
Let Kings that Fear, Forgive; Blows and Revenge for me.   [*Exeunt.*

[ACT V, SCENE III]

Enter Richmond, Oxford, Blunt, *Sir* William Brandon, *&c.*

Richm. The weary Sun has made a Golden set,
And by yon ruddy brightness of the Clouds,
Gives token of a goodly Day to morrow;
Sir William Brandon, *you shall bear my Standard.*
'Here have I drawn the model of our Battle,
'Which parts in just proportion our small Power.
Here may each Leader know his several Charge:
My Lord of Oxford, *you Sir* Walter Herbert,
And Sir *William Brandon,* stay with me:
The Earl of Pembroke *keeps his Regiment.*   10

Enter a Soldier.

Sold. Sir, a Gentleman that calls himself *Stanley,*
Desires admittance to the Earl of *Richmond.*
Richm. Now by our hopes, my Noble Father-in-Law,
Addmit him — My good Friends, your leave a while.   [*They retire.*

Enter Lord Stanley *in a Cloak.*

My Honour'd Father! On my Soul
The joy of seeing you this night is more,
Than my most knowing hopes presag'd — What News?
Ld. Stan. I, by Commission bless thee from thy Mother,
Who prays continually for Richmond's *good:*
'The Queen too, has with tears of joy consented,   20
'Thou should'st espouse *Elizabeth* her Daughter,
At whom the Tyrant Richard *closely aims:*
'In brief (for now the shortest moment of
'My stay is bought with hazard of my Life)
Prepare thy Battle early in the morning,

(*For so the season of Affairs requires*)
'And this be sure of, I, upon the first
Occasion offer'd, will deceive some Eyes,
And aid thee in this doubtful shock of Arms;
'In which I had more forward been e'er this,   30
'But that the Life of thy young Brother *George*
(Whom for my pawn of Faith stern *Richard* keeps)
'Wou'd then be forfeit to his wild Revenge.
Farewel: The rude enforcement of the time
'Denies me to revive those Vows of Love ——
Which so long sunder'd Friends shou'd dwell upon.
   Richm. We may meet again, my Lord ——
   Ld. Stan. Till then, once more farewel: Be resolute, and
     Conquer.
   Richm. Give him safe Conduct to his Regiment. [Exit Lord Stanley.
Well, Sirs, to morrow proves a busie day: 40
But come, the night's far spent —— Let's in to Counsel.
Captain, an hour before the Sun gets up
Let me be wak'd; I will in Person walk
From Tent to Tent, and early chear the Soldiers.   [*Exeunt.*

[ACT V, SCENE IV]

The Scene, before Richard's *Tent:* Richard, Ratcliff,
Norfolk *and* Catesby.

  Rich. Catesby!
  Cat.   *Here, my Lord.*
  Rich. Send out a Pursuivant at Arms
To Stanley's *Regiment: Bid him 'fore Sun-rise,*
Meet me with his Power, or young George's *Head*
Shall pay the forfeit of his cold delay.
What, is my Beaver easier than it was?
And all my Armour laid into my Tent?
  Cat. It is, my Liege: All is in readiness.

Rich. Good Norfolk, *hye thee to thy Charge;*
Use careful Watch: Chuse trusty Centinals.   10
   D. Nor. Doubt not, my Lord.
   Rich. Be stirring with the Lark, good Norfolk.
   D. Nor. I shall, my Lord.   [*Exit Duke of* Norfolk.
   Rich. Saddle White Surrey *for the Field to morrow.*
Is Ink and Paper ready?
   Cat.   *It is, my Lord.*
   Rich. An hour after Midnight, come to my Tent,
And help to Arm me. A good night, my Friends.   [*Exit.*
   Cat. Methinks the King has not that pleas'd Alacrity
Nor Cheer of Mind that he was wont to have.
   Rat. The meer effect of business ——————   20
You'll find him, Sir, another Man i'th' Field,
When you shall see him with his Beavour up,
Ready to mount his Neighing Steed, with whom
He smiling, seems to have some wanton talk,
Clapping his pamper'd sides to hold him still;
Then, with a motion swift, and light as Air,
Like fiery *Mars* he Vaults him to the saddle;
Looks Terror to the Foe, and Courage to his Soldiers.
   Cat. Good night to *Richmond* then; for, as I hear,
His numbers are so few, and those so sick   30
And famish'd in their march, if he dares fight us —
He jumps into the Sea to cool his Feaver.
But come, 'tis late: Now let's to our Tents,
We've few hours good before the Trumpet wakes us.   [*Exeunt.*

[ACT V, SCENE V]

Enter Richard *from his Tent. Solus.*
   Rich. 'Tis now the dead of Night, and half the World
Is with a lonely solemn darkness hung;

Yet I (so coy a dame is sleep to me)
With all the weary Courtship of
My Care-tir'd thoughts can't win her to my Bed;
Tho' ev'n the Stars do wink as 'twere, with over watching ——
I'll forth, and walk a while — The Air's refreshing,
And the ripe Harvest of the new-mown Hay
Gives it a sweet and wholesome Odour:
'How awful is this gloom — and hark from Camp to Camp   10
'The humm of either Army stilly sounds:
That the fixt Centinels almost receive
The secret whispers of each other's watch.
'Steed threatens Steed in high and boastful neighings,
'Piercing the nights dull Ear. Hark from the Tents,
The Armourers accomplishing the Knights,
'With clink of hammers closing rivets up
Give Dreadful note of Preparation; while some
'Like sacrifices by their fires of watch,
'With patience sit, and inly ruminate   20
'The mornings danger. By yon Heav'n my stern
'Impatience chides this tardy-gated night,
'Who, like a foul and ugly Witch, does limp
So tediously away: I'll to my Couch,
And once more try to sleep her into morning.
                              [*Lies down; a groan is heard.*
Ha! What means that dismal voice? Sure 'tis
The Eccho of some yawning Grave,
That teems with an untimely Ghost. — 'Tis gone!
'Twas but my Fancy, or perhaps the Wind
Forcing his entrance thro' some hollow Cavern;   30
No matter what — I feel my eyes grow heavy.   [*Sleeps.*
          King Henry's *Ghost, Lady* Ann's *Ghost, and the Ghosts*
                    of the young Princes rise.

     K. H. Gh. O thou, whose unrelenting thoughts, not all
The hideous Terrours of thy Guilt can shake,
Whose Conscience with thy Body ever sleeps:
Sleep on, while I by Heavens high Ordinance
In dreams of horror wake thy frighted Soul:
Now give thy thoughts to me, let 'em behold
These gaping Wounds, which thy Death-dealing hand

Within the *Tower* gave my Anointed Body,
Now shall thy own devouring Conscience gnaw   40
Thy heart, and terribly revenge my Murder.
    Pr. Gh. Richard, dream on; and see the wandring spirits
Of thy young Nephews, murder'd in the *Tower:*
Cou'd not our Youth, our Innocence perswade
Thy cruel heart to spare our harmless lives?
Who, but for thee, alas, might have enjoy'd
Our many promis'd years of Happiness.
No Soul, save thine, but pitties our misusage:
O! 'twas a cruel deed! therefore alone,
Unpittying, unpittied shalt thou fall.   50
    A. Gh. Think on the wrongs of wretched *Ann* thy Wife,
Ev'n in the Battles heat remember me,
And edgeless fall thy Sword — Despair, and Die.
    K. H. Gh. The mornings dawn has summon'd me away:
Now *Richard* wake in all the Hells of Guilt,
And let that wild despair which now does prey
Upon thy mangled thoughts, allarm the World.
Awake *Richard,* awake! To guilty minds
A terrible Example. ——
                  [All ghosts sink. Richard *starts out of his sleep.*
    Rich. Give me a Horse: Bind up my wounds!   60
'Have mercy, Heaven. Ha! — soft! — 'Twas but a dream:
But then so terrible, it shakes my Soul.
Cold drops of sweat hang on my trembling Flesh,
My blood grows chilly, and I freze with horror.
O Tyrant Conscience! how dost thou aflict me!
When I look back, 'tis terrible Retreating:
I cannot bear the thought, nor dare repent:
I am but Man, and Fate, do thou dispose me.
Who's there?
                  Enter Catesby.
    Cat. 'Tis I, my Lord; the Village Cock   70
Has thrice done salutation to the morn:
Your Friends are up, and buckle on their Armour.
    Rich. 'O *Catesby!* I have had such horrid dreams. ——
    Cat. 'Shadows, my Lord, below the Soldier's heeding.
    Rich. Now, by my this days hopes, shadows to night

Have struck more terror to the Soul of Richard,
Than can the substance of ten Thousand Soldiers
Arm'd all in Proof, and led by shallow Richmond.

   Cat. 'Be more your self, my Lord: Consider, Sir;
'Were it but known a dream had frighted you,   80
'How wou'd your animated Foes presume on't.

   Rich. Perish that thought: No, never be it said,
That Fate it self could awe the Soul of *Richard.*
Hence, Babling dreams, you threaten here in vain:
Conscience avant; *Richard's* himself again.

   Hark! the shrill Trumpet sounds, to Horse: Away!
My Soul's in Arms, and eager for the Fray.   [*Exeunt.*

[ACT V, SCENE VI]

      Enter Richmond, Oxford, *Soldiers, &c. Marching.*

Richm. Halt. —
Soldiers.   Halt, halt!
Richm. How far is it into the morning, Friends?
Ox. Near four, my Lord.
Richm. 'Tis well: I'm glad to find we are such early stirers.

   Ox. Methinks the Foe's less forward than we thought 'em.
Worn as we are, we brave the Field before 'em.

   Richm. Come, there looks life in such a cheerful haste:
'If dreams should animate a Soul resolv'd,
'I'm more than pleas'd with those I've had to night.
'Methought that all the Ghosts of them, whose Bodies   10
'*Richard* murther'd, came mourning to my Tent,
'And rous'd me to revenge 'em.

   Ox. A good Omen, Sir: Hark! the Trumpet of
The Enemy. It speaks them on the march.

   Richm. 'Why, then let's on, my Friends, to face 'em:
'In Peace there's nothing so becomes a Man
'As mild behaviour and humility:

'But when the blast of War blows in our ears,
'Let us be Tygers in our fierce deportment.
For me, the ransome of my bold attempt   20
'Shall be this Body, on the Earth's cold Face:
But, if we thrive, the Glory of the Action
The meanest here shall share his part of.
'Advance your Standards, draw your willing Swords:
'Sound, Drums and Trumpets, boldly and cheerfully.
The Word's Saint *George, Richmond,* and *Victory.*   [*Exeunt.*

[ACT V, SCENE VII]

Enter Richard, Catesby, *marching.*
Rich. Who saw the Sun to day?
Cat. He has not yet broke forth, my Lord.
Rich. Then he disdains to shine; For, by the Clock,
He should have brav'd the East an hour ago.
Not shine to day? — Why, what is that to me,
'More than to *Richmond?* For the self-same Heaven
'That frowns on me, looks lowring upon him.

Enter Norfolk *with a Paper.*
D. Nor. Prepare, my Lord, the Foe's in the Field.
Rich. Come, bustle, bustle; Caparison my Horse:
Call forth Lord Stanley; *bid him bring his Power.*   10
My self will lead the Soldiers to the Plain.   [*Exit* Catesby.
Well, *Norfolk,* what thinkst thou now?
D. Nor. That we shall Conquer; but on my Tent
This morning early was this Paper found.
Rich. [*reads.*] Jockey *of* Norfolk *be not too bold,*
For Dickon *thy Master is bought and sold.*
'A weak invention of the Enemy.
'Come, Gentlemen, now each man to his Charge.
And e're we do bestride our foaming Steeds,

Remember whom you are to Cope withal, 20
A scum of Britains, *Rascals, Run-aways;*
Whom their o'er cloy'd Country vomits forth
To desperate adventures and assur'd destruction.
If we be Conquer'd, let Men Conquer us,
And not these Bastard Britains, *whom our Fathers*
'Have in their own Land, beaten, spurn'd, and trod on,
And left 'em on Record, the Heirs of shame;
Are these Men fit to be the Heirs of England?

Enter Catesby.

What says Lord Stanley: *Will he bring his Power?*
   Cat. He does refuse, my Lord: He will not, Sir. 30
   Rich. Off with his Son Georges *head.*   [*Trumpet sounds.*
   D. Nor. My Lord, the Foe's already past the Marsh:
After the Battle let young *Stanley* die.
   Rich. Why, after be it then ——
A thousand hearts are swelling in my bosom.
'Draw Archers, drraw your Arrows to the head,
'Spur your proud Horses hard, and ride in blood:
And thou, our Warlike Champion, thrice Renown'd
St. *George* inspire me with the Rage of Lyons ——
Upon 'em! Charge! —— Follow me ——   [*Exeunt.*

[ACT V, SCENE VIII]

Several Excursions, Soldiers drove across the Stage by Richard.
Re-enter Richard.
   Rich. What, ho! young *Richmond,* ho! 'tis *Richard* calls.
I hate thee, *Harry,* for thy blood of *Lancaster;*
'Now if thou dost not hide thee from my Sword,
'Now while the angry Trumpet sounds Allarms,
'And dying groans transpierce the wounded Air.
'*Richmond,* I say, come forth, and single face me:

'*Richard* is Hoarse with Daring thee to Arms.   [*Exit.*

The Allarm continues: Enter Catesby, *and the Duke of* Norfolk
in disorder.

Cat. Rescue! rescue! my Lord of *Norfolk*, haste.
The King Enacts more wonders than a Man,
Daring an opposite to every danger: 10
His Horse is slain, and all on foot he fights,
Seeking for Richmond *in the throat of Death.*
'Nay, haste, my Lord: the day's against us.   [*Exeunt.*

   Enter Richard *and* Ratcliff *in disorder.*

 Rich. A Horse! a Horse! my Kingdom for a Horse!
 Rat. 'This way, this way, my Lord; below yon thicket
'Stands a swift Horse. Away, ruin pursues us.
'Withdraw, my Lord, for only flight can save you.
 Rich. Slave, I have set my Life upon a Cast,
And I will stand the hazard of the Dye.
I think there be six Richmonds *in the Field;*   20
Five have I slain to day, instead of him.
A Horse! a Horse! my Kingdom for a Horse.   [*Exeunt.*

[ACT V, SCENE IX]

   Re-enter Richard, *and* Richmond *meeting.*
 Rich. 'Of one, or both of us the time is come.
 Richm. Kind Heaven I thank thee, for my Cause is thine;
If *Richard's* fit to live let *Richmond* fall.
 Rich. Thy Gallant bearing, *Harry,* I cou'd plaud,
But that the spotted Rebel stains the Soldier.
 Richm. Nor shou'd thy Prowess, *Richard,* want my praise,
But that thy cruel deeds have stampt thee Tyrant.
So thrive my Sword as Heaven's high Vengeance draws it.
 Rich. 'My Soul and Body on the Action both.
 Richm. A dreadful lay: Here's to decide it.   [*Allarm, fight.*

Rich. Perdition catch thy Arm. The chance is thine: 11

> [*Richard is wounded.*

But oh! the vast Renown thou hast acquired
In Conquering *Richard,* does afflict him more
Than even his Bodies parting with its Soul:
'Now let the World no longer be a Stage
'To feed contention in a lingring Act:
'But let one spirit of the First-born *Cain*
'Reign in all bosoms, that each heart being set
'On bloody Actions, the rude Scene may end,
'And darkness be the Burier of the Dead.   [*Dies.*

   Richm. Farewel, *Richard,* and from thy dreadful end 21
May future Kings from Tyranny be warn'd;
Had thy aspiring Soul but stir'd in Vertue
With half the Spirit it has dar'd in Evil,
How might thy Fame have grac'd our *English* Annals:
But as thou art, how fair a Page thou'st blotted.
Hark! the glad Trumpets speak the Field our own.

Enter Oxford *and Lord* Stanley: *Soldiers follow with* Richard's *Crown.*

O welcome, Friends: My Noble Father welcome.
Heaven and our Arms be prais'd the day is ours.
See there, my Lords, stern *Richard* is no more.   30

   Ld. Stan. Victorious Richmond *well hast thou acquitted thee:*
—— And see, the just reward that Heaven has sent thee.
'Among the Glorious spoils of *Bosworth* Field,
'We've found the Crown, which now in right is thine:
'Tis doubly thine by Conquest, and by Choice.
'Long Live *Henry* the Seventh, King of *England.*   [*Shouts here.*

   Richm. Next to Just Heaven, my Noble Countrymen,
I owe my thanks to you, whose love I'm proud of,
And Ruling well shall speak my Gratitude.
But now, my Lords, what Friends of us are missing?   40
Pray tell me; Is young George Stanley *living?*

   Ld. Stan. He is, my Liege, and safe in Leicester *Town,*
Whither, if you please, we may withdraw us.

          Enter Blunt.

   Blunt. My Lord, the Queen and fair *Elizabeth,*
Her beauteous Daughter, some few miles of, are
On their way to Gratulate your Victory.

Richm. Ay, there indeed my toil's rewarded.
Let us prepare to meet 'em, Lords, and then,
As we're already bound by solemn Vows;
'We'll twine the Roses red and white together,   50
'And both from one kind stalk shall flourish:
England *has long been mad, and scarr'd her self.*
'The Brother blindly shed the Brother's blood:
'The Father rashly slaughter'd his own Son:
'The bloody Son compell'd, has kill'd his Sire.
'O! Now let *Henry* and *Elizabeth,*
The true Successors of each Royal House
'Conjoyn'd together, heal those deadly wounds:
'And be that wretch of all mankind abhor'd,
'That wou'd reduce those bloody days again: 60
 'Ne'er let him live to taste our Joys encrease,
 'That wou'd with Treason wound fair *England's* Peace. [*Exeunt.*

THE
Jew of Venice.
A
COMEDY.

As it is Acted at the

THEATRE in *Little-Lincolns-Inn-Fields,*

BY

His Majesty's Servants.

LONDON,
Printed for *BER. LINTOTT* at the *Post-House*
in the *Middle Temple-Gate, Fleetstreet,* 1701.

☞ *To morrow will be Published,* Anglia Libera: or, the Limitation and Succeffion of
the *Crown of England* Explain'd and Asserted, as grounded on, His Majesty's Speech ;
The Proceedings in Parlament ; The Defires of the People ; The Safety of our Religion ; The Nature of our Conftitution ; The Ballance of *Europe* ; and, The Rights of
all Mankind. Dedicated to the Duke of *Newcaftle.* By Mr. *Toland.*

ADVERTISEMENT
TO THE READER.

The Foundation of the following Comedy being liable to some Objections, it may be wonder'd that any one should make Choice of it to bestow so much Labour upon: But the judicious Reader will observe so many Manly and Moral Graces in the Characters and Sentiments, that he may excuse the Story, for the Sake of the Ornamental Parts. Undertakings of this kind are justify'd by the Examples of those Great Men who have employ'd their Endeavours the same Way: The only Dramatique Attempt of Mr. *Waller* was of this Nature, in his Alterations of the *Maid's Tragedy:* To the Earl of *Rochester* we owe, *Valentinian:* To the Duke of *Buckingham, The Chances:* Sir *William Davenant* and Mr. *Dryden* united, in restoring the *Tempest: Troilus* and *Cressida, Timon,* and King *Lear,* were the Works of three succeeding Laureats: Besides many others, too many to mention. The Reader may please moreover to take Notice, (that nothing may be imputed to *Shakespear* which may seem unworthy of him) that such Lines as appear to be markt, are Lines added, to make good the Connexion where there was a necessity to leave out; in which all imaginable Care has been taken to imitate the same fashion of Period, and turn of Stile and Thought with the Original. What other Alterations have been requisite as to the change of Words, or single Lines, the Conduct of Incidents, and Method of Action throughout the whole Piece, to bring it into the Form and Compass of a Play, would be superfluous to examin, every Reader being able to satisfy himself, if he thinks fit, by comparing.

PROLOGUE.

The Ghosts of *Shakespear* and *Dryden* arise
Crown'd with Lawrel.

Written by *Bevill Higgons*, Esq;

Dryd. *This radiant Circle, reverend* Shakespear, *view;*
An Audience only to thy Buskin due.
Shakes. *A Scene so noble, antient* Greece *ne'er saw,*
Nor Pompey's *Dome, when* Rome *the World gave Law.*
I feel at once both Wonder and Delight,
By Beauty warm'd, transcendently so bright,
Well, Dryden, *might'st thou sing; well may these Hero's fight.*
Dryd. *With all the outward Lustre, which you find,*
They want the nobler Beauties of the Mind.
Their sickly Judgments, what is just, refuse,   10
And French *Grimace, Buffoons, and Mimicks choose;*
Our Scenes desert, some wretched Farce to see;
They know not Nature, for they tast not Thee.
Shakes. *Whose stupid Souls thy Passion cannot move,*
Are deaf indeed to Nature and to Love.
When thy Ægyptian *weeps, what Eyes are dry!*
Or who can live to see thy Roman *dye.*
Dryd. *Thro' Perspectives revers'd they Nature view,*
Which give the Passions Images, not true.
Strephon *for* Strephon *sighs; and* Sapho *dies,*   20
Shot to the Soul by brighter Sapho's *Eyes:*
No Wonder then their wand'ring Passions roam,
And feel not Nature, whom th' have overcome.
For shame let genial Love prevail agen,
You Beaux Love Ladies, and you Ladies Men.
Shakes. *These Crimes unknown, in our less polisht Age,*
Now seem above Correction of the Stage;
Less Heinous Faults, our Justice does pursue;
To day we punish a Stock-jobbing Jew.

A piece of Justice, terrible and strange;   30
Which, if pursu'd, would make a thin Exchange.
The Law's Defect, the juster Muse supplies,
'Tis only we, can make you Good or Wise,
Whom Heav'n spares, the Poet will Chastise.
These Scenes in their rough Native Dress were mine;
But now improv'd with nobler Lustre shine;
The first rude Sketches Shakespear's Pencil drew,
But all the shining Master-stroaks are new.
This Play, ye Criticks, shall your Fury stand,
Adorn'd and rescu'd by a faultless Hand.   40
   Dryd. *I long endeavour'd to support thy Stage,
With the faint Copies of thy Nobler Rage,
But toyl'd in vain for an Ungenerous Age.
They starv'd me living; nay, deny'd me Fame,
And scarce, now dead, do Justice to my Name.
Wou'd you repent? Be to my Ashes kind,*
Indulge the Pledges I have left behind.*

---

* The Profits of this *Play* were design'd for Mr. *Dryden;* but, upon his Death, given to his Son.

DRAMATIS PERSONÆ.

MEN.

Bassanio. ⎤ Antonio. ⎦	Gentlemen of *Venice,* and Friends.	⎰ Mr. *Betterton.* ⎱ Mr. *Verbruggen.*
Gratiano.	Their Companion.	Mr. *Booth.*
Lorenzo.	In Love with *Jessica.*	Mr. *Baily.*
Shylock.	The Jew.	Mr. *Dogget.*
Duke of *Venice.*		Mr. *Harris.*
[*Salerio.*]		

WOMEN.

Portia.	A Rich Heiress.	Mrs. *Bracegirdle.*
Nerissa.	Her Friend.	Mrs. *Bowman.*
Jessica.	Daughter to the Jew.	Mrs. *Porter.*

Officers belonging to the Court of Justice, Servants and Attendants,

Men and Women.

Scene, *Venice.*

ACT I, SCENE I

Enter Bassanio, Antonio, Gratiano, *and* Lorenzo.

Anto. I hold the World, but as a Stage, *Gratiano,*
'Where every Man must play some certain Part,
And mine's a serious one.

   Grat. Laughter and Mirth be mine,
Why should a Man, whose Blood is warm and young,
Sit like his Grandsire, cut in Alablaster!
Sleep, when he wakes, and creep into the Jaundice,
By being peevish! I tell thee what, *Antonio!*
I love thee, and it is my Love that speaks;
There are a sort of Men, whose Visages   10
Do cream and mantle, like a standing Pond;
And do a willful Stillness entertain,
'Screwing their Faces in a politick Form,
'To cheat Observers with a false Opinion
Of Wisdom, Gravity, profound Conceit;
As who should say, I am, Sir, an Oracle.
Oh my *Antonio!* I do know of these,
Who therefore only are reputed wise,
For saying nothing; But more of this
Another time. 'Let you and I, *Lorenzo,*   20
'Take a short turn: Once more, my Friends, be merry.
'All have their Follies; merry Fools are best.
'*Lorenzo* come, Sir Gravities, Farewell,
I'll end my Exhortation after Dinner.   [*Exeunt* Gratiano *and* Lorenzo.

   Bass. Gratiano speaks an infinite deal of nothing;
More than any Man in all *Venice.* His Reasons
Are two Grains of Wheat, hid in two Bushels of Chaff,
You may seek all day e're you find 'em, and when
You have 'em, they are not worth the Search.

Anto. Well, tell me now, what Lady is the same   30
To whom you swore a secret Pilgrimage,
That you to day promis'd to tell me of.
   Bass. 'Tis not unknown to you, *Antonio,*
How much I have disabled my Estate
By something showing a more swelling Port,
Than my faint Means would grant continuance;
Nor would I now make suit to be abridg'd,
From such a noble Rate; but my chief Care
Is to come fairly off, from the great Debts
Wherein my Time, something too prodigal,   40
Has left me bound. To you, *Antonio,*
I owe the most in Mony and in Love.
   Anto. 'My Friend can owe me nothing; we are one,
'The Treasures I possess, are but in Trust,
'For him I love. Speak freely your Demand,
And if it stand, as you your self still do,
Within the Eye of Honor, be assur'd,
My Purse, my Person, my extreamest Means,
'Are all my Friend's.
   Bass. In my School-days, when I had lost one Shaft,   50
I shot his Fellow of the self-same Flight,
The self-same way, with more advis'd Regard,
And by advent'ring both, I oft found both.
I owe you much, and like a Prodigal;
That, which I owe, is lost; but, if you please
To shoot another Arrow, that self-way,
Which you did shoot the first: I do not doubt,
As I will watch the Aim, or to find both,
Or bring your latter Hazard back again,
And thankfully rest Debtor for the first.   60
   Anto. You know me well, and herein spend but Time,
To wind about my Love with Circumstance.
'Believe me, my *Bassanio,* 'tis more wrong
'Thus to delay the Service of your Friend,
Than if you had made waste of all I have;
'Is this to be a Friend? With blushing Cheek,
'With down-cast Eyes, and with a faltring Tongue,
'We sue to those we doubt: Friendship is plain,

'Artless, familiar, confident and free.
'Ask then as you wou'd grant, were yours the Power,   70
'Were yours the Power, so would I ask of you;
'No longer hesitate. Give me to know
'What you wou'd have me do, and think it done.
  Bass. 'Then briefly thus. In *Belmont* is a Lady
Immensly rich, and yet more fair than rich.
And vertuous as she's fair; sometimes from her Eyes
I have receiv'd kind speechless Messages.
Her Name is *Portia:* you have heard her Fame,
And how she's courted. O, my *Antonio!*
Had I but the Means —   80
  Anto. 'The Means be thine, if I can find the Means;
My present Fortunes are, thou know'st, at Sea.
No Money, nor Commodity is left me
'To raise immediate Sums. Therefore go forth,
Try what my Credit can in *Venice* do.
It shall be rack'd even to the uttermost
'To furnish thy Desires: Nay, no set Speech
'Of formal Thanks, which I must blush to hear.
Go, presently enquire. And so will I,
Where Money is: 'In Friendship, who receives,   90
'Obliges, by Acceptance, him that gives.   [*Exeunt.*

[ACT I, SCENE II]

Scene changes to Belmont.

Enter Portia *and* Nerissa.

  Port. In short, *Nerissa,* my little Body is weary of this Great
    World.
  Ner. It might indeed, if your Wants were as great as your
Plenty. For ought I see, they are as sick, who surfeit
With too much, as those who starve with too little;

'From whence I conclude, That Happiness is seated in
'The Mean: Superfluity brings Care, Care both
'Robs us of our Time, and shortens our Days;
'But Competency is the easiest and longest Liver.
  Port. Good Sentences, and well pronounc'd.
  Ner. They wou'd be better, if well follow'd.   10
  Port. It is a good Divine, who follows his own Teaching;
I could easier instruct Twenty, what were good to do,
Than be one of the Twenty, to follow my own Instruction.
The Brain may devise Laws for the Blood; 'but the hot
'Part will be sure to get the better of the cold; but what
Is all this to my choosing a Husband: Ah me! The Word
Choose: I am neither to choose whom I like, nor
Refuse whom I dislike; so is the Pleasure of a
Living Daughter restrain'd by the Will of a dead
Father. Was ever Woman ty'd to such hard Laws,   20
'*Nerissa?* Neither to choose, nor refuse?
  Ner. Your Father was ever virtuous, and holy Men at
Their Deaths have often good Inspirations; wherefore
Is this Lottery, which he dying devis'd, in these Three
Caskets of Gold, Silver and Lead, whereof who
Chooses his Meaning chooses you: I have Superstition
'Enough to believe the Benefit Lot is destin'd for
'The best Deserver.
'Love is at best, but a Lottery to all,
'Your Case looks different, but is in Effect the same   30
'With the rest of the World: For it is Fortune that
'Always decides. ——
And now pray discover to whom of this Retinue of Suitors
Stand your Affections most inclin'd,
'Never was Woman so surrounded as you are.
  Port. '*Penelope* was but a poor Princess to *Portia*,
But come, out with your List; Read me the Names,
And according as I describe, guess at my Inclinations.
  Ner. 'What a long List is here! Alas for poor Men, that
'Among so many, but one can be happy!   40
  Port. 'Alas! for poor Woman! that when she might have so
'Many, she must have but one; but come, a Truce
'To moral Reflections: Read, read.

Ner. Imprimis, here in the front, stands Monsieur *le Comte,*
Your French Lover.

Port. 'Of himself, thou mean'st: He has more Tricks than
'A Baboon: If my Bird sings, he strait falls a capering;
He will fence with his own Shadow; 'nor is his Tongue
'Less nimble than his Heels; I would as soon marry
'My Squirrel, or my Monkey.   50

   Ner. What think you then of your Englishman, he comes next.

   Port. 'The Frenchman's Ape: No, give me an Original,
Whatever it be. The Ape of an Ape must needs be a strange
   Monster.

   Ner. '*Myn Heer van Gutts,* the Dutchman, how like you him?

   Port. Very vilely in the Morning, when he is sober: And
More vilely in the Afternoon, when he is drunk;
At best, he is worse than a Man; and at worst, no better
Than a Beast: I will do any thing, *Nerissa,* e're I'll
Be marry'd to a Sponge.

   Ner. For any thing I find, this Lottery is not like to be   60
Fair drawn: For if he should choose the right Casket,
You'll refuse to perform your Father's Will.

   Port. Therefore, I prithee, Set a Bumper of Rhenish
On the contrary Casket; for if the Devil be within,
And the Temptation without, I know he will
Choose it.
'*La Seignora Gutts!* oh hideous! what
'A Sound would there be in the Mouth of an
'*Italian?*

Enter Servant.

   Serv. Some of the Strangers, Madam, desire to take   70
Their Leaves: And there are others just arriv'd, and
Alighting at the Gate.

   Port. Would some one, would come, to whom I could bid
Welcome, as heartily, as I can bid all these, Farewell.
'There is a Man, *Nerissa,* such a Man; But what we wish,
'Either never arrives, or is always longest in coming:
Fellow, go before: *Nerissa,* come: Whilst we shut
Out one Lover, another knocks at the Gate.

   Ner. 'This Lottery will certainly be drawn full.   [*Exeunt.*

[ACT I, SCENE III]

Scene returns to Venice.

Enter Bassanio, *and* Shylock *the Jew.*

Shyl. Three Thousand Duccats? Well.

Bass. Ay Sir, for Three Months.

Shyl. For Three Months? Well.

Bass. And as I told you, *Antonio* will be bound.

Shyl. Antonio bound? Well.

Bass. Will you oblige me, shall I know your Answer?

Shyl. Three Thousand Duccats for Three Months, and
Antonio bound!

    Bass.   Your Answer to that?

    Shyl. Antonio is a good Man.

    Bass. Have you heard any Imputation to the contrary?   10

    Shyl. No, no, no; my Meaning in saying he is a good
Man, is to have you understand that I think him
A sufficient Man. 'When a Man is rich, we say
'He is a good Man,
'As on the contrary, when he has nothing, we say a
'Poor Rascal: 'tis the Phrase, 'tis the Phrase. Let me
'Consider, one *Argosy* from *Tripoli,* another to the *Indies,*
A Third at *Mexico;* I understand moreover a fourth
For *England.* And other Ventures he has, scatter'd
Abroad; but Ventures are but Ventures, Ships are   20
But Planks, Sailers but Men: There are Land-Rats
And Water-Rats, Water-Thieves and Land-Thieves:
And then there is the Peril of Waters, Winds and Rocks.
The Man notwithstanding is a sufficient Man. Three Thousand
Duccats ———— humph ———— I think I may venture to take his
Bond.

    Bass. Be assur'd you may.

    Shyl. I will be assur'd; and that I may be assur'd, I will bethink
Me, where may I speak with *Antonio?*

    Bass. If you will please to dine with us.

    Shyl. Yes, to smell Pork, to eat of the Habitation, which   30

Your Prophet conjur'd the Devil into. I will buy
With you, Sell with you, talk with you, walk with you,
And so forth, —— but I will neither eat with you, drink
With you, nor pray with you, that's flat.

Enter Antonio.

  Bass. Here is Seignior *Antonio.*
  Shyl. aside. How like a fawning Publican he looks!
I hate him, for he is a Christian.
But more, for that in low Simplicity
He lends out Money *Gratis*, and brings down
The Rate of Usance, here with us in *Venice.*   40
If I could catch him once upon the Hip,
I would feed fat the ancient Grudge I bear him.
He hates our Sacred Nation; and he rails
Even there, where Merchants most do congregate,
On me, my Bargains, and my well-worn Thrift,
Which he calls Interest: Curst be my Tribe,
If I forgive him. ——
  Bass.   *Shylock,* do you hear?
  Shyl. I was debating of my private Stock:
And if my Computation's right,
I cannot instantly raise up the Gross   50
Of full Three Thousand Duccats, what of that?
Tubal, a wealthy Hebrew of our Tribe
Shall furnish me; but soft! How many Months
Is't you desire?
Rest you fair, good Seignior,
You were the last Man in our Mouths.
  Anto. Shylock, altho' I neither lend nor borrow,
By taking or by giving of Excess,
Yet to supply my Friend, I'll break a Custom:
Is he yet resolv'd, how much will serve?   60
  Shyl. Ay, ay, Three Thousand Duccats.
  Anto.   And for Three Months.
  Shyl. I had forgot, Three Months he told me so,
Well then, your Bond. But soft a little, methoughts
You said, you neither lend nor borrow
Upon Advantage.
  Anto.   I do never use it.
  Shyl. When *Jacob* graz'd his Uncle *Laban's* Sheep,

357

This *Jacob* from our holy *Abraham* was,
As his wise Mother wrought on his behalf,
The third Possessor, ay, ――― he was the third.
    Anto. And what of him? Did he take Interest?   70
    Shyl. No, not as you wou'd say, directly interest ―――
'You know the Story. 'Twas a way to thrive.
'And he was blest: For Gain is Blessing,
So Men steal it not.
    Anto. Was this inserted to make Interest good?
    Shyl. Note, my good Seignior! ―――
    Anto.   Mark you this, *Bassanio?*
The Devil can cite Scripture for a Turn,
An evil Soul producing holy Witness
Is like a Villain, with a smiling Cheek.
Oh, what a goodly Outside Falshood wears?   80
    Shyl. Seignior *Antonio,* many a time and oft
On the *Ryalto* have you rated me,
About my Monies and my Usances;
Still have I born it with a patient Shrug,
For Sufferance is the Badge of all our Tribe.
You call me Misbeliever, Cut-throat Dog,
And spet upon my Jewish Gaberdine,
And all for use of that which is my own.
Well then, it now appears, you need my Help:
Go to then, ―― you come to me, and you say   90
Shylock, we would have Monies;
You that did void your Rheum upon my Beard,
And foot me, as you spurn a stranger Cur
Over your Threshold: Mony is your Suit,
What shou'd I answer? should I not say,
Has a Dog Money? Can a Cur
Lend Three Thousand Duccats? or shall I bend down low,
And in a Bondman's Key, with softned Voice,
And whispering Humbleness, ――― Say thus!
Fair Sir, on Wednesday last, you spet on me   100
You spurn'd me such a day; another time
You call'd me Dog, and for these Courtesies
I'll lend you so much Monies?
    Anto. I am as like to call thee so again,

To spet on thee again, to spurn thee too.
If thou wilt lend this Money, lend it not
As to thy Friend; for when did Friendship take
A Breed of sordid Mettal of his Friend!
But lend it rather as to thy Enemy,
Who, if he fails, thou may'st with better Face   110
Exact the Penalty.
   Shyl. Why, look you, how you storm,
I would be Friends with you, and have your Love
Forget the Shames that you have stain'd me with,
Supply your present Wants, and take no Doit
Of Usance for my Monies —— And you'll
Not hear me, —— 'were this Offer kind?
   Bass. This were Kindness.
   Shyl. This Kindness will I shew; nay more, I'll take
Antonio's single Bond: And that we may henceforth   120
'Be Friends, no Penalty will I exact
'But this, meerly for Mirth ——
If you repay me not on such a day, in such a Place,
Such Sum or Sums as are exprest —— Be this
The Forfeiture.
'Let me see, What think you of your Nose,
'Or of an Eye —— or of — a Pound of Flesh
To be cut off, and taken from what Part
Of your Body —— I shall think fit to name.
'Thou art too portly, Christian!   130
'Too much pamper'd —— What say you then
'To such a merry Bond?
   Anto. The Jew grows witty; I'll seal to such a Bond,
And say there is much Kindness in the Jew.
   Bass. You shall not seal to such a Bond ——
'There is some Trick, some farther Fetch in this;
You shall not seal to such a Bond for me.
   Anto. Fear not, my Friend, within two Months, that is
A Month before the Bond expires, I expect Returns
Of thrice three times the Value of this Bond.   140
   Shyl. O Father *Abraham*, what these Christians are!
Whose own hard Dealings teach 'em to suspect
The Truth of others. Pray tell me, shou'd he fail

His Day, —— what should I get by the Exaction
Of the Penalty? A Pound of Man's Flesh?
Nor to be sold nor eaten. ——
To buy his Favour, I propos'd these Terms,
Such as I thought could bear no wrong
Construction; but since you're so suspicious,
Fare you well.   [*Going.*
    Anto. Stay, *Shylock*, I will seal as you propose.   151
    Shyl. Then meet me at the Notary's,   [*Returning.*
Give him Directions to prepare the Bond,
In the mean time, I'll fetch the Duccats;
See to my House, least some unthrifty Knave
Be on the Guard! Christian, thy Hand,
I'll presently be with you.   [*Exit Jew.*
    Anto. Thou'rt now a very gentle Jew.
This Hebrew will turn Christian, he grows kind.
    Bass. I like not yet the Terms,   160
'A Villain, when he most seems kind,
'Is most to be suspected.
    Anto. There is not the least Danger, nor can be,
'Or if there were, what is a Pound of Flesh,
'What my whole Body, every Drop of Blood,
'To purchase my Friend's Quiet! Heav'n still is good
'To those who seek the Good of others: Come *Bassanio,*
'Be chearful, for 'tis lucky Gold we borrow:
'Of all the Joys that generous Minds receive,
'The noblest is, the God-like Power to give.   [*Exeunt.*

ACT II, SCENE I

Enter Shylock *and* Jessica.
    Shyl. I am bid forth to Supper, *Jessica,*
There are my Keys; but wherefore should I go!

I am not bid for Love: They flatter me,
But then I'll go in Hate: To feed upon
The Prodigal Christian.
I am right loath to go, there is some ill
A brewing towards me: I dreamt last Night
Of Money-bags. *Jessica!* my Girl, look to my House,
They say, there will be Masques: Hear you me, *Jessica,*
Lock up my Doors —— And when you hear the Drum,   10
Or the vile Squealing of the wry-neck'd Fyfe,
Clamber not you up to the Casement then,
Nor thrust your Head into the publick Streets,
To gaze on Christian Fools, with varnish'd Faces;
But stop the Windows close; nor look, nor listen,
Let not the Sound of shallow Foppery enter
My sober House. By *Jacob's* Staff I swear,
I have no Mind of feasting forth to night:
Well, *Jessica,* —— go in, —— perhaps I will return
Immediatly. Do as I bid you, shut doors after   20
You. Fast bind, fast find.   [*Exit* Shylock.
    Jess. Alas! what Sin is it in me
To be asham'd to be my Father's Child?
'But how can he be said to have given me Life,
'Who never suffer'd me to know,
'What 'tis to live. O *Lorenzo!*
'Keep but thy Word to night, and thou shalt be
'A Father, and a Husband, both to me.   [*Exit.*
          Enter Lorenzo *and* Gratiano.
    Lor. Here she directs
How I shall take her from her Father's House,   30
What Gold and Jewels she is furnish'd with,
And how she'll be disguis'd; oh 'tis the kindest
Creature: if e're the Jew her Father comes to Heav'n,
It must be for his gentle Daughter's Sake.
Oh never may Misfortune cross her Foot,
For that she is the Issue of a Jew.
    Grat. 'Young, handsom, willing, with Gold and Jewels to Boot!
'Plague on't, when shall I have such Luck?
          Enter Jessica, *in the Balcony.*

Jess. Who are you? Tell me for more Certainty,
Albeit I swear that I do know your Voice,   40
I love the Repetition of your Name.
    Lor. *Lorenzo* and thy Love.
    Jess. *Lorenzo* certain, and my Love indeed;
For who love I so much? but ah, who knows
But you *Lorenzo,* whether I am yours?
    Lor. Heav'n and thy Thoughts are Witness that thou art.
    Jess. Here, catch this Casket, it is worth the Pains,
I'm glad 'tis Night; you look, but cannot see me,
For I am much asham'd of what I am,
'But Love is blind, and Lovers cannot see   50
'The Follies that themselves commit.
    Lor. Come down, my Love!
    Jess. I will make fast the Doors, and guild my self
With some few Duccats more, and then be with you.   [*Exit.*
    Grat. Now, by my Soul, a Gentile, and no Jew,
'She robs her Father with a Christian's Grace.
    Lor. Beshrew me, but I love her from my Soul!
For she is fair, or else my Eyes are false;
And true she is. What Proofs cou'd she give more?
'And oh she's kind; she loves me, and I love.   60
'A greater Bliss, scarce Heav'n it self can boast,
'Than mutual Love.

        Enter Jessica, *shutting the Door after her.*

    Jess. 'Shut Doors after you; fast bind, fast find,
'These were his last Words: Thus I avoid the
'Curse of Disobedience: Be thou shut till I
'Open thee.
    Lor. 'So whilst old *Laban* snor'd in Bed,
'*Jacob* with sprightly *Rachel* fled.
    Jess. 'His Gold, and Gems of Price they took,
'And eke the Flower of every Flock.   [*Holds up a Bag.*
    Lor. 'But not one precious thing was there   71
'That could with *Jessica* compare.

        Enter Antonio.

    Anto. Fy, fy, my Friends, why do you loyter thus!
Gratiano and *Lorenzo,* for Shame make haste:

Bassanio frets, that you are wanting,
He has sent twenty times to look you out.
   Grat. 'Matters of State, *Antonio,* Matters of State,
'A Rape and a Robbery: Matters of State,
'Matters of State, *Antonio.*
   Anto. Away, away, for Shame.   [*Exit.*
   Lor. Farewell *Gratiano:* Excuse me to *Bassanio.*   81
Come *Jessica,* this must be your way and mine.   [*Exeunt.*
   Grat. 'Jew, Turk and Christian differ but in Creed;
'In ways of Wickedness, they're all agreed:
'None upward clears the Road. They part and cavil,
'But all jog on ——— unerring, to the Devil.   [*Exeunt.*

[ACT II, SCENE II]

Scene opens, and discovers Bassanio, Antonio, Shylock, *and others,
sitting, as at an Entertainment. Musick playing: During the Musick,*
Gratiano *enters, and takes his Place.*

   Anto. 'This to immortal Friendship; fill it up ———
'Be thou to me, and I to my *Bassanio,*
'Like *Venice* and her *Adriatick* Bride,
'For ever link'd in Love.
   Bass. 'Thou joyn'st us well: And rightly hast compar'd;
'Like *Venice* on a Rock, my Friendship stands
'Constant and fix'd; but 'tis a barren Spot;
'Whilst like the liberal *Adriatick,* thou
'With Plenty bath'st my Shoars ———
'My Fortunes are the Bounty of my Friend.   10
   Anto. 'My Friend's the noblest Bounty of my Fortune.
'Sound every Instrument of Musick there,
'To our immortal Friendship.   [*All drink. Loud Musick.*
   Bass. 'Let Love be next, what else should follow **Friendship?**
'To Love, and to Love's Queen; my charming *Portia,*

'Fill; till the rosy Brim reflects her Lips;
'Then kiss the Symbol round:
'Oh, in this Lottery of Love, where Chance
'Not Choice presides: Give, give, ye Powers, the Lot,
'Where she her self would place it: Crown her wish,   20
'Tho' Ruine and Perdition catch *Bassanio:*
'Let me be wretched, but let her be blest.   [*Drink and Musick again.*
   Grat. 'Mine's a short Health: Here's to the Sex in general;
'To Woman; be she black, or brown, or fair;
'Plump, slender, tall, or middle-statur'd ——
'Let it be Woman; and 'tis all I ask.   [*Drink again, Musick as before.*
   Shyl. 'I have a Mistress, that out-shines 'em all ———
'Commanding yours —— and yours tho' the whole Sex:
'O may her Charms encrease and multiply;
'My Money is my Mistress! Here's to   30
'Interest upon Interest.   [*Drinks.*
   Anto. 'Let Birds and Beasts of Prey howl to such Vows,
'All generous Notes be hush'd: Pledge thy self, Jew:
'None here will stir the Glass ——   [*All Rise.*
'Nor shall the Musick sound: O *Bassanio!*
'There sits a Heaviness upon my Heart
'Which Wine cannot remove: I know not
But Musick ever makes me thus.
   Bass. The Reason is, your Spirits are attentive:
For do but note, a wild and wanton Herd   40
Or Race of skittish and unhandled Colts
Fetching mad Bounds, bellowing and neighing loud,
If they but hear by Chance some Trumpet sound,
Or any Aire of Musick touch their Ears,
You strait perceive 'em make a mutual stand,
Their savage Eyes turn'd to attentive Gaze,
By the soft Power of Musick: Therefore the Poet
Did feign, That *Orpheus* melted Stones and Rocks;
For what so hard, so stubborn, or so fierce,
But Musick for the Time will change its Nature.   50
The Man, who has not Musick in his Soul,
Or is not touch'd with Concord of sweet Sounds,
Is fit for Treasons, Stratagems and Spoils,
The Motions of his Mind are dull as Night,

And his Affections dark as *Erebus,*
Let no such Man be trusted. —— Mark the Musick.
> *Here to be a complete Concert of Vocal and Instrumental*
> *Musick, after the* Italian *Manner.*

[In Q, J, 3P, and 4P, II.ii.56SD is omitted, and *Peleus and Thetis, A Masque* follows. The masque is omitted here in the 1732 *Genuine Works.* See the discussion of the text of *The Jew of Venice,* below.]

[*PELEUS* and *THETIS.*
A MASQUE, *Set to* MUSICK.

The ARGUMENT.

Peleus, *in love with* Thetis, *by the Assistance of* Proteus *obtains her Favour; but* Jupiter *interposing,* Peleus *in Despair consults* Prometheus, *famous for his Skill in Astrology; upon whose Prophecy, that the Son born of* Thetis *should prove greater than his Father,* Jupiter *desists. The Prophecy was afterwards verify'd in the Birth of* Achilles, *the Son of* Peleus.

Persons in the MASQUE.

JUPITER.   PROMETHEUS.

PELEUS.   THETIS.

The SCENE *represents Mount* Caucasus; Prometheus *appears chain'd to a Rock, a Vulture gnawing his Breast.* Peleus *enters, addressing himself to* Prometheus.

PELEUS.

Condemn'd on *Caucasus* to lie,
Still to be dying, not to die,
  With certain Pain, uncertain of Relief,
  True Emblem of a wretched Lover's Grief!
    To whose inspecting Eye 'tis given
      To view the Planetary Way,
      To penetrate eternal Day,
    And to revolve the Starry Heaven.
To thee, *Prometheus,* I complain,
And bring a Heart as full of Pain.   10

PROMETHEUS.

From *Jupiter* spring all our Woes,
  Thetis is *Jove's,* who once was thine:
'Tis vain, O *Peleus,* to oppose
  Thy Torturer, and mine.
Contented with Despair,
  Resign the Fair,
    Resign, Resign,
Or, wretched Man, prepare
  For change of Torments, great as mine.

PELEUS.

In change of Torment would be Ease;   20
  Could you divine what Lovers bear,
Ev'n you, *Prometheus,* wou'd confess
  There is no Vulture like Despair.

PROMETHEUS.

Cease, cruel Vulture, to devour.

PELEUS.

Cease, cruel *Thetis,* to disdain.

      Thetis *entring, they repeat together.*

Cease, cruel Vulture, to devour,
Cease, cruel *Thetis,* to disdain.

THETIS.

Peleus, unjustly you complain.

PROMETHEUS *and* PELEUS.

Cease, cruel Vulture, to devour,
Cease, cruel *Thetis,* to disdain.   30

THETIS.

Peleus, unjustly you complain.
  The Gods, alas! no Refuge find
From Ills resistless Fates ordain:
  I still am true —— and would be kind.

PELEUS.

To love and to languish

To sigh and complain,
How cruel's the Anguish!
  How tormenting the Pain!
    Suing,
    Pursuing,   40
    Flying,
    Denying,
O the Curse of Disdain,
How tormenting's the Pain!
  To love, &c.

THETIS.

  Accursed Jealousy!
Thou Jaundice in the Lover's Eye,
Thro' which all Objects false we see,
  Accursed Jealousy!
Thy Rival, *Peleus,* rules the Sky,   50
  Yet I so prize thy Love,
With *Peleus* I wou'd choose to die,
  Rather than reign with *Jove.*
  A Clap of Thunder; Jupiter *appears, descending upon his Eagle.*
But see, the mighty Thund'rer's here;
  Tremble, *Peleus,* tremble, fly;
The Thunderer! the mighty Thunderer!
  Tremble, *Peleus,* tremble, fly.
  A full Chorus of Voices and Instruments as Jupiter *is descending.*

CHORUS.

But see, the mighty Thund'rer's here;
  Tremble, *Peleus,* tremble, fly;
The Thunderer! the mighty Thunderer!   60
  Tremble, *Peleus,* tremble, fly.
         Jupiter *being descended.*

JUPITER.

Presumptuous Slave, Rival to *Jove,*
  How dar'st thou, Mortal, thus defy
A Goddess with audacious Love,
  And irritate a God with Jealousy?

Presumptuous Mortal —— hence ——
Tremble at Omnipotence.

PELEUS.

Arm'd with Love and *Thetis* by,
  I fear no Odds
  Of Men or Gods,   70
But *Jove* himself defy.
Jove, lay thy Thunder down;
  Arm'd with Love, and *Thetis* by,
There is more Terror in her Frown,
  And fiercer Light'ning in her Eye:
    I fear no Odds
    Of Men or Gods,
  But *Jove* himself defy.

JUPITER.

Bring me Light'ning, give me Thunder,
  Haste, ye *Cyclops,* with your forked Rods,   80
  This Rebel Love braves all the Gods.
Bring me Light'ning, give me Thunder.

    PELEUS *and* THETIS, *holding fast by one another.*
Jove may kill, but ne'er shall sunder.

JUPITER.

Bring me Light'ning, give me Thunder.

PELEUS *and* THETIS.

Jove may kill, but ne'er shall sunder.

THETIS *to* JUPITER.

Thy Love still arm'd with Fate,
  Is dreadful as thy Hate:
  O might it prove to me,
So gentle *Peleus* were but free;
  O might it prove to me   90
As fatal as to lost consuming *Semele!*
  Thy Love still arm'd with Fate,
  Is dreadful as thy Hate.

PROMETHEUS *to* JUPITER.

Son of *Saturn,* take Advice

From one whom thy severe Decree
Has furnish'd Leisure to grow wise:
   Thou rul'st the Gods, but Fate rules thee.

[*The* PROPHECY.]

Whoe'er th'immortal Maid compressing,
Shall taste Joy, and reap the Blessing,
   Thus th'unerring Stars advise: 100
From that auspicious Night an Heir shall rise,
   Paternal Glories to efface
   The most illustrious of his Race,
Tho' sprang from him who rules the Skies.

JUPITER [*Apart.*]

Shall then the Son of *Saturn* be undone,
   Like *Saturn,* by an impious Son?
   Justly th'impartial Fates conspire,
   Dooming that Son to be the Sire
     Of such another Son.
   Conscious of Ills that I have done,   110
   My Fears to Prudence shall advise;
And Guilt that made me great, shall make me wise.
   The fatal Blessing I resign;
   Peleus, take the Maid divine: [*Giving her to* Peleus.
   Jove consenting, she is thine;
   The fatal Blessing I resign.   [*Joins their Hands.*

PELEUS.

Heav'n had been lost, had I been *Jove,*
There is no Heav'n, there is no Heav'n but Love.

PELEUS and THETIS, *together.*

   There is no Heav'n but Love,
     No, no, no,   120
   There is no Heav'n but Love.

JUPITER *to* PROMETHEUS.

And thou, the Stars Interpreter,
   'Tis just I set thee free,
   Who giv'st me Liberty:
Arise, and be thy self a Star.

'Tis just I set thee free,
Who giv'st me Liberty.

The Vulture drops dead at the Feet of Prometheus, *his Chains fall off,
and he is borne up to Heaven with* Jupiter *to a loud Flourish of all the
Instruments.*

              [Peleus *and* Thetis *run into each others Arms.*

PELEUS.

Fly, fly to my Arms, to my Arms,
Goddess of immortal Charms!
To my Arms, to my Arms, fly, fly,   130
Goddess of transporting Joy!
    But to gaze
    On thy Face,
Thy gentle Hand thus pressing,
Is heav'nly, heavenly Blessing.
    O my Soul!
Whither, whither art thou flying?
Lost in sweet tumultuous Dying,
Whither, whither art thou flying,
    O my Soul!   140

THETIS.

You tremble, *Peleus* — So do I ——
Ah stay! and we'll together die.
Immortal, and of Race divine.
My Soul shall take its Flight with thine:
Life dissolving in Delight,
Heaving Breasts, and swimming Sight,
Falt'ring Speech, and gasping Breath,
Symptoms of delicious Death,
Life dissolving in Delight,
My Soul is ready for the Flight.   150
    O my Soul,
Whither, whither art thou flying?
Lost in sweet tumultuous dying,
Whither, whither art thou flying,
    O my Soul!
               Both together repeat.

PELEUS *and* THETIS.

O my Soul!
Whither, whither art thou flying?
Lost in sweet tumultuous Dying,
Whither, whither art thou flying,
    O my Soul!   160

CHORUS *of all the Voices and Instruments Singing and Dancing.*

When the Storm is blown over,
   How blest is the Swain,
Who begins to discover
   The End of his Pain!
When the Storm, &c.
The Mask concludes with Variety of Dances.]

The Concert ceasing.

Anto. 'With such an Air of true Magnificence,
'My noble minded Brother treats his Friends:
'As hardly has been known to *Italy*
'Since *Pompey* and *Lucullus* entertain'd: 60
'To frame thy Fortune ample as thy Mind,
'New Worlds shou'd be created.

Enter Servant.

Serv. The Master of the Ship sends word the Wind is
Come about: and he desires you wou'd hast Aboard.
   Bass. turning to Anto. 'Oh my lov'd Friend! till now I never
      knew
'The pangs of parting Friendship.
'At distance I have tasted of the Pain,
'When the rude Morn has sunder'd us away,
'To our Repose: But, by my Soul, I swear
'Even then my Eyes would drop a silent Tear,   70
'Repugnant still to close, and shut out Thee.
   Anto. 'You go for your Advantage, and that Thought
'Shall keep *Antonio* comforted.

Bass. 'The Traject is from hence to *Belmont* short,
'And Letters may come dayly: Such Intercourse
'Is all the Cordial absent Friends enjoy:
'Fail not in that. Your Trouble shall be short,
'I will return with the best speed I can.
 Anto. 'Be not too hasty, my *Bassanio* neither;
Slubber not Business for my Sake, my Friend,   80
'But stay the very ripening of thy Love.
'Be gay, assiduous, and imploy such Arts,
'As best incline the Fair: Love is not seiz'd, but won;
'Hard is the Labour; you must plant and prune,
'And watch occasion just: This fruit is nice,
'Twill promise Wonders, and grow fairly up;
'Seem hopeful to the Eye, look ripe, and then
'A sudden Blast spoils all.

Enter another Servant.

 Serv. 'The Master of the Ship has sent agen.
 Bass. 'One more Embrace: To those who know not Friendship   90
'This may appear unmanly Tenderness;
'But 'tis the frailty of the bravest Minds.
 Anto. 'I ask but this, *Bassanio;*
'Give not your Heart so far away,
'As to forget your Friend.
'Come, is all ready? I must hasten you.
 Grat. 'If you were ready to part,
'Tis all we stay for now.
 Bass. 'Shylock, thy Hand: be gentle to my Friend,
'Fear not thy Bond, it shall be justly paid,   100
'We soon shall meet agen,
'Always, I hope, good Friends.
'Oh my *Antonio!* 'tis hard, tho' for a Moment,
'To lose the Sight of what we Love.
 Shyl. aside. 'These two Christian Fools put me in mind
'Of my Money: just so loath am I to part with that.
 Bass. 'Gratiano, lead the way: *Shylock* once more farewell.
'We must not part, but at the Ship, *Antonio:*
'Lovers and Friends, should they for Ages stay,
'Would still find something left, that they would say.   [*Exeunt.*

ACT III, SCENE I

Enter Portia, Bassanio, Nerissa, Gratiano, *and their Train.* Nerissa,
Gratiano *discourse apart.*

 Bass. Why if two Gods should play some Heav'nly match,
And on the Wager lay two earthly Beauties,
And *Portia* one, there must be something more
Pawn'd with the other; for the poor rude World
Has not her Equal: But alas, the while
Should *Hercules* and *Lychas* play at Dice,
Who were the better Man? The greater throw
Might turn by Fortune from the weaker Hand:
So were a Gyant worsted by a Dwarf;
And so may I, having no Guide but Chance,   10
'Miss that, which one unworthier may obtain,
'And dye with the Despair.
 Port. Therefore forbear to chuse, pause for a while,
Before you hazard; for in chusing wrong
You lose for ever: Therefore, I pray forbear;
For somthing tells me, but it is not Love,
I would not lose you: I could teach you
How to chuse right: But then I am forsworn,
So will I never be
'Yet should you miss me,   20
'I should repent that I was not forsworn;
I speak too much; tho' Thought will have no bound,
'A Virgin's Tongue should shame to hint a Thought,
'At which a Virgin's Cheek should blush.
Think it not Love, yet think it what you please,
So you defer a Month or Two,
'For fain I would detain you as a Friend,
'Whom as a Lover I might lose,
'Should you persist to venture the rash throw.
''Tis better still to doubt, and still to hope,   30
'Than knowing of our Fates, to know
'That we have lost for ever.

Bass. 'Doubt is the worst State: 'Tis better once
'To die, than still to live in Pain.
'Desire is fierce, nor brookes the least delay.
'Fortune and Love befriend me: I'm resolv'd;
My Life, and all my earthly Happiness
Sits on the chance: Where may I find the Casket!
   Port. 'Yet, let me perswade you: If for your self
'You cannot fear, tremble for her ———   40
'For her, to whom you have so often sworn,
'More than your self, you love her: Think! oh Think!
'On *Portia's* Fate: Who may not only lose
'The Man, by whom she wishes to be won,
'But being lost to him, remain expos'd
'To some new Choice; another must possess
'What Chance denies to you. O fatal Law!
'Lost to each other were a cruel Doom,
'But 'tis our least Misfortune; I may live
'To be enjoy'd by one I hate. And you   50
'May live to see it.
   Bass. 'To love, and to be lov'd, yet not possess,
'No greater Curse could be, but what thou fear'st,
'Yet I will on: With double Flames I burn,
'Knowing that *Portia* loves me; all my fear
'Was for her Love: Secure of that I go
'Secure of the Reward: Lead me to the Caskets.
   Port. Away then, and find out where *Portia's* lockt:
'Thy Courage is an Omen of Success,
'If Love be just, he'll teach thee where to chuse.   60
Nerissa, show him, since he is resolv'd,
The rest stand all aloft, whilst Musick Plays
That if he lose, like Swans we may expire
In softest Harmony: but if he win
Ah what is Musick then? Then Musick is
Even as the flourish, when true Subjects bow
To a new crown'd Monarch: Such it is,
As are those Dulcet Sounds at break of Day
That steal into the dreaming Bridegrooms Ear
And summon him to joy: See where he goes   70
With no less Presence, but with much more Love

Than young *Alcides,* when he did redeem
The virgin Tribute paid by weeping *Troy,*
To the Sea Monster: I like the Victim stand,
The rest aloof, like the *Dardanian* Wives,
With blotted Visages come forth to view
The Issue of the Exploit. Go *Hercules*
'Love that inflames thy Heart inspire thy Eyes,
'To chuse aright, where *Portia* is the Prize.
     [Portia *and the rest stand at a Distance observing soft*
     Musick. Till re-enter Bassanio *in each Hand a Casket.*
 Bass. Who chuses me, shall get what he deserves,   80
The like inscription bears this Silver Casket.
Shall get what he deserves; who chuse by outward show,
Entic'd by guilded Baits and flattering Forms,
Who look not to th' interiour: But like the Martlet,
Build in the Weather on the outward Wall,
Even in the force and Road of Casualty,
What may their Merit be? agen let me consider. [*Walks about thinking.*
 Grat. Take the Gold Man, or the Silver: plague on't,
Would I were to chuse for him.
 Bass. Shall get what he deserves: Let none presume   90
Without the Stamp of Merit to obtain.
Oh that Estates, Degrees and Offices,
Were not deriv'd Corruptly; and that clear Honour
Were purchas'd by the Merit of the Wearer,
How many then would cover who stand bare!
How many be commanded, who command!
How much low Peasantry would then be glean'd
From the true Seed of Honour! And how much Honour
Pickt from the Chaff and ruine of the Times,
To be new varnisht: Let me not be rash,   100
There yet remains a Third: well will I weigh
E'er I resolve.   [*Exit.*
 Grat. 'Take the Gold, I say; pox on Lead; what is it good
'For, but to make Bullets, 'tis the Image of
'Death and Destruction.
    Re-enter Bassanio *with a Casket of Lead.*
 Bass. The World is still deceiv'd with Ornament:

In Law, what Plea so tainted or corrupt,
But being season'd with a gracious Voice,
And cover'd with fair specious Subtleties
Obscures the show of Reason. 'In Religion   110
What damn'd Error, but some sober brow
Will bless it, and approve it with a Text.
There is no Vice so artless, but assumes
Some Mark of Vertue on its outward Parts,
Hiding the Grossness with fair Ornament.
How many Cowards with Livers white as Milk,
Have Backs of Brawn, and wear upon their Chins
The Beard of *Hercules* and frowning *Mars!*
Look even on Beauty: what are those crisped Locks
That make such wanton Gambols with the Wind?   120
What, but the Dowry of a second Head:
The Skull that bred 'em in the Sepulcher.
'Thus Ornament is as a beauteous Scarf
'Veiling Deformity. Therefore thou gawdy Gold,
Hard Food for *Midas,* I will have none of thee;
Nor, none of thee, Silver, thou common Drudge,
'Twixt Man and Man. But thou, thou Meager Lead,
'Which rather threaten'st, than do'st promise ought,
'Thy sullenness moves more than Eloquence,
And here I fix: Joy be the Consequence.   130
    Grat. 'Undone, undone: I'll not stand to't, *Nerissa.* I'll
'Chuse for my self.
    Port. aside. How all the other Passions fleet to Air,
As doubtful Thoughts, and rash, embrac'd Despair,
Tormenting fears, and Green-ey'd Jealousey.
O! Love! be moderate; allay this Extacy.
In measure pour thy Joy, stint this excess;
I feel too much thy Blessing, make it less,
For fear I surfeit.
    Bass. What find I here?   *[Opening the Casket.*
The Portraiture of *Portia.*   141
What Demi-God has come so near Creation, move these Eyes!
Or whether riding on the Balls of mine,
Seem they in Motion? Here are sever'd Lips,
Parted with sweetest Breath: 'The very odour

376

'Seems there express'd, and thus invites the Taste! [*Kissing the Picture.*
And here agen, here in her lovely Hair,
The Painter plays the Spider, and has woven
A Golden Snare, to catch the Hearts of Men:
'But then her Eyes!   150
'How could he gaze undazled upon them,
'And see to imitate: Let me peruse the Motto.
'*Reads.*] Who chuses me; let him whose Fate it is,
'Turn to the Fair, and claim her with a Kiss.
A gentle Schrole: fair Lady, by your leave,
I come by note, to give and to receive,
Like one of two contending for a Prize,
Who thinks he has done well, looks round to mark
(Hearing Applause, and universal Shout)
Whether those Peals of Praise are meant to him;   160
So stands *Bassanio,* full of Hopes and Fears,
'Still anxious what to trust, and what believe,
'Till you confirm his Hopes.
     Port. 'Had Choice decided, and not only Chance,
'As Fortune has dispos'd me, so had I.
My self, and what is mine, to you and yours
Is now converted. But now I was the Lady
Of this fair Mansion, Mistress of these Servants,
Queen o'er my self, even now, and in a Moment
This House, these Servants, and my self their Queen,   170
Are yours, my Lord. I plight 'em with this Ring,
Which when you part from, lose or give away,
Let it presage the Ruin of your Love,
'And stand, as a Record, that you were false,
'A follower of my Fortunes not of me,
'And never meant me fair.
     Bass. 'Dye first, *Bassanio,* my Mistress, and my Queen
'As absolute as ever shall you reign,
'Not as the Lord, but Vassal of your Charms,
'Not as a Conqueror, but Acquisition.   180
'Not one to lessen, but enlarge your Power.
'No more but this, the Creature of your Pleasure,
'As such receive the passionate *Bassanio.*

377

Oh there is that Confusion in my Powers,
As Words cannot express: But when this Ring
Parts from this Finger, then part Life from thence;
Then say, and be assur'd, *Bassanio's* dead.

                 [Gratiano *and* Nerissa *seem in earnest dispute.*

   Grat. 'I say, a Bargains a Bargain, and I will have Justice.

   Ner. 'I say, we drew Stakes.

   Grat. 'That was only in Case I had lost, Child.   190

   Port. A Dispute between our Friends! what's the matter, Cozen?

   Grat. I'll tell you, Madam, the matter in short, and you shall
    be Judge;

'I happen'd to say to this Lady, that it was her Destiny to
'Have me; she consented to put it to Tryal, and agreed
'To be determin'd by the Choice, my Friend should make;
'If he had you —— I should have her; and here
'Stand I to claim her Promise.

   Port. Is this true, *Nerissa?*

   Ner. 'Ay! but he recanted, and said afterwards, he
'Would chuse for himself.   200

   Grat. 'Why sure so I can, now I know the right Casket.
'What sort of a Tramontane, do you take me to
'Be? you are gone that way too, as I take it.

   Ner. 'Then Madam, all my Hope is, that you won't let
'Me keep my Word.

   Grat. ''Tis false, to my certain Knowledge she hopes
Otherwise —— *Nerissa!* we'll play with 'em the first
Boy for 1000 Ducats.

   Ner. 'Methinks, this looks like the last Act of a Play.
'All Parties are agreed; there remains nothing but   210
'To draw the Curtain, and put out the Lights.

   Grat. 'A good hint, my Love: Let you and I make our *Exit*
'About that same last Act, as you call it.

   Bass. 'I rejoice, *Gratiano,* that my good Fortune
'Thus included yours.
'Oh that *Antonio* knew of our Success,
'It would ore-joy him. Prithee *Gratiano,*
'Send a special Messenger to *Venice,*
'To inform him of our Fortunes ——

'*Shylock* shall now be paid, my Friend is safe,   220
'And Happiness, on every side surrounds us.

> [Gratiano *going out, meets* Lorenzo, Jessica, *and a*
> *Servant from* Antonio [Salerio] *entring.*

Grat. *Lorenzo,* and his pretty Infidel,
Salerio too, *Antonio's* Servant: If I mistake him not.
'Look here, *Bassanio;* here is News from *Venice.*

Bass. *Lorenzo,* Welcome! *Salerio* too! what News
'From my *Antonio?* Oh, 'tis the best of Freinds!
Y'are welcome hither. By your Leave, my Love,
Tho' my Interest here be yet but young, I
Take upon me to bid my Friends most welcome.

Port. So do I my Lord, they are entirely welcome.   230

Lor. We thank you, Madam: for my part, my Lord,
My purpose was not to have seen you here,
But meeting with *Salerio* by the way,
He needs would have me come.

Sal. I did my Lord desire it, and had a reason for it:
Seignior *Antonio* commends him to you.

Bass. 'How does my Friend?

Sal.   'This Letter will inform you.

> [Bassanio *reads to himself and seems concern'd.*

Grat. *Nerissa,* bid this pretty Stranger welcome;
Your Hand, *Lorenzo;* and yours, *Salerio.*
Whats the News from *Venice?* We are the *Jasons*   240
Who have won the Fleece: *Antonio* will rejoice
At our Success.

Sal. Would you had won the Fleece which he has lost.

Port. There are some shrewd Contents in that same **Paper,**
Which steal the Colour from *Bassanio's* Cheek:
'Some great Misfortune sure: No common Cause
'Could thus disturb him at this time. Still worse and worse.
With leave, *Bassanio,* I am half your self,
And freely must have half of any thing
That this same Letter brings you.   250

Bass. O my *Portia!* here are a few of the most fatal words
That ever blotted Paper ——
When I did first impart my Love, I told you

That all the Wealth I had ran in my Veins.
When I said Nothing, I should then have said
That I was worse than nothing: For indeed
I have engag'd my self to my best Friend;
Engag'd my Friend to his worst Enemy,
To feed my Fortunes. But is it true, *Salerio?*
Have all his Ventures fail'd? What! not one hit!   260
From *Tripoli,* from *Mexico,* from *England,*
From *Lisbon, Barbary,* and *India,*
And not one Vessel scape!
    Sal.   Not one, my Lord.
    Port. Is it your Friend who is thus troubled?
    Bass. The dearest Friend to me! the kindest Man!
The best condition'd, most unwearied Spirit
In doing Good; and one in whom
The ancient Roman Honour more appears
'For liberal Love and bounteous Courtesie,
'Than any that has breath'd in *Italy*   270
'Since *Antony* and *Brutus.*
    Port. What is the Sum?
    Bass.   For me 3000 Duccats,
'Rais'd to transport me hither.
    Port.   What! no more!
'And rais'd on my Account. 'Tis then my Debt;
Pay him 6000. double 6000.
And then treble that, before a Friend should suffer,
Or lose a Hair thro' my *Bassanio's* Fault:
You shall away to *Venice* to your Friend;
For never shall you lie by *Portia's* side
With an unquiet Soul. You shall have Gold   280
To pay the petty Debt 20 times over.
Nerissa and my self mean while will live
As Maids and Widows. Let none reply,
'For I will have it thus.
    Bass.   'O Love! O Friendship!
'Was ever Man thus tortur'd!
    Grat. 'What, not one quarter of an hour to pack up
'My Baggage?

Ner. 'Whereabouts is the last Act now *Gratiano?*
Grat. 'Faith, Child, I have the part ready,
'If I might have leave to play it.
    Port.   'Away ye Triflers.   290
'Nay then *Bassanio* I must thrust you from me:
"Tis hard for both to be divided thus
'Upon our Wedding-Day. But Honour calls,
'And Love must wait. Honour, that still delights
'To tyrannize or'e Love. Farewell, my Lord,
'Be chearful in this Trial: as you prove
'Your Faith in Friendship, I shall trust your Love.
              [*She conducts him to the Door. Exeunt* Bassanio, Gratiano.
  Lor. Madam, if you knew to whom you show this Honor,
How true a Lover of your Lord!
  Port. I never did repent of doing good;   300
Nor shall I now: But we have much to do
In other things: Therefore to you, *Lorenzo,*
And to this Lady, whose Pardon I should crave,
For having stood so much unnoted by me,
I will commit, as to my Lords best Friends,
The Husbandry and Conduct of my House
Until my Lord's Return: For my own part
I have to Heav'n breath'd a secret Vow,
To live in Prayer and Contemplation,
Only attended by *Nerissa* here,   310
Until her Husband and my Lord come back.
There is a Monastery two Miles off,
And there we will abide. I do desire you
Not to deny this Imposition, which
My Love and some Necessity
Now lays upon you.
  Lor. Madam, with all our Hearts;
We will observe your Pleasure.
  Port. Come on, *Nerissa;* I have Work in hand
That thou yet knowest not of. *Balthazar,*   320
Thou art honest; so let me find thee still.
Follow me in: I have some short Directions
For you all.   [*Exeunt.*

[ACT III, SCENE II]

Scene Changes to a Prison in Venice.

Enter Shylock *and* Jailer *with* Antonio *in Shackles.*

Shyl. Jailor, look to him. Tell not me of Mercy;
This is the Fool, who lent out Money *gratis:*
Where is that Friend thou hast so much oblig'd
Will own thee now? Jailor, I say,
Look to him.
    Anto.   Hear me yet, good *Shylock.*
    Shyl. I'll have my Bond: I have sworn an Oath, that
I will have my Bond: Thou call'dst me Dog,
Before thou hadst a Cause: but since I am a
Dog, beware my Phangs.
    Anto. I prithee hear me speak.   10
    Shyl. I'll have my Bond. I will not hear thee speak:
I'll not be made a soft relenting Fool,
To shake the Head, and sigh, and yield, and melt
To Christian Intercessors: I'll have no speaking,
I will have my Bond.
    Anto. Thou wilt not take my Flesh; what's that good for?
    Shyl. To bait Fish withal; if it will feed nothing else, it
Will feed my Revenge: Thou hast disgrac'd me,
Hindered me half a Million; laught at my Losses;
Repin'd at my Gains, scorn'd my Nation;   20
Thwarted my Bargains; cool'd my Friends;
Enflam'd my Enemies; and what's the Reason?
I am a Jew ——— Has not a Jew Eyes? Has not
A Jew Hands? Organs, Dimensions, Senses, Affections;
Passions? Fed with the same Food, hurt with
The same Weapons, subject to the same Diseases,
Heal'd by the same Means, warm'd and cool'd,
By the same Winter and Summer as a Christian?
If you prick us, do we not bleed? If you
Tickle us, do we not laugh? If you poison us,   30

Do we not dye? And if you wrong us, shall
We not Revenge? If we are like you in the rest,
We will resemble you in that: For if a Jew
Wrong a Christian, what is his Humility,
Revenge? If a Christian wrong a Jew, what
Should his sufferance be by a Christian Example?
Why, Revenge. The Charity you practise, I will
Imitate: And it shall go hard, but I will improve
By the Instruction.

   Anto. Thou art the most impenetrable Curr   40
That ever kept with Men.

   Shyl. My Daughter too! None knew so well as you of my
Daughter's Flight. Why there, there, there is a
Diamond gone, cost me 2000 Ducats in *Frankfort.*
A Ring too, it was my Turkis; I had it of *Leah,*
When I was a Batchelour; besides Gold, and many other
Precious Jewels. Would my Daughter were dead
At my Foot, so the Jewels were in her Ears;
Would she were Hears'd, so the Ducats were in the
Coffin. No News, and I know not how much   50
Spent in the Search: Loss upon Loss. The Theif gone
With so much, and so much to find the Theif;
And no Satisfaction, no Revenge: But thou art
Caught, and thou shalt pay the whole Theifs Bill.
Thou who wast wont to lend out Money for a Christian
Curtesy: Thou Christian Fool, pay thy Debts:
Jaylor, I say, look to him.   [*Thrusts him after the Jaylor and Exeunt.*

ACT IV, SCENE I

*A Court of Justice. The Duke and Nobles seated, Officers of the Court
attending* Antonio *as a Prisoner,* Bassanio *and* Gratiano.

   Duke. What is *Antonio* here?

Anto. Ready so please your Grace.

Duke. I am sorry for thee, thou art come to answer
A Stony Adversary; an Inhumane Wretch
Incapable of Pity. Go one and call the Jew
Into the Court.

Enter Shylock.

Make room, and let him stand before our Face.
Shylock, the World does think, and so do I,
That thou but lead'st this Fashion of thy Malice
To the last Hour of Act, and then 'tis hop'd   10
Thou'lt show thy Mercy, and Remorse, as strange
As is thy strange apparent Cruelty,
Glancing an Eye of Pity on his Losses,
That have of late so hudled on his Back,
Enow to press a Royal Merchant down,
And pluck Comiseration of his State
From stubborn *Turks* and *Tartars,* never train'd
'To Offices of tender Curtesy.
We all expect a gentle Answer, Jew.

Shyl. I have possest your Grace, of what I purpose,   20
And by our Holy Sabbath have I sworn,
To have the Due, and Forfeit of my Bond:
If you deny it, let the Danger light
Upon your Charter and the City's Freedom:
You'l ask me why I rather chuse to have
A weight of Carrion-Flesh, than to receive
3000 Ducats. I reply to that,
It is my Humour: Is that question answer'd?
What if my House be troubled with a Rat,
And I am pleas'd to give 10000 Duccats   30
To have it ban'd; What, are you answer'd yet?
My Humour is my Reason. Are you answer'd?

Bass. This is no Answer; thou hard-hearted Man.

Anto. I pray you think you question with a Jew;
You may as well expostulate with Wolves;
You may as well go stand upon the Beach,
And bid the Waves be still, and Winds be husht;
Forbid the Mountain Pines to stir a Leaf,

When the rude Gusts of Heav'n are whistling round.
You may as well do any thing most hard,   40
As seek to soften that, than which what harder?
His Jewish Heart: Therefore I do beseech you
Make no more Offers, use no farther Means,
But with all Brief, and plain Conveniency,
Let me have Judgment, and the Jew his Will.
    Bass. For thy 3000 Ducats here are Six.
    Shyl. If every Ducat in 6000 Ducats,
Were in six Parts, and every Part a Ducat,
I would not draw 'em: I will have my Bond.
    Duke. How mayst thou hope for Mercy, rend'ring none?   50
    Shyl. What Judgments shall I dread, doing no wrong?
You have among you many a purchas'd Slave,
Whom, like your Asses, and your Doggs, and Mules,
You use in abject and in slavish part,
Because you bought 'em: Shall I say to you
Let 'em be free: Marry 'em to your Heirs:
Why sweat they under Burdens? Let their Beds
Be made as soft as yours; and let their Pallats
Be season'd with such Dainties. You will answer,
The Slaves are ours; so do I answer you;   60
The Penalty which I demand of him,
Is dearly bought, 'tis mine, and I will have it:
If you deny me, shame upon your Laws,
There is no force in the Decrees of *Venice;*
I stand for Judgment. Answer; shall I have it?
    Duke. The Court will first advise. Here is a Letter
From fam'd *Bellario,* which does much commend
A young and learned Docter in our Court,
Whose Wisdom shall direct us. Where is he?
Call in the Council.   70
    Bass. Fear not, *Antonio:* This greedy Dogg
Shall have my Flesh, Blood, Sinews, Bones, and all,
E'er thou shalt lose one drop of Blood for me.
To Shylock.] Why dost thou whet thy Knife so earnestly?
    Shyl. To cut the Forfeit from that Bankrupt there.
    Bass. Can no Pray'rs peirce thee?
    Shyl. None that thou hast Wit enough to make.

Bass. Oh be thou damn'd, inexorable Jew,
And that thou liv'st, let Justice be accus'd,
'And Heaven accus'd that such a Wretch was born.   80
Thou almost mak'st me waver in my Faith;
To hold Opinion with *Pythagoras*,
That Souls of Animals infuse themselves
Into the Trunks of Men: Thy Currish Spirit
Govern'd a Woolf, who hang'd for Humane Slaughter,
Even from the Gallows, did his fell-soul fleet,
And whilst thou lay'st in thy unhallowed Dam,
Infus'd it self in Thee.
   Shyl. Till thou canst rail the Seal from off my Bond,
Thou but offends thy Lungs to speak so loud;   90
'Thy Curses fall on thy own Head, for thus
'Ensnaring thy best Freind, thou didst it, and not I.
'I stand for Law: Thy Prodigality brought him
To this.
   Bass. 'Inhumane Dog!
   Offic. Room for the Council there.

     Enter Portia *disguis'd like a Lawyer,* Nerissa *like her Clerk*
             with Bagg and Papers.

   Duke. Take your Place.
Are you acquainted with the Difference
Which holds the present Question in the Court?
   Port. I am instructed fully in the Case.
Which is *Antonio,* and which the Jew?   100
   Duke. Antonio and old *Shylock* both stand forth.
   Port. Is your Name *Shylock?*
   Shyl.   *Shylock* is my Name.
   Port. Of a strange Nature is the Suit you follow.
Is the Bond prov'd? Or does he confess it?
   Anto. I do confess it.
   Port.   Then must the Jew be merciful.
   Shyl. On what Compulsion Must I? Tell me that.
   Port. The Quality of Mercy is not strain'd;
It drops as does the gentle Dew from Heav'n
Upon the Place beneath: It is twice blest,
It blesses him that gives, and him that takes: 110
'Tis mightiest, in the mightiest: It becomes

386

The Crown'd Monarch, better than his Crown;
'It is the first of Sacred Attributes,
And Earthly Power does then seem most Divine,
When Mercy seasons Justice. I have spoke thus much
To mitigate the Rigour of thy Plea;
For if thou followest this strict Course of Law,
Then must *Antonio* stand condemn'd.
    Shyl. My Deeds upon my Head. I crave the Law,
The Penalty and Forfeit of the Bond.   120
    Port. Is he not able to discharge the Bond?
    Bass. Yes, here I tender't for him in the Court;
Twice, thrice the Sum; if that will not suffice,
I will be bound to pay it ten times over,
On Forfeit of my Hands, my Head, my Heart:
If this will not prevail, it must appear
That Malice bears down Truth.
    Port. There is no Power in *Venice*
Can alter a Decree establish'd;
'Twill be recorded for a President;   130
And many an Error by the same Example
May rush into the State. It cannot be.
    Shyl. A *Daniel,* a *Daniel:* So ripe in Wisdom,
And so young in Years! A second *Solomon.*
    Port. I pray you let me see the Bond.
    Shyl. Here 'tis, most reverend Doctor. Here it is.
    Port. Shylock, there's thrice the Money offer'd thee.
    Shyl. An Oath, an Oath; I have an Oath in Heaven:
Shall I lay Perjury upon my Soul:
No, not for *Venice.*   140
    Port. Be merciful, take thrice the Money:
Bid me tear the Bond.
    Shyl. It has appear'd you are an upright Judge;
You know the Law; your Exposition
Has been most sound. I charge you by the Law,
Whereof you are a well-deserving Pillar,
Proceed to Judgment. By my Soul, I swear,
There is no Power in the Tongue of Man
To alter me. I do insist upon my Bond;
The Time's expir'd; I claim the Penalty.   150

Anto. Most heartily I do beseech the Court
To pass the Sentence.
   Port.   Why then thus it is:
You must prepare your Bosom for the Knife;
For the intent and purpose of the Law
Has full relation to the Penalty,
Which plainly appears due upon the Bond.
   Shyl. 'Tis very true. O wise and upright Judge!
   Port. 'Prepare, *Antonio:* Officers, be ready
To lay bare his Bosom.
   Shyl. Ay, his Breast; so says the Bond: 160
Does it not, noble Doctor: nearest his Heart;
Those are his Words.
   Port. Have by some Surgeon, *Shylock,* at your Charge,
To stop his Wound, lest he should bleed to Death.
   Shyl. It is not nominated in the Bond.
   Port. Not so express'd in Words: But what of that?
'Twere good to allow so much for Charity.
   Shyl. I cannot find it: 'Tis not in the Bond.
   Port. Then do your Office.
   Duke.   'Hold awhile. *Antonio:*
Have you any thing to say to hinder Sentence?   170
   Anto. But little, I am arm'd and well prepar'd:
Give me your Hand, *Bassanio:* Fare you well:
Grieve not that I am fallen to this for you,
For herein, Fortune shows her self more kind
Then is her Custom: It is still her use
To let the wretched Man outlive his Wealth,
To view with Hollow Eye, and wrinckled Brow
An Age of Poverty, from which lingring Penance
'She kindly cuts me off: Once more farewell:
'Grieve not, my Friend, that you thus lose a Friend,   180
'For I repent not thus to pay your debt
'Even with my Blood and Life: Now, do your Office,
'Cut deep enough be sure, and whet thy Knife
'With keenest Malice; for I would have my Heart
'Seen by my Friend.
   Shyl. Doubt it not, Christian; thus far I will be Courteous.
   Duke. Antonio, is this all thou hast to say?

Anto. 'Tis all.

Bass. 'Stand off. I have a word in his behalf,
'Since even more than in his Avarice,   190
'In Cruelty, this Jew's insatiable;
'Here stand I for my Freind. Body for Body,
'To endure the Torture: But one pound of Flesh
'Is due from him: Take every peice of mine,
'And tear it off with Pincers: whatever way
'Invention can contrive to torture Man,
'Practice on me: Let but my Friend go safe,
'Thy Cruelty is limited on him;
'Unbounded let it loose on me: Say, Jew,
'Here's Interest upon Interest in Flesh;   200
'Will that content you?

    Anto.   'It may him, not me.

    Bass. 'Cruel *Antonio.*

    Anto.   'Unjust *Bassanio.*   *[Jew laughs.*

    Bass. 'Why Grins the Dog?

    Shyl. 'To hear a Fool propose: Thou shallow Christian!
'To think that I'd consent: I know thee well.
'When he has paid the Forfeit of his Bond,
'Thou canst not chuse but hang thy self for being
'The Cause: And so my ends are serv'd on both.
'Proceed to Execution.

    Bass. Then thus I interpose.   210

            [Draws and stands before Antonio: *The
              Jew starts back.* Antonio *interposes.*

    Anto. 'Forbear *Bassanio,* this is certain Death
'To both.

    Bass. 'In one, both dye: since it must be,
'No matter how.

    Duke. 'Before our Face this Insolence! And in a Court
'Of Justice. Disarm and seize him.

    Port. 'Spare him, my Lord; I have a way to tame him.
'Hear me one word.

    Shyl. 'Hear, hear the Doctor: Now for a Sentence
'To sweep these Christian Vermin, coupled
'To the Shambles. O 'tis a *Solomon!*   220

    Port. Heark you, *Shylock,* I have view'd this Bond,

And find it gives thee not one drop of Blood.
The Words expresly are, *A Pound of Flesh.*
No more. Take thou that Flesh,
But in the cutting it, if thou dost shed
One drop of Christian Blood, thy Lands and Goods
Are, by the Laws of *Venice,* mark you me,
Confiscate to the State.   [Shylock *starts surpriz'd.*
   Shyl.   Humph.
   Bass. O, upright Judge! Mark, Jew. O learned Judge!
'Forgive, most potent Duke, and Reverend Seigniors,   230
'That thus enforc'd by my Despair ———
   Duke. 'We do forgive thee, and admire thy Virtue
'More than we blame thy Passion. But proceed.
   Port. Shylock, thy self shall see the Act,
And Letter of the Law: For as thou urgest Justice,
Be sure thou shalt have Justice.
   Shyl. I take this Offer then; pay the Bond thrice,
And let the Christian go.
   Bass.   Here is the Money.
   Port. Soft! The Jew shall have all Justice: Soft, no haste!
He shall have nothing but the Penalty.   240
   Grat. 'A *Daniel!* A *Daniel!* Now Infidel,
We have thee on the Hip.
   Port. Why does the Jew pause? Take thy Forfeiture.
   Shyl. Give me my Principal, and let me go.
   Port. He has refus'd it in the open Court,
He shall have meerly Justice and his Bond.
   Shyl. Shall I not have barely my Principal?
   Port. Thou shalt have barely thy Forfeiture,
To be so taken at thy Peril, Jew.
   Shyl. Why then the Devil give you good of it;   250
I'll stay no longer Question ———
   Port.   Tarry Jew.
The Law has yet another hold of you:
It is enacted in the Laws of *Venice,*
If it be prov'd against an Alien,
That by direct or indirect Attempt,
He seek the Life of any Citizen,
The party against whom he shall contrive,

390

Shall seize on half his Goods: The other half
Comes to the privy Coffers of the State,
And the Offenders Life lies in the Mercy   260
Of the Duke only, against all other Voice;
In which Predicament, I say, thou stand'st;
For it appears by manifest proceeding,
That indirectly and directly too
Thou had'st contriv'd against the very Life
Of the Defendant; and therefore hast incurr'd
These several Penalties of Life and Goods.

   Duke. That thou may'st see the difference of our Spirits,
I pardon thee thy Life, before thou ask it;
But half thy Wealth shall be *Antonio's,*   270
The other half the States.

   Shyl. Nay, take my Life and all; pardon not that:
You take my House, when you do take the Prop
That does sustain my House: You take my Life,
When you do take the means by which I live.

   Duke. What Mercy can you render him, *Antonio?*

   Anto. So please my Lord the Duke
To quit the Fine of one half of his Goods
I am content, so he will let me have
The other half in use, to render it upon   280
His Death to young *Lorenzo,*
Who lately has espous'd his Daughter.

   Duke. He shall do this, or else I do recant
The Pardon of his Life.

   Port. Art thou contented, Jew? What dost thou say?

   Shyl. Pray give me leave to go from hence;
I am not well: send after me your Deeds,
And I will sign 'em.

   Duke.   Get thee gone; but do it.   [*Exit* Shylock.

   Port. Clerk, draw a Deed of Gift.

                  [*The Duke and Court rise.*

   Duke. 'Antonio, I rejoyce at this Conclusion;   290
'And I congratulate with you *Bassanio,*
'Your Friends escape: You will do well
To gratify that learned Councellor,
For in my Mind you both are in his debt.

            [*Exit Duke with his Train, the Court breaking up.*

Bass. 'Let me embrace the Man, by whom my Freind
'Has Life: For in that Life I live ——
3000 Ducats due on *Shylock's* Bond
I freely offer to requite your Pain.
    Anto. And stand indebted over and above
In Love and Gratitude for evermore.   300
    Port. He is well paid, who is well satisfy'd,
My Mind was never yet more Mercinary:
I pray you, know me, when we meet agen:
I wish you well, and take my leave.
    Bass. 'Not as a Fee, but as a small Remembrance;
'A Token of our Loves and Gratitude.
    Port. Give me your Gloves: I'll wear 'em for your Sake,
Or else that Ring ——
    Bass. This Ring! alas it is a Trifle;
'Not fit for me to give, or you to take.   310
    Port. I see Sir, you are liberal in Offers:
You taught me first to beg, and now methinks
You teach me how a Beggar shou'd be answer'd.
    Bass. There's more depends on this than on the Value;
The dearest Ring in *Venice* will I give you,
And find it out, by Proclamation;
Only for this, I pray you pardon me.
    Port. 'Such slight Excuses well I understand.
Well —— Peace be with you both.   [*Exit* Portia *and* Nerissa.
    Anto. My Lord *Bassanio,* let him have the Ring;   320
Let his Deservings, and my Love withall,
'Be valu'd against every other Scruple.
    Bass. Prithee *Gratiano,* run and overtake him:
Give him the Ring; and bring him, if thou can'st,
To my *Antonio's* House —— away, make haste.
                     [*Exit* Gratiano.
'Once more, let me embrace my Friend, welcom to Life,
'And welcome to my Arms, thou best of Men:
'Thus of my Love and of my Friend possess'd,
'With such a double Shield upon my Breast,
'Fate cannot peirce me now, securely Blest.   330
        [*As they go off, Re-enter* Portia *and*
        Nerissa, Gratiano *following.*

Grat. Sir, Sir, you are well overtaken;
My Lord *Bassanio,* upon more Advice,
Has sent you here the Ring; and does entreat
Your Company at Dinner.

    Port. For that he must excuse me: His Ring
I do accept with Thanks; and so, pray tell him:
And further more oblige my Clerk to show him
Shylock's House —— These Writings he must Sign.

    Grat. That I will do: 'Tis a pert pretty youth,
I had much talk with him, during the Tryal.   340

    Ner. aside. Now will I see if I can get a Ring
I gave him too at parting, which he swore
As much never to part from.

    Port. Thou may'st, I warrant: We shall have old
Swearing, that they gave these Rings to Men,
But we'll out-face 'em, and out-swear 'em too.
Aloud.] Make hast, I pray: Thou know'st where I will Tarry.

    Grat. 'Come on, Sir: The first Cause I have to split,
'You shall have all my Practice.

    Ner. 'That may be sooner than you dream of,   350
'Sir, I follow you.
'So many Shapes have Women for Deceipt,
'That every Man's a Fool, when we think fit.   [*Exeunt.*

ACT V, SCENE I

Enter Lorenzo *and* Jessica.

    Lor. The Moon shines bright. In such a Night as this
Did pensive *Troilus* mount the *Trojan* Wall,
Sighing his Soul towards the *Grecian* Tents,
Where beauteous *Cressid* lay ——

    Jess.   In such a Night ——
Sad *Dido* with a Willow in her Hand
Stood on the wild Sea-Beach, and waft her Love

To come again to *Carthage* ——
    Lor. In such a Night *Medea* gather'd the inchanted
Herbs, that did renew old *Æson*.
    Jess. In such a Night,   10
Did young *Lorenzo* swear to *Jessica*
He lov'd her well, and stole away her Soul
With many a Vow, and ne're a true one.
    Lor. In such a Night.⎫
    Jess. In such a Night.⎬*Both together.*
I would out-Night you. But hark!
I hear a footing.
                    Enter Portia *and* Nerissa.
    Port. That Light we see is burning in my Hall.
    Lor. 'Tis sure the Voice of *Portia.*
    Port. He knows me as the Blind Man does the Cuckow,   20
By the bad Voice. *Lorenzo,* is it you?
    Lor. Madam, you are most welcome.
    Port. We have been praying for my Lords Success,
Who fares, we hope, the better for our Pray'rs:
Is he return'd?
    Lor. Madam, not yet. But here are Letters from him,
Which give a good Account of his Proceeding,
And that he will be here to Night;
We were walk't out to wait his coming.
    Port. Give Order to my Servants, that they take   30
No Note at all of our being absent hence;
And let our Musick play, and every thing
So direct as we were here in formal Expectation
Of his return ——
This Night methinks is but the Day-light sick;
It looks a little paler. 'Tis a Day,
Such as the Day is when the Sun is hid.
           Enter Bassanio, Antonio, Gratiano, *and Followers.*
    Bass. We should hold day with the *Antipodes,*
If you would walk in Absence of the Sun?
'My *Portia,* this was kind to meet me thus.   40
    Port. 'O never more let any Cause of Grief
'Divide my Lord and me.
           [Gratiano *runs to* Nerissa, *who discourse apart.*

Bass. Nothing can: Here Madam is my Friend,
Let me present him to you: This is *Antonio,*
Whom, if you love *Bassanio,* you must love.
  Port. 'I should behold him with a Jealous Eye,
'Who has so large a Share in my Lord's Heart.
To Anto.] 'Having his Leave, you'll not deny me yours,
'To make a third in Friendship: I doubly joy
'That you are safe and here.
    Anto.   I thank you Madam.   50
  Port. 'Play all our Instruments of Musick there,
'Let nothing now be heard but sounds of Joy,
And let those glorious Orbs that we behold,
Who in their Motions, all like Angels sing,
Still Quiring to the blew-ey'd Cherubims,
'Join in the Chorus; that in Heav'n and Earth
'One universal Tune may celebrate
'This Harmony of Hearts. Soft Stilness, and the Night
Become the Touches of sweet Harmony.   [*Flourish of Musick.*
  Grat. By yonder Moon and Stars, I swear you wrong me,   60
By Heav'n, I gave it to the Lawyers Clerk.
  Port. A quarrel! what, already? What's the matter?
  Grat. About a Hoop of Gold, a paltry Ring she gave me,
Whose Poesie was, for all the World, like Cutlers
Poetry upon a Knife, *Love me, and leave me not.*
  Ner. No matter for the Poesie, or the Value.
When I gave it, you swore never to part with it:
If not for Love of me, yet for your Conscience sake,
For your Oath's sake, such vehement Oaths, you
Should have kept it. A Lawyer's Clerk! A fine   70
Invention! But well I know the Clerk who had it
Will ne're have Hair upon his Face.
  Grat. He will, if he but live to be Man.
  Ner. If! If a Woman live to be a Man!
  Grat. Now by this Hand, I gave it to a Youth, a kind
Of Boy; a little scrubbed Boy, no higher
Than thy self; the Judge's Clerk; a prating
Boy, that begg'd it for a Fee.
  Port. You were to blame, I must be plain with you,

To make so slight of the first Gift of Love;   80
A thing stuck on with Oaths upon your Finger,
'And rivited with solemn Protestations
'Of mutual Faith: A Pledge of Truth between you:
'Indeed you were to blame.
I gave my Lord a Ring, and made him swear
Never to part with it: And here he stands,
I dare be sworn for him, he would not give it,
Or pluck it from his Finger, for the Wealth
That the whole World contains.
    Bass. aside. Now were I best to cut my Left-hand off,   90
And swear I lost the Ring defending it.
    Grat. My Lord *Bassanio* gave his Ring away
To the young Smock-fac'd Lawyer, who begg'd it,
'And deserv'd it too: And then the Boy his Clerk,
'A little importunate Urchin, who took some pains
In Writing, would needs beg mine; and neither
Man nor Master would take any thing but the 2 Rings.
    Port. What Ring gave you, my Lord?
Not that, I hope, which you receiv'd from me?
    Bass. If I could add a Lye to hide a Fault,   100
I would deny it: But you see my Finger
Has not the Ring upon it; it is gone.
    Port. And even as void is your false Heart of Truth.
By Heav'n! I'll never come within your Bed
Till I have seen this Ring.
    Ner. Nor I in yours, till I see mine.
    Bass. If you but knew to whom I gave this Ring,
'For what I gave it, and for whom I gave it;
'How much compell'd, and how unwillingly,
'When nothing else would be accepted ———   110
    Port. If you but knew the Virtue of this Ring,
'If you had valu'd her, who gave this Ring,
Or your own Honour, bound by solemn Oath,
'To keep this Ring, you wou'd have dy'd, *Bassanio,*
'E're you had parted from it:
What Man is there so much unreasonable,
If you had pleas'd to have defended it
With any shew of Zeal, wanted the Modesty

To urge a thing, held as a Ceremony
'Sacred to Truth, and to Connubial Love.   120
Nerissa teaches me what to believe;
I'll dy for't; but a Woman had this Ring.
   Bass. No, by my Honour, Madam, by my Soul,
No Woman had it: but a generous Friend,
Even he, who had held up the very Life
Of my best Friend. What shall I say, my *Portia?*
I was beset with Shame and Courtesie.
Had you been there, you would your self have begg'd
'This Ring, to be dispos'd as I dispos'd it.
   Port. Let not that Man, whoe're he is, come near me: 130
Since he has got the Jewel that I priz'd,
I shall become as liberal as you,
And nothing can deny the Man that has it.
'A Ring it was of wondrous Mystery,
'And sanctify'd by Charms to rivet Love:
'Whoever has it, has the sure Command
'Of me, my Person, and of all that's mine:
'The dire Enchantment was so strongly wrought;
'One Mind directs us, and one Bed must hold us:
Know him I shall, I must; nay, I will know him;   140
'I feel the Effects already. Watch me like *Argos,*
If you do not, if I be left alone,
Now by my Honour, which is yet entire,
'That Man and I are one.
   Ner. 'Just such a Ring was mine:
'Methinks I love that Lawyers Clerk already,
'Just as I love my self.
   Bass. 'Forgive me this first Fault;
'I'll trust thy Honour above any Charms:
'My Love is built upon Esteem so strong,   150
'As cannot doubt your Virtue.
   Grat. 'I am not quite so liberal of good Thoughts;
'But this I'll say, if I can catch this Clerk,
'His Pen shall split for't.
   Anto. I am the unhappy Subject of this Quarrel
By my Perswasion ———
   Port.   Sir, grieve not you;

You're welcome notwithstanding.

> *[Walks about as in a Passion.*

    Bass. 'But hear me, *Portia;*
'Pardon this Error; by my Soul, I swear,
'By what is dearer to me than my Soul,   160
'Your precious self ——
    Anto.   I dare be bound for him;
'My life upon the Forfeit, that your Lord
'Shall never more break Faith.
    Port. 'You have been oft his Surety, and
'Have paid for't dearly.
    Anto. 'No more than I am well acquitted of.
    Port. 'Then be his Surety still: Here is a Ring,
'Of the same Virtue, and so qualify'd
'With equal Spells. This only can retrieve
'With Counter-Magick what the other lost.   170
Antonio, give him this: But make him swear
To keep it better.
    Anto. Here, Lord *Bassanio:* Swear to keep this Ring.
    Bass. By Heav'n!   *[Starts.*
This is the same I gave the Lawyer.
    Port. Why so it is; I had it from him: 'You see
'How quick an Operation is in Magick.
'We have met already.
    Bass. 'Met! how have you met!
    Ner. 'Met —— why by Art Magick, to lie together: 180
'Ask that same scrubbed Boy, the Lawyers Clerk.
    Grat. 'Why this is worse and worse.
    Bass. '*Antonio!* this was your doing.   *[Angrily.*
    Anto. 'Take your Revenge, and kill me.
    Bass. 'I am answer'd —— Is it then true?
'And can it be? That by the Secret Workings
'Of Mystick Words, and Spells, and dire Compounds,
'Potions and Invocations horrible,
'Nature can be so led? What then is Virtue?
'And what Security has Love or Reason,   190
'Thus subjected to every Hell-born Hagg,
'Who, by such Conjurations can disjoin
'United Hearts? uniting the Averse!

'How, wretched Man! how can'st thou boast free Will?
'If this in very deed be true. I'll not suppos't ——
'But then that Ring! How could she have it: 'tis Witch-craft!
'Damn'd, damn'd Witchcraft: And I will fathom Hell,
'But I will find a Fiend shall Counter-work
'The Devil that has done this.   [Portia *and* Nerissa *laugh.*

Port.
Ner. } Ha, ha, ha.   200

Grat. 'Is this true, *Nerissa!* are we then two Scurvy
'Cuckolds by Art Magick!
   Port. 'Ha, ha, ha. Well; since you grow so serious,
'I will be serious too: Read this *Bassanio,*
'The Adventures writ at large: Look not so sullen, Lord,
'But read it. *Lorenzo* here and *Jessica*
Can witness for me: I set out almost
As soon as you. And am but even now return'd,
'I have not yet enter'd my House: But
'For farther proof, Clerk, give *Lorenzo*   210
'The Writings sign'd by *Shylock.*
   Ner. I'll give 'em without Fee: Here *Lorenzo,*
Here is a Deed of Gift to you and *Jessica,*
Of all the Jew, your Father, dies possess'd of.
   Lor. 'See *Jessica,* is this his Hand?
   Jess. ''Tis his own signing.
   Lor.   'What prodigy is this?
   Bass. 'I am struck dumb with wonder.
   Grat. 'Was *Portia* then the little Smerking Lawyer,
'And *Nerissa* the Clerk: I'll never forgive such a
'Trick. Art-Magick do you call it?   220
   Ner. 'Nay, but *Gratiano.*
   Grat.   'Away, away.   [*Dispute aside.*
   Port. Antonio! Here are Letters too for you;
Ask me not yet, by what strange Accident
They fell into my Hands —— but read 'em.
   Bass. 'Amazement has bereft me of all Words.
   Anto. Why here I read, for certain, that my scatter'd Ships,
Are safely all arriv'd at *Rhodes,*
With their whole Cargo.
   Port. Doubt it not, *Antonio.* 'Tis most true.

'Virtue like yours; such Patience in Adversity,   230
'And in Prosperity such Goodness,
'Is still the Care of Providence.
    Anto. 'My Life and Fortunes have been all your Gift;
'Dispose 'em and command 'em, Madam,
'As you please.   [Gratiano *and* Nerissa *advance.*
    Ner. 'What can you bear no Jests, but of your own
'Making?
    Grat. 'You have so scar'd me with your Art-Magick,
'That I shall scarce be a true Man these two Days;
'But therein lies my Revenge: And so shake   240
'Hands. From this Day forwards,
    'As the most precious of all Gems, I swear!
    '*Nerissa's* Ring shall be *Gratiano's* Care.
    Port. 'All look amaz'd, in every Face I see
'A thousand Questions: 'Tis time we should go in,
'There will I answer all: Cease your astonishment,
'My Lord; by these small Services to you
'And to your Friends, I hope I may secure
'Your Love; which, built upon meer Fancy,
'Had else been subjected to Alteration.   250
    'With Age and Use the Rose grown Sick and Faint,
    'Thus mixt with friendly Sweets, secures it's Scent.
    Bass. 'The sweets of Love shall here for ever blow;
'I needs must Love, remembring what I owe.
'Love, like a Meteor, shows a short-liv'd Blaze,
'Or treads thro' various Skies, a wand'ring Maze;
'Begot by Fancy, and by Fancy led,
'Here in a Moment, in a Moment fled:
    'But fixt by Obligations, it will last;
    'For Gratitude's the Charm that binds it fast.   [*Exeunt Omnes.*

EPILOGUE.

Each in his turn, the *Poet and the †Priest,
Have view'd the Stage, but like false Prophets guess'd:
The Man of Zeal in his Religious Rage
Would silence Poets, and reduce the Stage.
The Poet rashly, to get clear, retorts
On Kings the Scandal, and bespatters Courts.
Both err; for without mincing, to be plain,
The Guilt is yours of every Odious Scene.
The present time still gives the Stage its Mode,
The Vices which you practice, we explode: 10
We hold the Glass, and but reflect your Shame,
Like Spartans, *by exposing, to reclaim.*
The Scribler, pinch'd with Hunger, writes to Dine,
And to your Genius must conform his Line;
Not lewd by Choice, but meerly to submit;
Would you encourage Sense, Sense would be writ.
    Plain Beauties pleas'd your Sires an Age ago,
Without the Varnish and the Dawb of Show.
At vast Expence we labour to our Ruine,
And court your Favour with our own undoing.   20
A War of Profit mitigates the Evil,
But to be tax'd and beaten, is the Devil.
How was the Scene forlorn, and how despis'd,
When Tymon, *without Musick, moraliz'd?*
Shakespears *sublime in vain entic'd the Throng,*
Without the Charm of Purcel's *Syren Song.*
    In the same Antique Loom these Scenes were wrought.
Embelish'd with good Morals and just Thought:
True Nature in her Noblest Light you see.
E're yet debauch'd by modern Gallantry,   30

---

* Mr. *Dryden,* in his *Prologue* to the *Pilgrim.*
† Mr. *Collier,* in his *View of the Stage.*

401

To trifling Jest, and fulsom Ribaldry.
What Rust remains upon the shining Mass
Antiquity may privilege to pass.
'Tis Shakespear's *Play, and if these Scenes miscarry,*
Let **Gormon *take the Stage* —— *or* ††*Lady* Mary.

** A famous Prize-Fighter.
†† A famous Rope-Dancer.

NOTES

Macbeth

Argument. Taken by Chetwin from Peter Heylin's *Cosmographie in Four Books,* printed in 1652, 1657, 1666, [1668]-69, 1669, 1670, 1674, 1677, and 1682 (Donald Wing, *Short-Title Catalogue,* 3 vols. [New York, 1945-51], H1689-H1696). Chetwin was involved in publishing the *Cosmographie:* see Harry Farr, "Philip Chetwind and the Allott Copyrights," *Library,* Fourth Series, XV (1934), 145-159. In the 1670 edition of the *Cosmographie* the passage is on p. 336.

Persons. All editions before 1710 give a cast that includes the characters Davenant omitted — copied, no doubt, from the 1673 quarto of Shakespeare's play. I have adjusted the cast to Davenant's adaptation. The playwright Nathaniel Lee (1653?-92) performed the part of Duncan so ineptly that he was *"ruin'd . . . for an Actor"* (Downes, p. 34). Philip Cademan (1643–after 1708), the youngest of Davenant's stepsons, was injured in a stage duel with Harris in 1673 and retired on a pension. Henry Harris (1634?-1704) often played romantic parts, including probably Ferdinand in the Davenant-Dryden *Tempest.* Davenant's changing "Seyward" to "Seymour" seems hard to explain unless he wished to compliment someone by that name. A possible candidate would be Henry Seymour (1612-86), like Davenant active in the royalist cause during the Civil War, and, as a messenger for Charles II, imprisoned in England 1654-57; after the Restoration he was Groom of the Bedchamber to Charles II. Mrs. Betterton (Mary Saunderson, d. 1712), "tho' far advanc'd in Years, was so great a Mistress of Nature, that even Mrs. *Barry,* who acted the Lady *Macbeth* after her, could not in that Part, with all her superior Strength and

Melody of Voice, throw out those quick and careless Strokes of Terror from the Disorder of a guilty Mind, which the other gave us with a Facility in her Manner, that rendered them at once tremendous, and delightful" (Cibber, *Apology*, I, 161-162). Q1 lists Sanford opposite the Ghost of Banquo; but as Y and the 1673 quarto indicate, he surely played the part of Heccate. Samuel Sanford excelled in villains' roles; he was a successful Iago. On Sanford see Robert H. Ross, Jr., "Samuel Sandford: Villain from Necessity," *PMLA*, LXXVI (1961), 367-372, and also my note on Cibber as Richard III below.

I.i.SD. The witches leave "flying" at the end of this scene and enter "flying" at the beginning of I.iii. They doubtless flew on other occasions as well: Downes, p. 33, refers to "flyings for the Witches" (such as the "machine" in III.viii.21SD); and much ridicule appears around 1673, as in the anonymous lines given by Thorn-Drury (*Some Seventeenth Century Allusions to Shakespeare* [London, 1920], p. 17): "Now empty shows must want of sense supply, Angels shall dance and *Macbeth's* Witches fly." Thomas Duffett's parody, "Epilogue spoken by the Witches, after the mode of Macbeth" appended to his *Empress of Morocco: A Farce* (1674), includes the stage directions "Three Witches fly over the Pit Riding upon Beesomes" and "*Heccate* descends over the Stage in a Glorious Charriott adorn'd with Pictures of Hell and Devils, and made of a large Wicker Basket." Performances at Dorset Garden in 1673 were undoubtedly more elaborate than those put on in Davenant's lifetime at Lincoln's Inn Fields. Since the early eighteenth century, however, the tradition has been for the witches to rise and sink or be discovered and disappear: see A. C. Sprague, *Shakespeare and the Actors* (Cambridge, Mass., 1948), pp. 225-228.

I.i.7SD. H. N. Paul, *The Royal Play of Macbeth* (New York, 1950), pp. 265-268, and C. Spencer, *Macbeth,* p. 63, suggest that the owl's shriek may be original stage business from Shakespeare's play.

I.iii.40. Assuming that Davenant would have wanted to make geographical sense, I follow Pope and succeeding editors of Shakespeare's play in altering *"Soris"* to *"Forres."*

II.iii.25. In a performance of *Macbeth* soon after the Great Storm of November, 1703, this line was applauded. In his "Dissuasive From the Playhouse" [1703], Jeremy Collier expressed his horror at the impiety of performing *Macbeth* and *The Tempest* soon after the storm: "Does it not look as if they had a Mind to out-brave the Judgment? And make us believe the Storm was nothing but an Eruption of *Epicurus's* Atoms, a Spring-Tide of Matter and Motion, and a blind Salley of Chance?" Quoted from p. 15 of Collier's essay by Sister Rose Anthony, S.C., *The Jeremy Collier Stage Controversy, 1698-1726* (Milwaukee, 1937), p. 191.

II.iv. In Y and Qq acts are divided; every act begins with a "scene i"; and scenes are divided from V.i through vi. This is the only other numbered scene division in the original texts.

II.v.29. Not only the absence of an entry for the witches, but also the Macduffs' reactions (ll. 43-48 and 69-76) indicate that the witches do not enter until l. 75. Then Macduff apparently sees them for the first time. C. Spencer, *Macbeth*, pp. 67-71, suggests that this First Song may have been written by Shakespeare.

The music to *Macbeth* — the subject of much controversy — has been well discussed by Edward J. Dent, *Foundations of English Opera* (Cambridge, England, 1928), pp. 128-136, and even more fully and lucidly by Robert E. Moore, "The Music to *Macbeth*," *Musical Quarterly*, XLVII (1961), 22-40. Robert Johnson probably wrote the original music for "Come away, Heccatte" and "Black Spirits": it is discussed by J. P. Cutts, "The Original Music to Middleton's *The Witch*," *SQ*, VII (1956), 203-209. Matthew Locke supplemented Johnson's music in 1666 or earlier: two of his dance tunes are extant. A score (1696) by John Eccles is extant in manuscript. The "Famous Music," printed by William Boyce in 1750 and carelessly attributed to Locke, has more recently been assigned to either Eccles or Henry Purcell; Moore, however, thinks it is by Richard Leveridge (1670-1758), who is known to have written some music for *Macbeth*.

II.v.75. Obviously the witches must enter before they can dance, though all texts place *"A dance of witches"* at the end of l. 75, before their entry. Probably the dance was indicated in the margin of Davenant's MS with no clear indication of its connection with the other SD. The quartos' *"Enter two Witches"* is unacceptable unless we were to assume that other witches have entered previously: see note to II.v.29.

III.iii.24. This line has often been quoted with punctuation similar to that of Q1 ("He, after life's short feavor, now sleeps; Well:") to show how bad Davenant's lines can be: e.g., H. Spencer, p. 174. Following Y (even though its pointing is often unreliable) and Q5, I have given Davenant the benefit of the doubt.

III.v.28SD. The Shakespearean First Folio places the Ghost's entry here, though later editors have usually placed the entry a few lines later. The second entry (80SD in Davenant) is, in F1, at the equivalent of Davenant's l. 76. The F1-Davenant first entry gives the Ghost time to take his place before his name is mentioned; the Davenant second entry permits the Ghost to enter and be seated when everyone is concentrating his attention on drinking the toast and will not notice the Ghost's arrival for a moment.

III.viii.19. Presumably this line is sung offstage and Heccate refers to it in "Hark." She speaks and another line is sung as the machine is lowered to take her away.

III.viii.56SD. The absence of the SD at the end of III.viii in Y and Qq and at the beginning of IV.i in Qq suggests that the two witch scenes might have been run together — indeed, combining the scenes might have been Davenant's reason for transposing III.vii and viii. However, evidence on the other side seems more compelling: at the end of III.viii the witches say they are leaving, and an act division and (in Y) an entry separate the scenes. Therefore, I have supplied the SD at the end of III.viii.

IV.i.1, 5. These lines, not in Qq, are written in a later hand in Y; they appear also in John Lee's adaptation of *Macbeth* (Edinburgh, 1753). They make couplets out of otherwise unrhymed lines.

IV.i.75. As H. Spencer, p. 163, observes, it seems odd that an adapter as interested in stage effects as Davenant should eliminate the Apparitions. Perhaps Davenant had more restraint than he is given credit for. The witches fly on and off, stir a cauldron which sinks, and provide a vision in a cave which later sinks. These fantastic happenings (1) are expected because they have happened before (the first), (2) suggest the hellish connections of the witches (the second and third), or (3) are a compliment to royalty (the third). The riddling prophecies themselves provide a hint of the future action without the Apparitions, which might have been considered too extravagant and which contribute neither to the serious moral of the play nor to the "operatic" singing and dancing. In his *Rivals* Davenant omits the scene in *The Two Noble Kinsmen* (V.i) in which the omens are seen and heard.

V.i.SD. Apparently only one Lady speaks; if Y(B) intended to divide the lines between two Ladies, he did not indicate his intention in the text beyond assigning the first line to "1 Lady."

V.i.37 ff. Wax marks in the margin of Y indicate that an addition was intended at the end of the scene, but the slip they attached is missing.

V.ii.2. Presumably Donalbain asks the question of Fleance about Lenox, who has come from a different direction, but with whom he had been onstage in II.iii. As rewritten, the scene is far from smooth.

V.ii.18-32. A possible explanation of the variants is as follows: Davenant meant to cancel the lines crossed out in Y(A), but did not make his intention clear; both Y(A) and Q1 made what sense they could of the passage. On rechecking Y, Davenant canceled the passage clearly and rewrote it with additions — Y(B).

V.ix.7SD. It would have been tactless to bring a monarch's head onstage before Charles II.

V.ix.31-34. Wax marks in the margin of Y indicate that an addition or a substitute for ll. 31-34 was intended here, but the slip they attached is missing.

The Tempest

Pref. 17. Davenant had died April 7, 1668.

Pref. 22-32. See also Pro. 15-18. Pepys saw two acts of Suckling's *Goblins* on May 22, 1667, and he refers to a performance on Jan. 24, 1667; it was also performed before the King on Nov. 21 (Nicoll, *History,* I, 344). Fletcher's *Sea-Voyage* was played before royalty on either Sept. 25 or 27, 1667 (*ibid.*) — probably this was the play (" 'The Storme,' a play of Fletcher's") Pepys saw on both the 25th and 26th. Pepys also saw *The Sea-Voyage* on March 25 (probably) and May 16, 1668. Although the tempest scene at the beginning of Fletcher's play reminds one of Shakespeare's — and even more, of Dryden's — the other resemblances Dryden mentions are not particularly striking. Suckling's play is indebted to several of Shakespeare's: see Ruth Wallerstein's rather general article, "Suckling's Imitation of Shakespeare," *RES,* XIX (1943), 290-295. The Goblins seem entirely unlike Ariel.

Pro. Like the Preface, the Prologue and Epilogue were published in 1670 with the Davenant-Dryden play. Both W. J. Lawrence and Summers (in both *Adaptations* and Shadwell's *Complete Works,* II) have reproduced another Prologue and Epilogue to *The Tempest* from

Egerton MS 2623, which seems to reply to Dryden's "Prologue" and "Epilogue Spoken at the Opening of the New House, March 26, 1674." Although Lawrence, p. 199, attributed these manuscript materials to Shadwell, his case was extremely weak: they are best considered anonymous. The Prologue (which I have transcribed from photostats of Egerton MS 2623) is as follows:

PROLOGUE TO YE TEMPEST.

Wee, as the ffathers of the stage have said,
To treat you here, a vast expence have made:
What they have gott from you in Chests is laid,
or is for purchac'd Lands, or houses paid.
You, in this house, all our estates may find,
wch for your pleasures wholly are design'd,
Twas foolish, for we might, we must confesse,
Value our selves much more, & you much lesse;
And, like those reverend men, we might have spar'd
And never for our Benefactors car'd:
still made your Treatment, as they do, more Coarse,
As if you did, as fast as they, grow worse:
But we young men, are apt to slight advice,
One Day, we may decrepid grow, & wise:
Then, hoping not to time to get much more,
Wee'l save our money, & Cry out wee'r poore.
Wee're young, & look yet many yeares to live,
& by your future Bounty hope to thrive;
Then let 'em laugh; for now no cost wee'l spare,
And never think we're poor while we your favours share:
without the good old Playes we did advance,
And all ye stages Ornament enhance:
To splendid things they follow in, but late;
They ne're invent, but they can imitate:
Had we not, for your pleasure found new wayes,
You still had rusty Arras had, & thredbare playes;
Nor scenes nor Weomen, had they had their will,
But some, with grizl'd Beards, had acted Weomen still.
Some restive horses, spight of Switch, & spurre,
Till others straine ag[ain]st 'em, will not stirr:
Envying our Splendid house, & prosp'rous playes,
They scoff at us, & Libell the high wayes.
Tis fitt we, for our faults, rebukes shou'd meet,
The Citty ought to mend those of ye street.
With the best poets heads our house we grac'd,
Wch we in honour to ye Poets plac'd.
"Too much of the old witt They have, 'Tis true:
"But they must look for little of ye new.

Persons. We do not know the original cast of either version of *The Tempest*. In the Davenant-Dryden play Edward Angell (d. 1673?) probably played Stephano (Summers, *Adaptations*, p. xlviii); Cave Underhill (1634-1710?) seems to have originated Trincalo in 1667 and to have played the role at his benefit on May 12, 1710 (John Genest, *Some Account of the English Stage* [Bath, 1832], II, 438); Henry Harris probably played Ferdinand (see note to III.v.23 below); Moll Davis, in the cast according to Pepys, presumably played Hippolito (Summers) or Ariel (J. H. Wilson, *All the King's Ladies* [Chicago, 1958], p. 140): Wilson suggests (p. 166) that Mrs. Jane Long played Hippolito. The role has traditionally been a "breeches part," although "Master Green," who played Prince Edward in Cibber's *Richard III* in 1735-41, took the role on May 15, 1741.

I.i. Three "scenes" are necessary for the play proper: the storm of I.i, "three Walks of Cypress-trees" with caves for I.ii, II.ii and iii, III.ii and vi, IV.i and iii, and V.i (also III.vii is at the mouth of one of the caves; and V.ii apparently begins at a cave mouth, from which the characters move forward at l. 4); and "the wilder part of the Island" or "A wild Island" for II.i and iv, III.i, iii, iv, and v, and IV.ii. Two further scenes are used in the masque, at V.ii.238SD and 323SD.

Usually the orchestra contained twelve stringed instruments ("violins") and sat in the gallery (E. J. Dent, *Foundations of English Opera*, p. 140); the twenty-four violins were "evidently the Royal Band, established early in his reign by Charles II, in imitation of the band of Louis XIV" (W. B. Squire, "The Music of Shadwell's 'Tempest,'" *Musical Quarterly*, VII [1921], 565-578). Nicoll, *History*, I, 356, prints the following warrant of May 16, 1674: "It is his Ma[ties] pleasure that Mr Turner & Mr Hart or any other Men or Boyes belonging to His Ma[ties] Chappell Royall that sing in ye Tempest at His Royall Highnesse Theatre doe remaine in Towne all the Weeke (dureing his Ma[ties] absence from Whitehall) to performe that service. . . ." These are the "30 Warbling voyces" of the Egerton MS 2623 Epilogue (see the note to the Epilogue below). Squire gives a full and relatively clear account of the music, but the subject is so complex that it needs the tabular listing that J. G. McManaway gives it on p. 87 of his "Songs and Masques in *The Tempest*," *Theatre Miscellany, Luttrell Society Reprints*, No. 14 (1953), 71-96. The tunes of the entries and some of the dances were composed by Giovanni Battista Draghi and are not extant. Matthew Locke wrote and published in 1675 the First and Second music (performed while the audience assembled), the Curtain tune, four Act tunes, and the Conclusion. *The Ariels Songs in the Play call'd the Tempest* [1674-75] contains settings by John Banister for "Come unto these yellow sands" and "Full fathom five" in III.i, "Dry those eyes" in III.iii, and "Go thy way" (see note to III.v.23 below) in III.v, as well as a setting by Pelham Humphrey for "Where the Bee sucks" in V.ii. Banister's music for "Dry those eyes" and "Go thy way" is reproduced from *The Ariels Songs* by Cyrus L. Day in *The Songs of John Dryden* (Cambridge, Mass., 1932), pp. 14-16. *The Ariels Songs* also includes one stanza of a song entitled "Dorinda Lamenting the loss of her Amintas," probably to be sung close to the end of IV.iii, but not in any text of the play. McManaway emphasizes (pp. 79-80) that the operatic parts of the play, at least, were constantly changing; this point is allied to that made by Thorn-Drury (see my Introduction above), that *The Tempest* was becoming more operatic before 1673. Music by Humphrey for "Where does the black Fiend" (II.iv) and the masque in V.ii survives in manuscript and was printed in part by Squire. "Arise ye subterranean winds" was set by Pietro Reggio and was published in 1680. Later, probably in 1695, Henry Purcell's music was substituted for that of the earlier musicians: this music is described by Robert E. Moore, *Henry Purcell & the Restoration Theatre* (Cambridge, Mass., 1961), pp. 188-203; Purcell's text of the masque is only about half as long as Shadwell's and its wording is different (Moore, p. 189). In 1755 John Christopher Smith wrote the music for Garrick's version (E. W. White, *The Rise of English Opera* [New York, 1951], pp. 228, 333).

I.i.2. hoaming. Summers says very rough; *OED* says meaning uncertain.

I.i.3. against. in anticipation of.

I.i.12. Capstorm. Capstan.

I.i.34. Seere-Capstorm. Stern Capstan.

I.i.38. Nippers. A piece of braided cordage used to prevent a cable from slipping (*OED*).

I.i.41. Vial. A large single-sheaved block through which the messenger passed when the anchor was weighed by the fore or jeer capstan (*OED*).

I.i.46. Anchor's a peek. I.e., the ship is vertically over its anchor (*OED*).

I.i.51. Catt. "Strong tackle, or complication of pullies, to hook and draw the anchor . . . up to the cat head" (Summers citing Falconer, *Dict. Marine*).

I.i.59. Mackrel-gale. A strong breeze (*OED*).

II.i.6, also II.i.10, 38, 54. soop. A sip or sup.

II.i.12. steal Custom. Cheat the custom-house (Saintsbury).

II.i.95. old *Simon* the King. A popular song mentioned also in *Tom Jones*, Book IV, Chapter 5 (Summers). The tune is used for Air LXII in Gay's *Beggar's Opera*.

II.ii.110. Hare in's Form. Hare in his nest or lair (*OED*).

III.ii.113. Callow-bird. Unfledged; hence, inexperienced (*OED*).

III.iii.36SD. Downes was impressed by (but also apparently confused about) this passage: he wrote of "one Scene Painted with *Myriads* of *Ariel* Spirits [I.i or V.ii.323SD]; and another flying away, with a Table Furnisht out with Fruits, Sweetmeats and all sorts of Viands; just when Duke *Trinculo* and his Companions, were going to Dinner" (Downes, pp. 34-35).

III.iv.45. old *Simon* the King. See note to II.i.95 above.

III.v.23. Pepys, who admired the "echo song" the first time he saw *The Tempest*, persuaded Banister to "prick [him] down the notes" on May 7, 1668, and four days later he went backstage "between two acts . . . and got [Mr. Harris] to repeat to me the words of the Echo, while I writ them down." William Van Lennep has written on Harris in "Henry Harris, Actor, Friend of Pepys," in M. St. Clare Byrne, ed., *Studies in English Theatre History in Memory of Gabrielle Enthoven* (London, 1952), pp. 9-23. As this song is printed in "The Songs and Masques in *The Tempest*" and as it is given in *The Ariels Songs* (see Day, *The Songs of John Dryden*, pp. 16-17), Ariel echoes every line through l. 33. In "The Songs and Masques" this song is listed as being in Act IV.

IV.i.116. The Scott-Saintsbury text begins a new scene here, but since Hippolito and Dorinda enter before Prospero leaves, the stage is not cleared.

IV.ii.22, also IV.ii.93. skink about. To pour out or draw Liquor; to offer or serve a drink (*OED*, quoting IV.ii.93).

IV.iii.57. Mount *Hecla*. The Davenant-Dryden play (1670) reads

"Mount *Hecla,*" referring to a volcano in Iceland; no Mount *Heila* (1674-92) is known.

V.ii.37-39. These lines are cited by M. E. Hartsock, "Dryden's Plays: A Study in Ideas," in Robert Shafer, ed., *Seventeenth Century Studies,* Second Series (Princeton, 1937), p. 102, in her discussion of Dryden's use of Hobbes's principle of mutation.

V.ii.43SD. As Summers points out, it should be Ferdinand's sword — the sword that made the wound — both according to tradition and according to Ariel (V.i.37).

Epi. See note to the Prologue above. The Epilogue (transcribed from photostats of Egerton MS 2623) is as follows:

EPILOGUE.

When feeble Lovers Appetites decay,
They, to provoke, & keep themselves in play,
must, to their Cost, make ye gay Damsells shine,
If Beauty can't provoke, they'l do't by being fine:
That pow'rfull charme, wch cannot be withstood
puts off bad faces, & adornes ye good.
oft' an Embroider'd Damsel have wee seen,⎤
ugly as Bawd, & finer then a Queen,   ⎬
who by that splendor has victorious been;   ⎦
She, whose weake Eyes had ne're one Victory gott,
m[a]y Conquer with a flaming petticoat:
Witt is a Mistresse you have long enjoy'd,
Her Beauty's not empair'd, but you are cloy'd!
And Since 'tis not Witt's fault that you decay,
You, for your want of appetite, must pay.
You to provoke your selves must keep her fine,
& she must, now, at double charges shine.
Old Sinners thus ——
When they feele Age, & Impotence approach,
Double the charge of furniture, & Coach;
when you of witt, and sence, were weary growne,
Romantick, riming, fustian Playes were showne,
We then to flying Witches did advance,
And for your pleasures traffic'd into ffrance.
From thence new Arts to please you, we have sought,⎤
We have Machines to some perfection brought,   ⎬
And above 30 Warbling voyces gott.   ⎦
Many a God, & Goddesse, you will heare, ⎤
And we have Singing, Dancing, Devills here;⎬
Such Devills, and such gods, are very deare.⎦

412

> We, in all ornaments, are lavish growne, ⎫
> And, like Improvident Damsells of ye Towne, ⎬
> For present bravery, all our wealth lay downe; ⎭
> As if our keepers ever wou'd be Kind, ⎫
> The thought of future wants we never mind, ⎬
> No pittance is for your old age designd. ⎭
> Alone, we on your Constancy depend,
> And hope your Love to th' stage will never end:
> To please you, we no Art, or cost will spare
> To make yr Mrs look, still young, still faire.

Epi. 9. *King* Richard's. Most editors assume that the reference is to Shakespeare's *Richard III*. However, the more immediate allusion is probably to Caryll's *English Princess; or, The Death of Richard the III,* which Pepys saw on March 7, 1667, about eight months before the Davenant-Dryden *Tempest,* and which, according to Downes, p. 27, was quite successful. The title page states that the play was licensed on May 22, 1667. Since the 1667 edition was succeeded by editions of 1673 and 1674 (Nicoll, *History,* I, 395), the lines might be expected to remind readers of Caryll's play in those years. In IV.ix Richard *"appeares in a distracted posture, newly risen from his Bed, walking in his Dream, with a dagger in his hand, and surrounded by the Ghosts of those whom he had formerly killed."*

King Lear

Ded. Thomas Boteler is identified by Arthur H. Scouten as a cousin of Aston Cokain, whose *Trappolin Suppos'd a Prince* Tate adapted in his successful farce, *A Duke and No Duke* in 1684 ("Aston Cokain and His Adapter Nahum Tate," unpub. dissertation [Louisiana State, 1942], p. cxii and note). Summers, *Adaptations,* p. 280, says "Thomas Butler, of the family of the Duke of Ormond," but the Duke's eldest son, Thomas Butler, Earl of Ossory, died in 1680 and in any case would not have been "Thomas Boteler, Esq."

Ded. 34. Dryden's *Spanish Friar* was advertised in mid-March, 1681 (Macdonald, p. 124), although it did not appear in *The Term Catalogue* until the Trinity Term (June); Tate's *Lear* was listed in the Easter Term (May).

Ded. 42. *Quaintness.* Highly elegant or refined (speech). See my Introduction above, pp. 12-13.

Pro. 21-24. In March of 1681, when Tate's *King Lear* was probably first performed, the controversy over the policy of Exclusion reached its climax in the Oxford Parliament.

Persons. Elizabeth Barry (1658-1713), for whom Tate may have tailored the part of Cordelia, was especially successful in "distressing" scenes; Cibber said of her, "In the Art of exciting Pity she had a Power beyond all the Actresses I have yet seen, or what your Imagination can conceive" (*Apology*, I, 160).

I.i. In the early texts and in Summers, scenes are not numbered and changes of "scenes" are not always indicated. I divide the scenes of Acts I and IV as does G. B. Harrison in *King Lear: Text, Sources, Criticism* (New York, 1962), who summarizes II and gives no divisions for it. I add a scene to III (scene iv) and to V (scene iv): at the beginning of each the stage is cleared. No "scenes" are indicated for Act I; but II.i-ii, III.ii, and III.v use a scene representing *"Gloster's House"* or *"Palace"*; III.i is *"A Desert Heath"*; III.iii-iv, IV.ii, and IV.iv employ *"The Field Scene"* (in bad and good weather); IV.i has *"A Grotto"*; IV.iii uses *"Goneril's Palace"* (doubtless used for I.ii as well); IV.v is in *"A Chamber"*; V.i has *"A Camp"*; V.ii employs a tent; V.iii uses *"A Valley near the Camp"*; V.v begins *"Enter before the Tents"*; and V.vi is in *"A Prison."* V.iv is not located, but was probably played before the scene used in V.iii. *"A Camp"* and *"before the Tents"* perhaps refer to the same scene.

I.i.281. wind. insinuate.

I.ii.19. Clatpole. Blockhead. The early quartos of Shakespeare's play read "clat-pole"; the Shakespeare folios and the later quartos of Tate's play read "Clodpole."

I.ii.21SD. The Servant must both exit and enter if l. 24 is to make sense.

II.ii.61. Muss-cat. Musk-cat: a term of reproach to a fop. In II.ii.254 Gonerill's Gentleman is called a "Fashion-fop."

II.ii.129. white minute. precious minute.

III.iii.40. fow. Dialect word meaning "foul" (Harrison).

III.iii.87-88. Summers, *Adaptations*, p. 281, suggests that Tate misread the folio spelling "wall-Neut" and "water-Neut" and emends to "Wall-Newt" and "Water Newt" (*sic*). However, "Water-nut" looks like a possible name for something, and it seems doubtful that Tate intended any other reading here.

III.iii.112. Summers, *Adaptations,* pp. 215 and 281, reads "dym," although he observes that the "Hym" of Tate's play and the Shakespeare First Folio should be "Lym." However, "Hym" is bracketed with "Brach," and the pair might have been taken to refer to female and male by Tate.

III.v.4. Ost. Host (Harrison).

III.v.60. Gonerill and Regan, married to the Dukes of Albany and Cornwall in Shakespeare, are married (respectively) to the King of Albany and the Prince of Camber and Cornwall in John Higgins' story of Cordila in *The Mirror for Magistrates* (1574), to the Kings of Albania and Cambria in *The Faerie Queene,* and to the Kings of Cornwall and Cambria in *The True Chronicle History of King Leir.*

IV.iv.59. The 1681 reading "Crow" is no doubt an error for the Shakespearean reading "Crown," rather than an error for "Brow."

V.v.75. Empericks. Quacks.

Epi. 16. Tangier was the property of the English from 1662 to 1684 and was used as a base of operations against the corsairs. From March to October, 1680, it was in danger of falling to a besieging army under Muley Ishmael; during the uneasy truce that followed, the English garrison's morals seem to have declined. Short of money, Charles was forced to abandon Tangier in March, 1684. See J. S. Corbett, *England in the Mediterranean . . . 1603-1713* (New York, 1904), II, 114-140.

Epi. 18. th' Alcade. I.e., the Alcayde, the commander of a fortress in Spain, Portugal, Barbary, etc.

Richard III

Ep. Ded. Henry Brett, Jun. of Cowley (d. 1724) "was the first [Gentleman] of any consideration since my coming to the Stage with whom I had contracted a Personal Intimacy" (Cibber, *Apology,* II, 33). Brett, who was assisted in his courtship by Cibber, married in 1700; according to Boswell, Cibber submitted his *Careless Husband* to Mrs. Brett for her approval: G. B. Hill and L. F. Powell, eds., *Boswell's Life of John-*

son (Oxford, 1934), I, 174n. Brett held the controlling share in the Drury Lane patent from June, 1707, to March, 1708.

Pref. 1-20. Remarking on the salutary effect of Collier's *Short View of the Stage,* Cibber in his *Apology* (I, 275-276) complained of the "zealous Severity" of the Master of the Revels (Charles Killigrew):

. . . a severe Instance of this kind falling upon my self may be an Excuse for my relating it: when *Richard the Third* (as I alter'd it from *Shakespear*) came from his Hands to the Stage, he expung'd the whole first Act without sparing a Line of it. This extraordinary Stroke of a *Sic volo* occasion'd my applying to him for the small Indulgence of a Speech or Two, that the other four Acts might limp on with a little less Absurdity! no! he had not leisure to consider what might be separately inoffensive. He had an Objection to the whole Act, and the Reason he gave for it was, that the Distresses of King *Henry the Sixth,* who is kill'd by *Richard* in the first Act, would put weak People too much in mind of King *James* then living in *France;* a notable Proof of his Zeal for the Government! Those who have read either the Play or the History, I dare say will think he strain'd hard for the Parallel. In a Word, we were forc'd, for some few Years, to let the Play take its Fate with only four Acts divided into five; by the Loss of so considerable a Limb, may one not modestly suppose it was robbed of at least a fifth Part of that Favour it afterwards met with? For tho' this first Act was at last recovered, and made the Play whole again, yet the Relief came too late to repay me for the Pains I had taken in it. Nor did I ever hear that this jealous Severity of the Master of the Revels was afterwards thought justifiable.

Wood, pp. 97-99, suggests that the first act was restored "about 1714," but an earlier date seems likely. R. H. Barker, *Mr. Cibber of Drury Lane* (New York, 1939), pp. 38-39, discusses "a tragical interlude of one act only called *The Death of King Henry VI*" in *The Medley* advertised in the *Daily Courant* for Oct. 21, 1702, and then canceled.

Pref. 29. Dryden, who died May 1, 1700.

Persons. Since Cibber prided himself on acting Richard as Sanford would have acted the part, Cibber's impression of Sanford is of particular interest.

[Sanford's] Voice had an acute and piercing Tone, which struck every Syllable of his Words distinctly upon the Ear. He had likewise a peculiar Skill in his Look of marking out to an Audience whatever he judg'd worth their more than ordinary Notice. When he deliver'd a Command, he would sometimes give it more Force by seeming to slight the Ornament of Harmony. In *Dryden's* Plays of Rhime, he as little as possible glutted the Ear with the Jingle of it, rather chusing, when the Sense would permit him, to lose it, than to value it.

Had *Sandford* liv'd in *Shakespear's* Time, I am confident his Judgment must have chose him above all other Actors to have play'd his *Richard the*

Third: I leave his Person out of the Question, which, tho' naturally made for it, yet that would have been the the [*sic*] least Part of his Recommendation; *Sandford* had stronger Claims to it; he had sometimes an uncouth Stateliness in his Motion, a harsh and sullen Pride of Speech, a meditating Brow, a stern Aspect, occasionally changing into an almost ludicrous Triumph over all Goodness and Virtue: From thence falling into the most asswasive Gentleness and soothing Candour of a designing Heart. These, I say, must have preferr'd him to it; these would have been Colours so essentially shining in that Character, that it will be no Dispraise to that great Author to say, *Sandford* must have shewn as many masterly Strokes in it (had he ever acted it) as are visible in the Writing it.

When I first brought *Richard the Third* (with such Alterations as I thought not improper) to the Stage, *Sandford* was engaged in the Company then acting under King *William's* Licence in *Lincoln's-Inn-Fields;* otherwise you cannot but suppose my Interest must have offer'd him that Part. What encouraged me, therefore, to attempt it myself at the *Theatre-Royal,* was that I imagined I knew how *Sandford* would have spoken every Line of it: If, therefore, in any Part of it I succeeded, let the Merit be given to him: And how far I succeeded in that Light, those only can be Judges who remember him. In order, therefore, to give you a nearer Idea of *Sandford,* you must give me leave (compell'd as I am to be vain) to tell you that the late Sir *John Vanbrugh,* who was an Admirer of *Sandford,* after he had seen me act it, assur'd me That he never knew any one Actor so particularly profit by another as I had done by *Sandford* in *Richard the Third: You have,* said he, *his very Look, Gesture, Gait, Speech, and every Motion of him, and have borrow'd them all only to serve you in that Character.* If, therefore, Sir *John Vanbrugh's* Observation was just, they who remember me in *Richard the Third* may have a nearer Conception of *Sandford* than from all the critical Account I can give of him. [*Apology,* I, 138-140].

Cibber seems to have been ineffective on the battlefield (see note to V.viii.14 below), but to have been successful in other scenes. Comparing Wilks and Cibber in *The Tatler* 182 (June 8, 1710), Steele asked, "can anything be . . . more exasperating, than [the behaviour] of Richard, when he insults his superiors? . . . To rally pleasantly, to scorn artfully, to flatter, to ridicule, and to neglect, are what Cibber would perform with no less excellence" than Wilks would perform certain other parts.

The cast published in the 1718 quarto (and repeated in later editions) has been assumed to be that of 1715 — e.g., Hogan, I, 379; *London Stage,* Part II, Vol. I, p. 379 — apparently on the ground that the parts played by Cibber (Richard), Wilks (Henry VI), Mills (Buckingham), and Mrs. Porter (Queen Elizabeth) were the same as those advertised for the Dec. 6, 1715, performance. However, these actors were performing the same four roles as late as 1728. I can find no evidence that eight of the total list of twenty actors were acting in 1715 (*London Stage,* Part II, Vol. I, p. 368, includes all eight in the roster of the Drury Lane company for 1715-16, but presumably because they are in the *Richard III* list). The following are the earliest references I can discover for them: W. Wilks received a benefit on May 16, 1716; Miss Lindar delivered a Prologue on May 27, 1717; Higginson appeared in a cast of Aug. 6, 1717; Diggs was in a cast of Jan. 31, 1718; Oates was listed in the cast of *The Play is the Plot* as it was printed in 1718 (*London Stage,* Part II, Vol. II, p. 483) and received a benefit on May 1 of that year; Norris Jr. and Wilson were in the cast of the 1719 edition of *Julius Caesar* (the Drury Lane company performed the play on Jan. 28 and April 24); and I can find no trace of Wright previous to 1720, when he appeared in the cast given in the 1720 edition of *I Henry IV*. The *Richard III* cast is probably that of the 1717-18 season, when the play was given at Drury Lane on Nov. 9 and March 15.

Misses Allison and Chock were child actresses who, beginning about 1695, were sometimes used to deliver Prologues and Epilogues; Miss Chock would have been about ten in 1699. See Montague Summers, *The Restoration Theatre* (New York, 1934), pp. 179-180.

I.i. The following "scenes" are indicated in the original text: "*A Garden within the* Tower" for I.i and "*A Chamber in the* Tower" for I.iii (I.ii doubtless used the garden scene, and so, probably, did IV.iii, introduced as "*The* Tower"; but IV.i, also "*The* Tower," seems better suited to the "Chamber"). II.i is at "*St.* Paul's"; at 53SD the "Scene *draws,*" revealing Ann and King Henry's body (see also the 1700 stage direction variant). II.ii and IV.ii employ "*the Presence*" scene. III.i and ii and IV.iv are unlocated; III.ii appears to be an indoor scene (see esp. ll. 68-71), but III.i might be indoors or out and IV.iv is outdoors.

In Act V, scene i is labeled "*The Field,*" scene ii "Bosworth *Field,*" and scene iv "*before* Richard's *Tent*" (1700) or "Bosworth *Field*" (1718 on). I have made a new scene of v, which begins with a clear stage and the stage direction "*Enter* Richard *from his Tent,*" and in which Richard "*Lies down*" and "*Sleeps.*" Rowe's edition of 1709 contains a frontispiece showing Richard sleeping in a chair inside a tent with the ghosts around him; one is sinking (or rising) through the floor. Hogarth's painting "Garrick as Richard III" (according to W. M. Merchant, *Shakespeare and the Artist* [London, 1959], p.

45, "probably the greatest theatre portrait painted in England") shows Richard awaking from his dream inside a tent. Grignion and Hogarth engraved the painting in 1746, and both the engraving and Rowe's frontispiece are reproduced by Merchant (Plates 6b and 7a). The other scenes in Act V are unlocated. I take it that the scenes in Richmond's camp (i, iii, and perhaps vi) were played before one "scene," and that those in Richard's camp (ii, iv, v, and perhaps vii) were played before another, which was probably also used for viii and ix. A tent was apparently erected, doubtless at Richard's command at the beginning of ii, and stood at least through V.v.69, when it might have been removed to make way for the battle. Merchant, p. 42, although he concedes that there is no "indication of the existence of a tent" for Richmond, thinks that "the subsequent action becomes more comprehensible if we suppose a pavilion to be erected on each side of the stage."

I.i.86. The stage directions do not indicate that Stanley has received news from anyone since his account of ll. 24-25.

I.i.101-106. Albert E. Kalson, "The Chronicles in Cibber's *Richard III*," *SEL*, III (1963), 253-267, points out that these lines are based on nothing in Shakespeare but correspond to details given by Holinshed, Stow, Baker, and Speed. From this and other points, some of which are listed below, Kalson concludes, p. 266, that "Cibber definitely consulted Speed, whose work, printed four times in the seventeenth century (1611, 1623, 1632, and 1650), was easily accessible," and probably Holinshed as well.

I.i.178-179. Kalson observes that King Edward's striking the Prince with his gauntlet is in the Chronicles, but not in Shakespeare. In Crowne's *Misery of Civil War* (1680), Edward uses his hand rather than a gauntlet.

II.i.100 ff. In an attack upon Cibber in the *Grub Street Journal* for Oct. 31, 1734, a correspondent wrote, "When he [Cibber] makes love to *Lady Ann*, he looks like a pick-pocket, with his shrugs and grimaces, that has more a design on her purse than her heart; and his utterance is in the same cast with his action."

III.ii.24 ff. Kalson (also Wood) points out that some details in this scene between Richard and Anne are similar to those in a meeting described by Holinshed and Speed, in which Richard comforts Ann even as he plans her murder. See also the comments of Lamb, Hazlitt, and A. C. Sprague, above, pp. 26-27.

III.ii.279-280. "Th'aspiring youth" was Herostatus, who, desiring to be famous even if by a great crime, burned the great Temple of Artemis at Ephesus. This act was allegedly performed in 356 B.C. at a time when Artemis was absent, assisting at the birth of Alexander the Great. Although he was interested in "acquiring" fame (1718 on), the 1700 reading seems the more precise.

IV.i.17-19. Kalson compares similar sentiments from Holinshed and Stow. He quotes, p. 262, the following from Stow: "Alasse, I would my Vncle would let mee enjoy my life yet, though I lose both my Kingdome and Crowne."

IV.i.109-113. Kalson quotes parallel passages from the Chronicles, and Wood cites *The Mirror for Magistrates*. The parallels are not striking, though Cibber apparently consulted the Chronicles and, therefore, might well have read the passages cited.

IV.ii.82. The alteration of "Henry" to "Harry," apparently made for the 1721 edition, may be vulgar, but it is thoroughly consistent with the vulgar person that Cibber the actor's Richard apparently was (see Steele's remark on Cibber in the note to the Persons above; see also II.i.276).

IV.iii.19-38. Apparently the first commentator to look at the first edition of Cibber's *Richard III* was Hazelton Spencer, who, according to A. C. Sprague, described the scene in his unpublished dissertation (Harvard, 1923, p. 594). The scene was printed by Sprague in "A New Scene in Colley Cibber's *Richard III*," *MLN*, XLII (1927), 29-32, who suggested two reasons for its omission: first, that reduction in the play's length was necessary when the first act was restored (however, the net loss is only eighteen lines and the original scene could have been shortened); and second, that the audience rebelled at the excessive horror of the scene. Perhaps the death on July 30, 1700, just after his eleventh birthday, of William, the only surviving son of Princess Anne, made even Cibber feel that the scene was in bad taste. The play seems not to have been performed again until 1704.

IV.iii.49-52. In Shakespeare the Princes are buried by the chaplain, and Tirrel does not know where. Kalson points out that Speed and Baker describe the coffin full of holes.

V.i. On the staging of this act see the note to I.i above.

V.viii.14. The author of *The Laureat: or, the Right Side of Colley*

Cibber Esq.; (London, 1740), p. 35, described the first night of Cibber's *Richard III* as follows: Cibber "screamed thro' four Acts without Dignity or Decency. The Audience ill-pleas'd with the Farce, accompany'd him with a Smile of Contempt; but in the fifth Act, he degenerated all at once into Sir *Novelty;* and when in the Heat of the Battle at *Bosworth Field,* the King is dismounted, our Comic-Tragedian came on the Stage, really breathless, and in a seeming Panick, screaming out this Line thus — *A Harse, a Harse, my Kingdom for a Harse.* This highly delighted some, and disgusted others of his Auditors. . . ." An anonymous correspondent of the *Grub Street Journal* for Oct. 31, 1734, did not admire Cibber at war either: "In Bosworth-field he appears no more like *King Richard,* than *King Richard* was like *Falstaff:* he foams, struts, and bellows with the voice and cadence of a watchman rather than a hero and a prince." Downes, p. 51, observed that Cibber's performance in tragedy would have been "not much Inferior" to that in comedy "had Nature given him Lungs Strenuous to his finisht Judgment."

The Jew of Venice

Pro. Bevill Higgons (1670-1735), poet, historian, and Granville's cousin, also wrote the Epilogue for Granville's *Heroick Love* (1698) and himself wrote an unsuccessful play, *The Generous Conqueror, or The Timely Discovery. A Tragedy, as it is acted at the Theatre Royal. 1702,* for which Granville wrote the Prologue. The Ghost of Shakespeare also appears in the Prologues to Dryden's *Troilus and Cressida* (1679) and Gildon's *Measure for Measure* (1700).

Pro. 11-12. Nicoll (*History,* II, 5) quotes E. Curll, *The Life of That Eminent Comedian Robert Wilks, Esq.* (1733) about conditions c. 1700: "The *English* Theatre was not only pestered with Tumblers, and Rope-Dancers from *France,* but likewise Dancing-Masters, and Dancing-Dogs; shoals of *Italian* Squallers were daily imported; and the *Drury Lane* Company almost broke."

Pro. 16-17. Dryden's *All for Love* was performed January 7, 1701.

Pro. 29. Stock-jobbing. Cheating. J. H. Wilson, "Granville's 'Stock-Jobbing Jew,' " *PQ,* XIII (1934), 1-15, discusses the implications of the term.

Epi. 1. In replying to "the parson" in his Epilogue to *The Pilgrim,* Dryden developed the thesis that the *openness* of vice came from the Court's example.

Epi. 16. The Epilogue is also printed among *Poems upon Several Occasions* in Vol. I of the *Genuine Works* (1732). There are a few variants, the most significant of which is the addition of two lines after l. 16 and the alteration of ll. 17-18 as follows:

> . . . Sense would be Writ.
> Good Plays we try, which after the first Day,
> Unseen we act, and to bare Benches play;
> Plain Sense, which pleas'd your Sires an Age ago,
> Is lost, without the Garniture of Show:

Epi. 21-22. The war is not only the attempt of theater people to balance their books; Granville doubtless alludes also to what the Tories considered the failures of King William's diplomacy.

Epi. 24-26. The masque of Cupid and Bacchus in Shadwell's *Timon of Athens* (1678) was set to music by Henry Purcell. H. Spencer, p. 98, quotes the Langbaine-Gildon *Lives and Characters* (1699) about *Timon:* " 'for a few Years past, as often acted at the Theatre Royal, as any Tragedy I know.' " Downes, p. 37, said of *Timon:* "the Musick in't well Perform'd; it wonderfully pleas'd the Court and City." Hogan lists a performance of *Timon* on Jan. 17, 1701.

TEXTS AND VARIANTS

The text of each play reproduces the spelling, punctuation, and capitalization of the copy-text with certain exceptions. In addition to ignoring the long *s*, display capitals, "Act ends," "Finis," etc., I have made *silent* alterations to achieve the following: all lines of verse begin with capitals, and all speeches and stage directions end with final punctuation; speech ascriptions are abbreviated consistently throughout each play, and each ascription is followed by a period; abbreviations in stage directions are usually expanded; entries are centered and exits are to the right, whereas other stage directions may be either to the left or the right; italics are used consistently, and usually the names of characters are spelled consistently throughout each play; when two or more part-lines of verse can be combined to make one line of five (or fewer) feet, I have generally made the combination. I have also made a very few alterations in spelling, principally correcting inverted letters, repairing transpositions of letters that produce nonsense, and adding obviously omitted letters (e.g., adding the *a* to "Prctise"); but in this respect I have been conservative. Similarly, I have made fewer adjustments in the lineation of the verse than I was tempted to make. Scene divisions are added to the plays, enclosed in brackets when they were not in the copy-text, but they are generally not mentioned in the variants unless the earlier editions themselves do not agree.

Although adjustments in verse lineation are made silently, I do record in the variants my alterations of verse to prose and prose to verse. Other modifications that I make and record are changes in punctuation when the original pointing seems to create an ambiguity in the sense or when it might well be momentarily confusing to a modern reader accustomed to reading seventeenth-century texts. Of course, substantive emendations of speeches, stage directions, and speech ascriptions are listed.

In addition to recording emendations and changes in punctuation other than final pointing, the variants list substantive and many semi-substantive differences from relevant later texts. The lemma is always the reading of my text, although, if I have adopted a reading from a text other than the copy-text, the lemma may not reproduce exactly the capitalization or spelling of that other text. For example, in *Macbeth,* IV.iii.41, only Q1 has the spelling "deceiptful": Y and Qq2-5 omit the *p*. However, I use the spelling of the copy-text in my text, and give the variant because of the comma: deceiptful, Y, Qq2-5] deceiptful Q1.

Macbeth

The texts of Davenant's *Macbeth* are discussed in detail in C. Spencer, *Macbeth;* only the conclusions and their application are given here. Entered in *The Term Catalogue* for the Trinity (June) Term, 1674, the play was published in two editions in that year, the first by P. Chetwin (Q1) and the second, which was printed from the first, by A. Clark (Q2). Editions followed in 1687 (Q3 — two issues), 1695 (Q4), and 1710 (Qq5-7 — three editions). However, preceding all the printed texts was the Yale Manuscript (c. 1663), which is referred to as Y or Y(A) for the original text and Y(B) for the additions in later hands on the original pages or on separate slips of paper. Y seems to have been a fair copy made from Davenant's manuscript and used in preparation of the prompt copy. As such, it was probably corrected by the adapter-manager, who, I think, was responsible for some if not all of Y(B): even though several hands seem involved in Y(B), some if not all of the additions were probably made at Davenant's instance. Q1, however, is not descended from Y; the printer's copy for Q1 was presumably either the source of Y or a transcript of that source. Both Y and Q1, then, have authority; but since Y shows signs of care and probably contains authorial revision, whereas Q1 was printed rather carelessly — it seems hurriedly — Y's text is more reliable. Q5, the first of the 1710 editions and the only quarto after the first with any authority at all, was based upon Q1 but seems to have been checked with a playhouse copy. Accordingly, substantive readings from Y(A) are normally preferred to Q1's, and a few readings are adopted from Q5. Also, I have included — but placed in brackets — the additions and most of the corrections in Y(B). Lines in Q1 but crossed out in Y(A) are included unless they are replaced by Y(B)'s additions; cancellations, substitutions, and additions are noted in the variants.

Nevertheless, in the interest of supplying a fairly consistent text with seventeenth-century pointing, I have chosen Q1 as the copy-text for accidentals: the pointing of Y is inadequate, and when it exists it is often hard to interpret (e.g., is the mark a period or a comma?). Moreover, since ten pages of Y are missing (containing I.ii.54–I.iii.57, I.iv.60–I.v.69, and II.i–II.iii.77), Q1 would have to serve for at least part of my text. This quarto, whose collation is A2, A-D4, F-I4, K2, contains irregularities in page numbers and catchwords; and several corrections were made in the course of printing. I give below the press-variants from eight copies: four copies at the Folger Shakespeare Library, and the copies at the Boston Public Library, Harvard University, the University of Illinois, and Yale University. Seven copies were listed in C. Spencer, *Macbeth*, p. 19n; in the course of comparing the Illinois copy with the Folger Kemble, Harvard, and Yale copies, I found two press-variants which I had missed previously and which are added here. The corrected reading is given as the lemma.

Corrected: BPL, Folger (3 copies including Kemble), Harvard, Illinois.
Uncorrected: Folger McKee, Yale.

   sig. A2 Arg 12 *at*] *to* (as Qq2-5)

            22 *hereupon* (Qq2-5)] *hereuprn*

            22 *caused to be* (Qq3-4)] *caused him so be* (*caused him to be* Qq2,5)

            25 Dunsinan (Qq2-5)] Dnnsinan

            35 *himself* (Qq2-5)] *himself,*

            37 *met in* (Qq3-5)] *met* (Q2)

            37 *taking*] *& taking* (*and taking* Qq2-5)

   sig. G1 III.vii.4 *pitti'd* (Q2)] *pitt'd* (*pitty'd* Y, *pity'd* Qq3-5)

In the BPL and Folger Kemble copies the catchword on A2v (Persons Names) has been corrected from "MACBETH." to "ACT."

Corrected: Folger Kemble, Harvard, Illinois.
Uncorrected: Yale.

sig. F2   III.iv.3   Traveller (Y,Qq2-5)] Travellers
Corrected: Folger Kemble, Yale.
Uncorrected: Harvard, Illinois.

   sig. H4   IV.v.39   Mans (Y,Qq2,5, Man's Qq3-4)] Manr
In this quarto as in others, especially *The Tempest* (1674), the collator is plagued with disappearing (sometimes, possibly, corrected) punctuation: for example, on sig. G2v, IV.i.24 ends "Gulf." in the Yale copy, but the period is absent in the Folger Kemble, Harvard, and Illinois copies; and further down the page (IV.i.41) "sing," in the Yale copy is "sing" in the Harvard and Illinois copies, and "sin" in the Folger Kemble copy ("And now about the *Cauldron* sin").

   The list of variants includes, in addition to departures from the copy-text, substantive and many semi-substantive variants from Y and Qq2-5, although variants in punctuation resulting from Y's inadequate punctuation are usually not given. Substantive changes in Y(A) made by Y(B) are also noted. Some readings from the Maidment and Logan edition of Davenant's *Dramatic Works* (1874), V, are included, but usually only when I accept the readings of neither Y nor Q1.

   Davenant's Shakespearean text was not F2 or F3: see Gustav Weber, *Davenant's Macbeth im Verhältnis zu Shakespeare's gleichnamiger Tragödie* (Rostock, 1903), pp. 11-14, and C. Spencer, *Macbeth*, pp. 55-56. The latter develops the thesis (pp. 58-71) that Davenant's Shakespearean text was a pre-Restoration manuscript rather than F1.

TP   Y *reads:* Macbeth | A | Tragedy | As it is now acted | at the | Dukes Theatre | [rule] | 1674 | [rule].
   Dukes Theatre Y,Qq1-2] Theatre Royal Qq3-4; QUEEN'S-THEATRE Q5.
   [double rule] Q1] [rule] | [ornament] | [rule] Qq2-4; [rule] Q5.
   LONDON, | Printed for *P. Chetwin* . . . 1674.] *LONDON:* | Printed for *A. Clark,* and are to be sold | by most Booksellers, 1674. Q2.
   LONDON, | Printed for *Hen. Herringman,* and are to be sold by | *Jos. Knight* and *Fra. Saunders* at the *Blue Anchor* in | the Lower Walk of the *New-Exchange,* 1687. Q3. (*Another issue of* Q3 *reads: LONDON,* | Printed for *H. Herringman,* and *R. Bentley,* and are to be | sold by *Thomas Chapman* at the *Chyrurgeons Arms* over | against the *Mewse* near *Charing-Cross.* 1687.)
   LONDON. | Printed for | *H. Herringman,* and *R. Bentley;* and sold | by *R. Bentley, J. Tonson, T. Bennet,* and | *F. Sanders.* 1695. Q4.

LONDON: | Printed for *J. Tonson:* And Sold by *John Phillips* at the *Black* | *Bull* over-against the *Royal Exchange* in *Cornhill.* 1710. Q5. (*Another edition has a similar imprint but reads: Philips.*)

Arg   *Om.* Y. *See also press-variants listed above.*

15   *with* Qq1-4] *with the* Q5.

16   *out in the former,* Qq2-5] *out, in the former* Q1.

22   *suspected* Qq1-2] *suspecting* Qq3-5.

26   *Consulted* Qq1-4] *consulting* Q5.

39   *Marching* Qq1-4] *marched* Q5.

41   *overtaken* Qq1-3,5] *overtaking* Q4.

44   *of* Qq1-3,5] *of a* Q4.

Pers   Y,Qq1-4 *include also Ross, Angus, Menteth, Cathnes, Doctor, Porter, Old Man, Seymour's Son;* Qq1-4 *include Macduff's Son. Seymour* Qq2-4] Seyward Y,Qq1,5. Maid] *om.* Y,Qq (*see II.v*). Mr. *Sanford. opposite* Ghost of *Banquo* Qq1-4. Witches Q5] *Three Wittches* Y,Qq1-4.

I.ii.7   the Y,Qq1-3,5] he Q4.

13   Isles Y] Isles: Qq1-4; Isles; Q5.

14   Gallow-glasses Qq] Gallow-grosses Y.

22   then Qq] when Y.

24   hope Y] hopes Qq.   rise,] rise Y,Q5; rise; Qq1-4,ML.

26   our Y] your Qq.

27   Heels, Q5,ML] Heels. Q1; Heels; Qq2-4.

42SD   Seyton ML] *Cap.* Y,Qq.

[*I.ii.54–I.iii.57 on pages missing in Y.*]

57   the Y,Qq1-3,5] the the Q4.

66   he has Qq1,5] he hath Qq2-4.

I.iii.9   without Qq1-3,5] without without Q4.

19   his Qq1-3,5] the Q4.

24   Yet it Q5] Yet Qq1-4, ML.

38   Command] Command; Qq1-4; Command, Q5,ML.

40   *Forres* ML] *Soris* Qq. (*Foris* Pope.)

53   hereafter. Qq2-5] hereafter? Q1.

63   favours Y] favour Qq.

69SD   *Going.* Q5] *Exeunt.* Y,Qq1-4; *om.* ML.

79   Ha! Gone! Y,Qq1-4] *om.* Q5.

105   that was the *Thane,* yet lives Y] who was the *Thane,* lives yet Qq.

107   lose. Q5,ML] lose, Qq1-4; loose Y.

112   Treasons Qq] Treason Y.

127   doth Qq] do's Y.

129   Deliver'd, . . . ill: Q5] Deliver'd; . . . ill. Y; Deliver'd: . . . ill, Qq1-4; Deliver'd . . . ill; ML.

145   late Y] past Qq.

I.iv.2   not they Y] they not Qq.

  10   been Qq] be Y.

  44-45   Now . . . *Enverness* Qq] *om.* Y.

  52   Prince Y] The Prince Qq.

  53   else Qq] *om.* Y.

[I.iv.60–I.v.69 on pages missing in Y.]

I.v.19   enough Qq1-4] *om.* Q5.

  35   leisure, Qq1-2] Leisure to Qq3-5.

  47   *rights* Qq1-4] *right* Q5.

  60   hither Qq1,5] thither Qq2-4.

  73SD   *Exit Servant.* ML *after 74*] *om.* Y,Qq.

  90   worthy Qq] worth Y.

  105   all Y,Qq1,5] *om.* Qq2-4.

I.vi.SD   Banquo Qq] *om.* Y.

  42   affections Y] affection Qq.

I.vii.10   his Y,Qq1,5] this Qq2-4.

  25   wakes Qq] wak'd Y.

  43   whilst Y,Qq1-4] while Q5.

  52   convince Y] convince; Qq1-2; convince, Qq3-5.

  68   I am Y] I'm Qq.

  71SD   *Exeunt.*] *om.* Y,Qq.

[II.i–II.iii.77 on pages missing in Y.]

II.i.18   Sisters; Q5] Sisters Qq1-2; sisters, Qq3-4.

  21   words Q5] wood Qq1-4.

  27   Allegiances Qq1-3,5] Allegiance Q4.

  30SD   *Exit Servant.*] *om.* Qq,ML.

  34   not, ML] not Qq.

II.ii.1   which Qq1-4] which hath Q5.

  14   don't. Qq4-5,ML] don't Qq1-2; don't, Q3.

  41   hurt minds; Q5] hurt; minds Qq1-4; hurt minds, ML.

  61   the Qq1-4] these Q5.

  70   shews Qq1-2] shew Qq3-5.

II.iii.20   gives Ease to it self. Q5] gives; Qq1-3; gives us joy; Q4; gives [no pain.] ML.

28   divers Ears; Q5] divers. Q1; divers, Qq2-4,ML.

38   a Qq1-2,5] the Qq3-4.

54   where. *Macduff*, Q5] where, *Macduff;* Qq1-4.

79   enter'd. There Y] enter'd there. Qq.

80   colour Y] colours Qq.

90   corner, Q5] corner Y; corner; Qq1-4,ML.

106-107   persons. | Where we are, [are ML] Q5,ML] persons | Where we are: [; Y] Y,Qq1-4.

II.iv.1   Three score and one Y(B)] *om.* Y(A),Qq.

9   Is't Y,Qq1,5] It's Qq2-4.   daies Qq] nights Y.

23   Is't Y] *Len.* Is't Qq.

28   secretly Y(B)] *om.* Y(A),Qq.

47   I'm in Qq] I am Y.

II.v.23   on foot Y] a foot Qq.

31   glasses Qq] *om.* Y.

32   slow Y] slow; Qq.

47   a Y] an Qq.

54   wheel, ML] wheel Y; wheel. Qq.

57   a Y] an Qq.

60   Beetle Qq] Beetles Y.

68   a Y] an Qq.

70   willingly Qq] willing Y.

72   how Qq] *om.* Y.

75SD   *Enter Witches* Y] *Enter two Witches* Qq.

78   those Y,Q1] these Qq2-5.

85   The Y,Qq1-4] *om.* Q5.   spake Y,Qq1-3,5] speak Q4.

88   these Qq] those Y.

92   take Y,Qq1-3,5] take take Q4.

III.i.13   commands Y] command Qq.

21   Twixt this and Supper; and Q5] twix't this and supper Y(B); *om.* Y(A),Qq1-4,ML.

37-40   *Crossed out* Y.

37   privately Y(B)] frowningly Y(A),Qq.

38-39   I have ... supper; Y(B)] *om.* Y(A),Qq.

40   Meet Y(B)] Embrace Y(A),Qq.

51   upon Y,Qq1-4] on Q5.

58-59   soul, | For them Y] soul | For them: Qq1-4; Soul: For them, Q5.

70   our Y,Q5] your Qq1-4.

89   on Qq] of Y.

91   Nor Y,Qq1-2,5] No Qq3-4.

III.ii.11 Justice Y] *om.* Qq.

31   your Y] our Qq.

32   Slavery, Q5,ML] slavery Y; Slavery. Qq1-4.

34   of Y] in Qq.

52   incur. Y,Q5] incur Qq1-4.

III.iii.20 nightly Y,Q5] mightily Qq1-4.

24   sleeps Well: Q5] sleeps well; Y; sleeps; Well: Q1; sleeps; Well, Qq2-4; sleeps well. ML.

26   No Y,Q1] Nor Qq2-5.

29   guests Qq2-5,ML] guest Y,Q1.

32   Tongue. Y,Qq2-5] Tongue, Q1.

33   honors Y,Qq1-4] Honour Q5.

37   mind, Dear Wife! Y] mind? Dear Wife Qq.

47   deed. Y,Q5] deed, Qq1-4. Night, Qq3-5] Night Y,Qq1-2; night! ML.

III.iv.3 Traveller Y,Q1*corrected*,Qq2-5] Travellers Q1*uncorrected.*

18   wandring Y,Qq1-4] wondring Q5.

III.v.10SD *To the Murtherer.* Q5] *om.* Y,Qq1-4,ML.

21   on Y,Qq1-4] upon Q5.

23   grown Y] ground Qq.

24-26 breed, | . . . Sting. To morrow, | . . . further *as* ML *except* ML *double* To morrow *as* Qq] breed | To morrow . . . further Y; breed. | . . . Sting, to morrow, | To morrow . . . further Qq.

35   upon Y,Qq1-3,5] upon upon Q4. will it Y] *om.* Qq.

47   passion. Y] passion Q1; passion, Qq2-4; passion; Q5.

52   your Y,Qq1-4] our Q5.

54   these Qq] those Y.

55   Impostors Y, Qq1-3,5] Impostures Q4.

69   Too horrid Y(B)] too terrible Y(A),Qq. times Y,Qq1,5] time Qq2-4. have Y,Q5] has Qq1-4.

79   here Y,Qq1-4] *om.* Q5. to him, and all Y] to all, and him Qq.

81   Begone Y(B)] *om.* Y(A),Qq.

83   this Qq] this this Y.

103   do you mean Y(B)] *om.* Y(A),Qq.

104   not to him; he grows] not to him he grows Y(B); [*blank space*] grows Y(A); not, he'l grow Qq,ML.

105   Question Y] Questions Qq.   enrages Y,Q1] enrage Qq2-5.
at once Qq] . . . Y.

III.vi.7   your Son Y] young Son Qq.

   19   greatest Y, Qq1-4] greater Q5.

III.vii.27   Malevolence Y] Malevolences Qq.   takes Y,Qq1-4] Take
Q5.

   31   *Seymour*] *Seyward* Y,Qq,ML.

III.viii.SD   *meeting* Heccate Qq] *om.* Y.

   24   With . . . may. Qq] *om.* Y.

   31   then Y,Qq2-5] the Q1.

   34   Cull Y,Qq1-3,5] Cup Q4.

   36   Air's Qq] aire Y.

   37   *Assigned to second witch* Qq.

   38   fair Qq] *om.* Y.

   54   hast, Y,Qq2-5] hast Q1.

   56SD   *om.* Y,Qq,ML.

IV.i.SD   Y] *om.* Qq,ML.

   1   Y(B)] *om.* Y(A),Qq.

   3   3. Y(B)] *assigned to second witch* Y(A),Qq.

   5   Y(B)] *om.* Y(A),Qq.

   6   And *Hecat* Y(B)] *Harpier* Y(A),Qq.

   15   Snake, Qq4-5,ML] snake Y,Qq1-3.

   24   Gulf Y,Qq2-5] Gulf. Q1.

   30   lips; Qq2-4,ML] lips Y,Qq1,5.

   37   a Y,Qq1,5] the Qq2-4.

   48   2. Y] *om.* Qq.

   49   *Hec.* Y] *om.* Qq.

   50   A round, a round, a round Y] A round, a round Qq.

   79   born Y,Qq2-5] born'd Q1.

   94   Extends Qq] Extend Y.

   98   that Y,Qq1-2,5] this Qq3-4.

   101   *Hec.* Y] *om.* Qq.

   119   Without there. Y,Q5] *as stage direction* Qq1-4.

IV.ii.3   much Y,Qq1-2,5] must Qq3-4.

   9   *Len.* Qq] Seat: Y.

   15   Madam, Q5,ML] Madam Y; Madam; Qq1-4.

   21   Sea Y] Sea. Qq.

   22   move. Y] more, Qq.   leave Y] way Qq.

   33   ones Y] one Qq.

IV.iii   *The Scene* Y,Qq1-4] SCENE II. Q5.

6   save Y] serve Qq.

19   Tiranny, Qq] Tyrannys Y.

37   rule Qq] meet Y.

41   bloody, Y,Qq2-5] bloody Q1.   deceiptful, Y,Qq2-5] deceiptful Q1.

47   Disownes Y] Disclaims Qq.

49   thee Y] you Qq.   her Y,Qq1-3,5] or Q4.

51   Evils Qq] evell Y.

52   hath Y,Qq1-4] Have Q5.

58   these Qq] those Y.

62   my Y] mine Qq.

72   a Y,Qq1-3,5] *om.* Q4.

IV.iv.7   in my Y] my Qq.

33   Methinks Qq] *om.* Y.

38   Actions Y] Action Qq.

39   does Qq] did Y.

51   commit? Qq2-5,ML] committ: Y; commit, Q1.   your Y,Qq
1-3,5] you Q4.

54   your Qq1-3,5] you Q4.

63   Breast Y,Qq1-3,5] Breath Q4.

66SD   Qq] *om.* Y.

71   grieve Qq] *om.* Y.

73-74   Y(B)] *om.* Y(A),Qq.

76   the Vipers Y] a Vipers Qq.

76SD   Y] *om.* Qq.

IV.v.7   can't Qq] cannot Y.

10   rend Qq] rent Y.

14   Dying Y] *om.* Qq.

15-16   Y(B)] *om.* Y(A),Qq.

17   *Crossed out* Y.

20   one Qq] *om.* Y.

35   *Seymour* Qq] SeyWard Y.

38   would Y,Qq1-4] should Q5.

43   alone Y] *om.* Qq.

46   it Y] they Qq.

49   Children Y,Qq2-5] Children, Q1.

56   *Macd.* Qq] *om.* Y.   too? Qq] too. Y.

58   Both Y] Both, both Qq.

59   my Wife too Y] my Two Qq.

60 *Mal.* Y,Qq2-4] *Macd.* Qq1,5.

61 revenge Y] Revenues Qq1-2; Revenges Qq3-4.

67 feel Qq] dispute Y.   as Qq] Like Y.

71 thee they Y,Qq1-3,5] the they Q4.

72 thine Qq] mine Y.

73-74 let . . . anger Y] *om.* Qq.

77 braggart Y(B)] brag on't Y(A),Qq.

78 Fiend Y] Friend Qq.

79 But Y(B)] *om.* Y(A),Qq.

80 minute Y(B)] hour Y(A),Qq.

V.i.SD *a Lady* Y(A),Qq] *two Ladies* Y(B).

1-5 Y(B)] *om.* Y(A),Qq.

1 *Lady.* Y(A),Qq] 1 Lad: Y(B).

7 ore Y] on Qq.

15 after Y] of Qq.

27 Out, out Y] Out, out, out Qq.

34 What, Y] *om.* Qq.

36 The Y] A Qq.

37SD *Exeunt.* ML] *om.* Y; *Exit.* Qq.

V.ii.8 I'm Y] I am Qq.

15 he's Y] he is Qq.

18-32 which . . . downe. Y(B)] Qq *om. and have instead:* and
he finds his Crown | Sit Loose about him: His Power grows
less, | His Fear grows greater still. Y(A) *has (crossed out):*
and he finds his crown | Let loose about him like a gyants
Pole | Upon a [*blank space*] shoulder; his power grows
less | His fear grows greater still.

V.iii.2 remove Qq] returne Y.

8SD *a* Qq] *om.* Y.

13 Coward Y] Coward too Qq.

17 Forces Y] Force Qq. with armd men ——— Y(B)] *om.*
Y(A),Qq.

19 Fear: Q5] Fear Y,Q1; Fear; Qq2-4.

20 born Y,Qq2-5] morn Q1.

24 departing Qq] departed Y.

25 fear; Y] fear Qq1-4; fear: Q5.

26 seems Y,Qq1-4] seem Q5.

28 Vapour Y(B),Qq] *om.* Y(A).

29 *Macb.* Y] *om.* Qq.

31   firm Y] firmly Qq.

32   out Y,Qq1,5] out my Qq2-4.

36   of Y,Qq1-3,5] with Q4.

43SD   *Aside.* Qq] *om.* Y.

V.iv.4 are Y] were Qq.

9   Forces Y] Force Qq.

24   like boughs Y] *om.* Qq.

26   fail; Q5] fail Y,Qq1-4; fail. ML.

V.v.SD *Souldier* Y] *Souldiers* Qq.

8   *Sol.* Y] *Ser.* Qq.

12   *Sol.* Y] *Ser.* Qq.

14   and Y] *om.* Qq.   Die Y,Qq1-4] Diet Q5.

15   To morrow, and Y] To morrow, Qq.

19   Eternal night Y(B)] Severall homes Y(A); Eternal homes Qq.   short Y(B)] that Y(A),Qq.

31   methought Y] me thoughts Qq1-4; methoughts Q5.

38   Forrests Qq] forrest Y.

39   before Y] of here Qq.

42   Fiend Y,Qq1-4] Fiends Q5.

47   staying Y] Tarrying Qq.

V.vi.12 Thief Qq] *om.* Y(A); sholders Y(B).

12SD   Y] *om.* Qq.

V.vii.1 'Tis Y,Qq1-2,5] 'This Qq3-4.

2   he Y,Qq1-2,4-5] *om.* Q3.

4   Heavens Y] Heaven Qq.   thee I have found thee here; [here Y] Y] thee; have I found thee here; [here: Qq3-4] Qq1-4; thee. Have I found thee here? Q5.

5   mayst Qq] must Y.

16   Punishment? Qq1-4] punishment Y; Punishment, Q5.   it. Qq1-4] it? Y,Q5.

17   thy Y,Qq1-2,4-5] the Q3.

20   I'm Qq] I am Y.

25   haunt Y, Qq1-2,5] hunt Qq3-4.

30SD   Seymour Qq] Seyward Y.

31   *Seym.*] Seyw: Y; *Sey.* Qq.

34   Cloud Y] Blood Qq.

36   *Seym.*] Seyw: Y; *Sey.* Qq.

37-38   *Crossed out* Y.

39   some Y] some Body Qq.

V.viii.1 Fall Y] Fall, Qq.
    20   a Y] *om.* Qq.
    21   Devil Y] Devils Qq.
    23   the Y] that Qq.
    25   Promise Y] Promises Qq.
    28   a Monster Y] a Monster, a Monster Qq.
    31   Witchcraft Y] Enchantment Qq.
    37   my Qq] thy Y.
    41   it, Ambition. [*Dies.* Y,Qq2-5] it, [*Ambition Dies.* Q1.
V.ix.SD   Seymour Qq] Seyward Y.
    3   *Seym.* Qq] Seyw: Y.
    6   Those Y] The Qq.
    11   yet Y,Qq1-4] *om.* Q5.
    17   Day Y,Qq1-4] Days Q5.
    26   all Y] us Qq.   Kinsmen Y,Q5] Kinsman Qq1-4.
    31-34   *Crossed out* Y.
    33   to shew Y] to shew | To shew Qq.
    35-36   Y(B)] *om.* Y(A), Qq.
    42SD   *Exeunt.*] *om.* Y,Qq,ML.

The Tempest

The Tempest was listed in *The Term Catalogue* for the Michelmas Term (Nov.), 1674, as printed for Herringman; and it was published by him in that year. The collation of this edition is A-L4, M2, with sig. A1 the title page, A1v blank, A2-A3v the Preface, A4 the Prologue, and A4v the Dramatis Personæ; the text of the play ends on M1 and the Epilogue is on M1v; M2 is blank. The first page of text (sig. B1) has the head-title "THE Enchanted Island" (the *E* of "THE" has dropped out in the Harvard and Clark copies); there is no running-title except on sigs. A2v-A3v, where it is "The Preface." There are imperfect catchwords on E2v and L4: on the former see the variants at II.iv.85; the L4 catchword is *"A short"* (for "A Symphony"). I have compared five copies of this quarto: the Halliwell-Phillipps copy at the Folger Shakespeare Library and copies at the William A. Clark Library, Harvard University, the Henry E. Huntington Library, and the University of Texas. There are two settings of the Preface, one in the Clark copy and the other in the other four copies that I have seen.

The differences between the settings are not substantive; the Clark copy reads: 1. *was, probably, invented* 13. *Argument* 25. *discern, that* 33. *pierceing* 34. *Design* 37. *that, by this means, those* 39. *contri- | vance* 62. *then* 64. *Writings* 69. *deterr'd* 69. *it,* [.] Comparison of several copies was extremely useful in establishing the punctuation of a number of lines, since many marks that barely printed in one copy were clear in another.

The 1674 quarto was succeeded by three editions dated 1676 and one dated 1690; my remarks on these later editions are based on the Folger copies. The first, which follows the 1674 quarto page for page, is Woodward and McManaway 331 and Macdonald 73c; it is identifiable by the spelling variants in the imprint, by having the collation A-L4, M2, and by having 81 pages of text. I refer to it as 76A. The "second" 1676 text (76B, Woodward and McManaway 333) apparently exists in a unique copy at the Folger Shakespeare Library; its collation is A3, B-I4, K1, in 65 pages. Of the "third" quarto (Woodward and McManaway 332, Macdonald 73e), Macdonald says, "Although dated 1676 on the title this edition is on inferior paper to the last, and bears every sign of being a much later production. It was probably printed about 1692, when the 4o sets of Dryden's Works were being made up." Short, part-line speeches are often printed two to a line; and, chiefly by such contraction of the text, the printer has crammed the play onto 57 pages (collation: A-H4). However, it was not printed from the 1690 edition; and, since it is textually close to the other editions bearing the date 1676, I refer to it as 76C and list it in the variants before the 1690 quarto. 76B and 76C are derived from 76A rather than 74, but these two later texts have so many distinctive readings in common that they cannot be explained as derived directly but independently from 76A. Although it is more likely that 76B served as copy for 76C than the reverse, such an explanation would not account for all the variants. However, the relationships of the 1676 quartos are of little importance in establishing the text, since there is no evidence of independent authority in them, and they are not directly related to the 1690 edition. The 1690 quarto (90) shows slight but unmistakable signs of care and of consultation of an outside authority (see variants to II.iv.85 and 123), but on the whole it appears to have been printed from the edition of 1674. I have also seen the edition of 1695, in which a few errors of 1690 are corrected, but which seems to have no independent authority.

A major problem in editing this text is adjusting the lineation of the verse and altering the verse to prose and prose to verse. Although I have changed between one-quarter and one-third of the lines in the play, I have been more conservative in this respect than Saintsbury, who remarked in irritation with some lines in V.i that they "may be versified in several ways, but all bad" (III, 207n). I alter the lineation of about 230 lines of verse. I also change about 490 lines of prose to verse as follows: I.i.83-91; I.ii.1-8, 14-15, 19-59, 63-78, 80-96, 99-121, 125-130, 145-149, 163-167, 169-175, 193-202, 212-280, 323-331; II.i.132-147; II.ii.115-121, 125-127; II.iii.36-39, 46-57; II.iv.1-28, 31-43, 46-47, 125-129; III.i.12-19, 29-31; III.ii.1-8, 15-21, 28-31, 35-38, 51-62, 84-87, 131-134; III.iii.31-32; III.iv.70-72; III.vi.1-29, 112-114, 136-137, 153-158; III.vii.19-24, 29-31, 49-54, 77-80; IV.i.10-28, 39-55, 58-69, 94-95, 109-115, 173-175, 199-200; V.i.21-22; V.ii.203-205. I alter about 70 lines of verse to prose: I.i.39-40, 49-50; II.i.5-11, 93-101, 118, 123, 127-129, 148-161; III.iv.42-45; V.ii.3-10, 29-30, 49-50, 54-64, 74-75, 109. It should be noted in connection with the mislineation that the stage directions are not handled consistently in the 1674 edition: many entries are at the right margin rather than centered. Much of the mislineation was inherited from the Davenant-Dryden version of 1670.

The variants include substantive and many semi-substantive differences from 76A-C and 90. They also include variants from modern editions when I depart from the copy-text (and, occasionally, elsewhere): from the Scott-Saintsbury edition (SS) of Dryden's *Works* (1889), III, which combines the 1670 and 1674 versions; from the Maidment and Logan edition (ML) of Davenant's *Dramatic Works* (1874), V, which gives the 1674 version; and from Summers' edition (Sum) in Shadwell's *Complete Works* (1927), II, in which there is no attempt made to improve the lineation. I do not list readings from the parallel texts of Shakespeare's play and the operatic version edited by F. W. Kilbourne in the Bankside-Restoration Shakespeare (1908), which gives the 1676A text of adaptation. "Songs and Masques in *The Tempest*," edited by J. G. McManaway in *The Luttrell Society Reprints*, No. 14 (1953), contains a few verbal variants and variations in speech ascriptions discussed by McManaway, pp. 84-86.

Hazelton Spencer, p. 238, cites Max Rosbund, *Dryden als Shakespeare-Bearbeiter* (Halle a. S., 1882), pp. 9-10, as favoring F3 as the Shakespearean text used by Davenant and Dryden, but as thinking that "a safe conclusion . . . cannot be drawn." Variants among the folios are comparatively few in this play, and the alterations made by the adapters are so extensive that only a very small number of folio variant readings are in lines that the adapters retained.

TP His Highness the Duke of *York's* THEATRE. 74,76A-C] Their Majesties Theatre IN *DORSET-GARDEN.* 90.
[rule] | [ornament] | [rule] 74,90] [double rule] 76A-C.
LONDON, . . . MDCLXXIV. 74] *LONDON,* | Printed by *J. Macock,* for *Henry Herringman* at the Sign of the | *Blew Anchor* in the Lower Walk of the *New Exchange.* | M.DC.LXXVI. 76A; *as 76A except: Blew-Anchor . . . New-Exchange.* 76B; *as 76A except: Priented . . . Blew-Anchor . . . New-Exchange.* 76C; *LONDON,* | Printed by *J. M.* for *H. Herringman;* and sold by *R. Bentley,* | at the Post-House in *Russel-street, Covent-Garden.* | 1690. 90.

Pref 13 *argument,* 74,76A,76C,90] *argument.* 76B.
   46 *The* 74,76A,90] *om.* 76B-C.
   62 *my due* 74,90] *due* 76A-C.

Pro *Island.* 74,90] *Isle.* 76A-C.

I.i.SD20 *and crossing* 74,76A,90] *om.* 76B-C.
   3 'twill 74,76A,76C,90] will 76B.
  17 Cabins 74,90] Cabin 76A-C.
  30SD *Exeunt.*] *Exit.* 74,76A-C,90,ML.
  34 Seere-Capstorm 74,90,ML,Sum] Steere-Capstorm 76A-C,SS.
  35 Capstorm Bar 74,76A-B,90] Capstorm-Bars 76C.
  86 now 74, 76A-C] *om.* 90.
  91SD *Exeunt.*] *om.* 74,76A-C,90,ML,SS,Sum.

I.ii.57 *Millan* 74,76A-C] in *Millan* 90.
  86 mine 74,76A-C] my 90.
 101 ride 74,76A,76C,90] rid 76B.
 107-108 Cabin, . . . amazement; ML,SS] Cabin; . . . amazement, 74,76A-C,90, Sum.
 132 where 74,76A-B,90] *om.* 76C.
 165 thou 74,76A,76C,90] than 76B.
 250 teach 74,76A-C] taught'st 90.
 259 dost 76A,ML,SS] does 74,90,Sum; do'st 76B-C.
 261 may 74,76A,90] *om.* 76B-C.
 276 wast 74,76A-C] was 90.

289   make 74,90] make me 76A-C.

337SD   *Exeunt.* 90,ML,SS,Sum] *om.* 74,76A-C.

II.i.SD   *at* 74,76A,90] *om.* 76B-C.

12   costs 74,76A-C] cost 90.

17   Fill's 76A-C,90,Sum] Fills 74; Fill us ML,SS.

22   *Bess* 74,76A,90] *Bless* 76B-C.

26   not 74,90] no 76A-C.   must 74,76A-B,90] had 76C.

49   Master 74,76A,76C,90] a Master 76B.

61   the Isle 74,76A,76C,90] this Isle 76B.

103   Assembly 74,76A-B,90] Assemble 76C.

129   declare 74,76A,90] declares 76B-C.

131SD   *upon* 74,90] *on* 76A-C.

132   who 74,90] whom 76A-C.

135   hear 74,76A,90] here 76B-C.

146   sent 74,90] *om.* 76A-C.

149-150   Isle; . . . painted,] Isle, . . . painted; 74,76A-C,90,
        Sum; isle. . . . painted, ML,SS.

II.ii.21   Stands 74,76A-B,90] Stand 76C.

36   have 74,76A-C] having 90.

102   but 74,76A-B,90] *om.* 76C.

118   forbidden 74,90] forbid 76A-C.

II.iii   iii ML,SS] *om.* 74,76A-C,90,Sum.

10   not it 74,76A,76C,90] *om.* 76B.

II.iv   iv ML,SS] iii 74,76A-C,90,Sum.

40   and 74,76A,76C,90] *om.* 76B.

51SD   *Sung* 74,90] *Sing* 76A-C.

59   *bear.*] *bear;* 74,76A,90,ML,SS,Sum; *bear?* 76B-C.

85   3. *Dev.* 74*catchword sig. E2v*,90,Sum] I. *Dev.* 74,76A-C,ML,
        SS; *"Songs and Masques" reads:* 4. *Dev.   No,* 90,ML,Sum]
        No 74,76A-C; *No;* SS; *"Songs and Masques" reads:* No:
        uneasily 74,90,SS,Sum] *do easily* 76A-C.

113   unmann'd.] unmann'd? 74,76A-C,90,Sum; unmann'd; ML,
        SS.

123   *Ant. . . . Fruit? as addendum after Epilogue* 90 *and in
        text in 1695 quarto*] *om.* 74,76A-C,Sum; *om. and assign
        120-122 to Ant.* ML,SS.

129SD   *and are* 74,76A,76C,90] *and art* 76B.

130   O] *Alonz.* O 74,76A-C,90,ML,SS,Sum.

III.i.15 Duke my Father's wrack; [, SS] ML,SS] Duke; my Father's wrack'd; 74,76A-C,90,Sum.

    23 *fade] fade.* 74,76A,90,Sum; *fade,* 76B-C,ML,SS.

III.ii.16 that 74,76A,90] than 76B-C.

    65 eat nor 74,76A-B,90] *om.* 76C.

    68 him 74,76A,90] him. 76B-C.

    74 as 74,76A,76C,90] at 76B.

    114 straggled 74,90] strangl'd 76A-C.

    148 beheld 74,90] behold 76A-C.

III.iii.11SD *sings.* 74,76A-C] *sing.* 90.

    24SD *Fruit* 74,90] *Fruits* 76A-C.

III.iv *New scene SS only.*

    6 fair 74,76A,90] far 76B-C.

    35-36 *Syc.* This is the drink of Frogs. | *Trinc.* Nay, if the Frogs of this Island 74,76A-B,90] *Syc.* This is the drink of Frogs of this Island 76C.

III.v v] iv ML; *not a new scene* 74,76A-C,90,SS,Sum.

    1 far 74,76A,76C,90] fare 76B.

    11 reply. 76A-C,90,ML,SS,Sum] reply 74.   I would 74,90] would I 76A-C.

III.vi vi] iv 74,76A-C,90,Sum; v ML,SS.

    32 young 76A-C,ML,SS] young, 74,90,Sum.

    69 what, 74,90] what 76A-C.

    70 think'st 74,76A,76C,90] think'd 76B.

    93 *Prosp.* ML,SS,Sum] *om.* 74,76A-C,90.

    134 you'l 74,90] you'd 76A-C.

III.vii vii] v Sum; vi ML,SS.

IV IV 74,76B-C,90] VI 76A.

IV.i.36 bear 74,76A,76C,90] Dear 76B.

    113 has 74,76A-C] had 90.

    116 SS *begins new scene here.*

    118 me all, all the 74,76A-C] me all the 90.

    172 needs must 74,90] must needs 76A-C.

    183 woman 74,76C,90] women 76A-B.

    186 know 74,90] knew 76A-C.

IV.ii.61 *New speech assigned to Trinc. begins with Caliban* 74,76A-C, 90.   *Exit* Caliban ML] *om.* 74,76A-C,90.

    65 friend 74,76A,76C,90] fried 76B.

    79 Scantum 74,90] Scanthum 76A-C.

IV.iii.16   Methink 74] Methinks 76A-C,90.

     50   meant 74,76A-B,90] mean 76C.

     57   *Hecla* ML,SS] *Heila* 74,76A-C,90,Sum(*in note says "a misprint for Hecla"*).

    124   you 76A-C,ML,SS] you, 74,90,Sum.

    199   satisfi'd. ML,SS] satisfi'd? 74,76A-C,90,Sum.

    232   that 74,90] the 76A-C.

    242   Accursed 74,76A,76C,90] A cursed 76B.

V.i.14   the Son 76A-C,90,ML,SS,Sum] thee Son 74.

V.ii.16   dream, 74,90] dream 76A-C. of 74,76A,90] to 76B-C.

    19   run 74,76A-C] run. 90.

   43SD   Ferdinand's] Hippolito's 74,76A-C,90,ML,SS,Sum.

    44   Who's] *Hip.* Who's 74,76A-C,90,ML,SS,Sum.

    46   Angel-Woman, ML] Angel, Woman, 74,76A-C,90,Sum; angel woman, SS; *see III.vii.79.*

   133   blessings 74,76A-B,90] blessing 76C.

   136   spoken 74,90] spoke 76A-C.

   150   is it 74,90] is 76A-C.

   167   *Daughters* 90,ML,SS,Sum] *Daughter* 74,76A-C.

   185   yet are 74,90] are yet 76A-C.

  238SD   ML,SS *add:* Scene II [*their second Scene II*].

   243   Element 74,90] Elements 76A-C.

   255   *Prisoners* 74,76A,90] *Prisones* 76B-C.

   270   *sing* 74,76A,76C,90] *sign* 76B.

  271SD   *Dance.* 74,90] *om.* 76A-C.

   272   *no* 74,76A-B,90] *on* 76C.

   275   *Passengers* 74,76A,90] *Passages* 76B-C.

   276   *Nept.* 74,76A-C] *om.* 90.

   291   *Down, down* 74,76A,76C,90] *Down* 76B.

   301   *Sound*] *om.* 74,76A-C,90,ML,SS,Sum.

  302SD   *wreathed* 74,76A-B,90] *wreathen* 76C. *Symphony* 74,76A, 76C,90] Symtom 76B.

   315   *backs* 74,76A-B,90] *back* 76C.

  323SD   SS *adds:* Scene III.

   328   wondrous 74,76A-C] wonderful 90.

   339   in 74,76A-C] the 90.

   346   mind 74,76A-B,90] mid 76C.

Epi 3   *abroad* 74,90,ML,SS,Sum] *aboard* 76A-C.

King Lear

"The History of King *Lear*" was entered in *The Term Catalogue* for the Easter (May) Term, 1681, and the quarto of that year (Q1) serves as the copy-text. I have examined five copies of this edition, those at Harvard University, the University of Illinois (two copies), the University of Michigan, and Yale University. In addition to the substantive differences among copies recorded in the variants below at I.i.92 and II.ii.314, the page number (11) does not appear on sig. C2 in the Harvard and Yale copies. The collation is A-I4, K2. Sig. A1 is the title page; A1v is blank; A2-A3v are the "Epistle Dedicatory.," as the running-title calls the dedication; A4 is the Prologue; and A4v is the Persons. Although the title page describes the play as a "History," the head-title on sig. B1 reads "KING LEAR. | A | TRAGEDY." Catchwords are missing on sigs. A4v and K2 (K2v contains the Epilogue), and the running-title throughout the text of the play is "King *Lear.*"

The variants include substantive and many semi-substantive readings from the quarto editions of 1689 (Q2), 1699 (Q3), [c. 1702] (Q4), and 1712 (Q5), as well as readings when I deviate from the copy-text from Summers' *Adaptations* (S), and from G. B. Harrison's edition (H) of part of the play in *King Lear: Text, Sources, Criticism* (New York, 1962). Each quarto seems to have used its immediate predecessor as copy, and there is no evidence of authoritative revision; Qq2-5 even repeat the absurd "Lond." for *"Loud"* in III.i.45SD and "beheaded" for "bareheaded" in III.iii.39. Woodward and McManaway, Wing in his *Short-Title Catalogue,* and Ford list no other editions between 1681 and the adapter's death in 1715; items with different dates listed elsewhere are apparently the quarto of c. 1702, recorded by Jaggard as [1690] and [1710], by the *Catalogue of the Barton Collection* (Boston, 1888) as [1692], and by Nicoll (*History,* I, 434) as 1703. On the title page of this edition is an advertisement for four works that have been "newly published": included among these is the two-volume octavo edition of Mrs. Behn's plays advertised in *The Term Catalogues* for the Trinity (June) Term, 1702, as published for Benjamin Tooke, and for the Easter (May) Term, 1703, as published for Wellington.

Of Tate's Shakespearean source, Hazelton Spencer says, p. 250, "Tate's source is certainly the text of the Quartos, not of the Folios, and seems to be Q2, but there are many exceptions, including Folio corrections, which point to some attempt at collation or to the existence of another text in the theatrical library. This may be a good point for Professor Nicoll." The reference is to the suggestion, first made in Nicoll's *Dryden as an Adapter of Shakespeare* (London, 1922), that some Restoration adaptations of Shakespeare were based on pre-Restoration manuscripts. (On this matter see C. Spencer, *Macbeth*, pp. 57-58.) H. Spencer also cites, p. 273, the opinion of R. Erzgräber in *Nahum Tate's und George Colman's Bühnenbearbeitungen des Shakespeare'schen King Lear* (Weimar, 1897), p. 14, that Tate used Q2 and F3. Tate uses a number of the approximately one hundred lines in the folios and not in the quartos (e.g., Tate's I.ii.99; II.ii.152a, 185-186, 216b-221a), but few of the lines not in the folios (however, see Tate's II.ii.102-103a). Many of the lines not in the folios are in longer passages or scenes that Tate omitted.

TP   Dukes Theatre Q1] Queen's Theatre Q2; Queens Theatre Qq3-5. *LONDON, . . .* 1681. Q1] *LONDON.* | Printed for *R. Bentley* and *M. Magnes* in | *Russel-street* near *Covent-Garden,* 1689. Q2. *LONDON,* | Printed by *H. Hills,* for *Rich. Wellington,* at the *Lute* in St. *Paul's Church-* | *Yard,* and *E. Rumbold,* at the *Post House, Covent Garden,* and sold by | *Bern. Lintott,* at the *Crass Keyes* in St. *Martin's Lane.* 1699. | [rule] | [advertisement] Q3. *LONDON,* | Printed for *Rich. Wellington,* at the *Dolphin* and *Crown* in St. *Paul's* | *Church-Yard,* and *E. Rumbold* at the *Post House, Covent Garden;* and *Tho. Osborne* at *Grays-Inn,* near the *Walks.* [n.d.] | [rule] | [advertisement] Q4. *LONDON:* Printed for *Richard Wellington,* at the *Dolphin* and *Crown* in | St. *Paul's Church-Yard.* 1712. | [advertisement] Q5.

Ded 3   *Perswasion* Qq1-2] *Perswasions* Qq3-5.

    9   *have* Qq1-4] *had* Q5.

   20   *whole, A* Q2] *whole A* Q1,H; *whole, as* Qq3-5,S.

   35   *an* Qq1-2,4-5] *and* Q3.

   43   *confess* Q1] *confess.* Qq2-3; *confess,* Qq4-5.

   44   *and partly* Qq1-2,4-5] *and and partly* Q3.

Pro 15   *his* Q1] *this* Qq2-5.

Pers   *The parts supplied in brackets are not in* Qq1-5; *all are in* S.

I.i.33   here Qq1-2] hear Qq3-5.

   49   Heaven Qq1-4] Heavens Q5.

   52   renders Qq1,5] render Qq2-4.

58 treasure Qq1-4] treasures Q5.

67 the Qq1-2] this Qq3-5.

71 *Albany,* Qq2-5,S] *Albany* Q1,H.

75 the Qq1-3] our Qq4-5.

78 valu'd, Qq1-2] valu'd Qq3-5.

92SD *Aside.* Q1 (Harvard, Illinois 1,2, Yale),Qq2-5,S] *om.* Q1 (Michigan),H.

104 I ought Qq1-4] ought I Q5.

114 never Qq1,4-5] never never Qq2-3.

118 there Qq1-3] their Qq4-5.

139 with Qq1-2] in Qq3-5.

154 thy Qq1-2] my Qq3-5.

200 that that Qq1-3] that which Qq4-5.

202 Sisters Qq1-4] Sister Q5.

233 Cold Qq1-2] could Qq3-5.

278 wake Q1] wak'd Qq2-5.

I.ii.4 here Q1] here. Qq2-5.

18SD *and Servant run]* runs Qq1-5,S,H.

19 Call Qq1-3] Call me Qq4-5. Clatpole Qq1-3] Clodpole Qq 4-5.

21SD *Enter Servant.]* om. Qq1-5,S,H.

30-33 *These lines come between Gonerill's entrance and 28b in* Qq3-5.

32 frontlet Qq1-2,4-5] frontless Q3.

36-37 bred Qq1-3] bred; Qq4-5. by their unbounded Riots, | I had fair hope Qq1-2] *om.* Qq3-5.

38 T'have had a quick Qq1-3] I thought t'have had a Qq4-5.

49 savour Qq1-2,4-5] favour Q3.

57 That H] The Q1; That which Qq2-5,S.

61 together; Qq4-5,S] together, Qq1-3,H.

65 approv'd Qq1-3] approv'd, Qq4-5.

97 Train Q1] Train. Qq2-3; Train, Qq4-5.

98 play Qq1-3,5] ploy Q4.

II.i.5 you are Qq1-2] your Q3; you're Qq4-5.

7 Have you Qq4-5,S] Have Qq1-3.

29 Stake Qq1-2] Stage Qq3-5.

II.ii.27 Ho! Qq1-2] *om.* Qq3-5.

28-30 *Kent.* . . . help. Qq1-2] *om.* Qq3-5.

34 you Qq1-2,4-5] your Q3.

65 wear Qq1-2,5] were Qq3-4.

116   of Qq1-2] on Qq3-5.

120   Escapt Q1] Escape Qq2-5.

124   my Griefs Qq1-3] the Griefs Qq4-5.

132   too, submit Q1] to submit Qq2-5.

139   Villages Qq1-2] Fillages Qq3-5.

141   *Tom* Q1] *Tom,* Qq2-5.

155   modest Qq1-2,4-5] moded Q3.

170   Coward Qq1-2] Cowards Qq3-5.

208   Tomb. Qq4-5] Tomb? Qq1-3,S.

221   clears Qq1-2] clear Qq3-5.

222   you are Qq1-2] your Q3; you're Qq4-5.

225   you yourself Q1] yourself Qq2-3; you self Q4; your self Q5.

234   half of Qq1-2] half Qq3-5.

248   put Qq1-2] but Qq3-5.

261   your sweet sway Qq1-2] you sweet saw Q3; you sweet Sir Qq4-5.

273   our Q5,S] your Qq1-4.

276   shall Qq1-2] all Qq3-5.

293   your Qq1-2,4-5] you Q3.

294   what! fifty Followers; Qq2-3] what fifty Followers Q1; what! fifty followers? Qq4-5,S.

314   hear Q1] here Qq2-5.   Plagues! Q1(Harvard, Illinois 2, Yale),Qq2-5,S] Plague Q1(Illinois 1, Michigan).

III.i.17   I will Q1] will I Qq2-5.

32   this Qq1-2] the Qq3-5.

34   hast Qq1,5] haste Qq2-4.

35   Hide, thou Qq1-2,H] Hide, that Qq3-5,S.

36   holy, holy Q1] holy Qq2-5.

40   begins Qq1-4] begin Q5.

42   me Qq1-2] *om.* Qq3-5.

45SD   *Loud* S,H] Lond. Qq1-5.

46SD   *Exeunt.*] *Exit.* Qq1-5,H.

III.ii.8   tread Q1] treat Qq2-5.

21SD   *Reads.* Qq2-5,S] *om.* Q1,H.

26SD   *Enter* Gloster. S] *om.* Qq1-5,H.

27-36   *Prose in all texts.*

48   his; Qq2-5,S] his Q1,H.

58   fall Qq1-3] *om.* Qq4-5.

59SD   *with* Arante S] *om.* Qq1-5,H.

60   all Q1] *om.* Qq2-5.

79   can ... Worse? Q1] *om.* Qq2-5.

111SD   *with* Arante. S] *om.* Qq1-5,H.

116   that Q1] *om.* Qq2-5.   a Q1] *om.* Qq2-5.

III.iii.7   Skin; so Qq2-5,S] Skin so, Q1; skin. So H.

13   punish home. Q1] punish; home. Qq2-5.

14   weep Q1] *om.* Qq2-5.

32-34SD   *Edgar in the Hovell. centered as SD (32 without speech ascription), 34SD om.* Qq1-5; S *adds 34SD, but otherwise as early texts;* H *adds speech ascription in 32, but otherwise as early texts.*

36   thy Qq1-3] the Qq4-5.

38-39   *Prose in all texts.*

39   bareheaded S] beheaded Qq1-5,H.

39SD   *Aside.* Qq1-3] *om.* Qq4-5.

48   cold. Qq2-5,S,H] cold Q1.

60   this Qq1-2] his Qq3-5.

75   the Boy, Q1] the Boy! the Boy! Qq2-3,5; the Boy the Boy! Q4.

81   self, unaccommodated Qq2-4] self, unaccommated Q1; self unaccomodated Q5.

90   Pool, Qq2-5,S] Pool Q1,H.

98   Yeoman Qq1,3-5] Yeomen Q2.

105SD   Qq2-5 *add: Aside.*

113   Tight Q1] Hight Qq2-5.

117   Se, se, se Q1] See, see, see Qq2-5.

135-140   *Prose in all texts.*

139   seek Qq1-3] to seek Qq4-5.

145   talk Q1] take Qq2-5.

151-152   *Prose in all texts.*

151   seek Qq1-3,5] seeks Q4.

156-158   *Prose in all texts.*

159   see Qq1-2] for Qq3-5.

III.iv.3   in Qq1-2] *om.* Qq3-5.

7   dog'd Qq1,3-5] dodg'd Q2.

11   this dear Devil Q1] this, dear Devil, Qq2-5.

23   dead Q1] dread Qq2-5.

32SD   Qq2-5 *add: Aside.*

44   thy Qq1,5] my Qq2-4.

45   hast Qq1-3] haste Qq4-5.

56   Blessings Qq1-4] Blessing Q5.

92   new Qq1-3] knew Qq4-5.

104   Triumph Qq1-4] Triumphs Q5.

III.v.4   Ost Q1,H] Host Qq2-5,S.

6   now Qq2-5,S] now, now Q1; we [have] now H.

36   I must Qq1-2] must Qq3-5.

42   shalt thou Q1] thou shalt Qq2-5.

67   *Regan,* I [*indented*] Q1] *Regan.* I [*indented as if speech by Regan*] Qq2-5.

67SD   *Exeunt.* Q1] *om.* Qq2-5.

IV.i.1   were Qq1-3,5] where Q4.

3   all Q1] *om.* Qq2-5.

8   thee Qq1-2] the Qq3-5.

17   ready Q1] already Qq2-5.

26   *so* Qq1-3] *om.* Qq4-5.

31   what thy Qq1-3] that thy Qq4-5.

48   Raise Qq1,3-5] rise Q2.

48SD   *Exeunt.*] *Exit.* Qq1-5,S.

IV.ii.11   afoot Q1] on foot Qq2-5.

45   a cold Qq1-4] cold Q5.

53   the Qq1-4] *om.* Q5.

58   There is Q1] There's Qq2-5.

68   Sea, Qq1-3] Sea Qq4-5.

73   To ... him, Qq1-3] *om.* Qq4-5.

91   ever Qq1-3] every Qq4-5.

IV.iii.7   *Albany?* Qq3-5,S] *Albany.* Qq1-2.

IV.iv.SD   *Field* Qq1-3] *The Field* Qq4-5.   *Enter*] *om.* Qq1-5,S.

10   am I Qq1-4] I am Q5.

14   Choughs Qq1-4] Coughs Q5.

38   Live Q1] lived Qq2-5.

40   how Qq1,3-5] how my Q2.

46   Hadst Qq1-4] Hast Q5.   Gosmore, Q1] Gosmore Qq2-5.

48-49   bleedst not, Speak'st, art sound; Q1] bleedst? Not speak! Art sound? Qq2-5.

59   Crown] Crow Qq1-2; Brow Qq3-5,S.

68   it Qq1-3] *om.* Qq4-5.

91   is't Q1] it's Qq2-5.

111   There's Qq1-3,5] There Q4.

125   What! Qq2-5,S] What Q1.

137   hold Q1] hold up Qq2-5.

148   mixt! Q2] mixt Q1; mixt? Qq3-5,S.

152   came Q1] come Qq2-5.

158   him, Sir, Q1] him, Sir: Qq2-3; him Sir: Qq4-5.

169   —— no Qq1-3] —— on Qq4-5.

191   I'ce Q1] I'st Qq2-5.

192   Out, Qq1,3-5] Our Q2.

193   vor your Q1] *om.* Qq2-5.

194SD *They fight.*] *om.* Qq1-5,S.

210   Sands Qq2-5,S] Sands. Q1.

IV.v.SD *Physician,* S] *om.* Qq1-5,H.

17   still Q1] *om.* Qq2-5.

37   Ignorant Qq1,3-5] ignorant; Q2.

70   Tempest Q1] Tempests Qq2-5.

73SD *Exeunt.*] *om.* Qq1-5,S.

V.ii.2 of the Qq1-3,5] of the the Q4.

V.iii.14 his Q1] the Qq2-5.

19   lay Q1] lie Qq2-5.

V.iv.77 in, Qq1-4] in, and Q5.

V.v.19 born a Q1] a born Qq2-5.

24   peruse Qq1-4] pursue Q5.

50   possibly Qq1-3] possible Qq4-5.

55   Heart. Qq2-5,S] Heart Q1.

63   Sir Qq1-5] Madam S.

68   too? Qq2-5,S] too. Q1.

109 deserv'd Qq1-4] deserve Q5.

V.vi.17 down, down Qq1-3] down Qq4-5.

22   sake's Q1] sake Qq2-5.

97   there Qq1-2] they Qq3-5.

109 be Q1] be a Qq2-5.

140 Heads Qq2-5,S] Head Q1,H.

148 cool Qq1-2] clo Q3; close Qq4-5.

Richard III

Between the first appearance of Cibber's *Richard III* and the death of the adapter in December, 1757, more than fifteen editions of the adaptation were published. The following list combines the dates of publication given by the *CBEL;* by the B.M. and Barton *Catalogues;* by *An Index to the Shakespeare Memorial Library* (Birmingham, 1903); by Nicoll, *History;* by Ford; by Jaggard; and by Mr. R. M.

Frye in a listing made for me of the Folger Shakespeare Library's holdings: [1700], 1718, 1719 (the British Museum copy of 1718 is in a collection dated 1719; only *CBEL* and Nicoll, *History,* II, 307, list 1719, and neither lists 1718, though Nicoll's supplementary list, *History,* II, 433, adds the 1718 edition), 1721 (in Cibber's *Plays*), 1731, 1734, 1736 (three listings in Ford), 1737, 1745, 1750, 1751, 1753, 1754, 1756, and 1757. From Ford's observations on "unrecorded plays," pp. 56-57, it seems likely that there are unrecorded editions of the adaptation, especially from around 1734-36; and Ford also lists, p. 98, as "advertised but not recorded," a quarto published by Wellington in "1704 or A[fter?]." The play was revived on April 4, 1704, as "not Acted these Three Years" (*London Stage,* Part II, Vol. I, p. 63). Jaggard, p. 370, lists the "Life and death of King Richard the third. . . . London: . . . 1709 8o," at the "Cambridge Public Library." However, the item cannot be found in the University Library, Cambridge, and is apparently not in the City Library either. Of the editions listed I have consulted those of [1700], 1718, 1721 (*Plays*), 1736 (one), 1737, 1745, 1751, 1754, and 1757.

The copy-text is the edition of [1700]. My collation of five copies of this quarto — those at the William A. Clark Library, the Folger Shakespeare Library, the Henry E. Huntington Library, the University of Illinois, and the University of Texas — reveals one press-variant: in V.vii.16 (sig. H3) "Dckson" of the Huntington, Illinois, and Texas copies has been corrected to "Dickon" in the other two copies. Among letters that did not ink or dropped out is the *I* of I.iii.13 in the Folger copy, in which the line seems to have shifted slightly to the right. The collation of this edition is A-H4. The title page is sig. A1; A1v is blank; A2-3 contain the "Epistle Dedicatory.," as the running-title calls the dedication; A3v is blank; A4 contains the Preface, and A4v the Persons; the text begins on B1. The quarto has neither head-title nor, after the front matter, running-title. There are four irregular catchwords: A4 PER- (The Persons.) E2 *And* (*Standing:* the Shakespearean original of Cibber's line — III.ii.110 — begins with *And*) E4v *D. York* (*Dutch. Y.* — anticipating at IV.i.30 the confusion in speech ascriptions on sigs. F1v and F2 in IV.i.71 and 114) G4 *Nor. My* (*D. Nor.* My).

The Preface of this edition is dated Feb., 1700; and *The Term Catalogue* for the Hilary (Feb.) Term, 1700, lists *Richard III* "Price 1s. Printed for R. Wellington at the Dolphin and Crown in St. *Paul's* Churchyard." It was advertised on March 16 (Nicoll, *History,* II,

307), and on the title page of the Illinois copy are written in ink *10d* and *18. March.* $\frac{1699}{1700}$. The imprint of the [1700] edition states that the quarto was printed for Lintott, but in the advertisement at the bottom of the title page is listed "The History of the Reign of *Lewis* XIII. King of *France* and *Navarre* . . . By Mr. *Michal le Vassor*," which is also listed in *The Term Catalogue* for the Hilary Term, 1700, as published for Wellington. (After the Epilogue is an advertisement for Howel's *Elements of History* "Printed for *Richard Wellington*"; this work is listed in the Trinity [June], 1700, *Term Catalogue* as printed for J. King.) Although the [1700] quarto was not very carefully printed, Cibber himself seems to have taken a considerable interest in the publication. Not only did he supply an Epistle Dedicatory and a Preface, but he also marked the lines he felt he had borrowed from Shakespeare (this feature was not repeated in later texts of the play). The stage directions are unusually detailed (e.g., the SDs from II.i.85-SD to 252SD) and describe action, costumes (V.iii.14SD), and properties (IV.i.83SD) more fully than those of other texts: they seem designed for a reader. The catchword on sig. E2 suggests that the printer's copy contained revisions actually made on it. Another distinctive quality of this quarto is the ceremony of both speech ascriptions and stage directions (e.g., *"K. Hen."* and *"Ld. Stan."* instead of *"Hen."* and *"Stan."*).

What is apparently the second extant edition — 1718 — contains the principal alterations in the play: Cibber substituted a new soliloquy for the scene in which the Princes are murdered onstage; he omitted four lines in IV.ii and two lines in IV.iii; he reworded V.vii.19 for the better and made not very extensive verbal alterations elsewhere; and he changed the staging of Ann's entrance with Henry's body, of the appearance of the ghosts in Richard's tent, and of the action at V.viii.SD and, perhaps, elsewhere. The stage directions are different: they are pruned of ceremony and character and are considerably reduced in number (eleven asides are omitted, along with *"Trumpet sounds," "Shouts here," "Kissing 'em,"* etc.). Two curious Latin stage directions are introduced at II.ii.105SD and III.ii.269SD. The edition of 1721 in Cibber's *Plays* agrees with 1718 against [1700] in all the matters mentioned above, and it seems to have been corrected with some care, presumably by Cibber himself (see, for example, II.i.256, III.i.155, and IV.ii.82, although the absurdity at III.i.127 was allowed to stand). Alterations were also made in others of the dramatic works included in the *Plays* of 1721. Dougald MacMillan in "The Text of *Love's Last Shift,*" *MLN*, XLVI (1931), 518-519, lists some changes made in one play in answer "to the new taste of audiences for refinement of language." Nettleton and Case, eds., *British Dramatists from Dryden to Sheridan* (Boston, 1939), p. 933, base their text of *The Careless Husband* on that in the 1721 *Plays* and remark that "the preparation of the collected edition [of 1721] . . . seems to have been taken quite seriously by Cibber: at all events, he made extensive alterations in *The Careless Husband.*" The best explanation of the texts of *Richard III* seems to be that the [1700] quarto was printed from a manuscript especially prepared for publication by Cibber, that the 1718 quarto was printed from another manuscript, possibly the current playhouse copy, and that the 1721 text was printed from a copy of the 1718 edition corrected by Cibber. However, it appears improbable that Cibber concerned himself with the accidentals of the 1718 or 1721 *Richard III,* and therefore the [1700] quarto is a better choice for the copy-text. In the speeches I incorporate the substantive variants of 1718-21, and when the two later texts disagree, I normally adopt the 1721 reading. The stage directions are those of [1700] except when different action or staging is suggested by the 1718-21 versions.

The list of variants gives the results of my collation of the three editions I have listed plus texts of 1736 (Ford 154) and 1757. These later editions show nothing new of significance: the dependence suggested by their offering the same list of actors' names as had been given in 1718 is confirmed by the texts of the play. The text of 1736 seems closer to that of 1718 (cf. I.iii.40-41) than to that of the 1721 *Plays;* and the 1757 text seems closer to that of the 1721 *Plays.* (Hogan, II, 525, cites a 1751 *Richard III* as "identical" with the [1700] text, but with "occasional minor restorations of the original, notably *IV.iv. 398-411*"; however, there are no additions in the 1751 edition [Copy 1] at the Folger Shakespeare Library, and IV.iv.398-411 are in every text of Cibber's *Richard III* that I have seen.)

In the first edition Cibber italicized those lines that he had borrowed from Shakespeare and placed single quotes before those that were "generally [Shakespeare's] thoughts." The accompanying table gives the results according to my count. The third column lists the number of lines italicized by Cibber minus those from Shakespearean plays other than *Richard III* and those for which I cannot find a Shakespearean source. The fourth column lists the number marked with quotes minus the same two groups. The fifth column lists lines borrowed from other Shakespearean plays (both italics and quotes). The sixth column lists the numbered lines that, in my opinion, Cibber should have marked (i.e., that he implied were his own but that in accordance with his general habits of attribution should probably be considered Shakespeare's). The seventh column lists the lines Cibber marked as Shakespeare's (italics and quotes), but for which I cannot find a Shakespearean source. The eighth column lists the number of lines remaining for Cibber (to which the lines in the seventh column might be added). Split lines are assigned to the column in which the largest part of the line belongs. H. H. Furness, in his *New Variorum* edition of *Richard III* (Philadelphia, 1908, p. 604), has a table of lines borrowed from Shakespearean plays other than *Richard III;* his figures differ somewhat from mine. Like other commentators before 1923, Furness apparently did not know the first edition, in which the non-Cibberian lines are marked.

	LINES	FROM *Richard III*		OTHER PLAYS		SH. UNATTRIB.	NOT SH.	CIBBER'S
		ITALICS	QUOTES					
I.i	240	0	0	III H VI	11	0	0	189
				R II	11			
				II H IV	29			
ii	28	18	0	III H VI	5	1	0	4
iii	89	4	0	III H VI	63	4	0	18
II.i	279	137	18	I H VI	5	0	1	107
				III H VI	11			
ii	140	9	12		0	2	3	114
III.i	178	79	17		0	1	5	76
ii	282	131	19	II H IV	4	6	2	120
IV.i	123	5	3		0	2	1	112
ii	104 (1700)	40	19		0	2	1	42
iii	96 (1700)	11	10		0	3	0	72
iv	208	101	39	II H IV	7	11	1	49
V.i	29	9	2	II H VI	3	4	2	9
ii	45	10	1	H V	5	0	1	28
iii	44	15	10		0	1	5	13
iv	34	14	0		0	2	1	17
v	87	9	3	H V	14	5	3	53
vi	26	5	8	H V	5	1	0	7
vii	40	22 (1700)	5		0	5	2	6
viii	22	10	1	II H VI	5	1	3	2
ix	62	10	10	II H VI	2	2	5	28
				II H IV	5			
	2156	639	177		185	53	36	1066

Cibber did not distinguish accurately between quotes and italics: perhaps 20 per cent of the italicized or quoted lines should have been marked in the other way. I have left all lines as they were marked in the copy-text, except that in the very few lines that were both italicized and marked with quotes, I have removed whichever seemed less appropriate.

Cibber's Shakespearean source has not been certainly determined. IV.iv.127-130 of the adaptation appear in the Shakespeare folios only, but V.v.73 is found in the quartos alone. Richard Dohse, *Colley Cibbers Bühnenbearbeitung von Shakespeares Richard III,* in *Bonner Beiträge,* II (Bonn, 1899), 12-13, concludes that Cibber used F3 with some assistance from Q1.

Richard III, [1700]	A
Richard III, 1718	B
Plays, 1721	C
Richard III, 1736	D
Richard III, 1757	E

TP The Tragical | HISTORY | OF | King RICHARD the Third. | CONTAINING | [*in double column*] The Distresses and Death of | King HENRY the Sixth. | The Artful Acquisition | of the Crown by King | RICHARD. | The Cruel Murder of | young King EDWARD | the Fifth, and his Bro- | ther in the *Tower.* | The Landing of the Earl | of RICHMOND, and the | Death of King RICH- | ARD in the memorable | Battle of *Bosworth-Field:* | Being the last that was | fought between the | Houses of *York* and | *Lancaster.* | *With many other Historical Passages.* | [rule] | As it is now Acted at the THEATRE- | ROYAL in *Drury-Lane.* | [rule] | Reviv'd, with Alterations, by Mr. CIBBER. | [rule] | —— *Domestica Facta.* | [rule] | *LONDON:* | Printed for *W. Mears,* at the *Lamb,* and *J. Browne,* | at the *Black-Swan* without *Temple-Bar,* and *W. Chet-* | *wood,* at *Cato's Head* in *Russell-Court,* near the *Theatre-Royal,* MDCCXVIII. B.

The TRAGICAL | HISTORY | OF | King RICHARD III. | As it is now Acted | At the THEATRE ROYAL | in *DRURY-LANE.* | [rule] | Alter'd from *SHAKESPEAR,* by Mr. *CIBBER.* | [rule] | —— *Domestica Facta.* | [rule] | [ornament] | *LONDON:* | Printed in the Year M.DCC.XXI. *in Vol. II of* PLAYS WRIT-TEN BY Mr. *Cibber.* In TWO VOLUMES. . . . LONDON; Printed for JACOB TONSON . . . BERNARD LINTOT . . .

WILLIAM MEARS . . . WILLIAM CHETWOOD . . . M.-DCC.XXI. C.
The Tragical | HISTORY | OF | King *RICHARD* III. | As it is Acted at the THEATRE- | ROYAL in *Drury-Lane.* | CON-TAINING | [The Distresses . . . *Passages as* B *but with different lineation*] | [rule] | Alter'd by Mr. *CIBBER.* | [rule] | —— *Domestica Facta.* | [rule] | *LONDON:* | Printed for J. TONSON, and J. WATTS, and | sold by W. FEALES, the Corner | of *Essex-street* in the *Strand.* | [rule] | MDCCXXXVI. D.
THE TRAGICAL | HISTORY | OF | King RICHARD III. | Alter'd from SHAKESPEAR | By COLLEY CIBBER, Esq; | —— *Domestica Facta.* | [ornament] | LONDON: | Printed for J. and R. TONSON in the Strand. | [rule] | MDCCLVII. E.

Ded   *Om.* B-E.

Pref   *Om.* B-E.

   27   different] diffe- A.

Pers   *Characters in brackets (except Rivers, Dorset, Lovel) not in* A, *added from* B *(also in* C-E*). Order of characters* B-E *different from* A. *Actors' names in* B *list also in* D,E; *no actors' names* C. Lord *Stanley,* A] *om.* B-E; C *lists Ratcliff as Ratcliff,* Lord *Stanley. Blunt,* B-E] *Blunt,* &c. A. *Rivers, Dorset, Lovel om.* A-E *(see II.ii.43SD, IV.ii.SD).* B-E *read:* Lady *Anne.* B-E *om.* Son . . . Third, *Cicely,* Mother . . . Third. married to *Richard*] married to *Rich-* A.

I.i.SD   *The Scene, A Garden within* A] SCENE *a Garden in* B-E. *the Lieutenant with a* A] Lieutenant, *and* B-E.

  6SD   *Knocking without.* B-E] *om.* A.

  15   Parent C] Parent, A,B,D,E.

  26   fear's A,C,E] fear, B,D.

  37   and wishes B-E] wishes A.

  42   them B-E] him A.

  45   Prayer; B-E] Prayer? A.

  47SD   *the Sixth* A] *om.* B-E.

  61SD   *Aside.* A] *om.* B-E.

  69   to that, 'tis possible, may owe C,E] from thence may happily derive A,B,D.

  73   Battle. B-E] Battle, Sir. A.

  83   soon —— B-E] soon? A.

  87   which C,E] who A; and B,D.

101   Eye A,C] Eyes B,D,E.

104   at B-E] of A.

111SD   *a Servant to the Lieutenant* A] Servant B-E.

117SD   *Exeunt. after* Farewell. *in 118* B-E; *Ex. Lord* Stan *after 117* A.

125SD   *Exit.* B-E] *om.* A.

132   *so Woe be gone* C,E] *to Woe be gone* A; so Woe to begone B; so woe to be gone D.

158   Trumpets A-C,E] Trumper's D.

164   he A-C] he a D,E.

185   was B-E] were A.

188   gripe! B-E] gripe? A.

208   now A,C,E] *om.* B,D.

214   that; B-E] that A.

220   must B-E] must, A.

224   Woes A,E] Vows B-D.

225SD   *an Order* B-E] *a Paper* A.

226   what B-E] what, A.

232   short, B,C,E] short A; short- D.

236   *thee* A,B] the C-E.

I.ii.SD   Richard *Duke of* Gloucester. *Solus.* A] Richard. B-D; Glo'ster. E [*throughout the play SDs and speech ascriptions have generally been changed from* Richard *to* Glo'ster *in* E; *this change is normally ignored in the variants*].

15   *this piping* A-D] piping E.

20   *to Orebear* A-D] o'erbear E.

28   step A,B,D,E] steps C.

I.iii.4SD   *Rising.* A] *om.* B-E.

13SD   *Sighing.* A] *om.* B-E.

14   Go A-D] *om.* E.

14SD   *Opposite 15* B-E.

17   *an* A] and B-E.

36   Then thou'rt B-E] Thou'rt then A.

40-41   *41 precedes 40* B,D.

50   *discords* A-D] Discord E.

57SD   *Opposite 58* B-E.

66   *remaining,* C-E] *remaining.* A; remaining B.

67SD   A *adds: stabs him again.*

78   *am like* A-C] and am like D; I am E.

II.i.SD   *The* A] *om.* B-E.

   26   nor A,D,E] not B,C.

  30SD   *Exeunt.* A-C,E] *om.* D.   *Enter* Richard *Solus.*] *Richard. Solus.* A; *Enter* Richard. B-E.

   33   far as A-D] as far as E.

   45   my A-C,E] than my D.

  45SD   *Lieutenant* B-E] *a Gentleman* A.

   46   *Lieu.* B-E] *Gent.* A.

   48   *Lieu.* B-E] *Gent.* A.

  49SD   *Exit Lieutenant.*] *om.* A-E.

   51   *Marrow, Bones* B-E] *Marrow-bones* A.

  53SD   *Scene draws* . . . Henry's *Body.* B-E] *om.* A.

   56   of A,C-E] of of B.

   63   sorrows A-C,E] Sorrow D.

  66SD   *He retires.* B-E] *He retires.* | *Enter Bearers with King* Henry's *Body, the Lady* Ann *in Mourning, Lord* Stanley, Tressel, *and Guards, who all advance from the middle Isle of the Church.* A.

  80SD   *Aside.* B-E] *apart.* A.

   84   *at her* B-E] *at the* A.

  86SD   Richard *comes forward.* A] *om.* B-E.

   96   *spurn* A-D] spurn upon E.   *this* A-D] thy E.

   97   thus, A,D,E] thus B,C.

  113   Lord's B-E] Lord A.

  119   thou A,C-E] thou thou B.

  140   my A-C,E] the D.

  153   *lov'd* B-D] *loves* A,E.   *thee* B-E] *the* A.

  160   *death,*] *death.* A; Death; B-E.

  161   aim Despair and Love; C-E] aim unpitied Love, A; Aim unpitied Love; B.

 168SD   *Aside.* A] *om.* B-E.

 178SD   *Aside.* A] *om.* B-E.

  182   *did provoke* B-E] *that provoked* A.

182-184   *Order of lines in* D *is reversed: 184, 183, 182.*

  183   *Nay* A,B,D] Or, C,E.

  189   Penitence. B-E] Penitence A.

 190SD   *lets fall* A] *drops* B-E.   *After 189* A.

 201SD   *Aside.* A] *om.* B-E.

  205   me A,C,E] *om.* B,D.

207   fleeting C,E] prostrate A,B,D.
209   despair: B-E] despair A.
219   *Wou'd* B-E] *I Wou'd* A.
230   Thy C,E] This A,B,D.
231   tun'd A-C] turn'd D,E.
250SD   *Exit with* Tress. *and* Berk. A] *Exit.* B-E.
252   *No,* B-E] *Now* A.
252SD   *Exeunt Guards* E] *Exit* A; *Exit Guards* B,C; *Ex. Guards*
        D.   Richard *Solus.* A] *om.* B-E.
253SD   *smiling.* A] *om.* B-E.
256   *his* C] *her* A,B,D,E.
264   *abase* B-E] *abuse* A.
266   *mishapen Thus!* B-E] *mishapen, Thus* A.
II.ii.SD   *Enter the Duke of* Buckingham *hastily, Lord* Stanley *meeting*
        him. A] *Enter* Buckingham, *hastily meeting Lord* Stanley.
        B-E.
6-7   impatience To acquaint him tho A,B] Impatience, To ac-
        quaint him, tho' C,D; Impatience To acquaint him tho, E.
18   ever. B-E] ever? A.
43SD   *Enter the Queen attended with* Rivers *and* Dorset, *and*
        others. A] *Enter* Queen, Rivers, *and* Dorset. B-E.
47   lov'd B-E] knew A.
51   I B-E] *om.* A.
56   griefs B-E] griefs, A.
60   and A-D] in E.
62SD   *Weeps.* A] *om.* B-E.
67   With all B-E] Withal A.   out A,B,D,E] *om.* C.
73   Good-morning B-E] Good morrow A.
73SD   *Weeping.* A] *Weeps.* B-E.
84   you B-E] your A.
104   you'd B-E] you'll A.
105   intent B-E] intents A.
105SD   *Exit with all but* Buckingham *and* Richard. A] *Exeunt*
        omnes praeter Buck. *and* [*ana* C] Richard. B-D; *Exeunt*
        all but Glo'ster *and* Buck. E.
113   doubt that A] doubt that, B,D,E; doubt, that, C.
127SD   *Exit* Buckingham. A] *om.* B-E.
128   wind; B-E] wind —— Let me see, A.
129-134   My Fortune . . . see —— B-E] *om.* A.

136 too, B,C] too A; too. D,E.

140SD *Exit.* B-E] *om.* A.

III.i.SD *with the Dukes of* Gloucester A] Richard B-D; GLO'STER E.

16SD *Aside.* A] *om.* B-E.

18 it B-E] I A.

25 will A-D] would E.

26 the B-E] his A.

33 I'll B-E] I'd A.

46SD *Enter Duke and Duchess of* York. B-E] *Enter the young Duke of* York *attended.* A.

47SD *Opposite 48* A.

64SD *Aside.* A,D,E] *om.* B,C.

69SD *Aside.* A,D,E] *om.* B,C.

75 *Ape,* B-E] *Ape.* A.

78 *sharp,* B,C,E] *sharp* A,D.

79SD *Aside.* A] *om.* B-E.

86 *What!* B-E] *What* A.

103 *to the* C,E] *to* A,B,D.

120 *now* C-E] *now in* A,B. *meeting in* C,E] *meeting at* A,B,D.

127 *him* A] *me* B-E.

148SD *Exit* Buckingham. A] *Exit.* B-D; *om.* E.

151 Catesby, *at end of 150* A, *below 151 on line by itself* B,D. Shaw, *and thence* | A-D] *Shaw,* | And thence E.

152 Haste, A-D] *om.* E.

153SD *Opposite 154* B-E.

155 out C,E] up A,B,D.

172 Crown'd A-D] Crown E.

III.ii.SD *Sola.* A] *om.* B-E.

3 Oh B-E] Ah A.

9SD *Soft Musick.* B-E] *Song here.* A.

23SD *Aloof.* A] *om.* B-E.

26 will not A,C,E] won't B,D.

27 hath B-E] has A.

28SD *Aside.* A] *om.* B-E.

30 mistake, A] mistake B-E.

33 Then A,C] That B,D,E.

36 now B-E] now, A.

62 have A-C,E] has D.

73   *say* A-D] says E.
95   *hath* B-E] *has* A.
98   *lower* A-D] th'lower E.
113   Seem, B-E] Seem A.
115SD   *Embracing.* A] *om.* B-E.
120SD   *Aside. Exit* Richard. A] *Exit.* B-E.
128   *wou'd he be* C-E] *wou'd be* A,B.
137   *lolling* B-E] *lulling* A.
140   *secret* A-D] Sacred E.
178   recure A-C,E] secure D.
180   *zealous* B-E] *vehement* A.   *Instigation,* C-E] *Instigation* A; Instigation: B.
187   *Glory* A,C-E] Birth B.
202   *happier* C,E] *happy* A,B,D.
219   Loyalty. B-E] Loyalty? A.
237   When A-D] till E.
239SD   Buckingham A] *om.* B-E.
240   *Sweet* B-E] *Call him again; sweet* A.
245SD   *Re-enter* A] *Enter* B-E.
250   *or* A,E] her B-D.
253   *all* A-C] *om.* D,E.
258SD   *Kneels.* A] *om.* B-E.
263   Majesty B-E] Grace A.
266   *Majesty* B-E] *Highness* A.
267   *we* B-E] *me* A.
269   *to* A-D] unto E.
269SD   *Exeunt* Buckingham *and Citizens.* Richard. *Solus.* A] *Ex. [Exit* C] *omnes praeter* Richard. B-D; *Exe. all but* Richard. E.
275   fills C,E] wraps A,B,D.
278   Fame not more A,B,D,E] Fame, not more, C.
279   aspiring A] acquiring B-E.
IV.i.SD   *The Scene* A] SCENE B-E.   *Enter the two Princes with the Queen, the Dutchess of* York, A] *Enter* Queen, P. [*Prince* E] Edward, D. [*Duke of* D,E] York, Duch. [*Dutchess of* D,E] York, B-E.
16   Innocence A-C,E] Innocents D.
22   thus A,C-E] *om.* B.
22SD   *to them,* A] *om.* B-E.

36SD   *to Lady* Ann A] *om.* B-E.

52   sorrow B-E] sorrows A.

58   *Men* A-D] Man E.

61SD   *Exit Lady* Ann *and* Catesby. A] *Exit with* Catesby. B-E.

71   *Dutch.*] *D. York.* A; *Dutch. York.* B,C,E; *D. York.* (*meaning Duchess in this text*) D.

83SD   *Enter the Lieutenant with an Order* A] *Enter* Lieutenant B-E.

97SD   *Gives 'em Lord* Stanley. A] *om.* B-E.

98   I not B-E] not I A.

108SD   *To her self.* A] *om.* B-E.

112SD   *Kissing 'em.* A] *om.* B-E.

114   *Dutch.*] *D. York.* A; *Dutch. York.* B,C,E; *D. York.* (*see IV.i.71*) D.

123SD   *parted* A] *om.* B-E.

IV.ii.SD   *The Scene changes to the Presence,* A] SCENE *the Presence.* B-E. *with* A] *om.* B-E. *other Lords and Attendants.* A] *&c.* B-E.

18   Friend A-D] kind Friend E.

32SD   Buckingham A] *om.* B-E.

61SD   *Aside.* A] *om.* B-E.

69SD   *Re-enter Duke of* A] *Enter* B-E.

82   Harry C-E] Henry A,B.

83   *be* B-E] *he* A.

84   *peevish* A-D] little peevish E.

90SD   Richard A] *om.* B-E.

92   A *has following 92:*

> Since he forgets the hand that lifted him,
> That seated still supports him; then 'tis time
> To loose my hold, and let him fall as low,
> As this contemn'd, this out-cast *Buckingham.*

IV.iii.3   *For.* B-E] *Digh.* A.

13SD   *Gives* A-D] *Giving* E.   *Opposite 12* B,C.

16SD   *Lieutenant* A] *om.* B-E.

17SD   *Giving them the Keys.* A] *om.* B-E.

18SD   *Exeunt severally. opposite 17* B-E.

18SD-41   *As in* B-E; A *om. and has instead:*

SCENE *a Chamber, the Princes in Bed. The Stage darkned.*
Pr. Ed. Why do you startle, Brother?
D. York. O! I have been so frighted in my sleep!

Pray turn this way?

    Pr. Ed. Alas, I fain wou'd sleep, but cannot

Tho' 'tis the stillest night I ever knew.

Not the least breath has stir'd these four hours[.]

Sure all the World's asleep but we.

    D. York. Hark! Pray Brother count the Clock!   *[Clock strikes.*

—— But two! O tedious night: I've slept an Age.

Wou'd it were day, I am so melancholy.   10

    Pr. Ed. Hark! What noise is that?

I thought I heard some one upon the stairs!

Hark! Again!

    D. York. O dear, I hear 'em too! Who is it, Brother?

    Pr. Ed. Bless me! a light too thro' the door! look there!

    D. York. Who is it? Hark! it unlocks! O! I am so afraid!

            Enter Dighton *and* Forrest *with dark lanthorns.*

    Pr. Ed. Bless me! What frightful men are these?

    Both. Who's there?   *Pr. Ed.* Who's there?

    Digh. Hist, we've wak'd 'em! What shall we say?

    For. Nothing. We come to do.   20

    Digh. I'll see their Faces ——

    D. York.   Won't they speak to us?

            *[*Dighton *looks in with his Lanthorn.*

O save me! Hide me! Save me, Brother!

    Pr. Ed. O mercy Heaven! Who are you, Sirs,

That look so ghastly pale and terrible?

    Digh. I am a Fool. —— I cannot answer 'em.

    For. You must die, my Lord, so must your Brother.

    Pr. Ed. O stay, for pity sake! What is our Crime, Sir?

Why must we die?

    Digh. The King, your Uncle, loves you not.

    Pr. Ed. O Cruel man!   30

Tell him we'll live in Prison all our days,

And, when we give occasion of offence,

Then let us die: H'as yet no cause to kill us.

    For. Pray.

    Pr. Ed. We do, Sir, to you. O spare us Gentlemen!

I was some time your King, and might have shown

You mercy: For your dear Souls sake pity us.

    For. We'll hear no more.

    Both Pr.   O Mercy, Mercy!   *[They smother them, and*

    For. Down, down with 'em.   *the Scene shuts on them.*

    38SD   *Solus.* A] *om.* B–E.

    39   A *has following 39:*

            'O the most Arch-deed of pitious Massacre

            'That ever yet this Land was guilty of.

    41   News C,D] welcome News A,B,E.

57SD   Tirrel A] *om.* B-E.

61   beauteous A-D] bounteous E.

70   confronted C-E] oppos'd A,B.

IV.iv.SD   *the* A] *om.* B-E.

4   perpetual; B-E] perpetual. A.

12   they do A-D] do they E.

17SD   *Trumpet sounds a march.* C-E] *om.* A; *Trumpet Sound a March.* B.

19SD   *Enter* Richard *with his Powers, the Dutchess meets and stops him, &c.* A] *Enter* Richard *and* Catesby. B; *Enter* Richard [Glo'ster E] *and* Catesby, *with Forces.* C-E.

22   *you mercy,* D] *your mercy,* A; you, Mercy, B,C,E.

53   *Dutch.* B-E] *om.* A.

61SD   *Dutchess.* A] *om.* B-E.

85-86   weep. On this present B-E] weep On this. Present A.

90   Uncle A-D] Uncles E.

106   *thy . . . mine* B-E] *my . . . thine* A.

114SD   *Aside.* A] *om.* B,C; *opposite 117* D,E.

134SD   *Opposite 135* A.

135SD   *Opposite 136* A.

139   *Inform* A,D,E] Informs B,C.

141SD   *Exit.* B-E] *om.* A.

147SD   *Enter Lord* Stanley. *follows 148* A.

153-154   *Rich. Well, as you guess?* | *Ld. Stan.* A-C,E] *om.* D. Morton, A,D,E] *Morton.* B,C.

178SD   *Exit* Stanley. A] *Exit.* B-E. *Enter* Ratcliff. B-E] *Enter a Messenger.* A.

179   *Rat.* B-E] *Mes.* A.

186   *Rat.* B-E] *Mes.* A.

197   fever-weakned B-E] favour weakned A.

208SD   *Exeunt.* A] *Exit.* B-E.

V.i   ACT V, SCENE I. B-E.

SD   *Scene, The Field* A] *om.* B-E.   *marching* A] *om.* B-E.

6   Posterity B-E] prosperity A.

13   Cheerly on, B-E] Cheerly, on A.

29SD   *Exeunt.* B-E] *Exit.* A.

V.ii.SD   *The Scene* A] *SCENE* B-E.   *in Arms, with* A] *om.* B-E.

10   certain A-D] *om.* E.

16   *D. Nor.*] *D. York.* A; *Norf.* B-E.

33   *direction.* B-E] *direction. Lead.* A.

38   tells A,D,E] tell B,C.

V.iii.3   *token* A-D] tokens E.

10SD   *a* A] *om.* B-E.

14SD   *They retire.* A] *om.* B-E.   *in a Cloak* A] *om.* B-E.

17   What A,C-E] what, B.

25   *thy* A-C,E] the D.

39SD   *Lord* Stanley A] *om.* B-E.   *After 38* B,D,E.

V.iv.SD   *The Scene, before* Richard's *Tent:* Richard A] SCENE, *Bos-worth-Field. Enter* Richard B-E.

13SD   *Duke of* Norfolk A] *om.* B-E.

18   *Cat.* B-E] *Rat.* A.

20   *Rat.* B-E] *Cat.* A.

29   *Cat.* C,E] *Rat.* A,B,D.

31   us — C] us. A; us, — B,D,E.

V.v.SD   *his Tent* A-C,E] *the Tent* D.   *Solus.* A] *om.* B-E.

8   Harvest A,C,D] Harvests B,E.

13   *other's* C-E] *other* A; others B.

31SD   *King . . . rise.* C,E] *Enter King . . . rise.* B,D; *The Ghost of* Henry VI. *rises.* A.

36   frighted A-D] frightful E.

41   A *has following 41: The Ghosts of the young Princes rise.*

50   A *has following 50: Vanish. The Ghost of* Ann *his Wife rises.*

53   *Sword —* B-E] *Sword* A.

58   awake! To A-D] awake to E.

59SD   *All ghosts sink.* B-E] *sinks.* A.   Richard . . . *sleep.* A] *om.* B-E.

60   *a* B-E] *another* A.   *wounds!* B-E] *wounds?* A.

87SD   *Exeunt.* A,E] *Exit.* B-D.

V.vi.SD   *Soldiers,* B-E] *om.* A.   *Marching.* A] *om.* B-E.

2   *is it into the morning,* A] is it unto the morning, B-D; into the morning, is it, E.

15   *Richm.* A,C-E] *Rich.* B.

26   *Exeunt.* A,E] *Exit.* B-D.

V.vii.SD   *marching.* A] *&c.* B-E.

7SD   *with a Paper* B-E] *om.* A.

13   Conquer; C] Conquer, Sir; A; conquer — B,D,E.

19   And e're we do bestride our foaming Steeds, B-E] *What shall I say more than I have infer'd:* A.

20   *you* A-C,E] we D.
23   *assur'd* A-D] *om.* E.
31SD   *Trumpet sounds.* A] *om.* B-E.
39   me B-E] us A.
V.viii.SD   *Several Excursions, Soldiers* [*Soldier* D] *drove across the Stage by* Richard. *Re-enter* Richard. C-E] *An Allarm is heard:* Richard *re-enters alone.* A; *Six Soldiers drove across the Stage by* Richard. *Re-enter* Richard. B.
4   Allarms B-E] Allarm A.
5   dying C-E] dead mens A,B.
6   single A-D] singly E.
7SD   *Exit.* B-E] *om.* A.   *The Allarm continues:* A] *om.* B-E.   *the Duke of* A] *om.* B-E.
13SD   *Exeunt.* A] *Exit.* B-E.   *in disorder* A] *om.* B-E.
14   *for a Horse* B-E] *for an Horse* A.
22   *A Horse! a Horse!* D] *An Horse! an Horse!* A-C,E.   *a Horse.* C,D] *an Horse.* A,B,E.
V.ix.5   spotted A,B,D,E] sported C.
10-11SD   *Allarm, fight.* Richard *is wounded.* A] *Fight;* Richard *falls.* B-E.
12   acquired A] acquired! B,C,E; acquired, D.
27   Trumpets speak A-C,E] Trumpet speaks D.
27SD   *and Lord* Stanley: *Soldiers follow* A] *Lord* Stanley, *and Soldiers* B-E.   Richard's A-D] *King* RICHARD'S E.
28   O B-E] *Richm.* O A.
36SD   *Shouts here.* A] *om.* B-E.
52   *scarr'd* A] scar'd B-E.
57   *Successors* C,E] *Succeeders* A,B,D.
60   those A-D] these E.
62SD   *Exeunt.*] *om.* A-E.

The Jew of Venice

The 1701 edition of *The Jew of Venice* is the copy-text for accidentals. Its collation is [A]-G4: sig. [A] is the half-title, "THE | Jew of Venice. | A | COMEDY."; [A1v] is blank; [A2] is the title page; [A2v] is blank; [A3-A3v] are the Advertisement; [A4-A4v] contain the Prologue, and [A4v] contains the Dramatis Personae as well. The

head-title on sig. B1 is: "[double rule] The Jew of Venice. [rule]";
and there is no running-title except on [A3v], "*Advertisement to the
Reader.*" The last page, sig. G4v, is a list of 93 plays and several other
books "*Sold by* BER. LINTOTT." On the date of publication of this
quarto, see note 73 to my Introduction above. I have collated five
copies of this edition: the Folger Shakespeare Library's Dobell copy,
and the copies at the University of Chicago, the University of Illinois
(missing pp. 42-43, sig. G2), the University of Michigan, and the University of Texas (p. 33, sig. F, imperfect). I found no differences worth
recording, except for the progressive decline of the title of Buckingham's *The Chances:* in the Advertisement, l. 11. The title and punctuation are clear in the Folger Dobell copy; the colon is missing in the
Illinois copy; the colon and the *s* are missing in the Texas copy; the
remaining title *The Chance* is faint in the Chicago copy; and the second word is illegible in the Michigan copy. Granville's distinguishing
between his own lines and the lines he borrowed from Shakespeare
indicates that the adapter paid some attention to the publication of
this edition.

Second among the texts of *The Jew of Venice* which I have collated is
that published by T[homas] Johnson at The Hague in 1711 (University of Texas copy). Jaggard lists editions of both 1711 and 1721 by
Johnson, but Handasyde, p. 272, states that the second listing is based
on an ink alteration of the date from 1711 to 1721 in the copy at the
Shakespeare Memorial Library at Stratford. According to Ford, who
discusses Johnson and his editions, pp. 46-56, *The Jew* was published
separately with the 1711 title page, was bound up in the second volume
of Johnson's *Collection of the Best English Plays* (12 vols., 1712-18),
and was also included in the "second issue" of that collection, 16 vols.,
undated, but "probably published from 1720 to 1722"; later, however,
Ford lists only one *edition* of *The Jew* published at The Hague, that
of 1711. This text, an octavo with the collation A-D8, E2, was presumably printed from the 1701 quarto and is a careful piece of work.
Some quarto errors are corrected, and of the other substantive devia-
tions from the quarto text, some seem to have been attempts to correct
what were thought to be errors. Most distinctive, however, are the
edition's printing some passages as prose (these are listed in the variants
below) and attempting to improve the lineation of the verse. At I.iii.
95-97 the wording was altered, perhaps in the interest of metrical
regularity. Although most of the changes in lineation are attractive to

the modern editor, they were not the intention of Granville, who evidently prepared the copy both for the quarto of 1701 and for the *Genuine Works* of 1732, and whose lineation I preserve with only a very few minor adjustments.

I also include the results of my collations with the texts of *The Jew* in Granville's *Three Plays* (1713), *Four Plays* (1732), and *Genuine Works* (1732). The 1713 edition included the "Masque of Peleus and Thetis" in the substantially altered version that had appeared in Granville's *Poems upon Several Occasions* (1712); and even the text of the play may have received very slight authoritative correction (e.g., I.iii.28). Except for the masque, this edition of the play seems to have been printed from the 1701 quarto, and the text in *Four Plays* seems to have been printed from that of 1713. The *CBEL* lists a separate text of 1713, and Jaggard includes a London edition of [c. 1720]. Neither Ford nor Handasyde mentions these dates, although Handasyde, pp. 281-282, does refer to editions of *The Jew* in *The English Theatre*, V (W. Feales, 1732) and *Plays* (F. Clay, 1732): she states that the former consists of sheets for *Four Plays* (1732) and that she has not traced the latter. Although I have not seen these editions, I have consulted the text of the play in Granville's *Genuine Works* published in 1736, the year after the adapter's death. Since there appear to be no authoritative changes from the text of the 1732 *Genuine Works*, I have not included variants.

The *Genuine Works in Verse and Prose,* published in two volumes in 1732, was accompanied by a Preface in which Granville protested against the "maim'd and imperfect" form in which his "Verses and Poems" had appeared; and he explained that in his "Leisure and Retirement" he had "been prevailed upon to give way to this present publication." According to Handasyde, pp. 221-222, "for this collection all his early poems, even the most trifling, were carefully gone over, and minute corrections made." Although Granville excepted *The Jew of Venice* (along with *Once a Lover*) from his repudiation of early editions of his works, it is clear that he revised *The Jew* too; his revisions seem even to have extended to the punctuation in a few instances. However, the variants point to the text in *Three Plays* of 1713 as the copy-text for the *Genuine Works;* and it seems more likely, therefore, that on the whole the accidentals of the 1701 quarto are closer to those of the adapter's manuscript than are the accidentals of the *Genuine Works.* As in *Richard III,* I have preferred substantive and some semi-substantive readings from the later, revised edition.

Granville stated in his Advertisement that he had marked with a single quote those lines that were his rather than Shakespeare's. Although it is extremely hard to be consistent about such matters, it does seem that, in addition to those lines he did mark, Granville should have claimed I.ii.53; I.iii.148-150; II.i.41, 80-82; III.i.25, 88-89, 101-102, 109, 191-192, 303-304, 322-323; III.ii.3-4 (added in the *Genuine Works*), 54, 56-57; IV.i.96, 150, 186-188, 210, 267, 340; V.i.32-34, 45, 200, 229. In addition, II.ii.99, unmarked in 1701, is correctly marked after 1713; and II.ii.13 and V.i.120, 147, and 215, all marked (as they should be) in previous editions, are unmarked in the *Genuine Works*. Lines that are marked but that should be considered Shakespeare's are I.i.2; I.ii.8; I.iii.17, 73; II.i.50-51; II.ii.81; III.i.11-12, 20-21, 110b, 123-124, 128-129, 150-151, 237; IV.i.18, 181, 241; V.i.94, 108-110, 112, 154, 158-159, 162-163, 209. Also, quotes precede incorrectly I.iii.128 in London editions after 1701 and I.i.76 and V.i.161 in editions before the *Genuine Works*. In the lines following I.i.79 in 1701, the fifth and sixth lines should probably not be counted Granville's. When quotes appear in the copy-text both at the beginning of a line and later in the same line, the second quote is silently omitted.

In the 1701 quarto the "Masque of Peleus and Thetis" begins at the top of sig. C3v with the head-title "Peleus & Thetis. | A | MASQUE."; the bottom half of the preceding page, after II.ii.56, is blank. The masque ends in the middle of sig. D2, and the play continues immediately without a space. "Peleus and Thetis" is similarly presented in Johnson's edition, in *Three Plays,* and in *Four Plays,* although it is in a considerably revised version in the last two. Meanwhile, the masque appeared regularly in Granville's frequently published *Poems upon Several Occasions.* In the *Genuine Works* of 1732 "Peleus and Thetis" was omitted from *The Jew of Venice* in Vol. II but was published in Vol. I along with the poems. My copy-text for the masque is that of the 1732 *Genuine Works,* Vol. I; however, I give the variant readings necessary to reconstruct the substantially different 1701 version and the slightly different version of 1713.

On Granville's Shakespearean source H. Spencer, p. 354, cites the suggestion of Otto Burmeister in *Nachdichtungen und Bühneneinrichtungen von Shakespeares Merchant of Venice* (Rostock, 1902), p. 19, that Granville used "Q2." H. Spencer continues, "I have not collated exhaustively, but I have reason to believe the source was probably F4." Granville wrote (and did not mark as his own) "He has sent twenty times to look you out" (II.i.76) — a line he probably would not have written without Shakespeare's line (omitted in Q2) "I have sent twenty out to seek for you" (II.vi.66). Two other variants are also relevant: Ff1-3 and Q1 read "one half his goods" (IV.i. 353), where Q2, F4, and *The Jew* (IV.i.258) read "on half his goods"; but Q1, Ff1-4 (III.ii.146) and *The Jew* (III.i.160) agree on "peales of praise" rather than "pearles of praise" (Q2). F4 does indeed seem to be the most likely source.

The Jew of Venice, London, 1701	Q
The Jew of Venice, The Hague, 1711	J
Three Plays, London, 1713	3P
Four Plays, London, 1732	4P
The Genuine Works, 2 vols., London, 1732	W

TP THE | JEW | OF | VENICE, | A | COMEDY. | *Written Originaly* | *By* Mr. Wm. SHAKESPEAR. | Now altered & very much improved, | *By the Hon.* M. GRANVILLE. | [ornament] | Printed for T. JOHNSON, | Bookseller at the Hague. | [rule] | M.DCC.-XI. J.

THE | *JEW of VENICE:* | A | COMEDY. | As it is Acted at the | THEATRE | IN | Little-LINCOLNS-INN-FIELDS. | BY | His MAJESTY's Servants. | [double rule] | *LONDON:* | Printed for *Benj. Tooke,* and *Bern. Lintott,* | 1713. *in* THREE PLAYS, ... Written by the Right Honble *GEORGE GRANVILLE,* Lord LANSDOWNE. *LONDON:* ... MDCCXIII. 3P.

THE | JEW *of* VENICE: | A | COMEDY, | As it is Acted at the | THEATRE | IN | Little Lincoln's-Inn-Fields, | BY | *His Majesty's Servants.* | [double rule] | *LONDON:* | Printed for BERNARD LINTOT, and for B. MOTTE, | at the Middle-Temple-Gate; and sold by HENRY | LINTOT, over against St. *Dunstan*'s Church in *Fleet-* | *street;* and W. FEALS, at *Row*'s Head over against | Clement's Inn Gate. 1732. *in* FOUR PLAYS Of the Right Honourable the LORD *LANSDOWNE.* .... *LONDON:* ... 1732. 4P.

[ornament] | THE | *JEW of VENICE.* | A | COMEDY. | [ornament] *in* The | GENUINE | WORKS | IN | VERSE AND PROSE, | Of the Right Honourable | *GEORGE GRANVILLE,* | LORD *LANSDOWNE.* | [rule] | VOLUME *the* SECOND; | *Which compleats his* LORDSHIP'S WRITINGS. | [rule] | [ornament] | *LONDON:* | Printed for J. WALTHOE, | over-against the | *Royal-Exchange,* in *Cornhill.* | [rule] | M.DCC.XXXII. ([*Vol. I*] *was printed for Tonson and Gilliver.*) W.

468

Adv   *Om.* W.

    11   *Chances:* Q] *Chances.* J; *Chance:* 3P,4P. *See description of*
          Q *above.*

    17   *mark't* Q,3P,4P] *mark't* (") J.

Pro 24   *genial* 3P,4P,W] *genal* Q,J.

    33   *or* Q,J,3P,W] *and* 4P.

    45   *scarce,* W] *scarce* Q,J,3P,4P.

  48-49   *The . . . Son W] *om.* Q,J; The Profits of this Play were
          given to Mr. *Dryden*'s Son. 3P,4P.

Dr Pers   *Actors' names om.* J,W.   *Salerio.*] *om.* Q,J,3P,4P,W.

I.i.19   this Q,3P,4P,W] this. J.

    37   now Q,J,4P,W] know 3P.

    56   self-way Q,J,3P,W] self-same way 4P.

    67   Tongue, Q,J,3P,4P] Tongue; W.

    76   And W] 'And Q,J,3P,4P.

  79-80   And ... Means —— W] Q,J,3P,4P *add:*

        From the Four Corners of the World; the Winds
        Blow in, from every Coast, adoring Crowds;
        The watry Kingdom, whose ambitious Head
        Spets in the Face of Heaven, is no Bar
        'To æmulous Love, as o're a Brook they come
        'To Anchor at her Heart: Her Sunny Locks
        Hang on her Temples, like a golden Fleece,
        For which these many *Jason*'s sayl in Quest.
        O my *Antonio,* had I but the Means
        To hold a Rival-Place with one of 'em.

I.ii   *Entire scene as prose* J.

    41   Woman Q,J] Women 3P,4P,W.

    53   it Q,J,3P,W] he 4P.

    68   would Q,J,3P,W] will 4P.

    77   Whilst Q,J,3P,W] while 4P.

I.iii.1-34   *Prose* J.

    1   Duccats? W] Duccats. Q,J,3P,4P.

    3   Months? W] Months. Q,J,3P,4P.

    5   bound? W] bound. Q,J,3P,4P.

    10   contrary? J,4P,W] contrary Q,3P.

    18   at Q,J,W] a 3P,4P.

    21   Planks Q,J,W] Plants 3P,4P.

    28   may I ... *Antonio?* 3P,4P,W] I may ... *Antonio.* Q, J.

    42   bear Q,3P,4P,W] beat J.

    55   J *adds: To Antonio.*

95   answer? Q,3P,4P,W] answer you? J.

96   Can Q,3P,4P,W] Or can J.

97   or Q,3P,4P,W] *om.* J.

101   day; another time J,W] day, another time; Q; Day, another time 3P,4P.

103   Monies? W] Monies. Q,J,3P,4P.

113   Love 3P,4P,W] Love! Q,J.

128   To Q,J] 'To 3P,4P,W.

147   propos'd Q,J,3P,W] propose 4P.

II.i   Scene i. 3P,4P,W] *om.* Q,J.

II.ii.13 ' Q,J,3P,4P] *om.* W.

37   not Q,3P,4P,W] not why J.

47   Poet Q,3P,4P,W] Poets J.

56   no Q,3P,4P,W] *om.* J.

56SD *Here . . . ceasing.* W] *om.* Q,J,3P,4P, *which have masque here; variants for the masque follow:*
        Set to MUSICK 3P,4P,W] *om.* Q,J.

        Arg   Jupiter 3P,4P,W] Jupiter, *also in love with her,* Q,J. *afterwards* Q,J,W] *afterward* 3P,4P. *Son of* Peleus W] *Son of* Thetis *by* Peleus Q,J,3P,4P.

        SD   *The* SCENE *. . .* Prometheus. W] *Prometheus* is seen upon Mount *Caucasus* chain'd to a Rock with the Vulture at his Breast. A Flourish of all the Instruments. Then plaintive Musick. *Peleus* Enters to *Prometheus.* Q,J; Prometheus *appears upon Mount* Caucasus *chain'd to a Rock, with the Vulture at his Breast.* Peleus *enters, addressing himself to* Prometheus. 3P,4P.

        16-18 Resign . . . prepare W] *You must, you must resign* | *Or wretched Man prepare* Q,J; O wretched Man! resign | Whom you adore, or else prepare 3P,4P.

        19   3P,4P *add after 19:* 'Tis vain, O *Peleus,* to oppose | Thy Torturer and mine.

        25   Q,J *add after 25:* If for the Pleasures of an Hour | We must endure an Age of Pain, | Love give me back, my Heart again.

        25SD-30 Thetis . . . disdain. W] Q,J *have following order:* 26, 27, *Enter* Thetis. 28, Pel. *Give me back my Heart again. om.* 29, 30; 3P,4P *have:* Thetis *enters. om.* 26, 27, *have* 28-30.

35-45 Q,J *om. and have instead:*

Pel. *Despair tormented first my Heart,*
Now Falshood a more cruel Smart!
  O for the Peace of Human-kind,
Make Women [Woman J] longer true, or sooner kind!
  With Justice, or with Mercy reign:
Or give me, give me back my Heart again.
                        Both together.
The. ⎱ Peleus *unjustly you complain.*
Pel. ⎰ *Give, give me back my Heart again.*
          The. *Accursed Jealousie!*
Thou Jaundice in the Lover's Eye,
Thro' which all Objects false we see;
      Accursed Jealousy!
Pro. *Love is by Fancy led about.*
From Hope to Fear, from Joy to Doubt:
  Whom we now a Goddess call,
Divinely grac'd in every Feature,
Strait's a deform'd, a perjur'd Creature;
  Love and Hate, are fancy all.
'Tis but as fancy shall present
Objects of Grief, or of Content,
    That the Lover's blest, or dyes:
Visions of mighty Pains, or Pleasure,
Imagin'd want, Imagin'd Treasure,
    All in powerful Fancy lyes.

37   cruel's W] killing's 3P,4P.
46   THETIS. 3P,4P,W] *CHORUS.* Q,J.
50   Thy 3P,4P,W] The. *Thy* Q,J.
51   I so Q,J,3P,W] so I 4P.
53   reign W] llve Q; live J,3P,4P.
53SD *A Clap . . . Eagle.* W] *Jupiter* appears descending
        Q,J,3P,4P.
56   The Thunderer Q,3P,4P,W] *The Thunder* J.
57SD *of Voices . . . as* W] of all the Voices . . . while
        Q,J,3P,4P. Q,J *add:* Thunder the while.
81   Q,J,3P,4P *add after 81: And every Hour by Love is*
        made | Some Heaven-defying Encelade.
82SD-84 PELEUS . . . Thunder. W] The. Jove *may kill,*
        but ne'er shall sunder. | [Pel. *and* The. *holding*
        by each other. | All three repeat. | *Bring me . . .*
        Thunder. Q,J; 3P,4P *as* W *except om.* holding
        . . . another.

86   *to* JUPITER W] *om.* Q,J,3P,4P.

92-93   Thy . . . Hate. 3P,4P,W] *om.* Q,J.

94   *to* JUPITER W] *om.* Q,J,3P,4P.

98   [*The* PROPHECY.] Q,J,W] *om.* 3P,4P.

99   Joy W] *the Joy* Q,J,3P,4P.

102   efface W] *outshine* Q,J,3P,4P.

103-104   Q,J,3P,4P *substitute: And be the foremost*
[*Greatest* 3P,4P] *of his Line.*

105   JUPITER [*Apart.*] W] Jup. 3P,4P; [Jupiter *during
the* Chorus *seems to stand considering.* Q,J.

106   Like *Saturn* 3P,4P,W] *As* Saturn *was* Q,J.   impious
3P,4P,W] *Aspiring* Q,J.

112   Q,J *add SD:* [Turning to *Peleus.*

114SD   3P,4P *place after 113; om.* Q,J.

116   The . . . resign. 3P,4P,W] *om.* Q,J.

116SD   *Joins their Hands.* W] *om.* Q,J,3P,4P.

117   PELEUS. 3P,4P,W] *Peleus receiving Thetis.* Q,J.

118   there is no Heav'n but Love W] *like mutual Love*
Q,J,3P,4P.

119-121   PELEUS . . . Love. W] *om.* Q,J,3P,4P.

122   *to* 3P,4P,W] *turning to* Q,J.

125   Arise 3P,4P,W] *Arise, arise* Q,J.

126-127   'Tis . . . Liberty. 3P,4P,W] *om.* Q,J.

127SD   *Instruments* Q,J,W] *Musick* 3P,4P.   Peleus . . .
Arms. W] *om.* Q,J,3P,4P.

128-163SD   Q,J *om. and substitute the following ending:*

> Peleus and Thetis together.
>
> Pel. & ⎱ *Be true all ye Lovers, whate're ye endure,*
> The.   ⎰ *Tho' cruel the Pain is, how sweet is the Cure!*
> *So Divine is the Blessing*
> *In the Hour of possessing,*
> *That one Moment's obtaining*
> *Pays an Age of Complaining:*
> *Be true, all ye Lovers, what'ere you endure,*
> *Tho' cruel the Pain is, how sweet is the Cure!*

144   its W] her 3P,4P.

160SD   *Voices and Instruments* W] *Instruments and
Voices* 3P,4P.

165SD   *The Mask . . . Dances.* W] *om.* 3P,4P.

61   Fortune W] Fortunes Q,J,3P,4P.

96   is all ready? Q,J,3P,W] all is ready; 4P.

99   ' 3P,4P,W] *om.* Q,J.

100   Bond, 3P,4P,W] Bond Q,J.

III.i.SD   Nerissa, Gratiano *discourse* Q,J,3P,W] Nerissa *and* Gratiano *discourse* 4P.

3   *Portia* one, J,4P,W] *Portia,* one Q,3P.

8   from Q,3P,4P,W] to J.

21   Q,J,3P,4P *add after 21:* 'For oh, what heavier Curse for perjury | 'Could Heav'n provide, than losing all my Hope?

33   State Q,J] Estate 3P,4P,W.

62   aloft Q,3P,4P,W] aloof J.

64   softest Q,J,3P,W] softer 4P.

87SD   *Walks* Q,J,3P,W] *Walking* 4P.

95   then Q,J,W] than 3P,4P.

103-105   *Prose* J.

114   its Q,J,3P,4P] its it's W.

118   Beard 3P,4P,W] Beards Q,J.   *Mars!* W] *Mars,* Q,3P; *Mars.* J,4P.

126   Drudge, W] Drudge; Q,3P,4P; Drudge J.

164   Chance, J] Chance. Q,3P,4P,W.

172   from J,3P,4P,W] 'em Q.

180   Acquisition. Q,3P,4P] Acquisitor J; Acquisition; W.

185   this 3P,4P,W] the Q,J.

193   it Q,3P,4P,W] is J.

193-213   *Prose* J.

195   make; J] make Q,3P,4P,W.

196   he Q,3P,4P,W] be J.

221SD   Salerio] *om.* Q,J,3P,4P,W.

223   not. W] not, Q,J,3P,4P.

238   pretty Q,J,3P,4P] *om.* W.

243   has 3P,4P,W] had Q; hath J.

270   has Q,J,3P,W] hath 4P.

296   prove] prove, Q,J,3P,4P,W.

297SD   *Exeunt* W] *Exit* Q,J,3P,4P.

III.ii.3-4   Where . . . now? W] *om.* Q,J,3P,4P.

7   call'dst W] call'st Q,J,3P,4P.

17-39   *Prose* J.

42-57   *Prose* J.

48   Ears; 3P,4P,W] Ears Q; Ears. J.

IV.i.7 Make] *Duke*. Make Q,J,3P,4P,W.
20 purpose Q,J,W] propose 3P,4P.
28 answer'd? J,3P,4P,W] answer'd, Q.
38 Forbid . . . Leaf, W] You may as well forbid the Mountain pines | To wag their Tops, and dance about their Leaves, Q,J,3P,4P.
43 farther 3P,4P,W] father Q,J.
49 draw Q,J,3P,W] have 4P.
56 Heirs: W] Heirs Q,3P,4P; Heirs. J.
77 hast 4P,W] has Q,J,3P.
81 mak'st W] make Q; makest J,3P,4P.
102 Name. 4P,W] Name? Q,J,3P.
106 Compulsion J,W] Compulsion? Q,3P,4P.
119 Deeds Q,J,3P,W] Deed's 4P.
137 the Q,3P,4P,W] the the J.
141 the W] thy Q,J,3P,4P.
149 my Q,J,3P,W] the 4P.
164 his Q,J,3P,W] the 4P.
169 awhile. W] awhile Q,3P; a while: J; a while, 4P.
180 not, 4P,W] not Q,J,3P.
237 Bond thrice, J,3P,4P,W] Bond, thrice Q.
278 Goods W] Goods. Q,J,3P; Goods, 4P.
286 from Q,J,3P,W] *om.* 4P.
306 Loves Q,3P,4P,W] Love J.
342 at Q,3P,4P,W] a J.
V.i.17SD Nerissa J,W] Jessica Q,3P,4P.
26 Letters Q,J,W] the Letters 3P,4P.
51 our Q,J,3P,W] your 4P.
59SD *Flourish of Musick* W] *Musick* Q,J,3P,4P.
70-71 A fine . . . Clerk Q,J,3P,W] *om.* 4P.   well I know W] well I know, J; well, I know Q,3P.
81 Finger J,W] Fingers Q,3P,4P.
120 ' Q,J,3P,4P] *om.* W.
121 believe J,3P,4P,W] be believe Q.
139 directs Q,J,3P,W] direct 4P.
147 ' Q,J,3P,4P] *om.* W.
157SD *as* Q,J,3P,4P] *om.* W.
161 I W] 'I Q,J,3P,4P.
164 oft his 3P,4P,W] of this Q,J.

208   even Q,3P,4P,W] *om.* J.

215   ' Q,J,3P,4P] *om.* W.

240   lies W] ly Q,J; lie 3P,4P.

241   Hands. From . . . forwards, J,W] Hands from . . . forwards. Q,3P,4P.

251   grown Q,J,3P,W] grow 4P.

256   wand'ring J,3P,4P,W] wond'ring Q.

Epi   *Printed between Prologue and Dramatis Personae* J.

36-39   Mr. *Dryden* . . . Rope-Dancer. 3P,4P,W] *om.* Q,J.